Heads and Hearts

Heads and Hearts

An Inquiry into Integrity

ANNE LAMB

To Susan with respect & love —

Anne Lamb.

St. Lukes. 2008

Designed by Louise Millar

Published by Calder Walker Associates
2 Umbria Street
London SW15 5DP
alangw@copperstream.co.uk

Printed by Bain and Bain, Glasgow G46 7UQ

ISBN 0 9541275 4 4

For

Charlie, Tommy and Emily
16/5/02   16/9/04   8/2/07

Author's Note

The original subtitle of *Heads and Hearts* was 'A Beginners Exploration'. The explorers' journey arose from insatiable interest in words and has proceeded, one way and another, all my life.

A new category of words, **donouns**, derived from Performatives (see Introduction) has been identified.

Thirteen sections emerged, **I – XIII**, with sub-sections. This structure forms the Contents, which appears on pages 25-29.

There have been times when the text resembled a 'common place book' rather than a systematic Exploration. Inter-dependence between heads and hearts is challenged when experiences associated with them, thoughts and feelings, become separated. When and why this happens raises need, urgent need, to renew their association; to recognise and reclaim their interdependence. This led to change the subtitle: 'An Inquiry into Integrity'.

A caution to you, the reader: sections overlap, sometimes repeat, and range from simple obvious observation to occasional excursions of special interest such as stimulated by *The Consolations of Music, Logic, Theology, and Philosophy* (see References) and some of many social, economic and political consequences during fifteen hundred years since.

A late addendum: to thank Caxton who established his printing press (using Gutenberg technology) at Westminster. Monks and friars, imps and devils (including boy Benedictines, who became black with ink) worked with and for Caxton in the Chapples, which housed his presses.

FONT, word into PRINT, is clear on the top bar with WORD, VIEW, EDIT, WORK: baptism of literacy renewed in our new world of Information Technology.

Acknowledgements

In my head and heart, heart and head, are very many friends; wise erudite elders, lifelong teachers, particularly Peggy and Henry Chadwick, faithful, learned explorers.

Young and ageing students, vividly remembered, are valued and appreciated. Essential questions, often unanswerable, require to- and fro- curiosity, wonder, doubt and faith. Far, far more continues to be received than offered from these and from my beloved family.

The George Bell Institute (GBI), founded and directed by Andrew Chandler, now in its tenth year and increasingly world-wide, has brought new friends — Fellows, Scholars and Trustees, earlier connections renewed and new ones formed. Melanie Barber, encyclopaedic archivist/librarian, GBI Trustee, introduced me to Andrew Chandler, editor of Humanitas, the GBI biennial journal. His encouragement, generous, support, accompanied by the IT skill of Andrew McClosky, have been unfailing. Jan Ross, GBI Fellow with powerful Anglo-US literary perspectives, has offered sustenance and invaluable suggestions.

The exigencies and necessities of publishing such work have demanded much courage as well as skill and expertise. Alan Gordon Walker has met them despite many versions, alterations, complicated by eccentricities of different software and hardware to produce this volume. New thoughts and connections occur: compelling, hard to repress. I value and appreciate his experience, patience and expertise, midwife of a long and strenuous process.

Friends: Christopher Sinclair Stevenson, Peter and Brenda Duffell of St Gabriel's Trust, have helped.

I hope that among the words gathered and set down, some will stimulate discussion and further inquiry since integrity is central to human goodness and happiness.

Anne Lamb
London, April 2007

Introduction

'Words are man-made things which men use, not persons with a will and consciousness. Whether they make sense or nonsense depends upon whether the speaker uses them correctly or incorrectly.'

(W. H. Auden, *Notes on the Comic*, 1948)

'For last year's words belong to last year's language
And next year's words await another voice.'
(T. S. Eliot, *Little Gidding* II (CPP, page 194))

'In the beginning was the Word '
(*John* 1.1)

i

Why is so much written here, now, about such ordinary everyday ingredients of human being as head and heart, mind and will, work and play, by a non-specialist ageing beginner for beginners? Is there a story?

'Integer' is a whole quantity, intact. 'Integral' is gathering integers, quantities, parts, to integrate them into a whole. Heads and hearts, integral in living being, cannot be weighed and measured, quantified, until and unless pathologists have reason to examine them after death, but 'integrity' is a quality of personality and character expressed in actions and is the subject of this inquiry: none can estimate their own. The scope is far reaching, general in range, uneven when special excursions occur.

The Contents, included in this introduction, present the whole. Each section, subsection, is intended to be, like an integer, intact, investigated to be read for itself; then integrated within the whole: larger than the sum of the parts. Quotations and persons provide references within sections and sub-sections; subjects which are topics as well as themes.

1

Heads and hearts are visible and invisible entities: organs that embody thoughts and feelings, seen and unseen, which characterise thinking and feeling. Nobody, no body, is alive without both. External physical stimulus promotes internal response in each person distinctively, and with others. Reactions prompt impulse, feeling, then thought. Memory stores and remembers. Ideas occur in the head where sight, hearing, smell and taste communicate and interact. Senses prompt reactions, emotions, capable of expansion and development — with news, informed intelligence for intelligence. The fifth sense, touch, extends throughout healthy living bodies, outsides and insides. Emotion is said to 'touch' the heart; realised, acknowledged, considered in mind towards definition, understanding, remembered. Feeling, initial sense-response, engenders reaction with emotion, positive and negative, thought-provoking. All this follows and is promoted by emergence of **word**, singular, plural; infinitive, definitive, definite, infinite.

Knowledge grows when experts develop specialities. These diverge and appear to lose connections with each other. This tends to *limit* our apprehension of the whole. Nevertheless, the '-ologies' and '-ographies', theoretical, graphical and practical, need each other, inwardly and outwardly. The '-ics' and '-isms', (aesthetics and aestheticism, ethics and ethicism, romantic and romanticism) are experiences in search of principles: realised, understood then methodically applied. Recognising interdependence need not, ought not, surrender consciousness of the high value of ever increasing specialisations. Fact engages heads to discern theory, discover principle which enhances practice.

Shakespeare characterises Moth, a page, and Costard, a clown, discussing the hazardous folly of words studied and used in affectation rather than understood in lived experience:

> *Moth:* They have been at a great feast of languages, and stolen the scraps.
> *Costard:* O! they have lived long in the alms-baskets of words. I marvel thy master hath not eaten thee for a word; for thou art not so long by the head as honorificabilitudinitatibus: thou art easier swallowed than a flap-dragon.
> (Shakespeare, *Love's Labour's Lost*, V.1)

Theory, of a kind and practice, fuse in proverbs: 'the proof of the pudding is in the eating'; 'don't bite off more than you can chew'; 'fed up to the teeth'; 'I'll eat my hat'.

Frontiers and limits, recognised for precise definition and for concentration on particularities, endanger realisation of the whole if they exclude what is relevant to it. Motive lies in feelings and in thought moving action in any sphere, and level. Thought scrutinises, seeks to evaluate, to judge, plan and decide. Distinctive casts of mind tend to form and call on Heads and Hearts; interrelated, inter-dependent to integrate them.

ii

> 'Tell me where is Fancy bred,
> Or in the heart or in the head?
> How begot, how nourish'ed?
> Reply, Reply.
> It is engender'd in the eyes,
> With gazing fed; and Fancy dies
> In the cradle where it lies .
> Let us all ring Fancy's knell:
> I'll begin it, - Ding, dong, bell!
> ALL: Ding, dong, bell.'
> (Shakespeare, *The Merchant of Venice*, III. 2, lines 63-70)

Bassanio (friend of the Merchant, Antonio) loved Portia: beautiful, talented, 'richly left'. Her father determined to distinguish qualities of character among suitors courting his beloved daughter by inviting each to choose a casket, gold, silver or lead. Bassanio sings of fancy before reviewing the caskets. He prefers lead to gold or silver. It contains Portia's portrait. Bassanio becomes 'giddy in spirit'. Fancy, like thistledown, floats in breezes, dances in wind, is blown away. It has developed many meanings, illusions, delusions. Bassanio's fancy did not flee away; he loved Portia and would have to survive her severe tests too.

Heads (visible externally), hearts (unseen), are vital in living being. The challenge to wonder, consider, explore, think and feel, is enduring, but specialists explore further, farther. Talk of heads now includes brain and psyche; cognition, sense reception, perception and intelligence, mind and memory. Hearts, meanwhile, beat, pulse with breath and blood, more than core physical organs. 'Heart trouble' may mean unresolved, uncertain, contradictory emotions, desires, feelings, complications of intention.

Why should a generalist attempt to find more, fresh, words about heads and hearts, objects and subjects of expanding specialization? Things, words, understood in everyday realities draw on all manner of cultural sources, memories and associations interacting between body and mind, feeling and thinking. Personal consciousness awakens instantaneously and gradually throughout life as externals prompt internal reactions in feeling and thought. Search for meaning explores far beyond primary sense perception, obvious, and reason, thoughtful, assisted by recollection, connections in memory. Undigested experience requires digestion for coherence and understanding.

These interrelationships raise questions not simply of comprehension, but of individual characteristics: capability to evaluate and *act* accordingly, integrated into 'character'.

Where does this integration, 'integrity' come from? Can it be cultivated, like a healthy plant, a fruit-tree? It is surely more than fancy. How do we learn to trust? To become trustworthy? Learning to discern what is beautiful, true and good? Integrity, recognisable in others, cannot be claimed for ourselves however much hoped for.

Specialists concentrate on increasing their expertise. Some become inward-looking and remote from each other. Definition concentrates on distinctive particularities but a concept can become a tyranny. Human beings experience immense diversity. Personal and communal cultivation, culture, promotes civilizations recognisable when they acknowledge and integrate diversity coherently, creatively and successfully.

iii

There is a new word/concept: DONOUN. Donoun sounds odd at first, but it means what it says and says exactly what is meant.

Donouns bridge the gap between intention and action: inwardly considered, decided, possibly in action done: potential union in being and doing. **Many donouns are in *italics*, but not all.**

Mind and *Work*, prototype donouns, reflect the possibility, reality, of **unity in being and doing**. As soon as this train of thought gets going, many **donouns** emerge:

present, find, mix, paste, digest, dream, muse, dance, praise, act — all express potential union: intention to do with something done.

As verbs, donouns are 'doing words', but as a donoun, the same word is used for what might, could, be done: the thought, word, deed: the name of the intended *purpose*, **the** *object* **becomes the thing done, a noun e.g.** they *dream* of a place where the *dream* will come true.

An idea thought of in mind moves from *conceived* to *envisaged* to *planned* and, possibly, *performed: achieved, realised, done*. **DONOUN** unites in one word, to BE and to DO simultaneously; when you *dream* a *dream*, run a *run, act* an *act*.

Many words change or need another word formulated for action, performance. To think a thought, sing a song, do a deed, speak (make) a speech, modify the verb.

DONOUN is a NEW WORD/CONCEPT, derived from PERFORMATIVE UTTERANCE, explored by J. L. Austin. Austin uses the word PERFORMATIVE to unite statement with action: saying as doing. (*How to do Things with Words, page 4.*) (See Appendix **B** Perfomatives; Appendix **C** Donouns.)

Performatives and **donouns** assist this inquiry. A **PROMISE** is a performative utterance: something done by saying it: **'I promise'**.

An **Act** is not performed until done, so *act* is not a 'performative'. Speaking of it does not do it. Also, ***will*** (see **IX**) signifies 'I will act' or will not, or fail to.

ACT, like *mind*, is a donoun. An act is inward (e.g. ***resolve***), outward, (e.g. ***done***), **acted out, integrated when intention resolved is done consistently: simultaneously, or sooner or later.**

To think is ability to *act* **in** *mind*. Sometimes I *act* before I think. Sometimes I think before I *act*. Do I, do you, understand what that *act will mean*: means? What do you think? *Mean*, mathematical, measurable, also signifies ***purpose*, intention, meaning.**

I think a thought but thought is not a **donoun**. Words spoken have been called linguistic acts. Unity in being and doing, is the essential, significant, potential quality in **donouns** as in 'happy' performatives. A broken ***promise*** is unhappy.

Human acts occur at different levels: in practice (evident), in feeling, in thought, in evaluation of quality and purpose, moral. These may integrate in 'the spirit' of the act: the feeling, thought, value. (See Appendix **A**.)

The simple method to recognise distinctions between levels of meaning shows in ordinary **donouns** in common use, e.g. *smell, dig, mix, kiss, present* etc: integral actions in themselves, also capable of further meaning. *Form, judge, plan, purpose, promise, hope* ***need*** more than one level of meaning, for significance. (See Appendix **A**.)

Primary **donouns**, e.g. *will, work, struggle, fight,* engage more than first level: ordinary, practical, primary, in emotional, intellectual, moral contexts.

Elemental **donouns**, e.g. *LIGHT, EARTH, AIR, FIRE, WATER, SPRING,* known physical realities, practicalities, are realised, understood to descend, e.g. *light* **from sun, long before life lived to recognise and enjoy it.** Sun is source of the reality of *light*.

Another category: **electrifying donouns**, includes *switch, wire, fuse, ring, plug,* with other meanings, some puns. More will occur.

FIT: **vital, exemplary, dangerous donoun**; fascinating prefix and suffix: *try* it!

DONOUNS assist the motive and the dynamic of inquiring into integrity since they recognise potential integration in being/doing, *intent* achieved, or at least, intended to. (See Appendix **C**.)

iv

Words enable communication. To identify, *name*, describe, discuss each and any material thing: practical, emotional, thoughtful theoretical, quality experienced in heads and hearts, discovers and stimulates ideas and beliefs: some with *power* capable of transforming lives and conditions of life towards culture and civilisation. High risks occur in challenging strenuous **WORK**. Insulation, isolation — sometimes protective, protecting — isolated lives may need *rescue*, *repair*, friendship, *humour*, joy to *laugh*, *cry*, *SAVE*, deliver, redeem, restore. Deliver becomes deliverance, redeem redemption, restore restoration.

Individuals at *work*, singly, alone, and together with another, others in a group, *need* and use words. Hearing is inward and outward; heard and/or spoken; intimately, privately, publicly: connected, consciously directed. **WILL**, personal or another's, includes imperatives: indicative, tense, tenses, tensions, interactive, manifest, paradoxical, *embodied experience* — stimulating, frustrating, metaphysical and mysterious with transforming visions: glimpses of *glory*; rumour; concern for the future; occasional *promise* of continuity, possible eternity.

Words, particularly performatives and **donouns**, draw together and integrate *work* with words. This is unending, continuing, inexhaustible since words began simply; are simply here to be explored and increase exponentially. Here, now, this inquiry is the effort of a slightly literate English castaway on Prospero's Island, neither *desert* nor deserted. Insularity, first person singular, requires appetite and will to survive: intuition accompanies formation and development of individuality. Shakespeare knew the works, words of Homer and Plutarch, Alfred the Great, Chaucer: of Coverdale, Tyndale, Cranmer: translators who made the English Bible and Common Prayer that encompass the highest and lowest, breadth and depth of most intense and extreme experience in head and heart, body and soul. *Love* and *hate*, *hope* and *fear*, *delight* and *despair*: *hope* confident to enjoy liberty; to suffer and experience tragedy, comedy, glory.

Mind scrutinises; needs and seeks criteria for quality, for comparison, reference and terms of reference. A *cast* of *mind* tends to *form*: fanciers fancy – cats, birds, pigeons. Hearts, symbols of emotion distinct from heads, intellect, *move* towards conscious, occasionally dynamic, reaction in notions, ideas, concepts worked out in *mind*. *Will*: mysterious ingredient beyond impulse, sometimes diagnosed as determination or denied as pre-determined, inevitability, leads to action. Freedom realised, assumed, suggests initiative to *lead*, follow, obey or disobey. *Head* may advise and assist *will* to *rule*; to overrule heart. Heart is capable of disparaging thought and disregarding *head*. Criteria clarify and enable evaluation in effort to *resolve*, decide, *act*. Context, circumstances, other people, discourage exclusive introspection, self-protecting isolation, danger of self-invention. Cross currents produce whirlpools of uncertainty, *fear*, inertia, inaction, sometimes unmanageable.

Heartlessness suggests absence of feeling. Headlessness (not a word, but colloquially referred to, unkindly, as 'bone from the neck up') implies little ability and/or will to think, now recognised as 'learning difficulties.'

Numb senses; emotional, mental, moral blindness, remain ignorant until *hunger* for nourishment; for mending and healing is awakened. Heads and hearts interact in every direction, up and down, down and up, adjacent, crosswise, diagonally. Appendix **A** invites you to *find* your own words. Individual *face* and *voice* are similar but unique: personal. Common denominators, low; and factors, high and low, (not numerical) engender tension and conflict. **WILL,** conscious or not, absent or present, weak, strong; wild, cultivated, personal, social, intuitive, instinctive, conscientious, inspired, divined engages faculty of decision for intended, purposive activity. (See **VIII** and **IX**). Those who believe themselves prisoners of genes; of circumstance including imprisonment, poverty, disability, may find liberty and joy in making ordinary simple decisions which *help*, and *work*. Obedience, disobedience and subjection, liberty and freedom, wisdom and folly, good and evil occur, realised or unrealised, at every level of consciousness, cognition and re-cognition. Attitudes to *will* involve belief.

(See **XIII I**.) Questions of liberty and freedom, virtue, **order**, regulation, law and citizenship open landscapes of humanity to individuals who discover and explore them. Heart and **head**, body and **mind** generate energy for growth, exploration, spirit of adventure, for good and ill.

Great questions concern **initiative**, **change: initiation**, **quality**, **value** and **effect.**

Is **change**, rise and *fall*, *progress* and regress, beyond personal responsibility, decision and **control**? Natural changes occur in natural cycles, one leading to another. Sun, earth and moon **move**, give **light** and darkness. Tides, seasons, measured in **time**, **space**, **place**, are predictable; occasionally extreme, devastating. Scientific method is systematic observation, from evidence; experiment verified with reason.

Will, *purpose* and intention in human doings continues to challenge individuals and society afresh. War and peace, **power** in different forms, variously exercised, characterise the **rise** and *fall* of social/political/economic systems. Evaluation raises questions about the nature and criteria of value. These involve interests, law, virtue, good and evil, true or false. To diagnose the true nature of things, circumstance, situation, motive, requires cultivation, **control**, and conscience at every **level**. Civility nurtures and is nurtured, cultivated, towards civilisation characterised by qualities valued. Sure foundations of knowledge and responsibility include differentiating between wisdom and folly, virtue and vice. Heads and hearts *need* **will** — for good order.

V

DONOUN, is emphatic repetition. (c.f. phonic, -phatic, -rhetic.) Donoun: a word used as a verb, a doing word, and an action, something done.

A name or a personal pronoun identifies the doer of an action done. Places and things as well as persons are nouns.

I **work** the **work**; you **switch** the **switch**; we **hope** the **hope**, they **plan** their **plan**.

Donouns draw attention to **intention** to do and **action**, **act** done. Being and doing become *integrated*. Otherwise, an intention, possibly not genuine, is delayed or remains undone. Does this test integrity ?

Use and understanding of DONOUN is essential in the **plan** of this **inquiry**. **HEAD and HEART often intend to co-operate in action**, but do not always do as intended: **plan**, **purpose**, *not* **achieved, do not integrate.**

Donoun communicates **potential integrity of intention and action, in** **practice.**

Donouns disclose useful, functional, fruitful, helpful co-ordination: integration.

MIGHT and *POWER*, **donouns** of energy, connect reaction to initiative: *WILL*. An idea in *mind* moves from imagined to envisaged to planned: capable of being done. This possibility extends the concept of **PERFORMATIVE, to do as said** (e.g. I promise, bet, bequeath, etc: performed and achieved by saying so).

Performatives and donouns identify and recognise INTEGRATION of being and doing, thence INTEGRITY: *purpose* **trusted to be achieved.**

Act, like *mind*, is a **donoun**. An act is performed inwardly, outwardly, both together. To **think** is ability to *act* in *mind*. Sometimes I *act* before I think. Sometimes I think before I *act*. Do I understand what that *act will mean*: means? What do you think? I think a thought but thought is not a **donoun**.

Unity in being and doing is the quality, the potentiality; disclosed and emphasised in donouns and in happy performatives.

Prototype **DONOUNS**, *WILL* (IX) and *WORK* (XII), demonstrate possibility and reality of unity in doing and being. More categories will occur.

A Per*form*ative can be noun and adjective as well as verb. *Form*, singular, plural, tense and participle, becomes the *form*, formed to *form* up and so on. Studies of words are consequent and subsequent from their origin. (See Appendix **B**.)

A word **spoken** outwardly is heard inwardly. To speak or write what is known by name, heard of, remembered, is recalled in memory and adopted as known. **Writing** is imitated, copied, reproduced, to be read. Words for feeling: *desire*, *gain*, loss, reject, *hope, fear, trust, love* and *hate* involve personal response. Thought and thinking process advance from naming things; responding with feeling; then considering: 'notions', 'ideas', 'concepts', theoretical: evaluated for *purpose*, stored in memory, return to practical use.

To suppose, presuppose, reason, and explain needs and includes objective description, as accurate as possible. To think about things, about actions considers what to do; something or nothing. The levels of experience make much more *sense* together, integrated. Evaluation before action saves mistakes and time. Thinking about future plans, actions, involves *hope* and *fear*, expectation and *dread*, inclination, preference; hopeful — or not. Prospects raise questions of value, commitment, cost and responsibility; what next to expect and prepare for; sooner or later.

Words emerge to refer to any and everything 'under the sun' and beyond: outside and inside ourselves, to spheres where conjecture, imagination, *wonder* and discovery reach regions conceived in mind wherever intelligent theory, theoretical calculation, lead.

Mind work assisted by high technology enables projection beyond limits of direct *sense*. Ordinary day to day concepts of time and space prepare mind to re-appraise, to conceive of immeasurable vastnesses and unimaginably minute entities, cells, sub-atomic ingredients, reactions, needing new names: words.

Languages live and die. Linear B, deciphered, opened understanding of inscriptions excavated at Knossos. To articulate and remember occurs within, in and out of consciousness. From silence to silence is stillness without or beyond words. Grains of sand on the sea shore; stars, familiar constellations, remote galaxies, black holes, red giants; invisible minutiae, atoms and protons, neutrons and neutrions, extreme in size and scale beyond sight. Seeds, infant plants, great trees, insects, bacteria, embryos of life, fishes, birds, animals, all creatures evolved and evolving; some devolving towards extinction. Words needed are found.

Plato's Line (See Figure 1, **XIII I**) illustrates transition from wondering to believing; **to awaken to know the good**. This awakening may be slow, gradual, instantaneous. Interest, curiosity, confident *trust* encourage *will*. (See Figure 2, **XIII I**.)

Problems with *will*, with *desire* and duty; with *power*, energy and conscience are not solved by *knowing* good and evil, true and false. *Power* to *ACT* is needed.

Form leads to formation, intrinsic form, active energy in *will, act*. Actions according to spoken form are performed. Performance is visible or invisible, seen and unseen, heard and unheard.

Perform joins formative into performative. Actions such as to breathe, *drink, sleep,* are indispensable for life. Action performed, to do or not to do, to obey or disobey, quote or misquote, affirm or deny, depends on the *will* **of the performer: free, forced or unforced. The moral significance of J. L. Austin's recognition is so significant that it cannot be exaggerated.** Some readers may not need repetition but emphasis may help others. Sections and subsections, sequential, are supported within themselves.

An action spoken and done by saying so is performative: 'I name this ship'. Looking for what is true, performative and performance depend on *motive*: prior *intent*: *will* to do. A performance may derive from essential nature of being in being; such as *stand, drink, grasp, state*: facts. A performative states, announces, speaks, 'utters' intention as commitment to do.

Personal performance derives from primal ability, instinctive, and/or deliberate *will*; yours, mine, by, with or from inherent source of being human due to another **WILL** which may or may not be known, known of, acknowledged, willingly obeyed requiring us to *sleep*, awaken, *move, stand* etc. Such actions are 'ordered' as instinctive, composed, imitated, reproduced, eventually decided obediently, independently, or not, at different levels of experience. A performative is stated. The speaker who makes the statement does what is stated: I *estimate*, *value*, *locate*, *swear*, *bet*, *repudiate* and *conclude*.

A performative utterance is defined in saying which causes action to take place **in speaking the word only**: to say is to do. Promise, assess, diagnose, recommend, calculate, define (and many others) are examples. It is not necessary to say 'I am performing an assessment'; 'I *assess*' is sufficient. That is the simple test for a performative, always a verb. I refer, hope, understand (or hope I do, and keep repeating the principle of performatives to emphasise it). If I have missed something that limits your understanding, and betrays my incomplete understanding, that will be very unhappy. (Critics please observe and mention). The integrity of performatives depends on dependable speaker-performer, who keeps the spoken word: assumed, believed, sure. The guarantor is the utterer: the speaker who will perform. Failure raises questions of responsibility, of *trust*, of *fault*, of **integrity**. This inquiry engages destructive as well as positive factors.

What factors damage integrity? Levels of deception, of *not being true* to oneself, to another, to ultimate source(s) of what is **true. The question of what is true hangs over the performer whose intention tests integrity in action.** (See **XIII II.**)

Performatives are intended, expected, to be trustworthy and reliable. When they are not, Austin's word for them is **'unhappy'**. Limited knowledge, unintended error, incomplete assessment, partially informed diagnosis, distorted understanding, prejudice, unexpected intervention are among many possible causes of such unhappiness. An assessor, aware of uncertainties, makes the best of what is known and may include provisos. An assessment is approximate; generalised as carefully and accurately as possible. More may be known than the assessor realises; new information relevant to the assessment awaits discovery. A third fallibility is in the motive of the assessor (diagnostician, recommender, evaluator, judge, prescriber) who utters the performative. An assessment intended to mislead, exaggerate, falsify will have **unhappy consequences**.

Performatives depend on these three aspects of what is true: first knowing; second known to and from the speaker; third, intention to do as said. Resolution and energy are needed to perform; either may fail. Trust-worthy *trust* is reciprocal: 'My word is my bond.' Is it? Are you sure? Can you or I be sure? Whose word are you sure of?

To *define* is itself origin of *performative*. Words stand for, state, describe and speak of. Some words define and are defined in more than one way. *Long, post, point, work,* among many others, have many uses and meanings, food for puns as well as thought. Definition may be incomplete, partly true, true sometimes, but capable of distortion, falsity, to mislead. A 'false' definition contradicts the term. It is not true. Who to *trust* and what to believe? Performatives are personal, singular, as when you or I say what we are doing and will do. To promise, covenant, plan, bet, enact, proclaim, agree, vote are performed, with or without assistance. An **order** to be obeyed by another, others, is performative.

Order does not depend only on word spoken but on authority communicated in a word. 'Let there be **LIGHT**!'

Donouns show, link, join, integrate, being and doing. To span the abyss of our ignorance, a *bridge* will link natural practicality, actual, with theoretical principle. A *bridge* connects two sides, practical and abstract, practice with theory, outward to inward; a feature of realistic thought, of thoughtful realism. 'Symbol' is not a **donoun** because it represents something which endows experience with meaning. 'Symbol' is not a verb but *bridge* is a symbol, noun and verb. It is, in the first instance, a *structure*. As a concept, a bridge connects; to cross and be crossed over rivers, railways, chasms; over misunderstandings, doubts and disbelief experienced. To *plan* and build a *bridge* offers *benefit* from the *process* of to-ing and fro-ing. This is its *function*; a real achievement as a material thing embodied, and as a concept, a *construct* for two-way communication. *Tunnel* is an underground version of *bridge*.

Collective performatives occur when one voice speaks for all and commits people to act together in, for, under **ORDER**, sovereign *will*. Each individual **link** in the **chain** is tested in collective action when a community is conscious of and respects corporate identity: family, village, school, business, public corporation, city, nation, alliance: 'thrones and dominations'. Consensus enables one to speak for all in common *hope*, and accepts constitutional *process*, representation, to determine *consent*. Policies stated, decisions announced, tax imposed, treaties signed, war declared, peace made, celebrations planned, involve collective performatives. Bad behaviour defined, proclaimed, needs law, legislation, Acts enacted. The same qualifiers apply. Unhappy performatives occur, infelicities of policy, injustices in administration and law; maladministration, deceptions, misleading spin, follies. To breathe is essential for life, indispensable obedience to the way life is. Goodness is direct responsibility, not automatic, nor sole. The cleaner the air, the better.

Many utterances, verbs, derive from impersonal activities. **To *form* a natural crystal, *brew* a storm, *blow* a gale, a hurricane; *grow* a tree do not originate or depend only on personal human will or action, although** Prospero found *power*, and prospered. No ordinary human being is able to form, brew, invent or empower forces of nature. To speak of these is not to do them, but recognises that they happen, are done, caused, witnessed, experienced. Some are inimitable, but **many are imitated**. To plant a tree is done with intention, hope, that it will take root and grow. Natural process, imitated, engage selecting plants, trees, for their seeds, nuts, fruits, flowers and wood; cuttings, grafts grow better in some cases but success varies. Genesis concerns beginnings, origins, generating, generations. Francis Bacon paraphrased the emergence of Eden: 'God Almighty first planted a garden; and, indeed, it is the purest of human pleasures': continuing delight from simplest border, bed, hedgerow for cottage to high grandeur of palace and park, increasingly publicly enjoyed. Music, cosmic, of the spheres, is also 'food of love', and:

> 'Orpheus with his lute;
> With his lute made trees
> And the mountain tops that freeze,
> Bow themselves when he did sing...'
> (Shakespeare, *Henry VII*, III, lines 1- 3)

The life of the mind develops *power* to think, remember, associate, distinguish and reconcile intelligence as information; with tension between responses, felt/thought. Mixing, arranging and rearranging thoughts for appraising, judging, deciding, willing, seeks and intends wise action. New ideas occur. Nuclear research unleashes energy; recognition of DNA opens previously unimagined possibilities to identify.

Performatives such as reckon, analyse, concede are less obviously connected with natural processes. Others known in and by nature include plant, lay, strike. **Judge** engages all levels. Union of thought and act, intention done as stated, achieved in saying so; is in effect an ordered act, the *order* given and done in one word. Nevertheless, failures occur. Dangers are not always foreseen: suffering is endemic; effort is costly; injury needs healing, forgiveness, mercy, reconciliation, divinely human; highest and best possible.

To *catch* and imitate echoes, original sounds; then to order, reproduce and develop; to make a song to sing, an instrument to play makes music. David on his *harp*:

improvising, composing and performing, plucked harp and heart strings. Melody and harmony, scale, octave, chord and discord appear for composing and making music. Pattern and theory discerned in sounds enable notation. Compositions noted, written, read, can be repeated, rehearsed, practiced, performed. Personal participation, direct, witnessed — we hear with our ears and see with our own eyes — arouses response in sense, mind and spirit; nourishing the soul. Music enables participation in the fire, sound and light of life; a form of energy moving to creative and performing art: composed, danced, dramatised, staged, performed; depicted, painted and written about. Experience returned to us moves, disturbs, soothes, inspires, ignites appreciation and understanding from sense impressions filtered through heart and mind into other, revealing, digestible matter.

Language increases. Words and phrases, absorbed by listening are caught rather than taught but more complex communication raises questions in the mind of speaker, listener, reader or writer. Grammar emphasises principles as rules to memorise, not always understood. Instinctive communication needs grammar, not as indoctrinated straitjacket but to liberate meaning with clarity; correct but flexible usage; constructions needed to communicate difficult concepts. Performatives offer this challenge. Disregard of right and wrong usage causes inadequate, inappropriate, unsuitable, even false communication. What is true is obscured, hidden, disguised, eventually lost. Superficial use evaporates words spoken without commitment and responsibility. Words adopted, adapted, applicable as far as they go, go only so far as the limits of the user's knowledge of grammar and knowledge of vocabulary, necessary as they are for comprehensive clarity, draw power and energy from source to speaker, writer, true to the good, believed and acted upon.

The skeleton of language structure, the bones and joints that give form and shape to body and limbs, are clothed with muscles and sinews for fluent movement; skin, sensitive to touch and to protect. Strength and agility of mind voiced into words develops quality of speech. Inward personal *form, shape* are of living organs, the heart and lungs of receiving and giving experience, nerved and minded, sensibilities of consciousness, conscience to *filter*; to *reflect*, remember, formulate, evaluate, *judge*, describe and attempt to find words. Each person, free and able, may do this for themselves, more and less effectively. We are fortunate when introduced to words well and truly spoken, well-constructed to nourish appetites of enthusiasm, enjoyment and understanding, from early age.

Each new voice in English — poets, philosophers, translators, some already mentioned – Chaucer, Langland, William Tyndale, Cranmer, Shakespeare, Milton, George Herbert, Dryden, Alexander Pope, Browning, T. S. Eliot, renew and extend resources of language which refresh and reinvigorate the common tongue. User confidence increases the powerful gift of words; consider an exclamation overheard during a performance of Hamlet: 'This play is just made up of quotations'.

'Icon' has been adapted for a processor symbol. 'Icon' 'personifies' a trend setter, a leader of fashion, style and taste. This is not new or unimportant. Access to increasingly profound experience through icons has divided believers in deep *rift*, schism. Performatives involve the speaker making good the action performed in speaking, understood when heard. It is **the spirit in the will of the speaker as performer** which makes an utterance happy or unhappy. Integrity integrates when PRINCIPLES are recognised, acknowledged, respected and followed.

DONOUNS are considered with participles, junctions, conjunctions in **XIII II**. Finding words follows need to express something in **context**: nouns, verbs, adjectives, conjunctions, prepositions and so on. *Search* is active to discern, identify, verbalise and *name*.

Activity, events, happenings and doings require a distinctive word, not a *noun* but a *verb*. To quote 'verbatim' means repeating exactly, without adding or subtracting. To report without describing, discussing or embellishing has regard to origin; true source and source of what is true. Addiction to adjectives and adverbs, exaggeration, hyperbole, can obscure simple source and origin and dramatise beyond reality. To *play* down is to 'understate'.

A noun plus a doing word, a verb, make a sentence. The briefest sentences are two words. **I am. It is. You do. We see.** (See **II iii**.) **They tell. I hear. I wonder. I might. I will. Will you? Austin suggested going through a dictionary for more performatives.** Once you look for them, they occur again and again. Some are **donouns** but not all; agree becomes agreement, argue argument, apologise apology but a *judge* is the *judge*. **The will of the speaker/doer to perform defines performatives. Austin's work, commended by a very revered and learned friend, is a discovery of this inquiry. Austin renewed moral philosophy.**

'A **noun**: the name of a person, place or thing.

A verb: a **do**-ing word.'

Simple definitions memorised, learnt 'by heart' at school, remain in mind, trip from the tongue, are tapped into the processor. To re-emphasise: a **donoun** is both a noun and a verb.

Personal pronouns (I, you, etc), definite or indefinite article (the, a, any); and appropriate adjective(s) accompany **donouns** in sentences. He *will* make his *will*. You *smile* with a *smile* of welcome. I *cry* with a *cry* of joy; or anguish.

Verbs adapted as nouns becomes **gerunds**. Add '-ing' to the verb 'to add' is action of addition. 'Adding' (gerund) is a verbal noun (like telling, swimming, skimming, slimming). You think and might say 'I am having a think' or 'I was/am thinking' (gerund): or 'I thought' (past tense but referring to present thinking). Think is not a **donoun**. It does not make sense to say 'I think a think' but 'I had a thought' or 'a thought came into my mind'; I *thought* a *thought*, (not) but 'I had a thought' or 'a thought came to me'; an idea is more usual. Thought, past tense, conditional, may not reach conclusion. **Conclude** is performative. A jury concludes guilt or innocence, a verdictive performative.

Participles of verbs are used as adjectives for nouns. 'Participle' originates from a person partaking, participating **in two natures**. A participle as a verb adds more about being, essences, characteristics described: lighting, planting, weeping, meditating. A jumping flee, a running rabbit, a sitting duck, a scintillating, or tiring person, a loving friend use participles as verbal adjectives. Two natures are **emphatic** in hopping mad, sailing clouds, raging sea, healing hand, **living word. Theological implications are powerful, as in electrifying energy,** *charge* **and charging. Living word charges and is charged, divinely human.** (See **XIII II 2 iii.**)

A finite verb can occur on its own in a main clause with variations in tense, number, mood. (They race; he is racing.) The infinitive, base form of a verb: to race, jump, swallow, is non-finite. Many **donouns** occur as both. **Donoun**, gerund and participle overlap, but each has distinctive qualities. **Donoun** is of itself; not a gerund or participle but duality in unity, being and doing. **Donouns** express this unity, this capability to be and do, will-in-act, intrinsic capability in a word. Experts in linguistics, not always the same as expert linguists, may comment on these, and other differentiations.

Performatives presuppose intention to do by saying: saying as doing: *promise, estimate, consent.* Sometimes a performative fails; a promise is not kept, an estimate not adhered to, or wrong; consent withdrawn or denied. Austin's discussion of performatives as felicities and infelicities, happy or unhappy, is essentially profoundly **MORAL**. A false promise is untrue; a lie, not intended to be performed. Circumstances alter cases, but intention was or was not, is or is not genuine. Alice in Wonderland meant what she said and said what she meant. Hearing precedes saying until words said are heard. To believe relies, depends on **trust** tested and found genuine in performance. This involves trusting the person who utters the word, words. 'Happy' and 'unhappy'; 'felicities' and 'infelicities' depend on intention, genuine or not, of the utterer. Austin is wary of saying 'true' and 'false' because of possibility of 'fetishes'. His analysis of the principles of performatives includes recognition that rules broken cause misfires, abuses, misinvocations, misexecutions, flaws due to insincerity. (*How to do Things with Words*, page 18.)

Being/doing unites two 'parts of speech', two aspects of life in one word, **donoun**. Finding words to state intention moves from present and past to intended future. To formulate, express, explain, inform, encourage or warn are performatives: commitment to do by saying. **Donouns** unite being/doing.

Inward being and doing includes *wonder, stress, doubt, range, rage*: **donouns** of felt/thought prior to speech and action, but occasioning awe, *fear*, tears, exclamation, utterance, eventually, with will, performative. To articulate is action and Austin's discussion of performative utterances starts there. Some performatives are **DONOUNS**. The most obvious are practical: *rate, rule, value, cost*. Give, thank, assess need modification; you *walk* the *walk*, *run* a *run*, *stage* on *stage*, *stake* the *stake*, *hold* a *hold* need no new commitment to be involved: the same word is doing and deed. *Read* is used in discussing 'A Good Read' (BBC Radio 4). 'Runs may read' puns 'runs'. *Play* the game has many variations, inverse, converse, diverse etc.

Donouns disclose and reflect essential union, real and potential, in being and doing. They do not depend on what someone means to do by saying so but they reflect reality, **what is as it is. *Water* is *water* is wet, elemental and primal. Being begins in the thing itself in origin and *power*. Its function may be encouraged, promoted, cultivated, imitated by doer, doing. WILL is capability, doing done; or left undone. *Purpose* in, as, for and on purpose; deliberated, deliberately, deliberate; comprehensively evident in each and all levels of human experience expressing *will*, with or without integrity.**

Readers who recognise **donouns** as uniting, unifying being/doing will want to qualify, modify, and add to *preliminary classification*. (See Appendix **C**.)

Original intelligence engages inward recognition. We *need water* and unless we *find, drink, take* it in some *form* or other, we de-hydrate and expire. Primal **donouns**, subsequent to elemental, are primary in nature, principles discovered in processes and realised through function in action.

Some, both primal and elemental, in substance and activity are sovereign

donouns. *Water* is agent of process as well as an element. *Rain* washes away, erodes. *Water* will *find* its own *level, flow* as a stream, *drain, stream* into rivers, lakes and seas. Falling from *cloud, rain* supplies *water* to *drink*, to irrigate. Moving *water* has potential *power*, with and without *control* until we *work* out how and *find* ways and means to *harness* waterpower. *Wind power*, horsepower, electric and nuclear *power* have *source* outside ourselves. *Desert* people learn to live with little water but do not survive without *drink*. (*Desert* is an adjective, noun and verb). *Drink* quenches *thirst*; essential to bodily *functions*: saliva, *blood, sweat*, tears, juices of human body. **Salt** is specially needed in hot weather and climate. Surplus liquid is **waste**, recycled inwardly or ejected outwardly; liquid or moisture, vaporised, distilled and purified, re-cycled in the atmosphere. **Water supply**, originally natural, is essential for life; cultivation rewarded by *increase* and improvement.

It has taken much *time* to learn, to observe, imitate, co-operate with and reproduce natural cycles experienced in climate, growth, renewal of life. Impure *water*, noxious *waste*, poisonous plants and creatures are identified to *cause harm*; evil rather than *good*, but capability to purify recycles again. A good **wash** and a good **drink** use **water** to cleanse the outside as well as the inside of a body. *Water* distilled through evaporation returns as sweet refreshing rain and other precipitation.

Cause and *effect* are clues to *reason*; essential to learn, follow, and imitate *process*; to anticipate and to direct **WILL**, to **move**. This underlying power of cause and effect is given and available to human beings, inherent, imitable and imitated. *Raison d'etre* is a succinct expression. What is true of **power**? We *wonder, doubt*; may believe, presuppose, begin to know. Static and dynamic; moving, still and still moving, *time* and *change* are continuing elements of consciousness, increasingly conscious of **WILL** *power*; natural, human, devised mechanisms: was there a starting gun? The **START** is personified by the STARTER; **the person who signals with arm, flag, shot, shout: 'Ready, steady, GO'. (Big Bang setting off processes to evolve.)**

Personal necessities, to *drink, wash, water* the garden with *water* from convenient source: a pond, river, *stream*, well, tank, reservoir, *tap, hose*. Meaning of signs and symbols, give clues and hints, many anticipate **name**. **Donouns** embody being/doing, in and out, out and in. The outward, external is discerned inwardly, internally, internalised but not interned. The word gives the word; a word is of that word. Talent and virtue qualify doing but are not verbs.

Looking for **donouns** discovers them everywhere. Many *stem* from vegetation: *seed, bloom, climb, spread, harvest*. Animal activities: *neigh, snort, trot, gallop; growl, bark; purr,* *pounce, hunt, kill,* not done often by plants or vegetables, but *poison* is exception. Sounds provide many: a *sound* uttered, heard, may *call* for a word. *Question, doubt, plan, plead* are not known activities of plants and animals. Natural vegetation has survival powers, including multiplication, adaptation. Hi-tech cameras *watch, catch,* magnify and disclose them. Growth preceded human existence but knowledge and cultivation promote it. Sticks for peas, beans and clematis to *climb*; straw for strawberry plants to *spread,* safe from slugs; *trench* for potatoes to swell under cover of darkness. Plants were not being secretive; not deliberately protecting their privacy but finding fresh, different ways to adapt, survive and develop. Movement of animals with legs resembles human mobility: *step, pace, walk, jump, leap, attack, escape, race.* People move instinctively, like animals, but also in response to reasons, purposes, other wills. Motives add *design, shape, order* from *mind,* memory at work. Instinctive beginnings are supplemented by thoughtful, controlled reaction and deliberate *purpose.* Inspiration, *cause, start, light,* ignite *will* to *fire, burn, move* and motivate.

Fish *is quintessential* **donoun**. 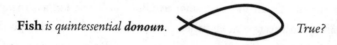 *True?*

Vegetables, animals, humans are interdependent and each dependent on elements: *heat, water, air* and *earth.* (*Earth* becomes **donoun** in knowledge of electrical energy, made safe.) *Breath* breathed in and out, out and in, balances oxygen and carbon-dioxide inhaled and exhaled by foliage, photosynthesis, a formidable recognition. *COUNT, measure, distance* are essence of *size* and of morality.

Conjunctions are reflected in parallel, paradigm, paradox, parable, paradise. (See **XIII II**.)

Para-phrase summarises. A parachute-regiment soldier, trained to drop from an aircraft, is called a Para. The prefix means alongside, pass above, below and parallel to. Variants include para-medic, para-military, parapet, parabola. A French umbrella, *parapluie,* not parasol, but both offer overhead protection from rain or sun. Para- is not neo-, quasi-, change, revival, substitute or imitation but need from or for natural hazards.

Intangible *change*, inward and invisible, shows one thing by means of another through figures of speech: simile, metaphor, analogy and allegory.

Keats' morale is very low, as if drugged, until he hears a nightingale:

'Was it a vision, or a waking dream?
Fled is that music: do I wake or sleep?'
(Keats, *Ode to a Nightingale*)

Participles of verbs are used as adjectives for nouns. 'Participle' participate, participation, originate from a living persons willing activity.

Things, feelings, ideas, hopes and fears occur in work and play, local, extended from countries and continents, increasingly global. Personal memories include some knowledge, less or more. People interact harmoniously and furiously, closely and interdependently; inseparable but separate. Description, spoken and written, promotes analysis. Subjects, topics, themes, problems, infinitely extensive, paradoxical, comical and tragical, promote laughter and tears, pleasure and pain, joy and sorrow, coexisting delight, misery, challenge.

On large scale maps, outline is stronger than detail but maps on any scale need to be true to best information available: not imagined, supposed, invented. Many regions, areas, are unmapped. A map being drawn needs to reflect change during surveys of land and water; mountains, hills, valley and plain. Belief that change is compatible with expectation and tradition requires respect for folk memory plus well tried practice, not necessarily immutable. Imperfection and failure inspire critical dissent, not necessarily revolt or revolution. Exploration itself becomes an attitude of open mind and hopeful heart essential for renewal. Cultivation promotes innovation at every level, tested, informed.

A generalist's scheme forms to profess an underlying philosophy. Extremes become absurd. In Voltaire's *Candide*, Dr Pangloss's determined optimism glossed over calamities and catastrophes, disasters, misery, pandemonium, tragedy, distress without hope, prosperity without compassion. Is all for the best in this best of all possible worlds? Acts of hatred, cruelty, duplicity, depravity cause suffering. Fear, horror, repulsion, revulsion extend from victims to witnesses with *reason* to despair. *Hope* in heart concentrates mind and strengthens *will*; promotes courage for constructive initiative, responsible action, good purpose, compassion; **just** appraisal followed by effort to overcome misery, to relieve distress, with mercy and generosity.

Geoffrey Chaucer went to Canterbury as pilgrim in 1388, aged forty-eight. His *Canterbury Tales*, unfinished when he died, were copied but unprinted until circa 1476-7. (See Appendix **D**.) The vocabulary of its time, renewed, continues embedded in English consciousness, ignored or considered, repelled or digested. Chaucer's parson offers his own scheme of language, experience, salvation. God, he writes, desires no one to perish; there are many spiritual ways to the celestial city. One noble way is Penitence, lamenting for sin and *will* to sin no more. The root of the tree of Penitence is contrition; the branches and leaves are confession; the fruit, satisfaction; the *seed* is *grace*; the *heat* in that seed is the Love of God. Chaucer presents a world where right and wrong, good and evil, true or false, illuminate value and clarify alternatives. Error requires the person who errs, (sins) to embrace contrition. Pride, envy, anger, sloth, avarice, gluttony and lechery cause error. Confession becomes necessary, freely willed in faith, for one's own sins; spoken truthfully, without subtle words; considered, frequent. Satisfaction consists in alms-giving, penance, fasting, its fruit is 'endless bliss in Heaven'.

FONT became the word used for style of letters in **PRINT** because Caxton's printing press was situated at Westminster, worked by youths learning from and taught by the monks, Benedictine. The *Canterbury Tales* were unfinished when Chaucer died and unprinted until Caxton set up his press, in 1476, using technology as new and as significant at that time as Information Technology today.

Caxton's father lived nearby the Abbey, centre of Church and State. Kings lived in the Palace of Westminster. Parliament, attended them there when summoned. Representatives of Shires and Boroughs added to the Great Council (Lords Spiritual and Temporal, plus Treasurer, Chancellor and Judges) when consent was needed for taxation beyond normal feudal dues, increasingly demanded. Orders in Council, later the Privy Council, were promulgated; dissemination of news, information, accelerated when Caxton's printing press became available.

At the root, curiosity stimulates people to explore, investigate, discuss, record and read what is written. Human society has its systems: school and university to offer opportunities to study what is known; to consider and debate, to discover delights and discern dangers; to enjoy friendships and realise abilities to explore new ideas. These are life-long quests. Independent while interdependent, discerning capability in others awakened in ourselves.

Four levels of response, physical, emotional, thoughtful and evaluative, contribute towards balanced wholeness. Frailty in one or more level limits, disables, until sightless eyes or unhearing ears open to compensate. Sense, first level of consciousness, finds response in heart engaging appetite and desire for food for thought. Heartlessness suggests absence of feeling; headlessness the absence of ability and/or *will* to think. Lack of criteria for evaluation includes ignorance and/or denial.

These levels interact through conscious activity in heads and hearts, up and down, down and up, crosswise and diagonally, positively and negatively. (See Appendix **A**.)

Heads and hearts, individual and infinitely variable, have common denominators and shared factors, often in conflict and tension. **WILL**, conscious or not, weak or strong, wild or cultivated, offers challenges acuity of decision, fundamental questions of motive, determining, resolving precede action, doing. (See **VIII** and **IX**.) **WILL** engages energy and power, control and subjection, wisdom and folly, good and evil — all potentially present at every level of consciousness with cognition and recognition, ability to *control*. It is tempting, and not uncommon, to regard change as unavoidable, inevitable, coming and going like natural cycles but primary questions and problems continue to challenge each person in social, culture and society afresh.

The rise and fall of political, economic and social systems appear to confirm the unpredictable nature of human affairs and cause wonder as to what sort of future may be hoped and worked for. We struggle to evaluate, and evaluation itself raises questions about the nature and criteria of value. Contexts in time and place: of family, social groups at work and play, local and extended, countries and continents vary but how we think and feel together, as social beings with particular codes and patterns, ideas and visions requires language commonly understood.

Words are best read in sequence if there is an unfolding saga. This anthology of exploration invites you to 'dip' in and out. Fragments excavated, become pieced together by archaeologists who look for larger patterns. The edges of a jigsaw puzzle set limits; detail is built up within them. Heads, like globes, encompass experience lived in expanding concentric spheres intersected, interrupted by others. Exploration becomes an attitude to sustain and be sustained by open mind and responsive heart. Looking for a beginning is an end in itself with curiosity and imagination.

vi

There are thirteen sections.

First communication occurs without words through senses, signs and symbols, essential connectors, messengers outward, inward and circumstantial. Words are needed, required, nominated, to explore connections, in sections **I**, **II** and **III**.

Things, sources of things: elements and substance, emerge in **IV** and **V**, material in every sense, at every level. Words themselves are symbols. Movement, *change*, is natural at every level. Metamorphic, metamorphosis, metaphysical, **VI**, is continuing theme in exploring words, words within worlds and worlds discovered through words to detect meaning and significance.

Light, sense and energy enable observation, identification, recognition; diagnosis and evaluation; involve judging, preparing for deciding, **VII**, is a simple attempt to explore possibility and responsibility of judging in order to decide and raises questions of wisdom in deciding and finding energy of *will* to do.

Deciding towards doing what could, should be done involves willing, **VIII**.

WILL, **IX** engages dilemmas, complexities, difficulties, fear of danger, of ill-will, leading to realisation and recognition of **EVIL**, **X**, of **CONSCIENCE**, **XI**, interacting in **WORK**, **XII**.

The final section, **XIII**, concerns wondering what is true. To question 'is it true?' presupposes belief that knowledge attainable, verified, is true, since what is not true is not knowledge. This last is in three part: external, internal and in unison, returns to the start: realisation of outward and inward in union.

Simple interest and delight in words, as they are coined, grows and alters our understanding. For Humpty Dumpty: 'When I use a word, it means just what I want it to mean — neither more nor less.' But Alice did not think of her words like that. Humpty Dumpty fell off his wall.

By what criteria can we examine language? This book proposes a scheme of its own. The **DONOUN** unites being and doing, the doer and the deed done. The name of what IS, is a noun. To name is itself an action. You name it, do it. Doing requires a verb: *Look! Act!!*

Donouns help us to discern what is real; emphatic reality. The Appendices are intended to help. Appendix **A** summarises the framework of levels in knowledge and experience; **B** amplifies J. L. Austin's analysis of 'performatives'. **C** is a 'preliminary' on '**donouns**'. The fourth, **D**, summarises Chaucer's *Parson's Tale* in Neville Coghill's modern English.

The Contents, overleaf, sets out the plan, introduced above.

Contents

I

Looking for Words

Eggs, Hats, Stars and Hearts

I i Process and Change

To 'know by heart' means remembered in mind.

Specialists in medicine, building, engineering and technologies need new words: coined, usually connected and derived from origins. Appetite and enquiry add knowledge, fruit of experience increasing expertise assisted by digestive juices of intelligence and storage capability of memory. Practicalities, written records, become inscriptions, codices, scrolls, texts. Interchange between direct and indirect experience, physical sense and inward comprehension nourishes. Proverbs connect them: 'the proof of the pudding is in the eating'; 'don't bite off more than you can chew'; 'fed up to the teeth'; 'I'll eat my hat'; if the seemingly impossible occurs and the unbelievable happens, becomes real, realised. Sometimes, words pass us by; 'go in one ear and out of the other', with no pause for thought or digestion. Sometimes we are 'stitched up' with laughter at an inappropriate word, a silly joke like the bore who couldn't find oil and was told he had better stop boring.

Activities need and find words for common talk; cooked up, overdone, burnt out, boiled dry, steaming, roasted, frizzled and fried. 'Own goal' is recognised by spectators and players. 'Caught out', 'hit for six' and 'it's not cricket' are used by people who neither watch nor play the game themselves.

Word processing is changing ways of learning and communicating. Space, place, time are transcended by this fast developed and developing technology. Memory resources extend and revitalises interest in words. '*Process*' is progenitor of processing, procedure and procession. It is **noun** for the doer and **verb** for what is being done: the processor who processes in action on a processor. A professor professes, makes and works professing profession with huge benefit from using word-processors.

In primary school literacy hour, the revived word 'kenning' concerns being aware of something, someone: John Peel the huntsman, sung to rollicking tune 'Yes, I **ken** John Peel, at the break of day...' To '**con**' is to learn, probably after being told, but systematic instruction, formal teaching method, has been modified by tactile, sense-based discovery since infants and children respond to sights, sounds, smells, tastes and touches, first level experience before encountering a bright star, new planet kenned with awa**ken** personal appetite to wonder and explore.

Word processing generates new words and new meanings for old. The machines, the processors have parts: screen, keyboard (not typewriter, itself a newish word) are 'hardware' with 'mouse' and 'modem'; software, programmes on disk (or disc?), hard and floppy (but soon hard no more). Vocabulary of *function* includes dialogue-box, window, clipboard, headers and footers (from older printing language) *click, scroll, drag*: actions and things that unite *cause* and *effect* according to instruction, to *order* by *command* and *command* to *order*. The earlier meaning of 'computer' as a person who computes has become the instrument operated to do the ***work*** with speed and accuracy, processing words and numbers.

Word Processor applies to the machine. The person at work, in *command*, is a processor engaged in writing, assisted by a processor ('er', or 'or'?). The functions of author, scribe, secretary are changed. A person who errs makes an error, a mistake — hence 'terror'. ***Process*** is a verb and a noun: another **donoun**. The messy business of rubbing out, erasing, becomes '***cut***'. A mistake on screen can be corrected, clicked at sight. The processor may check spelling, organise and reorganise layout and contents ahead of printing, commitment to paper, in ***print***. The Internet is a resource of limitless possibilities. Time and veracity are continuing, enduring considerations.

New words occur as well as old words with new meanings. What is a bitmap font? — a bit, a map, a font, are familiar. Is it safe to guess? Not in this case, since imagination fanciful rather than enlightening — leads into confusing thickets which disable the most obliging system. New vocabulary must be acquired, conned: correctly, truly understood. Technical knowledge of what goes on inside the processor is not essential. A car can be driven without knowing how the engine works under the bonnet or 'hood'. A competent driver drives; a word-processor works to process. Short, simple journeys, routines, enable longer expeditions. Familiarity in practice benefits from newish term 'user-friendly' and astonishing operational capabilities become familiar, used, habitual.

Is this processor just a machine? Is 'Artificial Intelligence' a genuine definition of what a processor makes available to user? Its memory stores words and figures which can be recalled at touch or a few clicks. Without initiative or ideas, a system works according to the design of its designers. Their intelligence offers resources. Problems are anticipated; *'help'* helps. Learning to word-process engages user to search out the designer's patterns, the secrets of the 'Ghost in the Machine', accessible through signs and symbols on screen responding to **command** through keyboard commands; a mouse that clicks. It is necessary to be clear and unequivocal although warning, question, statement come up in dialogue box. *Help* and *search* are available. **Save** is indispensable.

The processor is empowered by electricity and a chip. Like the genii of Aladdin's lamp, it awaits *command,* **click** rather than **rub**, to obey. The operator must operate within rules and scope of the machine. The ghost is of amazing resourcefulness, well-connected and in good working order to serve beginner and expert, young or old who learn its ways. Sometimes a *bomb* appears on the screen. 'Danger: this is too much. I am warning you to find another way of asking me to do this. You are close to causing the system to blow up'. The bomb must be taken very seriously. The screen can 'freeze'. It is too late to ask oneself 'Why? What mistake have I made? What went wrong'. The only thing to do is to switch off. Total loss of work occurs if not 'saved'. Words saved are still there when thaw occurs, the ghost and the machine recover and order is restored. Why did the screen freeze? Answers need to be worked out by going back to a beginning, first cause, consulting an expert or a manual written. 'Know-how' books do not always answer the questions asked. They go back to other starting places to be followed step by step. Gradually there are fewer freezes and bombs. Similarly, a learner-car-driver discovers how to avoid stalling the engine, grinding gears, forgetting to free the hand brake, remembering indicators, looking in mirrors and so on. We learn by doing, by realising causes of failure, remembering and overcoming them. Hope to improve is encouraged by *'practice* makes perfect', if this is believed. *Practice,* good practice, accuracy, encourages confidence, improvement and progress. Word processing is personal used individually, on a PC. (These initials have come to connote 'politically correct' meaning ideas, ideology, of and approved by a leader whose 'vision' is 'willed', communicated 'on-line'.)

Widening networks, the Net, increase personal, public, professional and political resources. The hardware, the machines; the software programmes are valuable and invaluable; costly and profitable. All four levels are needed to operate IT, information technology. *Use* includes learning the language and acquiring skill for these are interdependent. Users begin from intention, *plan* and *purpose* and from interest stimulated by curiosity: 'IT is there so let's do it', but good and evil intent, subversive purpose, are ever present dangers. (See **X** and **XI**.)

The word icon has been adopted and much used. I-con? Is it Ikon? The key to unlock a required *function*; a 'window' to open; a function to perform looks for a small diagrammatic picture on screen to click. Is the 'bomb' an icon in this sense? Shapes, graphics and illustrations are available too. Zapf, the ingenious Swiss designer, developed 'dingbats' to add to the vitality and intelligibility of Word. On the 'Mac Classic' a pair of eyes could be called up to roll, then settle to indicate direction of the next step. While processing proceeded happily, the eyes closed, the ghost snoozed, until woken by a 'click' when needed. These eyes simulated familiar natural function of eye 'pupils' without words. Pupils need them. They are not ikons, icons, in original Greek meaning, but illustrative personification; like a hand with indicative finger; symbol such as sword, spear, halo. (See **XIII II 2 i**.)

I ii Word

An utterance, a sound heard or unheard, voiced in song or speech occurred long before signs and writing developed. It might mean something to whoever hears it. Voiced intentionally to communicate, a sound becomes a word. An echo repeats.

Cry out: voice: give tongue: make music: sing like Orpheus, with his lute: to make trees. Words identify, name, order, define, exclaim, explain, discover and soon a vocabulary grows into a language. The very first physical sound could have been a hissing of an excited or angry snake. The similarity between IS, EST, word-sounds for 'is' are sensibly similar in various tongues, essentially of the essence, suggesting common source. The 'snakiness' of 'S' looks as symbolic as its sound sounds. Shoosh is intended as a silencer, hush-hush for secrets. Psssssssssst.

As a new word emerges and joins others, groups gather into recognisable categories: things, actions, feelings, ideas, hypotheses, concepts, sentence, statement. These reflect function and activity such as to sense, feel, think, evaluate. Individual words with a common function of being, doing, describing, are recognised as parts of speech: nouns and then pro-nouns, verbs (with and in tense, time); adverbs, adjectives, conjunctions and so on. Collections of words relate to each other in phrase, sentence and paragraph, clarified by punctuation. Emerging structures of the spoken and then the written word are discovered to follow principles capable of formulation: grammar.

Speech begins, often continues, without consciousness or knowledge of form and syntax but communication and literacy develop and benefit from them. The first condition of this potential was and is present in existence: the very nature of living being: alive among other living beings; people, creatures capable of utterance and with something to exclaim about. Questions follow.

The trouble with the old riddle as to which came first, the chicken or the egg, is that neither is a sufficient answer. When the egg was forming inside the chicken — before she laid it — she herself was the entity, the unit, a potential mother-hen advancing in expectation. Conceived in an instant, invisible from outside, the egg was undivided from her until it she laid it, when her egg separated from her to become an entity in itself. Cockerels act; seen; were, are, involved. Without them eggs do not hatch into chicks. The hen has capability, once done, to do it again, a repeating process, procreating, adding to and multiplying the poultry population of the earth. Someone who saw one of these beautifully formed life-containing objects uttered the sound, EGG, to name and identify it. Heard through other ears, understood and accepted, 'egg' continues to apply not only to effort of hens but to the product of a vast, varied collection of birds and creatures who reproduce in that way. Expressions like 'egging on' and 'good' or 'bad' egg reflect their achievement. The riddle provokes thought. Salmonella results from human failure, not hens.

Is it possible to conceive of, to imagine, to think of an event which has neither cause nor effect? Moving from poultry to cosmic experience, there is comparable search for primary reality, elemental, original. Out of a sense of infinite mystery accompanied, perhaps, by awe and fear of the unknown, of darkness, even chaos, stars are observed, seen. Sun and moon raise recognition of dependable, orderly, repeating sequences. Light follows darkness, night becomes day. The source of light is outside our earthly habitation until realised to be part of a knowable system. Sun, moon, stars, can be trusted to re-appear, visible from earth when the sky is clear. Even if cave dwellers in permanent darkness deny them they are still there, shining on, illuminating, awaiting cognition and recognition.

Event, occurrence, **will** to begin, first *act* like the sound made by firing a starting gun, concentrates *cause* and *effect*, consequence. Utterance, 'first word' emerges in sound: voice into song with words: words born and borne out, to resound, grow, change. Utterly original at the beginning; seeking uttermost limits at last, as more words emerge, new life from uterus of creation, from cataclysmic experience and continuing gestation in and from the womb of word, the pre-existent world of life, external and internal. Big Bang and Continuous Creation are distinct functions in conception, pregnancy and birth: the Event. Things come to exist, live, are identifiable and become identified, named. Sight makes for views, interpretations, opinions, increasing or decreasing possibility, probability. Affirmation believed and verified uncovers knowledge of what is true. False trails fail as routes to what is true. Events stir debate and may issue in conflicting interpretations. Things themselves: eggs, hats, stars and heart, each itself, is an event in a word. Head and face are unique but hats are human inventions. First *sight* of hats delighted native Australians.

Differences in origin, function, meaning and significance emerge from reflection. Living hearts and the insides of heads are normally invisible. Eggs break when a chick hatches, may be broken by accident, must be broken to see inside the shell, to use, to eat. Broken hearts continue to beat but dead hearts have failed. A broken head may mean a cracked skull; perhaps an uncertain, undiagnosed disconnection, unusual erratic behaviour. Words adapt and are adapted with astonishing range and subtlety and are expressed in music. To recognise a little of what is already known and realised stimulates curiosity as to what has, might, may, could become so. A new vocabulary is developing with investigation and description of the birth and death of stars.

Constellations, seen from earth, seem to move with repetition and regularity; varied brightness and intensity of light. Occasional streams of meteors, 'shooting stars', comets, make the night sky a spectacle of glory, mystery and fascination. The heavens, the celestial sphere, carry curiosity beyond sight. Exploration leads to and continues to find more knowledge and understanding.

First light indicates approaching sunrise and cockcrow, familiar in the countryside but rare in towns and cities. Its meaning dawns in mind. Early light makes long shadows which shorten and sharpen until noon after which they lengthen again until, by sunset, they disappear as dusk merges into darkness. Consciousness of time: regular and measurable, to *keep, pass, spend, save, plan* and remember adds pointing to existence, to memory, to recollection, thinking back in order to learn by and from experience. Linking past with present and future leads to realise the transforming faculty of anticipation, looking forward with *hope* and *fear*. The fourth level becomes the first; plans can be initiated. (See Appendix **A**.)

Regular re-appearance of daylight with degrees of warmth is a fact of sense experience. The possibility of measuring *time*, timing, prediction, leads to question the cause and nature of time itself. The evidence of experience suggests a system. How does the system work? Is there a 'grammar' of the universe to assist comprehension of its order, patterns and structures? This is a long, unfinished exploration. Horizons open up others unless they disclose limits. Universe and universals inspire questions about cosmic discovery; moment to millennia. Clues offered by the roundness of sun and moon, their cyclical appearances together with the behaviour of shadows suggested rotating relationships. Long before the shape and behaviour of earth was discerned and understood, the daily re-appearance of light was worked out, predicted, together with seasonal variations. Stonehenge is an early observatory. That the earth seemed flat, though with ups and downs, did not prevent recognition of order and regularity in the apparent movements of sun, moon and stars. When these patterns became known and understood, they could be held in mind, remembered, measured, anticipated. From first *sight*, immediate and transitory, accumulating experience suggests explanation. From guess to idea to conjecture to theory visualised; checked until verified or disproved, knowledge and understanding grow. The joke is that it turns out to be the earth that is in a *spin*, not the heavens. What was known of has become known.

The seashore and sea posed and pose questions of their own: movement of water, horizontal drift, changing levels, vertical, effect coastlines. Investigations led to realise connections within the system: coincidental regularity of tides with the shape and position of moon and sun were observed as 'spring' and 'neap' tides. How were these connected? When, how, why do eclipses occur? Was the earth really 'flat' although surface irregularities were obvious? Was it still, or could it be moving? Revolutionary ideas proposed as theories were, are, tested by observation and reason to find sense from experience. Calculations were needed, devised, worked out for solutions to problems posed; authenticated answers to questions asked. Apollo, Neptune, Poseidon personified heavenly and earthly powers.

Spheres of knowledge continue to expand. Number and study of number, shape and size led to mathematics, astronomy, physics — general specialisms begun with counting and sizing from simple shapes and patterns, geometrical, numerical, still, and still moving, concern movement, are dynamic. The round sun gives light and heat; the changing size and angles of shadows; measured in span, foot, yard-arm and pace remind of early methods to *size*, to work out practicalities of *time, place, space* and *change* until measurement became standardised. Implications and consequences continue to increase scope and complexity. The coherent dependability of the system is as astonishing as its dynamic magnitude, elegant simplicity and infinite, balanced complexity.

Tense: past, present and future, exposes contradiction, tension of opposing forces. Weighing up works well with salt, sugar, rice, silver and gold, tangibles, but emotions, ideas, theories, intentions, initiatives usually include uncertainties and intangibles. Dynamic energy empowers movement, speed and strength like the wind. For human beings, normal sense responses to outward conditions cause inward reactions: sensitivity to surprise, shock; excitement arouses wonder, hope and fear in the face of present dilemmas, curiosity and/or need. Inward activities respond to and receive outward stimulus. The process of questioning and reflecting re-commences. These few are among infinitely many inward processes which engender thought. Deliberate outward action may follow inward deliberation. This interaction between need and working out how to meet it sets up tensions and concentrates attention. Perplexing? Bothering? Bewildering? Such reactions engender functions of designing and making which depend, in their turn, on thoughtful ingenuity and practical skill in responding to necessity and taste with actual things, materials, words. Human need requires supply for survival. It provides motive for enquiry to proceed and action to follow.

Word processors are as far from clay tablets as jet-planes from camel trains; both serve desire and need to travel, communicate and transport. One thing leads to another. Use of Word Processors is neither instinctive nor intuitive. Intuition and instinct, together with high mathematical talent, contribute to engineering and developing them into applications which assist in making use.

I iii Being and Doing

Interaction between things and thoughts moves from senses to word, to words; from static to active and dynamic.

That which IS is as it IS, unless, until, *change* occurs. Within itself, awaiting recognition of form and structure, is possibility not only to understand but to reproduce: to DO and to MAKE. At the simplest level, DOING requires BEING and CREATING.

Doings are evident in the nature of things. They are there, consequent on that which IS. They may *change*. The evolution of a landscape, usually so slow as to be imperceptible in a lifetime, is sometimes violent, dramatic, immediate, like the great eruption of Vesuvius, the California earthquake, a cliff collapsing, an inundation. Also, there are natural doings of plants and animals — the astonishing variety of life on earth — surviving, adapting or dying out; extinct like dinosaurs. Such events seem inevitable when human effort was, is, absent or powerless. Nature, whatever the source and energy of that word, took and takes its course unless living beings modify, alter, attempt to dominate it.

Human beings have physical needs in common with those of many animals; natural, essential, inescapable; breathing, drinking, eating and sleeping, production and reproduction. Developing a further, additional doing, inward beyond instinctive, includes thinking, willing, evaluating, intending. These require *control* if they are to become dependable. To dream and imagine, visualise and envisage stimulate activity in *mind*. To think, discuss, prefer and deliberate about what is to be done develops confident ability to decide what to do, and to act accordingly. This sort of doing differs from the first since it may enable a person to over-ride instinctive desires and needs, not with disregard but with concern for quality and benefit; to serve longer term interests and purposes. Words are required for articulate speech, reasoned thought, debate with others and with ourselves. Human minds become able to analyse and then to employ testing capability of experiment, for use or abuse, thought before action.

Experiment involves examining the first sort of doing, asking a natural process if this is how it works. To light a fire, find clean water and maintain a supply; to recognise and use the force of gravity; to realise nourishment of milk and learn to keep and milk a healthy cow.

The doing words, verbs, join the identity words, nouns, to unite activity and function in present presence, doing and being: things and people: a 'stones throw', a 'water fall', 'as the crow flies', sunset and sundown, last post, night-watchman, night nurse, reveille. Once, continually, repeatedly: these are words for doings that monitor consciousness at all levels, some measurably. 'Now', 'from time to time', 'permanently', describing experience understood in living. Nouns are words which name and symbolise things, places and persons. Verbs represent activity, still and moving. Either may display or veil, disclose, disguise, conceal essentials. For instance, at sea: 'as far as you can see: that is the horizon.' 'mist hides the horizon', 'the horizon seems near when it is misty'. Is there a change in the position of the horizon? What is visibility? Is it determined by mist rather than by distance? Does the quality of eyesight lengthen visibility or alter measurable distance of the horizon? Such problems revive the question of what defines 'horizon' and why, on a clear day, to climb up a ship's mast to the 'crows nest' or, on land, to a cliff-top, enables the same eyes to see further. These clues suggest the difference between 'as far as the eye can see', subjective, and 'as far as is visible from a given point', objective, independent of weather for visibility or quality of eyes. Lenses, telescopes, binoculars intensify vision of detail but do not alter horizons.

Realisation of *process* follows recognition of first cause as when exploring a stream to the source of running water enables discovering where it springs from. Nature originates and offers boundless scope for words into language to name, describe and to explain. Like tomorrow which never comes and the horizon of one moment giving way to further prospects as it is approached or by heightening viewpoint. Wondering and wandering from unknown, known of, knowable and eventually experienced joy of knowing even a little, curiosity leads through processes of learning in order to understand, enjoy, appreciate and, possibly, to develop, to improve.

We assume that through observation, discovery and thought, knowing overcomes ignorance as light dispels darkness. Ultimate knowledge, itself objective, is elusive, like horizon. Subjected to learning in a particular sphere: the subject which is the object of investigation, a search is a means to an end, like finding water to drink and use – an end in itself – for thirst quenched, necessaries washed. What else is there to learn about *water*? As more and more is discovered, increased recognition of categories, structures, topics and aspects of water are realised. It, and they exist because of what they are and life is, even when unknown: not yet known. Blood, derived from water, is subject for investigation, tests, 'count', analysis: indicating health and wellbeing.

Explorers discover, uncover, recover what is already there: to benefit, improve or to ruin. Each voyage which achieves its destination, or objective, finds much else on the way suggesting topics and ideas for further exploration. Each questing purpose arises from curiosity in search of further knowledge and informed experience; hunger calling for food; wise eating to satisfy it. Questions represent appetites of the mind, to find interesting answers, 'food for thought', not only to satisfy, nourish, but to stimulate curiosity to learn. Enjoying the tastes is part of appetite and digestive process. Reasoning reflection, 'chewing it over', nourishes more thought and imagination, extra digestive juices preparing to swallow, reject or accept, change.

Thinking compares with using word processing in head as hardware. Inside the skull is the brain, 'grey' matter, mind and memory to respond to sense messages, nerve connections setting up software programmes in memory which open ways to register, record and formulate sensible communication. That is a minimal statement. Human and artificial intelligence are as different as organic and mechanic, living and robotic.

Gathering information as a function of 'intelligence' informs thinking and planning. Actual decisions, at best, also require sustained JUDGMENT and determination of **WILL**. Within the thinking, informed MIND — again at best — the three unite as one. One head contains them and one personality embodies these three functions. DOING has moved beyond natural instinct to include considered assessment and deliberation. To act deliberately unites motive, thought out method and practicable means.

Huge questions of evaluation — for good or ill — await consideration.

Kipling named, said he kept, 'six honest serving men who taught him all he knew. Their names were What? Why? When? How? Where? and Who?' Assembling these words of enquiry, the poet recalls a child's curiosity: listening because wanting to hear and to know immediately. A literate person can, may, read to learn, study and think; listening in the inward, inner ear of mind when these possibilities are cultivated.

The delight of Kipling's verse spoken or read is its rhythmic, rhyming recognition of first compelling curiosity. It gets better.

> 'I know a person small
> who keeps ten thousand serving men
> who get no rest at all.'

This reminds of the Elephant's Child whose cur(t)iosity is (in)satiable and who will never forget. Elephants grow to immense strength and can be trained to co-operate with purposes other than their own. They do not become literate in human ways, speaking, reading and writing, but they surely react to, absorb and follow their mahout who directs and inter-acts with their sensibilities recognised, respected, cultivated for powerfully strong cooperation. Horses and dogs extend human range and speed with sense, speed and strength of their own. Cats respond to human being and doing but their own interests come first. They enjoy food, appreciation, affection, share comfort, catch mice while maintaining independence, their private life, until ill or old.

Infants are instinctive and learn instinctively. First needs supplied are often accompanied by words heard, spoken, absorbed, remembered. The cries of infancy soon become talk: the first word, words as names to identify and respond to. Words together into sentences, question and answer, converse, conversation; stimulating and thought promoting lead to the question 'why'. Learning to read and write, like talk, starts with imitating. Careful copying to make a shape, a letter until words make a message, a '*note*', another sort of letter. In a word, to write as well as to speak, comprehends instinctive will to communicate.

All this may seem so obvious as scarcely to need description. In the high-tech audio-video-disco-assisted environment of many children, natural sequences have become obscured, inverted, ignored, out of sight and mind. It was not and is not obvious that the earth spins daily on its yearly journey round the sun nor that stillness is itself relative and conditional. For ages people thought that the sun was moving because it appeared so: to rise and set. A great leap into theory, demonstrably evident by systematic practical observation, occurred when the principle of earth's behaviour — in daily spin on its yearly path round the sun — was discerned. Cosmic organisation realised and imitated in living experience measures time and, by degrees, distance. Keeping watch, waiting until the time was ripe for sun to ripen without scorching. Sundial, hour-glass, eventually clocks captured the sequences of movement: time-keeping and keeping time. Timetables and plans, calendars and diaries, tide-tables, timetables of dawn and sunset at different seasons are calculated. Sun, moon and stars for navigation at sea became as valuable as surveying instruments for mapping of land and coastlines. Limits of visibility, of uncertain weather have stimulated study of meteorology (not of meteors as such) and weather forecasting, together with knowledge of climates, to enable well-informed cultivation of crops. The music of the spheres transposes to reflect and be reflected into sounds and rhythms of experience; life, birth, death, terrible and glorious, towards timelessness, eternity.

This inheritance could evaporate unless understanding, partial and incomplete as it is, of its original framework and processes continues affirmed. Questions as to meaning and purpose challenge individuals to build, to contribute to their culture rather than destroy it. Wealth of experience becomes available through participation of mind and senses together; interaction of knowing with being and doing, heart and body, head and mind together.

II

Personality

'The lunatic, the lover, and the poet,
Are of imagination all compact;
One sees more devils than vast hell can hold,
That is the madman; the lover, all as frantic,
Sees Helen's beauty in a brow of Egypt:
The poet's eye, in a fine frenzy rolling,
Doth glance from heaven to earth, from earth to heaven
And, as imagination bodies forth
The form of things unknown, the poet's pen
Turns them to shapes, and gives to airy nothing
A local habitation and a name.
Such tricks hath strong imagination...'
(Shakespeare, *A Midsummer Night's Dream*, V. 1, lines 7-18)

An old lady persuaded by her family to use the telephone for the first time felt obliged to put on a hat. Unaccustomed to speaking to anyone outside her house without being appropriately dressed, a hat was felt necessary.

Styles of dress change even faster than those of speech. Hats went out, almost, outdoors, and in, for a time but they are coming in again at least for going out to something special. A hat protects from weather; cold, sun, snow, rain. Some are worn to do nothing more than enhance appearance, a degree of powerful, stylish conformity among men — or disguise. A feminine hat may express personality and style; taste; and in critical opinion, ghastly or elegant.

To put on a hat to speak on the telephone followed sense of custom, habit of time and place. The hat fitted sense of propriety. Perhaps conversation could not be unseen. Her descendents re-tell the story with affection. Policemen and women now wear 'riot-gear' when incidents of violence are likely. Demonstrations: against the poll tax, miners against stiffer picket laws, became violent. Terrorism intensifies danger.

Hats, helmets, head coverings frame faces of wearers and offer clues to activity and personality: conventional, protective, ritualistic: functional uniformity, expressive individuality.

A living language is adapted and developed by people who speak and think with originality and vigour about life in their time and place. Awareness of the past, a sense of history, nourishes understanding and strengthens stability despite present discontents, to express hope for the future. Apathy can be as dangerous as revolt. Cycles of renewal, foliage in spring, seasonal perennials in garden and park, provide refreshing change within continuity. Looking back in memory constructively, with and without anger, offer comparisons to look forward, ahead, beyond. Yesterday adds to today and both await tomorrow until days stretch into months, years into centuries. An Irishmen asked a Spaniard what he meant by *mañana*. 'Tomorrow. Don't you say that?' 'No', said the Irishman, 'no such definite a notion do we have here', but that is changing in both countries and in other parts of Europe. Consciousness of continuity, of unchanging strength and steadfastness contributes to communal wellbeing as surely as weakness and fear undermines it.

Personality cannot be dissected as if it were a dogfish. To propose a post-mortem of personality is absurd since a body, at death, loses the vitality which is its essence. What 'remains' turns to dust or ashes. A personality lives on in memory, occasionally with such strength as to offer continuing influence in the life and work of later generations. Words of recollection are set down. Reminiscences, biography and, in personalities of outstanding significance, are revised again and again, assisted by best available resources; letters, diaries, memoirs.

Personality known personally, in life, brings response in feeling remembered and thought about in mind. Characteristics, actions, achievements, friendships are recollected with particular care. Each person's essential characteristic appearance, speech, behaviour opens to whoever encounters them. Every baby born, every body, is a potential personality whose body is the starting place, the personal beginning.

II i Body

No clothes at first or last but wrapping: a shawl and then a shroud.

To 'body forth' suggests conception in mind with thought as filter of imagination;

mind to body, made flesh; in and with mind. Recognisable outside by face, eye, and fingerprint, the inside of a body is hidden from direct sight sheltered within the skin. The system of senses and nerves which receive from the outside world works in reverse when pain locates trouble and pleasure gives delight. Infants express themselves vigorously in hunger and discomfort. Satisfaction is palpable in eyes, smiles and gurgles.

Dissection of human remains for medicine, science and art has opened up the form and function of the human body to increasingly precise particular and general knowledge. A living heartbeat is felt but not seen. A body dies when the heart ceases to beat. Autopsy adds knowledge of heart failure. Surgical operation enables internal investigation and can sometimes correct life-threatening symptoms. The heart is enabled to resume its essential functions if ingenious by-pass and implant techniques provide maintenance to lengthen life.

Specialisms multiply: heart, lungs, blood, eyes as well as bones, cells and nerves — every part is more and more intensively examined and analysed. The life of the mind is applied to the life and functions of the body as it is to the external world, earthly, planetary. New words accompany new discoveries and doctors are challenged to explain diagnosis and propose treatment to suffering patients who listen, want to understand the name and nature of both ailment and cure, if any. Yesterday's insights, the best in their day, lead on to fresh thinking and require fresh teaching. Doctors of medicine find that earlier 'doctrine' changes, required by developments in knowledge and experience.

Each life, measurable though not always measured, changes in stages. Infancy, childhood and youth merge into adult life and the process of ageing. Strenuous activity accelerates: marvellous, miserable, sometimes both — when time is said to 'fly'. At other times, it seems to 'stand still'. Both are metaphors, comparative words for bodily experience of speed and of stillness.

Organs in normal organisation inside the body assist understanding of health and wellbeing, disease and sickness. Body and mind are evidently interdependent but distinguishable, ordered to realise and command attention for essential functions; weary for rest, hungry for nourishment. Other infinitely varied, subtle relations develop between organs, senses, nerves, feelings and thoughts. The HEART is heart of this organisation, vital organ of vitality, of lifeblood, and has come to represent not only pumping, thumping heartbeat but feeling; core dynamic of emotion, motivation. To lose heart, take heart, learn the secrets of another's heart, give one's heart; these are moments of consequence in living experience. Knowing and understanding about hearts grows in head from heart. Writing requires considering, head and mind applied to questions about heart, in that order, but living heart sends life blood to mind to think, speak, write.

Language develops to identify and name, discuss, explain, record, read, using words peculiar to each speciality. Old words are adapted and new words invented, coined for fresh discoveries. Doctors in general practice face people, personalities, whose bodies are subject to dis-ease at the moment of consultation. The doctor's objective knowledge is crucial. People anxious or ill enough to consult want to know and understand what is the matter, the complaint, and to benefit from treatment. Cure as mending, restoration, healing, starts with diagnosis, clues, patterns of symptoms, and continues with what is prescribed. Some cases involve a specialist, a 'consultant'. External symptoms are examined again; internal suspicions investigated through tests, samples, techniques, instruments such as X-ray, scan, biopsy. Each body in each case calls on knowledge, expertise gathered by observation, heard from others, found in books, which together increase skill and professional competence. Wisdom comes with sympathy, intelligence, knowledge and evaluation, four levels together.

Pain is a primary symptom and clue. Unacknowledged symptoms remain hidden, untreated. Sudden, unexpected seizures, a stroke, a heart attack, can be fatal. Doctors consider each individual, ailing, failing, and hope to revive health.

The OUTWARD-INWARD-OUTWARD process of examination matches INWARD-OUTWARD-INWARD personal thought and experience. Good health is reflected in appetite, vitality, energy, vigour, delight; balanced mental and physical wellbeing. Countless positives and negatives between body and mind compose head and heart of personality.

Horizons of mind, beyond eyesight, lead towards vision in mind's eye. Sights seen, remembered, occasionally recur in dreams; in wondering, contemplating, and in conversation. Imagination is inventive, fanciful, and stimulates vision. Feeling, emotion, connects with will. Hope assists mind to conceptualise, to analyse and explore further.

Interchangeable words from practical into theoretical and back again pervade our world. *Table* and volume are among them. Numerical information is stored in lists, 'tables' (like those first learned for multiplication and division) then volumes, three dimensional as in cube; solid books such as a dictionary or the *Nautical Almanac*. Words stored in dictionaries assist speech and thought, thinking and writing. When words emerge as names into actions from mind, they acquire an additional level of meaning. Some can be memorised. Table, a piece of furniture with a flat surface used to eat or work at, is also a table of information; a tide-table predicting times of high and low tides; a time-table for day or week, for planning transport: bus, train and plane time-tables, useful if reliable services are maintained. Stores of information, ready like a well-stocked meal table, larder or 'fridge, can be available in home, office, library (liberating from ignorance as food from hunger) and through information technology (word processors again) with vast, fast accessible memory. When a meal or document is 'on the table' it is ready to be devoured, to nourish or be discussed for decision. To describe use appeals to familiar action. It is a way of picturing, illustrating, 'bodying forth': called a table, what a table is used for, in different senses.

Mental activity moves far beyond physical limits. Mind is at work within them, situated in the head, within the skull. The actual grey matter, cells, nerves and the veins which fuel them is BRAIN, an organ, average in size and weight of a super-market chicken, about 3 lbs, or 1.4 kilos. Eyes are visible intermediary: receptive, responsive, discerning.

The senses are our information and 'intelligence' service receiving messages to transmit to mind. Practicalities interpreted in mind become known, digested, food for thought, to BRAIN which, for this function, is MIND. Intelligence is also capability of mind, 'brain power', potential for processes of thought, analysis: recollection and memory and of imagined and dreamt hopes and fears. To separate out even these few aspects of MIND points to differences between one and another to show the tensions and contradictions of their coexistence; variable, sometimes at variance, in each personality. Debate may occur between bodily hunger and the question of what is good to eat. The informed mind foresees dangers but appetite refuses delay or avoidance. This fruit looks delicious; irresistible: too tempting for words. Experience leads to knowledge; to matters of *taste*, choice, judgment and *will*, recurring.

II ii Body and Mind

Independent aspects of interdependent functions are obvious in a living human body. Each part, quiescent or active, belongs together with all the others in unity for use, growth, replenishment and wellbeing. The brain is nourished from other parts of the body, re-vitalised by heart and lungs which sustain the intelligence system: information through the senses.

This, in turn, stimulates and sustains capability of mind to work towards distinctive mental effort of analysis and objective thought: thinking, developing theory before testing: trying out in practice. Mind, like body, gets tired.

Doctors of medicine listen first to a patient's words, if any, then question the body itself for symptoms, all senses alert, using testing techniques known and available to them. Connections are made that help to make sense of the complaint, complained of. A correct diagnosis may be simple or it may be immensely complicated to reach. Two minds as well as two bodies, personalities, patient and doctor, interact together. The condition that led the 'patient' to consult needs recognition before possibility of effective treatment. A doctor gains knowledge and experience from any new 'case' that adds to personal store of medical memories. These grow through combining sympathetic care with clinical skill. Hitherto unrecognised ailments and/or cures add to what is known.

Mind is unseen but its activities register in looks, reactions, as well as in words. Facial expressions and gestures can be revealing. Insights gained from listening, reading, thinking about our own mental processes lead to comparison with those of others. Minds vary in their capabilities and range of interests: numerate, literate, visual, tonal, musical; and in qualities: quick, slow, open, closed, well stocked, empty, generous, mean; sometimes all and many more, simultaneously. Qualities of personality and of character develop as activities of mind interweave with practicalities, into habits. Mind is a noun and a verb, I *mind*, you *mind*, he and she *mind*. The active, doing, **mind** links with whatever is minded about — the subject minded. This is a double function. The two functions operate together as one when **integrated into unity**. It deserves a word category of its own, one word to distinguish this dual nature. **Donoun** sounds odd at first, but it says exactly what is meant, means what it says and is memorable. (See the Introduction and Appendix **C**.) It helps to bridge the gap between hand work and mind work; *work* in union of *mind* and body, essential in this exploration, and repeated.

Mind and *work* are prototype **donouns**. They reflect possibility and reality of unity in doing and being. As soon as this train of thought gets going, many **donouns** emerge: *present, find, mix, paste, digest, dream, muse, dance, praise, act:* to do with something done. As verbs, these are 'doing words', but as **donouns** the same word is used for what is to be done, function subject and object. They *dream* of a place where their *dream* will come true. An idea in mind moves from imagined to envisaged to planned and, possibly, achieved, realised, done. **Donouns** unite in one word, to *BE* with to *DO*, simultaneously when you *dream* a *dream*, *act* an *act*. Many words *change* or need another word when formulated for performance. To think a thought, sing a song, do a deed, speak (or make) a speech are modified from the verb to the act itself.

Where does an idea come from? A connection in mind? Something seen, which suggests and is taken as a model? Heard of? Inspired? An idea as a thought thing traces back to whatever gave it birth. Like the egg from the hen, conceived in the hen's body, ideas are conceived in mind. Some minds seem to be particularly fertile: responsive, imaginative, self-fertilising as ideas bubble and emerge from them. Where, then, does, did, mind come from?

Dance is an OUTWARD-INWARD-OUTWARD activity. Delight in sound which creates response of rhythmic movement of body: pulse, breath, patterns repeated in steps and gestures that *hum* in music, song and *dance*, dance was — and is — cultivated. *Mind* recognises form and repetition, ideas to work out and try out as next **step**. The person who found her or himself dancing for joy or sorrow continues, first experimentally, then systematically, to elaborate, improve and discover more movements to perform. These add *dance* to existing *dance*, fresh innovative achievements, variously interpreted.

They will **dance** that **dance** again; **dance** is another donoun. What about **step, stage, design, plan, perform**?

Dreams are a distinct source of ideas, creative and destructive. They do not occur to order. Remembered, they become food for thought and feeling, happy or miserable, comforting or terrifying, glad or appalling. Imagination and dreams nourish ideas occasionally realised through combined effort of mind, **will**, and ingenuity with material, activity in making. Creative designers and makers use ideas from dreams re-presented differently, combining vision, originality and skill. The overlap between imagination and dream is indistinct. Dreaming happens during sleep, but memory of intense visual experience dreamed is assimilated consciously, sometimes through daydreaming. Familiar people and places appear in dreams, modified, enhanced, exaggerated, distorted, to delight or terrify the dreamer. Some dreams are fantasy; unreal but not unimaginable: fantastic, haunting and enchanting: some communicate power of foresight and inspire action: others illuminate hindsight. Signs, wonders, prophetic gifts, divine intervention are associated with dreams. (See *The Oxford Dictionary* and *Biblical Concordance*.)

Creative work grows with discovery and re-discovery of existing elements, substance, *form* and *process* to *move* into *mind* from observation to analysis, interpretation, contemplation. Physical senses promote reactions; **wonder** and curiosity; for consideration, thinking. Methodical experiment, valid evidence, verifies and justifies communication of discovery. Further critical analysis, re-examination, thoughtful return to practice, promotes revision, improvement, regeneration.

Poets, artists with words, distil and translate from direct perception and inward response to capture reflections: to express beauty and ugliness; to formulate reactions which reflect and express happiness and misery, horror, tragedy and glory of lived experience. Their comprehension helps listeners and readers to transcend day-to-day pre-occupations, frustrations; encounters with evil and fear; and to look beyond accepted limits, frontiers and horizons. Poets benefit from the insights of science, of engineers, as these may benefit from those of poets, reciprocal enrichment.

In Greek legend, Apollo was believed to personify the divinity of the sun and be the source of music. Zeus (Jupiter to the Romans), divinity of weather (derivative of sun) fathered nine daughters with Mnemosyne, each a *muse*. Their doings expressed *order* and *pattern*. Three emerged: Dance, Music and Poetry, believed to dwell on Mount Parnassus, high above the Castalian spring, with the Sun, Apollo, as Zeus, their father, and inspired festivals, celebrations at Delphi; at Olympus: and elsewhere.

Electricity, identified source, resource, of energy, travels as current, wired from place to place, using a *switch* to turn on and off. A person is 'switched off' when absent in mind or asleep. A *fuse* causes failure of current. Lights go out when a particular fuse blows, whatever the reason. **WIRELESS**, without wires, carries *sound* for huge distances by radio, using waves. Nerves transmit energy into, within, and out of each body and mind.

FUSE, a powerful contemporary **donoun** practical and electrical; fuses being and doing, head and heart in action together; unless will re-fuses.

As soon as we think about it, the physical life of our body is being accompanied by the thinking life of mind. Primary sense experience, outward-inward, stimulates immediate mental apprehension, increasing intellectual activity abstracted, capable of objectivity, in any sphere. Some 'think on their feet' — we all have to sometimes — but many find that concentration is stronger when they are still, if that is possible in their circumstances. Practicalities learned early introduce mind work: wondering, thinking, calculating, discerning, recognising, discovering. If we are fed with mind work which seems to have nothing to do with 'real life' it can seem irrelevant. We lose interest when 'fed up' with it. Perversely, sometimes, efforts to learn confuse rather than clarify. Facts and ideas get muddled, difficult to distinguish, indigestible and unreasonable until and unless, by one means or other, illumination enables thought and understanding to restore meaning, to disclose sense from nonsense. Being, doing, thinking are re-united. If not, there is danger of confusion, even despair. Unless confidence is recovered, a person finds it difficult to believe that learning has any treasures to offer, especially when rigorous effort to learn and think are forcefully demanded. Curiosity evaporates and motive dissolves. This is 'inoculation' against study and happens all to often when boredom, indifference, negation, suffocate ignition. Conversely, a fresh injection of curiosity, delight in discovery and understanding, create an enthusiastic appetite which grows and grows, expanding confident capability in and of resources of mind.

II iii Sense and Mind

Of the five senses, three are **donouns**. Can you *smell* that fragrant (or foul) *smell*? They *touch* with gentlest (or roughest) *touch*. You *taste* that sweet (or bitter) *taste*. The senses of eyes and ears need other words: I see a *sight*; hear a *sound*. Sight and sound, already noted, stimulate memory and promote thought beyond immediate sense. Much to be seen and heard existed before human eyes and ears evolved to perceive and receive. Thought with memory, pictures in mind, a tune or poem 'on the brain' stimulates mind to *look* (meaning to envisage and think), to ponder, wonder, contemplate and try to foresee consequences including different courses of action. Eyes and ears are special agents, eyes particularly so since they can give as well as receive. Also, they stimulate vision as well as receiving it. Some see stars showing in their eyes.

The distinction between intellectual activity and immediate mental reaction emerges in comparing sight and hearing with taste, touch and smell. For example, one cannot taste the food that another has already eaten. It has gone into a mouth, to be chewed, swallowed, digested, uniquely. Even from the same dish, what one has swallowed can not be eaten by any one else. It may be transformed into mother's milk of a mother who is breast-feeding. He and she may touch, but each experiences a different sensation. They cannot touch an outside object in the same place at the same moment, however nearly, and although they feel the wind blowing and the heat of the sun at the same time, neither of these is itself touched in direct physical contact although effects are received at the same time from the same source. *Smell*, like *touch*, is direct, subjective, impermanent, unique to each nose although of common origin and is extinguishable. Hearing may be communal, collective; simultaneously personal. Several people hear music together and interpret similarly or differently. Sounds, like smells, come and go but may be shared at the same time. Basic sounds, if they repeat as when a baby is crying, call for action. A telephone bell means someone calling, for whatever reason, until the *ring* is answered or ringer rings off without *reply*. **Sound** is capable of carrying for great distances and of containing complex, distinct ingredients in voices, cries, words and music. When written, the words can be seen and read repeatedly, silently or voiced, audible as well as visual. Music also can be read and heard in the inward ear, sung to oneself in memory or as silent sight-reading. **Score** is a **donoun**.

Eyes give access to sights which are permanent as well as to those which are temporary and transitory. From daily, simple things, to that which energises life through heat and light, eyes can see the sun itself, but it is harmful, dangerous, to gaze at it open-eyed. The sun is our constant, continuing, permanent star: centre of earth's solar system. Life, including human life, depends on the sun for light, heat and water. The sun is now known to belong within ('in' seems insufficient) the greater universe. The night sky, when clear, displays constellations in familiar configurations continuing since named in antiquity; their patterns of apparent movement predictable. We know, now, that it is our planet, Earth, which is moving, travelling round the sun while rotating on its own axis. North and South poles themselves are calculated places rather than natural land or ice marks. We learn that the universe itself is less constant than the stars in their constellations suggest. Sight draws our understanding beyond immediate, local, transitory limits. Sight develops into vision, to remotest distances beyond here and now and into deepening consciousness, knowledge, inward insight. Blindness of any sort is a serious handicap. A window blind, on the other hand, is protective from cold or heat, darkness or light; for privacy and sense of security. Eyelids close for rest and sleep but also to avoid seeing. A child was heard to say 'I'll shut my eyes: you can't see me.' Another 'I've gone, I'm out of your sight'.

Our five senses, gatherers of information, relate together as common sense like five fingers in one hand exercised to make music together, joining wrist with pulse and artery, beating heart and lungs. Focussed in the mind's eye which sees — we may learn to discern. **Practice** is a musical and a medical **donoun**: essentially practical.

Smoke is another **donoun**. An old man liked the smell of *smoke*, the *feel* of a pipe, the *taste* of smouldering tobacco, the soothing effect of smoking. He became a smoker who enjoyed a *smoke*. Whenever he wanted to *smoke*, a familiar pattern of action was followed: cleaning and filling his pipe with moist, brownish yellowish textured tobacco of preferred *blend*, then lighting and drawing until the bowl glowed and clouds of *smoke* billowed as from a human volcano. Perhaps it is simply an acquired pleasure. Certainly smoking is addictive and becomes a habit. Perhaps it assists mind at work on worrying problems by promoting calm reflection and deliberation. It sends signals to family, friends and colleagues. No *smoke* without *fire*, says the proverb. To *smoke* is a deliberate activity, involving all senses except hearing. To *light* a *fire* is deliberate too. J. S. Bach's *Tobacco Cantata* is peculiarly soothing.

Donouns clarify. A *shadow* cast between the idea and its realisation is overcome. Some friends are leaving and they *wave*. If you or I *wave* to them, they may see the *wave*. What does the *wave* mean? A *wave*, in this sense, is visible gesture of invisible motive. Why did, or didn't, he *wave*? Doubts and misunderstandings are possible. Was it feeling, reason, or polite formality? Have I reason, confidence, to *wave* back? Puns suggest themselves, wavering. Waves on the sea, breaking on a shelving beach, are not human gestures and have none of the ambiguity or ambivalence possible in *waves* as gestures but their regular rhythms reflect disturbance − like emotion, calm and stormy. The feeling ingredient is not always clear in gestures or actions, but **donouns** affirm this potentiality. Adjectives add quality, colour and style, also open to interpretation.

Donouns indicate interconnection of mind and body in unanimity. Many verbal-nouns, derived from gerunds, need adapting. **Donouns** do not. One word (as illustrated by *smell, touch, taste, smoke, mix, wave*) like MIND, shows the possibility, the essential quality of unity: active and objective at once. They are BEING-DOING-BEING words.

Study to discover the nature and capabilities of *MIND* is more and more specialised. Presence of mind is common need. Each mind has potential to develop according to innate ability and circumstances of need, stimulus, resource and opportunity. Your mind and mine are, like our faces, similar but unique, alive in independent inter-dependence.

Human life begins in total dependence. Simple physical necessities: drinking, feeding, washing, cleanliness and *rest* enable survival during early years. An infant body communicates need by cries. Other symptoms of aches, pains, sickness convey their messages. As already described, words are soon learned by listening, connecting in experience to show meaning which nourishes life of the mind to thrive and grow: doing, watching, asking, understanding and remembering. Kipling's 'six honest serving men' answer as best they can. Their **honesty** is crucial. The dependent infant becomes a questioning child, a doubting and uncertain teenager (since adolescence involves powerful, intensified, contradictory changes) who may emerge towards independent responsibility of an adult. This involves more than thought, and there is more and more to think about. *MIND* is the means, in our heads, centring and connecting the intensifying senses which are themselves co-ordinated, potentially presided over, by common sense. Whereas bodies tend to stabilise in size and shape, including heads, the mind possesses astonishing capacities of development within but without physical enlargement. Nothing is wasted or lost while mind activity proceeds. Recall tends to become less total, frailer, in old age.

Derived from *munde* meaning *world*, *mind* is our personal universe. Like a university, mind has many faculties offering entry into limitless spheres of study. The more intensively active the *mind*, the more extensive its development and capability. To encounter greatness of *mind* in a living person — a scholar, teacher, doctor, expert in their sphere — is profoundly stimulating and mind enlarging. So too, writings which live in the power of continuing communication, evergreen classics waiting to be opened, re-opened, and appreciated from generation to generation, century and millennium.

Investigation by one *mind* of another starts with interest and search for evidence of activity. Questions are devised, spoken or written, whose answers might provide clues to minds-ways: the range of mind-work providing evidence of knowledge and understanding. Questions of what is **good, virtuous, wise** require more developed investigation; consideration of evil and folly. The ultimate question, ever present at all stages: **'Is this true?'** will recur. (See **XII I** and **II.**)

Self provides an echo chamber where words, concepts, ideas resound as one *mind* seeks to understand another and to know subjects, objects and itself better. Questions suggested by introspection yield layers of apprehension according to capabilities, heights, depths, within each human being. There is a take-off point when a subject becomes objectified, depersonalised, universalised when a structure of principle co-ordinates and makes sense of known details. For example, theory of ***shape***, geometry, defines triangles, squares, circles, ellipses, parabolas — any shape known — discovered to have perennial characteristics and qualities. 'Theorems' investigate, explore and discover elegant demonstrations, originally worked out by Euclid and Pythagoras. This is also the point at which a general theory can show so many exceptions as to be doubted, perhaps invalidated. To generalise is to look from definitions to connections, classifications; matter(s) considered, discussed, perhaps disputed from opinion to become established fact. True? Is a shape ever perfect? During that time, activity of *mind* is both subjective and objective. (Coincidently, **matter, subject, object** are **donouns**.) From perception to original conception, a concept was, is, conceived. Many are received from elsewhere, tested to avoid danger of being deceived; firmed, confirmed as true. A straight line is the shortest distance between two given points but it is not always the best, even the only possible way. Stringent surveyors, mapmakers, know the challenge of curves, irregularities, between measuring, drafting, drawing. Non Stop.

III

Activities of Mind

To explore and cultivate the life of the mind concerns a thoughtful person at any age. A philosopher aims to think clearly and reasonably about present and ultimate matters, to ask questions and explore possible answers to them; to speculate and conjecture; to seek what is true, good, beautiful and wise. (See **III v** and **XIII**.) That was, as it is, the original far reaching brief of exploring words.

Activities of mind are evident in action and inaction, prompted by sense, into thoughts, words, works: doings.

Since experience precedes knowledge thought emerges as a 'post mortem' of it. Words are, at first, more memorable when they concern or represent something seen or pictured. An elephant, not necessarily seen alive, is recognised. Some undertake long journeys to see real elephants, giraffes, whales, pyramids, reported by explorers. Words are material of literacy; numbers of numeracy. Grammatical and mathematical systems emerge as principles and ingredients of thought, of philosophy, in any sphere of mind's activity with necessary and compelling interest and, when available, are followed, learned, understood, digested.

Thoughts are not heard unless communicated; and doings do not always match intended purpose. Inconsistent, unpredictable actions are difficult to explain, control, respond to. Mind distinguished from will (see **IX**) leads to recognition of limits: inability, nervous disturbance possibly due to inward or outward difficulties, exceptional sensibilities, mental and physical illness: common causes of human suffering.

Mind's activities, for description, are as intimately organised to function, co-operate and co-ordinate as organs of digestion. To 'chew it over', 'spit it out', 'swallow it whole' apply to ideas and concepts in words as food. Mind responds spontaneously when stimulated by outside resources, mouth watering, with inward appetite of interest, curiosity, hunger to know. Activity of mind is work to digest and can be encouraged, sustained, increased, improved, intensified by personal effort and concentration stimulated, encouraged at home and school; schooled by teachers, tutors, supervisors who may inspire as well as inform. Some minds expand like the universe as they feel and find greater and more minute detail.

Distinctive activities of mind are, at best, heartfelt: sympathetic understanding, thinking about feeling towards possible objectivity, discovered and analysed. Performatives and **donouns** identify integration.

Unlike brain and guts, mind cannot be dissected directly, nor can its contents be inspected like those of the stomach, by pathologists. Discovery of mind begins from what it does for you, me, other persons, in emerging consciousness observed to disclose evidence of characteristic activities. Coherent practicalities with systems, systematic, from such functions as using words, add to perceived activities of other minds.

Simple activities of mind are the start. Identification grows from conscious consideration, from particular to general, towards expert and specialist. Mouths open to breathe, to accept nourishment, to make sounds, to voice and to speak words. A mind opens to wonder; to receive impressions, words, messages, information, ideas and begins to form them; to conceptualise, to work out, explore and try to reply to questions we ask ourselves and are asked. First levels of consciousness and imagination are stimulated and the two combine as generator and dynamo of mind's energy. Mind is personal apparatus for apprehension and thought and can be empty or full, poor or rich, occupied, busy or static, idle, dormant without motive for activity. The storehouse of each mind feeds upon and feeds from the wealth of the common mind and, in its turn, has access to available wealth of culture and of civilisation, inherited, but only activated by personal, critical effort.

Seven activities spring to mind as they emanate and radiate from the hub of personal consciousness and imagination, the generator variously referred to as heart, soul or psyche. Like the spokes of a wheel they connect to and from the circumference to rejoin the hub and inter-connect with one another, still and moving in and out of mind: *first:* memory; *second:* thought (including purpose and intention); *third:* being in mind; and *fourth:* realisation in and yet beyond mind. These four have universal and personal features, general and individual, outward and inward including sensed, felt, acquired, learned and experienced content of knowledge.

Three further activities depend on these four; they concern digesting, ordering and using knowledge; thinking simply and generally is mind's *fifth* activity. A philosopher thinks about thinking and from such thoughts philosophy emerges. Bearing in mind that general exploration proceeds a step at a time, and that inspiration (from consciousness and imagination) encourages ideas to be examined with REASON, this *fifth* activity explores thought forming notions, ideas and concepts towards discerning patterns, until a grammar of thought emerges, develops, by one philosopher and another, helpful for systematic study and understanding. *Sixth* is the forward looking activity of VISUALISING, the capability to envisage, to activate vision and belief as well as reason.

The *seventh* activity is COMMUNICATING, first and last, since any attempt to explore mind's activities, outward and inward, involves communication: using words, word for word. Nevertheless, without memory, there would be nothing remembered to communicate, nor with which to define and refine communication.

Consciousness and imagination, hub of heart and mind in union, are pervasive, sometimes overwhelmingly intense vital existence. Situations and scenes imagined suggest ideas, desires, possibilities of uniting dream with reality. Sparked at first in immediate sense experience, especially sight, but from any source of emotional impact; stored in memory, conceptualised in thought, cultivated in thought processes, imagination offers anticipation; to look forward with **delight** and **dread**, **hope** and **fear**. Imagination is a generic, stimulating link between doing and being, being and doing: aspiration as actuality, a dream come true. *Dream* and *act, plan* and realise include imaginative ideas. JUDGING, RESOLVING and WILLING: essentials in responsible doing, filter out illusion and romanticised fantasy. All these, and many others assist transmission, interaction between mind and body to **temper**, refine and qualify the fruits of consciousness and imagination into vision and memory.

The life of the mind co-ordinates functions, activates capabilities to work together, orchestrated in and out for this and any other exploration. These seven familiar activities of mind are not sent out like Kipling's 'six honest serving men' to bring in information. They are innate and cultivable endowments; able to become active: to supplement, to develop and illuminate inward consciousness. Mind can operate in semi-detached, near independence from bodily constraints while mental activity, intellectual and contemplative, is paramount; at least for the time being. Any of these statements promote thought, provoke contradiction and invite further investigation.

III i Memory

Remembering and being remembered happens in mind; not out of *mind*, absent, unknown. If something is forgotten or lost, recollection, reminding, is possible. Remembering returns by being reminded plus inward will to rediscover, re-learn, retrieve, recollect. Writing it down, making a note, is a form of self-help: word.

Memory provides a storehouse of immeasurable resource concerning every aspect, detail and generality of knowledge and experience. Recollections occur and connections are made in this interior realm of mind. The next task is to remember, describe, record and even try to write, always aware that the farther you seek, the more and more is to be found in detail and in extent. Unexpected connections occur and suggest, sometimes, that a discovery is curiously familiar. Some see this as encountering intrinsic order in creation, an aspect of searching un-searchable riches. Jung thought of it as realising the presence of the collective unconscious, a universal source of common memory.

Without memory and words, there could be no spoken or written record of past events: no store or inventory for identification and names, of pains and pleasures, no available history or means of cultivating a sense of history. The activities characteristic of human minds: to verbalise, consider critically, debate, articulate and write, distinguish humanity. **Language** is the transforming supplement of instinct enabling memory to record, renew, recognise, describe, recreate.

Remembering is personal, immediately practical as well as infinitely long term. Families, streets, parishes in villages and towns, counties, countries and continents have common memories. Cycles are registered in time and strengthened in memory by natural recurrence of days, seasons, years, and by personal events: birthdays, anniversaries, centenaries that mark growth and achievement in present and past life. After death, these change into commemorations; celebrations of particular lives, continuing occasions for feasting with joy and abstaining in sorrow. Death brings grief and mourning to those bereaved and intensifies appreciation of the life remembered, of life itself. Memory enables digestion in context and perspective. Like ending a day, reaching a destination, departure at death seems to be, and in bodily terms is, a conclusion but appreciation of personal quality and influence, good and ill, continues.

Collective memories of powerful significance lead to public remembrance. Peace, cessation of war, armistices; Founders' days, Jubilees, Centenaries, Millennia will continue as long as communities, great and small, enjoy and appreciate inherited benefits as debts to those whose lives were lived to give, supply, preserve what continues valued, remembered, and worth preserving. Benefactions, endowments which enrich at every level, continue from past into present with hope for the future. Ceremonies strengthen appreciation by renewing memories and perpetuating them. At best, there is communication between all ages and generations in reminding and remembering together what is known, felt and thought to be worth commemorating. The sense of continuity assists understanding and promotes stability but events are remembered because they happened and not because they are invented to popularise non-events. The twenty-first century, so far, has included great memories as well as new calamities: disasters, some brought upon ourselves.

III ii Thought
(Including Purpose and Intention)

This trio compose and are composed for performance to incline a person towards 'making up their mind'; stimulating in order to *act, play,* make music. All that comes to mind, too little and too much, contributes to a view, a reasoned evaluation of motive, inclination, formation of opinion, thought clarified and resolved; to determine purpose and intent. ***Will*** will be considered further. (See **IX**.)

Purpose and intention do not always coincide with inclination and desire. Conflict between thought and feeling needs to be recognised, distinguished in mind, if control and resolution are to refine intention. Fulfilment suggests achievement but frustration feels like failure and failure is often frustrating. Both are assessed by others in action done, and by ourselves; what is refrained from or left undone. Thinking ahead is to pre-meditate, to recognise purpose intended. Thinking it over includes afterthoughts; aspects remembered as successful, fortunate, lucky, chancy, disastrous or not; wise, unwise, foolish. In perplexity, thought rotates like this paragraph, commenting rather than resolving.

Performatives and **donouns** are helpful. *Act*, like *mind*, is a **donoun**. An *act* is performed inwardly, outwardly, both together. To think is ability to *act* in *mind*. Again, sometimes I *act* before I think. Sometimes I think before I *act*. Do I understand what that *act will mean*: means? What do you think? You think a thought. Words spoken have been called linguistic acts. Unity in being and doing, integration, can occur in

donouns as in happy performatives. (See the Introduction.)

Thought is private, secret, until disclosed in words or actions and is a formidable activity of mind. We are aware of our own thoughts and can work to inform and organise them, to sort out motive, purpose, intention before outward action. Others' thoughts about unknowns engage supposition. Sympathy, intelligence and familiarity may enable another mind to be read, warily.

Since mind is the living centre of thought, a well exercised mind promotes speed and power of activity. Through learning, a mind graduates from first things and words to enjoy a degree of independence and maturity. Memory, increasingly well stocked storehouse, benefits thought. Mental vigour and agility, flexible to discern purpose, strengthens intention with knowledge and experience; *will* to perform. Purpose and intention define motive; motive provides live current between thought and action. **Will** sparks effort to *switch* on and transmit from mind to body received and obeyed into action. There is a report-back process between body and mind. This recognises that *will* is distinct from thought and can accept or refuse mind's orders, directions, control. (See **IX**.) The orders may come from other sources, another mind or will; significant to be consulted, considered, obeyed; postponed or disregarded. Dissociated sensibilities need reconnection.

III iii Being in Mind: Psyche

Some personalities are mainlanders with comparatively easy communications. Others are islanders, like Wight, Arran, Scillies, separated by water, protected by proximity, occasionally disturbed by weather and stormy seas. Some have a connecting strip, like Portland, others are accessible at low water like Lindisfarne. Most persons have areas more or less dormant, hidden rather than exposed, unconscious, sub-conscious awaiting awakening and realisation. Taking consciousness as at the core of personality, it is the heart where responsive being becomes aware of and experiences growth; ability to cultivate and become cultivated by vitality of increasing consciousness. Inward response to outward encounters; necessities, places, people, feelings and thoughts: all contribute to expanding consciousness. Eyes, face, look at, and receive from the outside world. Each face has features common to all but is like no other. Expressions show more than words can tell, reflecting what cannot, need not, ought not for the time being, be articulated.

Consciousness develops with perception, more and more alive with cognitive and emotional powers nourished in experience and memory. Areas of consciousness awaken gradually, sometimes prematurely, instantaneously, dramatically. An area awakened, might be, was, is, or becomes suppressed, numbed, silenced, lost for the time being; unresponsive until shocked or coaxed to surface. Senility is a common word for loss of response, worn out connections of memory; retrieval system in mind, different to denial.

If heart represents feeling and head represents thought, human consciousness embraces, exists in, and has need of both. A hard heart and/or a dull mind *limit* thought and action. Heart and head, best when operating in confident union, are capable of contradicting each other. Fortunate people know in childhood, without self-consciousness or anxiety, that heart is the place of repose, personal home. When heart and mind disagree, oppose seriously, there is inward conflict. Tension contained constructively becomes creative. Extreme, unbearable, unmanageable, stress can becomes distress, un-ease capable of disturbing nerves of behaviour, control of temper, outlook, balanced reactions.

This centre of well-being or disturbance is the **psyche**. It is the confluence, formed and formidable, of consciousness and imagination. Originally a Greek word encompassing soul as spirit with body, psyche is sometimes regarded as part of personality not quite of the body, flesh, blood or bone, yet distinct from mind. Connected with mind but not of it, psyche depends on and is assisted by pneuma, breathing breath of life, intuitive like instinctive action of lungs yet nourishing to and from the oxygen of consciousness. Greek genius for personification associated Psyche with Cupid rather than with rational faculties. Aristotle discussed the soul as that which animates. If it is the inspiration, the motivator, the creative core and energy of mind, psyche helps to identify and move **WILL**. Pneuma, pneumatic breathing in and out, is breath and spirit of life; ventilated by fresh air, the wind of the soul to breathe freely, healthy; making whole.

The expression 'psyched up' has come into common use. 'Ready and willing', 'determined to do', 'going ahead now', 'roaring to go' are similar indications of intent into act: of personal mobilisation to do. All indicate pre-considered purpose over instinctive reaction. The mind is 'made up', the body is in gear to obey (reluctantly perhaps, perhaps with good reasons). The complexities of psycho/mental processes suggest a sort of frontier between recognition and action: thinking 'yes' rather than 'no', qualified by 'perhaps': clear in mind but not quite at the next stage, able and willing to actually go to, and do. The psyche engages intensity of purpose with sense and sensibility as well as thought.

Observed, tested and investigated through listening and discussion, psyche is studied as psychology, academic and clinical. Analytical and therapeutic, counselling is intended to offer help in managing unmanageable problems; analysis seeks to plumb the depths of inner life. Both explore human nature and behaviour. MIND includes active capability for thought, doing the thinking, mind itself in activity: like the processor doing the processing. Psyche is where interaction occurs, fusion of response between heart and mind for sympathy and understanding, comprehension and action. When psyche is thought of as soul, nourishment is supplied, needed, from heart as well as mind: emotion, passion, reason plus metaphysical recognition: dynamic faith.

'Psychic' suggests highly developed intuition. Exceptional insight into unusual, abnormal, 'para-normal' occurrences which fascinate, breed fear and tempt towards superstition. Extrapolating a 'spirit world' leads claim of being a 'medium'. What is called 'spiritualism' attempts to communicate with the 'spirit' of someone dead, perhaps desperately missed, through the agency of the 'medium' or 'spiritualist' to find comfort. Advice in the form of prediction is sought from astrology. Necromancy and witchcraft attempt to minister to, sometimes exploit, personal uncertainty, insecurity, guilt, anguish and *fear*: destructive.

To say that two people are 'on the same wave length' recognises sympathy, empathy, intuitive understanding of soul, psyche: deep friendship balanced in feeling and thought, *trust* and *reason*, personified *reason* to *trust*.

III iv Beyond Mind

An 'open mind' suggests readiness to listen, to read, consider new ideas and discoveries; to think about, discuss and attempt to comprehend their significance. It includes recognising differences and limits of response, opinion and interpretation, including will and judgment. Common usage of indifference, prejudice and intolerance refer to conditions thought to, perhaps inclined, even disposed to, oppose an open mind able and willing to re-think. Denial of fact and repudiation of new insight are forms of disbelief. Belief, unbelief and disbelief as to what is true are indispensable to constructive conclusions, affirming or denying, in theoretical and practical matters filtered in mind with conscience (see **XI**) and reason. All these are among mind's conscious activities. Beyond them, horizons extend and, if the soul develops antennae open to mystical reception, it reaches regions where consciousness and imagination engage in contemplation rather than analytical thought, mind finds extraordinary resources. The traditional words for such access are prayer and meditation.

III v Mind with Philosophy

Philosophy, thinking about thought, leads to stating thoughts: ideas, notions, concepts about thinking. It takes place in mind and requires words for expression. Exploring words leads to sources, the things and ideas behind the words. To distinguish between appearance and reality; to recognise, identify, and name; to express differences of meaning and means of distinguishing them; to find thought forms and ways of thinking: these are among the functions of philosophers.

Philosophy, speculative exploration, concerns ideas and language as a grammar of thinking vital in any studies. Ethics, politics and aesthetics, the traditional domain of moral philosophy are hived off towards law, to 'sociology', to the creative and performing arts including matters of taste. Philosophers wrestle abstractedly with words and meanings in ways which have brought them to linguistics, philology, etymology. Good and Evil seem in danger of being thought personal preferences, convenient or inconvenient. To define, to analyse, to classify requires general and universal personal responsibility; necessary, vital and careful as thinking about meaning and intention.

What differentiates natural philosophy from moral philosophy? Discussion of nature and of morality began with science, *scientia*, meaning knowledge, until study of natural material things and processes by observation, test and experiment became regarded as different, distinct, from study of mind. Human thought and behaviour, mental and moral categories considered, discussed, analysed, include social, civil, political questions. Not suspect as un-scientific but other than the turn taken when speculative thought is primarily concerned with studying vegetable, animal, mineral and all physical things: practicalities of nature and of natural life.

In antiquity, a philosopher was a lover of wisdom seeking to discover and understand what is true. Sophism identified the specious but fallacious arguments seen through by the wise. To sophisticate was to pervert. Science concerned only nature — if that means material, mechanical and embodied practicalities — shifts theoretical, speculative; imaginative work in the mind of scientists as philosophers in search of what is true but concerned with 'natural' rather than 'moral' spheres of thought. **This rift led to dissociation of sensibility: the one essential area of experience and knowledge separated from the other.**

First and last, anatomy unites physique of living life, an-atom-y of physical form other than physic. Heat, light and sound, known in and through observation and experience of nature, promote and condition life in the natural given world. Abstracted for analysis, discovered not invented though inventive ideas, methods, theories and techniques lead to comprehensive, comprehendible disclosures. Physics suggest physicians on one hand and metaphysicians on the other (as tempting an excursion here as was 'infinity' beyond MIND. (See **VI iii.**) Convergence between energy and numeracy stimulates study of philosophy with mathematics: integrating words, used differently, with mathematical methods.

Differentiation precedes, then enables integration. It is not dis-integration. An elliptical issue has two centres rather than the one of a single circle, rotating in orbit of equidistant radius. The ellipse, elliptical shape, with reference to two points, is static or orbital.

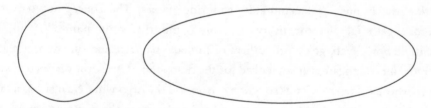

A start is made on any journey even if the route is unknown. Explorers look for uncertain destinations, planning and hoping to find it. (***Plan*** is a **donoun**.) If conclusion is achieved, the end invites new beginnings, further exploration. Priority and order are indispensable to proceed; in theory as in practice. The range of considerations grow, multiply and challenge the mind, the philosophy of a philosopher, who explores thinking about thought and finds and depends on such great words as ***reason***, analysis, logic, fallacy, conclusion. Systems are systematic; methods have become 'methology', themes 'thematic', helpful frameworks and structures; until formalised to the point of suffocation, obfuscation, rather than liberation.

III vi Visualising

Accurate map making depends on surveys. Measuring distances, ups and downs, directions, features and details was undertaken for defence by the Ordnance Survey. Landscape is visualised by reading a large-scale map. Maps of imagined places, like *Treasure Island*, make fiction more like reality. The imagination of the writer strengthens the plot visualised in the mind of the reader.

In settled regions, people find and reflect sense of identity. Communal needs lead to political development more or less stable, viable when their community is visualised and realised as an entity. Natural feature: islands, peninsulas, inlets, rivers valleys and mountain ranges are landscapes affecting and affected by latitude, altitude, sea, which condition climate from tropics to ice-caps, as do surface rocks. Vegetation and animal life followed, preceding human habitation, and are visualised as 'pre-history'. Exploration often promotes colonisation; settlement, cultivation and development: constructive or destructive exploitation.

Personality, infinitely varied, inverts to see natural phenomena as personification. Early astronomers visualised forms in star patterns and named constellations after their heroes. Heroic characters: Perseus, Andromeda, Cassiopaeia, Castor and Pollux, Orion the hunter, are memorable, enduring names. The concept of terrestrial-become-celestial equator in twelve zones, months, took names of adjacent constellations; crab, goat, bull; others of human character and function, Aquarius, Virgo, Libra. Navigators at sea looked for the first point of Aries, the distinctive Ram's horn whose golden fleece was sought by Jason and the Argonauts. Navigational tables calculated for the *Nautical Almanac* since 1765 make use of the first point of Aries.

E. C. Brewer, encyclopaedic collector of phrase and fable, made a rhyme to connect the signs of the zodiac, each a twelfth of the celestial equator, with months and seasons:

'Our vernal signs the RAM begins
Then comes the BULL, in May the TWINS;
The CRAB in June, next LEO shines,
And VIRGO ends the northern signs.
The BALANCE brings autumnal fruits,
SCORPION stings, the ARCHER shoots;
December's GOAT brings wintry blast,
AQUARIUS rain; the FISH come last.'

The idea of the influence of star positions at time and date of birth is very old. The beauty, glory and mystery of the night sky, the apparently steady patterns of stars, in stillness and movement, the moon waxing and waning, hold imagination in wonder and awe and rouse questions as to the origin and meaning of life and of human destiny. This has promoted supposition, speculation, of the significance of astrology. Visualising influences and calculating on 'astral' basis, significance, leads to notions of inevitability closer to fatalism, superstition, than to clear light of reason, opportunity and responsibility.

Early visualisation searching for meaning in experience drew on terrestrial growth as well as celestial patterns; on fertility, ancestry, work and prosperity, fortune and misfortune, as influences on character and characteristics.

When words move into patterns and rhythms that include but transcend essential grammar, a poem is being made. The mind of the poet visualises in words what has captured personal vision and experience. A reader may enter into that experience. Drawing, painting, sculpture draw their inspiration from seeing, visualising, interpreting their responses. Composers of music listen, hear, echo, adapt and enrich sounds from inward resonances including remembered musical experience. To give oneself up to work of art: a poem, a picture, a statue, a song or symphony is to enter into the visualisation of the artist, empty of distractions, to concentrate upon, respond to and receive it.

III vii Communicating: Signs and Symbols

Discovering that we are equipped to receive and transmit, to communicate, is an activity of mind that requires and depends on physical expression. Signs are received and given. A *sign* is a thing which of itself makes some other thing come to mind. Some signs are natural such as buds on plants and trees, mould on stale food; some are literal, direct words, *HALT*; others move; waving or beckoning. All signs can be expressed in words but not all words in signs. A **sign** indicates, significant when recognised, capable of positive and negative; invitation and barrier. Sign writing, the first stage of language development, leads to words with or without an alphabet. Clouds showing signs of rain have led to improved, now high quality, weather forecasting. Clouds themselves range from exquisitely beautiful, high cirrus, mackerel, mare's tails, tinged at dawn or sunset sometimes in every shade of pink red into purple. Deep, dark greys, gloomy, threatening rain or storm; low, dull, limiting visibility; fog.

Symbols provide another degree of communication, more than indicative. Symbols are what they are because they do what is in their nature to do: in being as well as to show meaning. A *seed* grows and signifies growth. The life of a *seed* is spent in reproducing. The plant reproduced makes more seeds which will die, then live. Symbols unify being and doing, to communicate more than signs. Eggs are themselves symbols, already mentioned; new life which signifies and symbolises the cycle of reproduction and of nourishment. Symbols communicate what is true. Beyond themselves, they offer metaphor and practical approach to metaphysical insight.

IV

Elements

IV i In General

Elements are irreducible, primary, 'elemental' factors: Aristotle thought, taught, that the universe itself consisted of four: **earth, water, air, fire**. Each has in its turn become 'natural science' multiplying into branches of increasingly specialist study.

Any topic, subject, theme and process has elements. Study of things themselves, their practical use, physical characteristics and qualities precede recognition of theory and principle. We observe and receive; first, through senses. Perception offers 'material' evidence. Second response is to name and find words to describe things. Third, to discover governing principles to understand and experience their use, for need, pleasure and power. Thinking about elements leads to analysing form, shape, process and change. The fourth stage, appreciation, involves appraisal and evaluation, possible control; use and abuse.

Lavoisier (1743-1794), lawyer, scientist of genius, identified and connected different forms of *matter*. His table of ELEMENTS has grown since. William Smith (1769-1840), 'father of geology', observed, examined, tested, analysed and classified rocks by origin and characteristics of earth's surfaces. Those deposited in **water** he called 'sedimentary'. Beneath the cooling crust is Earth's heart of *fire*: molten material, volatile, leaking out of fissures, sills, lava, or exploding as volcanoes, known and feared since antiquity. Slowly cooling material emerges as 'igneous' rock such as Dartmoor granite. Rocks changed by heat, e.g. limestone into marble, or compressed, e.g. clay into slate, are called 'metamorphic'. Smith's self-appointed geological survey began when surveying for railway cuttings between Bristol and London exposed sediments which enabled him to draw the first authentic geological map. His method extended, eventually, to the whole of this island where every era, age, and type of rock occurs and discloses the evolution of landscape and of life fossilised in strata. Mapping outcrops and exposures in cuttings enabled Smith to visualise underground structures and draw cross-sections of them, invaluable for quarrying and mining. His grasp of the elements of geology contributed to and was assisted by other specialisation: botany, zoology, chemistry, physics in field and laboratory, stratigraphy, palaeontology, chemical elements in mineralogy, petrology, now reuniting as Earth Sciences.

New knowledge sometimes strikes dramatically, as did the electric shock experienced by Benjamin Franklin when flying his kite. Some discoveries retain the name of who recognised, discovered and understood them: Euclid's geometry of shapes, (geometric cousin of geology), Descartes for Cartesian mathematics and philosophy, Newton's laws of motion, Linnaeus for names and classification of plants, Darwin for gathering, observing, connecting specimens to recognise natural selection and theory of evolution.

Light and *strike*, *watch* and *face*, simultaneous in being and doing, are vulnerable to human and to mechanical failure and to individual deceit or obfuscation. *Space* and *time* are measured reciprocally on earth: seconds, minutes, hours *match* longitude: 0 - 180°, 2 x 180° (West and East) =360°; 24 hours. Vast cosmic distances are reckoned in 'light years'. *Time*, infinitely expandable, *is* simultaneously, immediately present: now, at this moment, and forever. *Time* encompasses continuity, infinity, eternity. Does this **conceive**, anticipate, world without end?

Not regarded as an element in antiquity, *time* has always fascinated people. We speak of spending and saving time; making, gaining and losing it; we suggest comparisons between time and money and have sought ways to measure and mark experience of it. Sundial and hourglass, clock-working by *spring*, weight, pendulum; quartz and digital timers. The round *face* of a clock or *watch* with moving hands or blinking figures register time now. Wound up or otherwise empowered, they match the rotation of earth; noon and midnight, dawn and sunset.

WATCH is kept by open eyes, being and doing, for conditions, dangers, positions, routes.

Compass direction responds to earth's magnetic poles, at sea and elsewhere, and indicates North and South in unknown territory. A compass, or rather a pair of compasses, draws arcs, circles, to form and to divide; to make pattern and plan. Like instruments marking passage of time, compasses draw circles resembling and representing the sun, full moon and shadowed phases, the globe and precisely drafted lines to represent intersecting arcs of latitude and longitude.

Steady patterns of constellation in the night sky with their predictable seasonal positions and apparent regular circular movement suggest an awesome degree of

ORDER. Measured by observation from the first point of the constellation, ARIES, or from Greenwich, 0° degrees, by chronometer, accurate positions are reckoned. Twice a year, equinoxes occur when time 'stands still' at North and South Poles. Patterns of heat and cold on land are experienced as cycles of seasons: spring, summer, autumn, winter. Seed-time and harvest, determined by varying degrees of sunlight, warmth and cold, wet and dry, became familiar long before time and space were measured or weather and climate understood.

Informed guesses propose theory, hypothetical until verified. Subsequent exploration, further discovery, if it upsets this or that theory, calls for revision. *Change*, conclusively demonstrated, continues 'for the time being' until fresh insight arouses further question and debate, reopens reasoned criticism, revision justified or denied. Theories verified continue to be challenged but if they emerge unshaken, continue to be accepted, believed true.

IV ii In Particular

Words are sought, developed, to communicate expanding, intersecting spheres as they become known to us. When a mind is weaned from dependence on sense perception, conceptual ability develops. At any age, a person of honest mind, interest, intelligence and willing power of concentration may experience this change. Speaking and writing enhance our use of language. Moving from one level to another by analogy and metaphor releases potential for analytical thought. Counting moves from numbers into more complex mathematics, increasingly abstract intellectual activities: consideration of form, formulae, applications static and dynamic. Talk, dialogue, engages recognition of other points of view. Characteristic humility fosters mature deliberation and guides towards sound judgment, wise and true. Far beyond source, knowledge, are possibilities of great benefit in life: of joy through freedom to explore and discover: new responsibility through freedom to overcome ignorance: to learn that *control* liberates and life flourishes within it.

An **element** is an irreducible component of a complex whole; distinct within substance of existence. *Control* changes the fabric of elements in personality to reveal areas of *will*: of conscience, evaluation, decision, and needs additional sources of insight: **moral philosophy** which emerges in and though experience of natural elements.

Particularity, in particular, differentiates **part**. Like **form**, **part** is also syllable, prefix or suffix. To *part* segments of an orange separates them. Two people part, willingly or not; by force of circumstance, material, emotional preference, political, legal, any reason *part*icular to personal or communal conditions. De-part, im-part involve will. Partial, participate, partner, party and partisan imply involvement, possible commitment.

Particular relationships include ingredients, elements that exercise various faculties. Each tree, leaf, plant, moss, fungus and inhabitant of a wood contributes to and enhances understanding. Comprehending a forest: its enjoyment, value, use, long term care may precede or follow appreciation of its beauty and mystery; enchanting combinations of colour, light and shade; different scents, sounds and qualities of quietness. A forest may become a refuge, somewhere to hide as for *The Children of the New Forest*; a place to lose one's way in; a place of despair as Dante's *Wood of the Suicides*; a place of tryst and romance, the Forest of Arden in *As You Like It*; of fear where grotesque shapes and unfamiliar sounds assume threatening personification of unknown danger told by the Brothers Grimm; a place of peace where filtered sunlight, quiet leaves and soft mosses are accompanied by multiple birdsong; re-creative. The whole is infinitely greater than the sum of particular parts. Each **element** in being has its meaning clarified when perceived to function in unity with the whole.

IV iii Transformation

This dynamic word is movement for *change* as in **trans**late, **trans**fer, **trans**pose, **trans**port. If *form* is being changed, it becomes trans**form**ed into something else by growth (acorns into oak trees) by deliberate *work* (wool spun and woven into cloth), by effort, personal mechanical, chemical; and by emotional, intellectual and moral determination: will-power. *Form*, (**donoun**), is exceptionally versatile. It may be prefixed with con-, de-, in-, per-, re-, or itself extended as **form**ula, **form**ulate, **form**ed, **form**idable. It is an aspect of 'element'.

Each of Aristotle's four elements are symbols in every level of experience. (See Appendix **A**.)

Fire heat Ignite	destroying/refining/purifying	inflame, *power*
Water wet	*flood, drain, wash* away, quench, cleanse...	renew
Air move, wind, *wind,*	blow, breathe, ventilate/precipitate/transport	breathe, sound/resound
Earth ground place foundation	base, build/bury ... up/down, soil	firm, nourish/sustain, stabilise

Order circulates in ocean currents, air, and atmospheric pressure systems. Fire and earth, first and last, are last and first: Prometheus alive before he could capture fire.

Elements interact and may move to change and become transformed. Wind, movement of air parallel to earth's surface, circulates in its atmosphere, provides breath of life, symbol of will and spirit, creative and destructive. Purpose, place, season and time vary with starting place and priorities.

Many chemical 'elements' have been recognised and named since Aristotle's classification, and Lavoiset's. (See Appendix **A**.)

V

Substance

'Throughout the world, if it were sought,
Fair words enough a man shall find
They be good cheap; they cost right nought;
Their substance is but only wind.
But well to say and so to mean,
That sweet accord is seldom seen.'
(Thomas Wyatt, 1557, published posthumously)

From limestone to marble, from water to ice or steam, from maggot to fly, from caterpillar to moth or butterfly, from bean-seed to bean-bearing beanstalk, from girl to woman, bride and mother, these changes are commonplace and astonishing. Observing change as natural process opens questions of how, when and why it happens: to promotion and cultivation, to prevention and control.

How and why do things, persons, powers, being of one substance become another?

A metamorphosis is a particular change. When the process is understood and if the change is desired it may become an everyday procedure such as boiling or refrigerating water. Unpredictable natural phenomena which cause dramatic change: a flood or a volcanic eruption for example, suggest super-human power. When linked to relief or catastrophe, they seem to imply benevolent or malignant intervention in customary experience, creative and destructive. Remembered in saga, myth, fable and legend, their consequences are interwoven with heroism and frailty in human behaviour which involve dimensions of judgment, of moral significance, for good and evil. Suspicion and fear are elements in superstition. What can we do to be saved, from drought, flood, disease, hatred, war, or any of the conditions dangerous to our wellbeing?

If metamorphoses occur in natural things and in our bodies, do they offer models for change of mind, head, and change of feeling, of heart?

METAPHOR is a way of describing something in terms unusual, even impossible, as it is. Fly, meaning hurry rather than go by aeroplane. Squeeze a soaking cloth and limiting credit. You **see** the inexhaustible body/mind metaphor, eye to sight as well as to understanding, uniting appearance and insight, surface and depth.

Breath receives air, wind. The same air, oxygen, can be breathed once only. Once breathed out, it is carbon dioxide. Vegetation absorbs carbon dioxide and exhales oxygen. Natural scientists discovered this process. Thomas Wyatt's verse is an epigraph for **donouns** 'in sweet accord' of being as doing, unifying, integrated. 'In the beginning' creative wind breathed: 'moved upon the face of the waters' (*Genesis* 1. 2) and 'divided the waters' to make land. Earth science and divinity speak also of union, natural and moral philosophy, being and doing 'seldom seen', but, once recognised and acknowledged, as **substance**. 'Faith is the substance of things hoped for, the evidence of things not seen.' (*Hebrews* 11.1.)

Not one of the five senses can do the work of any other one. Each is, in this *sense*, elemental. Functions may overlap; *smell* and *taste* supplement *sight*. 'Common sense' combines distinctive senses towards intelligence within a general view; seeing the forest, the wood as well as each tree. Where and when *sense* joins consciousness towards the whole includes seeing the forest as totality of each and every tree. Looking forward, visualising, mixes memory with desire and imagination. Recollection rediscovers memories of things past. Intuition, sometimes called a sixth sense, thrives on sense with sensibility. Sense offers a semblance, but common sense looks further for resemblance, assembly, the whole. Intuition discerns beyond information learned, sensed, taught, read. It is conscious realisation, made more nearly whole by looking from form to substance to see the unseen and invisible, to meaning itself. Intuition includes visualisation; a looking forward enriched by recollection.

The underlying source, the essence of anything under consideration, involves more than form. *Form* itself is something more than *shape*, size, and surface appearance. Thinking about *form* and elements leads from **substance** to *value*, to appraisal, criticism, evaluation, apprehended together. We co-ordinate sense with feeling and thought to discern meaning and significance, the qualities and functions of **substance**: the intricate, infinitesimal detail of pattern and composition and, altogether, the principle of the thing; the spirit of the act.

Speaking of a 'person of **substance**' suggests *integrated* qualities of well-being; substantial and balanced, independent yet dependable; responsible and trustworthy.

Of course, **substance** may include, and be limited to, property possessed; as well as properties, as qualities of personality and character.

Physical substance, material, has essence, external and internal. Ideas raise essential questions concerning personality, principle, irreducible matters of substance. Discussion continues but the substance of a matter becomes clarified. 'I think, therefore I am' does not include the substance of what is thought about; good and evil, strength and weakness for example; but that there is something to think about, outside and beyond myself. To say 'I am therefore I think' makes thought dependent on ability to think rather than having something that requires thought. Clarification of substance goes beyond proposing and supposing. These assist thought processes with reason but do not plumb the substance of being that awaits us beyond ourselves.

The overwhelming question and ultimate concern here is for, and of, **what is true**. **Reason is an indispensable agent**. Substance is substantive and offers food for thought. Visualisation helps, expands, but requires consciousness, perception, emotion. Recognising limits asks: are you sure? Can I depend on it? If it was so, is it still so now? Will it continue to be so in future? Do you believe so? Affirmation and *Trust* challenge.

Personal hopes and fears encourage subjective reactions. Does 'it' suit your and/or my personal interest? A clear, objective view of cause and effect is hoped for when human beings are intelligent, articulate, reasonable, virtuous, responsible: and all these things are qualities contributing to **integrity**: substance: but readily distorted. Action is more than physical. Stature concerns maturity beyond height. In public life, those who act justly and administer justice are expected to be objective: to listen, to hear, to be fair. To seek for substance is to enquire into the very nature, the heart and soul of what is or is not true: the good.

Looking for such underlying sources of being suggests five areas to explore. Separate for description, but interdependent in experience of substance there are dangers in isolating them from each other.

SOURCES   ## Processes

Natural
Immediate perception   Direct evidence of each sense, practical, tactile,
audible, recognised: contributing to,
and, joined in common sense

Historical
Experience, memory.   Oral. Art. Archaeology.
Personal, family,   Any sources with evidence of the past:
communal, recorded   built, written, excavated

Theoretical
Ideas, abstract, analysis,   Guessed, reasoned, evaluated,
theory and principle   Verified authenticated

Speculative
Forethought, envisaged   Wonder, imagine, intuitive assessment
Recognised aim, possibility,   of cause and effect
Idea   2nd, 3rd etc guessing, formulation of policy

Believed
Pre-supposed, trusted,   Tried, tested in action,
reasoned,   verified in experience, surviving
accepted, affirmed, confident   doubt: undoubted
expectation   expectation, to be prepared for

The summary above suggests enquiry nourished by any one of the five sources with reference to each of the others; in case any source(s) is absent or ignored. The significance of each sharpens contrast with its opposite:

i.   Unnatural, deniable, out of touch, insulated, isolated, ignorant: ignoring evidence.
ii. Absence of history — lacking benefits and warnings from past experience, remembered tradition.
iii. Lack of analysis — 'not thought through', is present idiom.
iv. Absence of vision — plan or policy; no aim or forward criteria for assessing.
v.   Disbelief, unbelief, no belief — no will to pre-suppose; 'denial' of potent power of trust.

To assume that what true is discoverable depends on its being believed or denied. Enquiry proceeds in confident expectation of discovering **an** — if not **the** — answer. This simple statement of process shows affirmed purpose: 'I have started and I will finish'. 'I believe and see.' 'I see because I believe'. No other person can speak for you or for me. Your voice is of you, your personality, your potential **substance** in being, knowing and willing. Individuality, individuation for confidence, coexists in family, community, culture, in harmony and discord.

Heart, head and tongue in harmony are happy; but they are not always so. The accord is rare particularly when its possibility is not recognised, not thought significant.

Belief, like *hope*, engages confidence. Belief affirmed affects every *level* and aspect of living: needs, desires, aspirations, plans. Denial, disbelief and unbelief are linked with absence of *hope* which begins in indifference and ends, at worst, in *fear* and despair.

Transformation involves will to reconsider, to reopen and a question. A *change* of attitude may lead to *change of mind*, from denial to recognition. This, too, is of **substance**. 'Stance' is the basis of an underlying attitude, a position taken, an attitude adopted. Sub-, underground, is substantial, on sure foundation, even when underground, but never exempt from danger of natural or human violence.

Genuine responsibility involves acceptance or rejection. Thinking requires terms of reference, aims and ideals, presuppositions upon which to formulate, design, a new pattern within familiar tapestry of common life. Political as well as personal questions rest on moral and economic concerns. Karl Marx (1818-1883) thought in practical as well as theoretical terms. His system of thought was not simply postulated and examined but **believed**.

To discuss and affirm something true in experience is, in this instance, opinion believed to be sure, true. That 'every truth has become so' is a philosopher's statement rather than an article of faith, but converges. Hitler's Nazi creed inspired and 'carried conviction' enabling him to impose it as the National Socialist system in Germany until defeat in 1945.

What can be learned from questioning these experiences? The post mortem about what is past searches to contribute to understanding present problems, difficulties, strengths and weaknesses calling upon assistance from philosophy and faith; philosophers who believe, believers who reason. Looking backwards or forwards, wisdom is needed to discern what is true: to hope to recognise, comprehend, begin to understand. These are questions of **substance**.

Belief, like *hope*, engages *trust* and expectation. Intention, immediate and longer term, needs scrutiny at every level in every aspect of living. To explore, evaluate and judge, unites inward and outward to transforming practicalities into knowledge and thought.

Performatives and **donouns** pin-point union of being/ doing.

In his long life, C. G. Jung (1875-1961), doctor, academic teacher, psycho-therapist, described his explorations in papers and special studies: twenty volumes of *Collected Works*. His examinations of consciousness, of the sub-conscious and 'the unconscious' include clinical and pastoral experience. *Memories, Dreams, Reflections* (Vintage Books, 1989) weave together a chronology of personal development with accounts of self-examination, including dreams:

'My life has been permeated and held together by one idea and one goal: namely to penetrate into the secret of personality. Everything can be explained from this central point, and all my works relate to this one theme.' (Page 232.)

'As I worked with my fantasies, I became aware that the unconscious undergoes or produces change...that the psyche is transformed or developed by the relationship of the ego to the contents of the unconscious. In individual cases that transformation can be read from dreams and fantasies. In collective life it has left its deposit principally in the various religious systems and their changing symbols. Through the study of these collective transformation processes and through understanding of alchemical symbolism I arrived at the central concept of my psychology: the process of individuation. (Page 235.)

Jung regarded himself by education and inclination as a scientist. His experimental experience concerned himself, his patients, and his concern for humanity. What he called 'individuation' was for him, intensely introspective. He was exceptionally capable of dreaming, recalling his dreams and subjected his recollections to high intellectual analysis and so moving towards constructive self-awareness. In such a language Jung was not alone.

T. S. Eliot, his contemporary, was as acutely aware of European culture, its psychology of anxiety, misery, war, post-war 'waste land' despair, and interest in psychotherapy. As a young Harvard-American philosopher/poet, Eliot was in Paris, 1910-11, Germany, in 1914, then England. These two twentieth century giants bequeathed a formidable literature in different works of perennial impact. Questions of substance and of the working of *mind* are as old as thought. Eliot diagnosed the 'dissociation of sensibility' in English culture particularly as expressed in poetry. (See *Clark Lectures*, Cambridge, 1926, published 1993, Faber and Faber, edited by Ronald Schuchard, pages 220-228.)

Questions concerning every aspect of pain and suffering; of healing and forgiveness, life, death, were addressed to Jesus. His responses enlarge and deepen the thinking and understanding of the questioner. Bewildered, uncertain listeners, later readers during centuries since, discover transforming news when the law, the law of Moses, (summarised in *Deuteronomy* 6) is fulfilled in **love**; 'heart, soul, mind and strength' together in **love** of God and of neighbour (*Mark* 12. 28-31). Jesus added **MIND to heart, soul and MIGHT**. *Might engages strength of* **purpose**. Listeners then, readers since, encounter selfless love, forgiving, merciful, foreseen by Isaiah in the suffering servant who redeems.

John records the conversation between Jesus and Nicodemus ('a man of the Pharisees, a ruler') who is baffled by 'rebirth', 'being born again', obviously literally impossible. Union: reunion between flesh and spirit, earthly and heavenly, head and heart of the good news, (the Gospel) of Jesus Christ: being of one substance, human and divine, divine and human, born, manifest Christmas birth, unspeaking baby accompanied by superhuman coincidental events; songs of glory, peace on earth, good-will are unfolded. (*John* 3), remembered and celebrated year by year. Deeply troubled hearts, fearful and needy, experience **trust**; are drawn, called, invited to **believe** (*Matthew* 11. 28) and assured of ever present experience of continuing presence, 'comfort' (*John* 14-17).

At last, going, knowingly, to be crucified, Jesus reveals identity of being in one substance, Son of man as Son of God; one in *will*, **one** in union: Father and Holy Spirit: eternal Presence, Creator, Comforter: shepherd, master, teacher, friend. Early Christians thought of the Comforter as grace, strength of soul: the Holy Spirit, as the ENERGY of God.

VI

Movement and Change

'For last year's words belong to last year's language
And next year's words await another voice.
(T. S. Eliot, *Little Gidding*, part 2)

VI i Natural Change

Natural change has been observed and imitated for human purposes since earliest people found ways to cultivate, to promote improvement and deter deterioration in natural things useful to them. Consciousness of necessity, benefit or delight lie deep in folk memory and legend. Paradise garden, recalled in our imperfect world, speaks of a sense of loss, of the reality of failure and urge to retrieve and succeed. Persons and communities change too, sometimes gradually, sometimes rapidly and dramatically. *Change*, measurable in size, shape, is not transformation of character but sometimes affects outlook, attitude and perspective, intention and *will*. Events and circumstances challenge *will*; characteristics and character form in response to them.

Change: desired, intended, predictable or unpredictable, avoidable or preventable, has causes and effects. Living things change in size as they grow. Cultivation, co-operating with normal, anticipated conditions of weather, climate and seasons, rock, soil quality, landscape, relief and climate promotes growth. Decay and disintegration are natural too. Methods to postpone or prevent them may be devised. Change happens also by mishaps, accidents, unintended, unforeseen, genuinely accidental.

Earth itself, the ground of living existence, vegetable, animal, human, is reproductive and fruitful; enhanced when cultivated. Our original elements are continually, repeatedly at work: creating and destroying, forming and modifying things, events and circumstances:

Fire and *heat* energise, modify and transform matter. Promethean flame ignites practicalities. To light, cook and bake; to mould, smelt, purify, burn and destroy, incinerate and cremate need *fire*. Soon a word such as *spark* applies not only to physical but to emotional and intellectual interests, to our zest for life.

Air to breathe ventilates leaves and lungs. The process of osmosis balances.

Wind has power to transport, to *blow*, to dry, to precipitate, to *move* and to *change* temperature, moisture, due to presence, absence, intensity of Sun's radiant energy.

Water to *drink*, to cleanse, irrigate, *sail* on, is indispensable to life: *fish*. *Water* distilled is purified, uncontaminated, like clean *rain*.

Materials such as rock, flint, skins and bones, grasses, reeds, wood were and are shaped, adapted to change from their original functions. Sand and stone make walls, clay is turned into bricks and tiles, material for building, marking, recording. From caves and simple shelters, a hut becomes a cottage, house, castle, villa, palace, a dome for pleasure, wonder and worship. Every *stage* is enhanced for needs or desires including security, comfort and style.

Change requires energy. Diamond, pure carbon, crystallizes in perfect form in intense heat. Skilled cleaving, cutting, polishing and setting maximize its ability to refract and sparkle. Many minerals have potentially perfect geometric form, precisely configured shape and faces co-ordinated. Quartz, fluorspar, galena are examples. Clay and slate, early used for inscribing, writing, changed from one to the other by compression, shrinking folding of original sediment. Limestone into marble provides sculptors with material of monumental beauty. All these things, the elements themselves; the principles reflected in them; their characteristic functions; the order and pattern which enable human minds to discern and learn of them are *given, inherited, and capable of movement and change.*

Personal determination to harness elemental energy has transforming consequences. Natural processes are imitated to produce change. Farmers, builders, scientists, artists use techniques applied, engineered, from natural material adapted for scientific purposes and for the art of living itself, for particular and general improvement within constraints and opportunities. Prosperity and poverty vary human well-being and misery. Sufferings caused by ignorance, privation, natural disaster intensify if wealth brings greed; if conflict brings war. Prosperity is forfeit until the opportunity for balance is found again. All living creatures, animal and human, inhabit this paradigm. Need and desire to discover and to change are continuing themes of the exploration of nature, self and society, imperfect, to visions of perfection, at every level.

Meta- is prefix of change, a developed difference. **Ortho-** prefix of form; **para-** of comparison.

Metamorphic is material change, from static to differently static, but moved, e.g. rock having been heated, folded, faulted, squeezed, stretched, altered.

Metamorphosis occurs in living being; in nature, circumstance, and by decision, *will*. It is personal, impersonal; subjective, objective, inner and outer change.

Metaphor uses words to compare, communicate change. Music reflects sounds metaphorically, e.g. bands for dancing, marching; Beethoven's Pastoral Symphony; choral singing: word enhancing, despair, devotion.

Meta-physic: intense inward experience: pain, fear, loss, grief suffered; healing as mending, making whole, finds restored union of substance and form, energy and power explicating metaphysical consciousness. Such change is envisaged and realisable through conscious endowment and cultivation: pastoral, clerical, medical, juridical, artistic, vocation, profession and commitment.

VI ii Metamorphoses

Repetition is intended and needed to assist description of change.

Metamorphosis is *change* of *form, shape* and *function* — sometimes all three — that occurs naturally, without human intervention. Such process, understood and desired, may provoke action or series of actions to set it in motion. Planting, cultivating, harvesting: keeping chickens for eggs, cows for milk, cream and butter: all involve deliberate, beneficial purposeful *change*. Natural metamorphosis is imitated and reproduced: such as heating or refrigerating. Power stations recycle one sort of fuel into another; coal and oil are turned into electricity. Successful production improves produce, and encourages specialisation. Self-sufficiency overflows to make a market: supply, demand, sale, profit, balance or loss. In turn, mechanised, 'industrialised' mass-markets lead to selling in 'super-markets'. Food produced, prepared, pre-prepared, is eaten, digested, to repair, renew, make energy to do and to make; to produce and reproduce. All these activities involve simple metamorphoses, no longer mysterious, often beneficially multiplied to meet increased need and rising standards of living. Change in some cases is dramatic. This and other words suffixed with –ic: metamorph-ic, encapsulate change; describe action that is sudden or gradual: frantic, artistic, antic, manic, panic, chronic, comic, tragic, myopic, mechanic, anthropomorphic, cosmic.

Change evident in the histories of human societies tends to be propelled by danger, inspiration and by material discoveries. Before we learned to reproduce energy, survival depended on ceaseless drudgery. Leisure for the few required co-operation or compulsion of slaves, serfs, servants. Individuals who discover and enjoy liberty, freedom, opportunity find that freedom includes responsibility, effort and suffering. Some communities are led towards ordered civilisation. This metamorphosis is no less dramatic than any in the natural order. Earliest recorded societies see such change consequent on the lives of exceptional individuals: Hammurabi, Achilles. Joseph, enslaved, became advisor and effective ruler in Egypt. Leadership inspires more than personal, metamorphoses. A crowd, a rabble, becomes a tribe, an army, for good or evil with disciplined leadership. Stalin and Hitler were twentieth century examples who enforced totalitarian ideology.

Early writers convey fear, even terror, when describing metamorphosis. In Homer's *Iliad*, a snake is turned to stone. (*Iliad* 2. 319.) In Hebrew history, Moses' staff becomes a serpent and then back to its original form. (*Exodus* 4. 1-4.) The power to cause such change is mysterious, awe-inspiring, unaccountable in terms of normal human experience. Imputed to gods and goddesses, immortals believed to intervene in human activities; invisible to human kind, provoked life-changing interventions; such as storms and war. Ted Hughes's translation of Ovid's *Metamorphoses* discloses fatalism, inevitability, ineluctable consequence; forms of judgment gathered within irredeemable destiny.

Magic engages magicians, wizards and witches who frighten, deceive, enchant into spell-binding reactions intended to subjugate, even destroy. In contemporary fiction their practices fascinate young readers. The practice of witchcraft intensifies in times of ferocious religious and political controversy; hell-fire preachers and rabble-raisers who initiate witch-hunts when their opponents fight back. Moderate voices, advocates of toleration, are difficult to hear, become reluctant to engage in such extremes as in sixteenth to seventeenth century England. Shakespeare drew off poisonous elements by dramatising enchantment, as in *A Midsummer Night's Dream*. Oberon has his own Kingdom, the Royals enchanted, endeavour to rediscover each other and theirs, and the artisans (led by the carpenter) make high comedy. In *The Tempest*, Prospero exemplifies fatherly devotion and, shipwrecked on his island domain, engages magic powers until rescue and release are achieved. The Tragedy of *Macbeth* opens with the three witches boiling up recipes and pronouncing incantations. They are feared for their power to invoke hostile elements and brew deep trouble. Macbeth, power hungry, superstitious, fearful of ghosts as well as of witches, bends to the murderous scheme of Lady Macbeth, and nemesis.

Cruelty which exploits ignorance and superstition is not funny, but 'magic' amuses through illusion, sleight of hand, special equipment, tricks; Houdini, disappearing, reappearing; contrived apparent metamorphoses. Clowns, in contrast, entertain with comic humour disguised in clowning. They do not intend to hurt or harm themselves, each other, but follies, mishaps, contortions and confrontations involve antics that promote astonishment, pity and mirth in their audiences. The costume and make-up of a circus clown metamorphoses the wearer. White face, bulbous nose, frightened eyebrows, enlarged red-painted mouth, baggy garments, head topped by conical, comical hat decorated with pom-poms. Movements mix clumsiness with amazing acrobatic agility: juggling, tumbling, stilted, grotesque; acting without malice in hilarious contests of water, whitewash, flour, pudding messes carried on between themselves. Our own follies and frailties become laughable in the face of such clowning: pathetic, comic tinged with tragic; folly without threat.

'Miracle' is mysterious change for the better, inexplicable beyond reason, expectation, practical possibility. Dramatic change: recovery from sickness to health, from wickedness to virtue, from failure to success, from crime to good citizenship: deliverance from any affliction or pattern of conduct thought or known evil, enslavement, beyond hope of deliverance may be regarded as miraculous. This is something far greater than the magical, sourced in normal virtues: care, skill, knowledge, understanding, kindness, sustained effort, exceptional sympathy: a vital spark that ignites confidence, faith that enables a miracle to happen. Medical practice is realised as humane art with a scientific method plus insight and intuition. Doctors, like poets, need metaphor and metaphysic to understand and communicate with a patient whose confidence and respect, in turn, promotes healing. Extraordinary recoveries are described, truly, as miracles, with and without medical expertise.

Mastery of material things through sense and effort of mind generates further enquiry fulfilled by discoveries in practice. Codes cracked disclose 'secrets' of nature. Galileo measured acceleration from the top of the tower of Pisa; Newton watched an apple fall from a tree in his garden. Gravity and stability known are measured, and knowledge enables us to erect buildings with sufficient material strength to stand ; some with beauty, grandeur, magnificence. All these are forms of reversed metamorphoses, of concepts realised. Architects, like doctors, unite art with science with respect for what is true in the inner nature of things. The urge to create, recreate, integrate, renew, enhance: to *form, design; plan*; all involve deliberate effort with expectation of success; metamorphoses.

VI iii Metaphor

Words, names as nouns and doings as verbs, often communicate **change**. Sentences spoken and written, some verdictive and prescriptive, become poetic when rhythm and rhyme point and dramatise them. Metaphor spoken, written (in prose, verse, poetry) uses comparison, analogy, particularity and personification.

In antiquity, powers personified as gods and goddesses were imputed to determine human functions and intentions with benevolent and malevolent purposes: power to change. **Belief in one all-powerful deity, creator and maker, able and willing to share and delegate creative power, marks a change from fatalism to willing effort. This brings new *hope* of shared purpose with obedience: voluntary, willing liberty to serve.** Individuals realise initiative, opportunity to lead, to accept action with responsibility, felt/thought engaged with instinct but looking further. Presence of deity engages this confidence. The four levels (see Appendix **A**) rightly ordered, simplify and exemplify this humane divinity experienced in engaged faith: in imitation of Christ's personification of *love*: divine and human, for good; of thought **preceding** action arising from need to act. This impetus, impulse, spark, instinctive urge involves *reason, intention, purpose* and *plan, power* to decide and *act*.

Metaphor captures maternal impulse (distinct from paternal) urgently protective of dependent offspring:

> 'In panic, she flew.
> Though not literally true:
> Not a witch on a broomstick nor angel who sings
> But seeking her child, for whose safety she wings.'

Personification of feeling unites doer with deed, poetically:

> 'Sport that wrinkled Care derides,
> And Laughter holding both his sides'.
>
> (Milton, *L'Allegro*)

Metaphor communicates richer, deeper understanding when faith brings knowledge of the supernatural, not as superstition but of Divinity. A fanciful personification, not far from 'deification' among imaginative romantics, needs thoughtful and practical criteria to match intention and realisation. 'Abysmal ignorance' is a metaphor.

A metaphor of vision, not necessarily fanciful, is intensely concentrated, inspired foresight:

> 'To see a World in a grain of sand,
> And a heaven in a Wild Flower,
> Hold infinity in the palm of your hand,
> And eternity in an hour'.
> (William Blake, *Auguries of Innocence*)

Metaphor expresses an idea, by uniting it with a quite different idea, experience, or thing. The contrast arrests attention and liberates through disclosure. We are surprised and caught by incompatibles, impossibilities.

'Go and catch a falling star', says John Donne.

A ship rides the waves. Surfers, wind-surfers, dinghy sailors, know this as did the Vikings, merchant adventurers and Icelandic writers of sagas. Gliders and hand-gliders ride in up-currents of air: thermals. 'The balloon has gone up' means battle joined.

Metaphor surprises with contrasts. Unrealised feeling is released in listener or reader when expressed; emotional pain is relieved and mental bewilderment clarified. Reflective phrases rich with metaphor integrate feeling with thought in ways which assist digesting the indigestible.

Kathleen Raine's *Envoi* concludes:

> 'In rose with petals soft as air
> I bind for you the tides and fire-
> The death that lives within the flower
> oh gladly, love, for you I bear!'

Hail, rather than farewell, in Robert Herrick's *Corinna's Going a-Maying*:

> 'Get up, get up for shame! the blooming morn
> Upon her wings presents the god unshorn.
> See how Aurora throws her fair
> Fresh-quilted colours through the air:
> Get up, sweet slug-a-bed, and see
> The dew-bespangled herb and tree.'

(Dylan Thomas, in *Fern Hill*)

> 'And the sun grew round that very day.
> So it must have been after the birth of the simple light
> In the first, spinning place, the spellbound horses walking warm
> Out of the whinnying green stable
> On to the fields of praise.'

There speaks a modern man: the stable before the horse in metaphor of creation, power spontaneous, disordered metaphor.

T. S. Eliot reclaimed ancestral connections in time and place. *The Four Quartets* are rich with metaphor of living, sailing, learning, building, healing. Andrew Eliot, baptised at East Coker, Somerset, 1627, last mentioned there, 1668, joined First Church of Beverley, Massachusetts, 1670 and received liberty to cut two loads of timber on the town's common to be used to build a ketch. His son, Andrew drowned off Cape Cables, 1688, c.f. third of Four Quartets, *The Dry Salvages*. The New England Eliots became, continue, a remarkable family across the USA from New England.

Thomas Browne in *Religio Medici* proposed the metaphor: 'For the world, I count not an Inn but an Hospital; a place not to live but to die in'.

This 'absolute' paternal care personifies and embodies, concern for loss, ruin, recovery, redemption, restoration. (T.S. Eliot, *CPP*, page 181.)

Mixed metaphors produce insight, occasionally dramatic and comic. 'He left no stone unturned until he reached the top of the tree.'

Shakespeare conveyed Hamlet's bewilderment with mixed metaphors:

> 'Whether 'tis nobler in the mind to suffer
> The slings and arrows of outrageous fortune,
> Or to take up arms against a sea of troubles.'
> (Shakespeare, *Hamlet*, III. 2)

VI iv Metaphysical

This word, used by Aristotle, can cause nervous reaction, uncertainty, denial. Some philosophers have spoken and written of 'metaphysical fallacies'; others, Aristotle himself, considered 'Poetics'. English poets with transforming genius with words offer metaphysical delight. Some 'scientists' may not find *time, taste, will* to consider metaphysics as more than fanciful irrelevance. Literacy, limited to literal interpretation of material practicalities: physical evidence, inhibits appreciation of metaphysics. Exaggerated literal interpretation becomes 'fundamentalist'.

Metaphysics require willingness to entertain a change in normal familiar practicalities sensed in commonsense-based climate of the mind; to realise movement of sure, definite, practical foundations regarded as immovable. Nervousness often accompanies uncertainty; we fear change as leading to instability. Ideas and thoughts considered over-subtle, not altogether reasonable or unconfined by reasoning, are sometimes referred to as 'metaphysics' to imply occult rather than cultivated, 'cultured' fantasy rather than reasonable, philosophical.

There are difficulties, dangers, in attempting to define, to pin down, metaphysical. 'Physical' usually means a natural, bodily form examined by physicians. The multiplication of physical things in direct sense experience soon become innumerable. Need for definition and limits leads to recognising and examining for emotional, theoretical and moral significance. (The levels again.) 'Meta-', change, joins 'physical' to make one word, metaphysical, to identify distinct, different, often opposite conditions. Is this an impossibly unsatisfactory paradox? Does it comprehend, contain, two mutually exclusive conditions, contradictory but true?

Thinking 'scientifically' and/or 'rationally' often appears to mean thinking without metaphysics, with disregard for metaphysical consciousness. Metaphor is accepted because it helps to understand by verbal contrast and illustration. 'Simile' is similarity by comparison but without changing one thing into another (though that is manageable as metamorphosis when raw cake mixture cooked becomes a cake and food eaten and digested fuels all sorts of energy for things initiated by impulse, need, desire, interest and will). Food for thought, digested, enables extraordinary human 'being and becoming'.

What, then, is the opposite of physical? Is it abstract? Does that mean abstracted, theoretical, theorised? Is it simply non-physical, un-physical, un-real? Non-existent?

Immaterial? Some, unhesitatingly, say 'spiritual'. Others deny any such concept; separable, distinct, other than experienced as living body. 'Spiritual body' seems nonsensical.

First literacy achieves but stops at literal interpretation; refusal to enlarge; to withstand signs, symbols, metaphors, towards metaphysics. 'Property' is remarkably metaphysical. Physical material: of belongings, things personal and social, of and for people, of places to live, *produce* to *produce* has use, meaning, significance. Across the Atlantic, houses, apartments and land are 'real estate', claimed, possessed and lawfully held. But property is also in and **of** *mind*, in thoughts and ideas defined, organised, spoken, written, recorded. Hence, copyright and 'intellectual property', hugely expanding through communication by information technology. 'Moral properties' concern quality and value rather than cost and price are spoken of. These move through all levels of experience. Properties refer to physical features – of things, shapes, places; to people: of personality, temper and character, to beauty and ugliness, vice and virtue. When aspects of 'property' combine, its meaning extends to the whole, actual and potential: something far greater than that of separated parts. Proper and properly, propriety as *order* and *form*, manners and allocations, enjoyment and duty, these also merge together. The state of things, ideas, people are not static but status described at a time may change: reaching for integration.

Light is spectacularly metaphysical. Scientists experience *light* in *time* and *space*, *space* and *distance, fire*, sun, on earth. Physics includes study of *heat, light* and *sound. Light* is itself invisible but enables us to see. We can of course see and describe sources of light: the sun (dangerous to look at directly), moon and stars, candles, lamps, torches and electric light bulbs, sunrays and laser beams. Physicists discuss the properties of light and offer explanations as they master some of its mysteries. Inward *light*, enables *mind* to learn, know and understand; judgment enables us to evaluate towards illuminating right purpose: *will* to *act*. In **light**, properties become illuminated for comprehension. The **spirit of the thing**, disclosed, is realised. What we think of as the soul, the psyche, is where metaphysics warm and develop consciousness. The fourth level emerges as the first.

Light discloses, promotes growth, enlightens response in *mind* to question, to **work** out, puzzle from sight to insight, clarified for decision and effective action, 'seeing it through'.

Light-giving life is at one with life-giving light. (See Thomas Traherne, *News*.) Darkness does not overcome light but light may fade and fail.

Shakespeare used personification and symbol to project interaction of energy as power. Puck would 'put a girdle round the earth in thirty minutes'. (*A Midsummer Night's Dream*, II. I, line 175.) Ariel, spirit of the air, was obedient to Caliban, until Prospero released him from subservient bondage. Then he became able to sing ecstatically of superhuman freedom (*The Tempest*, V. I, line 88.) Both personify metaphysical immediacy. Telepathy, from *mind* to *mind* without use of **senses**, was first used in 1882. Thinking intensely of someone often produces a telephone call from them.

Heat, light and sound, distinct, interact together, change into each other. One source of electric current will power a heater, cooker, light bulb and re-produce sound by radio, TV or record player. The energy itself is hidden from sight, physical perception, but its effects are sensational. Faults can cause *shock, fire,* failure of energy supply. 'Physic' as medicine; physician as healer; intend to mend pain of loss of physical energy in human beings. Sense and feeling, re-action and action, taste and judgment, desire and need, passion and control require unifying cohesion; integration. Metaphysical experience is primary in human life, even if not identified or realised as such. Realisation and renewal may follow. Follow, not a **donoun**, is definite step.

Beyond sense the norms, appearances, dimensions of origin, creation (natural and supernatural) are accessible in inward vision by metaphysical light. **Let them be called 'eyes of faith'.** Consciousness of unseen, mysterious presence in souls pervades metaphysical poetry to become mystical as well as metaphysical. The Greek word 'hymn' was for a song in praise of divinities or heroes. Many Hebrew psalms are songs, poems, of praise (*Psalms* 19. 146); expressions of metaphysical unity (*Psalms* 24. 100), yearning for self knowledge (*Psalms* 139), for relief from guilt and shame, pleading for mercy and forgiveness (*Psalms* 130, 143). In Christian culture, transformation of personality: longed for and experienced through faith, is a central characteristic of personal hope, elusive but longed for above anything. Life realised and recorded by *love* and by *love* of life: confronting evil, suffering, unjust accusation, mockery, torment, even agonising death, transforms fragile mortals filled with virtue to become good. The word 'saint' is applicable.

Dante refined his poetic method to describe human experience through exact sense equivalent: darkness of utter despair: hot hell of infernal depths of tormenting destruction contrasted with brilliant, unfailing, *light*. Purged in experience, purgation brings him to everlasting delight. Dante is strengthened in the company of Virgil (reason) and devotion to Beatrice, his beatific vision of personal love; radiant disclosure of **head and heart together as if falling in love is followed by rising in love.** Having survived hell: infernal regions of experience, he finds himself at the foot of Mount Purgatory. Seven stages, terraces, challenge him to take steps, to ascend from terrace to terrace, where each deadly sin is overshadowed by encouraging angels of appropriate virtue who represent cleansing, healing, restoration. First, he must face himself truly. This self-reflection is symbolised in mirror image from three steps, polished to reflect, each a decisive embarkation. His resolution is sustained as on, up; no longer in company with Virgil, he is drawn by vision of divine and human love awaiting fulfilment in Paradise. Heaven, glorious unity they experience together.

Dante's poetic allegory is inexhaustible, perennial, metaphysical and mystical.

In Christian faith, life after death offers vision of human being imitable and yet inimitable: Jesus was, is, lives and continues to exemplify new life personified: divine power to transform. New love in faith and hope: common ground to poets of all ages, past to present, narrative and metaphysical: Chaucer, Langland, Richard Rolle, Richard Crashaw, John Donne and George Herbert, Thomas Traherne, Robert and Elizabeth Browning, Gerard Manley Hopkins, T. S. Eliot, Geoffrey Hill, among them. Identifying inward experience with something practical derives from parable; is powerful in Mystery plays; becomes modified, adapted, into pageant, then theatre, poetic drama, renewed by Ben Jonson, Shakespeare, in the sixteenth to seventeenth centuries and in metaphysical poetry. Metaphor nourishes and is itself nourished by symbols. A symbol, curiously called a *conceit*, is conceived imaginatively as well as observed in nature and applied poetically. Feeling and thought diverge, become aware of loss, desire to rediscover unity and need to be illustrated in sense equivalent: a ring, a rock, a tree, a cross. Love, human and divine, physical and spiritual, envisaged and known, recovers unity, wholeness, 'holiness'. Sometimes, not always, this fusion transforms to make ultimate sense within: new life as ***change***: 'conversion': profound integration of sensibilities.

Poetry may express an accelerating heart beat of metaphysical power: passion-emotion-thought-reality; unity realised in union with another: John Donne in *The Ecstasy*; Robert Herrick in *To Julia*. Human love believed to reflect divinity is fused, infused, into words: discontinuity between them is dissolved. Natural, physical desire filtered and sublimated in poetic description produces words of exquisite intensity. Both men were capable of deep devotion, physical and intellectual sensibility; clergymen in whom flesh, natural, physical appetites, were sometimes more willing than conscience, will and spirit could, should, allow. Their fancies, their hopes, like those of Shakespeare, belong in union of *living heart and head*, **soul** stimulated in soaring imagination while acutely aware of dangers, tempting to depths, deep evil: in life imperilled. They were not puritans. Joy and delight are in their hearts stronger than fear and suppression, rigid rules and dangerous, unacknowledged appetites: inhibitions. *Light* accompanied by *hope* and *love* makes manifest reality in metaphysical wholeness. The obligation to celibacy of the clergy had been the formal rule in England until 1549. For Donne and Herrick this was within living memory.

George Herbert (1593-1633), clergyman, in *The Elixir* glimpses beyond the arts of alchemy to realise philosophy and divinity in fusion:

> 'A man that looks on glass,
> On it may stay his eye;
> Or if he pleaseth, through it pass,
> And then the heaven espy,
> This is the famous stone
> That turneth all to gold;
> For that which God doth touch and own
> Cannot for less be told.'

Herrick, only two years older than Herbert, lived longer and survived the English Civil War:

> 'There is no evil that we do commit,
> But hath th' extraction of some good from it:
> As when we sin; God, the great *Chymist*, thence
> Draws out th' *Elixar* of true penitence.'

But:

> 'When once the Soule has lost her way
> O then, how restless do's she stray!
> And having not her God for light
> How do's she err in endless night!'

Metaphysical allegory continues to inspire explorers. *The Waste Land* is T. S. Eliot's Inferno; *Ash Wednesday* his Purgatory; *The Four Quartets* his Paradiso. There is no end of life, aware but wary of burnt out cases whose candle flickers to extinction in emptied romanticism, sensuality without emotion, nothing, emptiness, mixing metaphors of earth, earthy as hell. Eliot's Clark Lectures, (Cambridge, 1926, published by Faber and Faber, 1993, edited by Ronald Schuchard, as *The Varieties of Metaphysical Poetry*) are classic analysis; introducing the definition by examining the work of poets. Donne, pre-eminent subject in four of the eight lectures, from the Middle Ages, then Crashaw, sixth, to 'Cowley and the Transition' where Eliot identifies the *'dissociation of sensibility'* (thought and feeling; intellect and emotion), indexed in the Schuchard edition.

The Clark lectures set out the reading, critical thinking and writing achieved by Eliot as American student from New England, St Louis and Harvard who came to Europe to discover his, their, cultural roots: philosophical, literary, musical, political and theological of European civilisation. Poetry and criticism, already published, took on momentum when Christian faith, commitment, led to him to explore the implications and consequences of conversion. From *Gerontion* (1919) and *The Waste Land* (1922) to *The Hollow Men* (1925), he embarked on *Ash Wednesday*, completed 1930, *The Idea of a Christian Society* (1940), outcome of association with George Bell (Dean of Canterbury, later Bishop of Chichester, who had commissioned *Murder in the Cathedral*,) and Archbishop William Temple. *The Four Quartets* were composed under the storm clouds of Hitler's Germany. Ideas, words in *Burnt Norton* are used in 'Murder...': from *East Coker* into *The Family Reunion* concern his personal 'erinyes' and homage to Robert Browning. The devastating fires of the London blitz, witnessed by Eliot, an Air Raid warden and Church warden at St Stephen's, Gloucester Road, recur in *Little Gidding*. In 1944, last year of the war, Eliot addressed the Virgil Society: *What is a Classic?* (published by Faber, 1945). *Notes towards the Definition of Culture* (1949) represents, combines and includes, social, political, philosophical and theological criticism, head and heart in union, plus the advantage and power as a publisher.

Since initiating *The Criterion*, Eliot introduced new writers to English reading readers, including Marcel Proust. His written drama *Sweeny Agonistes* (drafted, 1923, published 1926, the year of the Clark lectures) contrasts with verse for *The Rock* (1934) and *Murder in the Cathedral*, (1935), directed by E. Gordon Browne. *The Family Reunion*, drafted 1937, was first performed in 1939. Post-war plays included *The Cocktail Party*, commissioned for the Edinburgh Festival, 1949.

Dichotomy between head and heart, endemic in thoughtful, conscientious persons, with and without knowledge of philosophers; differently expressed by poets; is worked out and expressed by performing artists in dance, drama, music and in tactile creative artistry. Detective work, engineering, architecture, are distinctive art forms. Consciousness of mysteries; mystical awareness associated with faith recur in practice of faith, in prayer and contemplation. Metaphysics, identified by Aristotle, fundamental to Dante, 'philosophical poet', are discussed in the first and second Clark lectures.

Early Christianity grew among and from those who listened, trusted and believed; 'devout' persons, from every nation, Parthians, Medes, Elamites, dwellers in Mesopotamia, Cappadocia, Pontus, Asia , Egypt, parts of Libya; Greeks and Romans, Jews and Gentiles addressed by Peter, witnessed and described by Luke (*Acts* 2) at Pentecost, harvest, fifty days after Passover of Christ's crucifixion and resurrection. Persecution followed. Leaders returned to Jerusalem to consider relations between Gentile and Jewish converts. The Council at Jerusalem (*Acts* 15), prototype of subsequent deliberation: Nicea, Chalcedon, Arles, Whitby, Florence, Canterbury, Lambeth, reflect early, repeatedly reinvigorated, vision of consultation, consent, cradled democracy. Concern for unanimity in faith raises questions of what is just and fair among citizens: renewed idea of citizenship until Augustine, faced with the end of the Roman Empire: law and administration, wrote *City of God*.

The Christian record militant and peaceable, strengthened by war, defended, changed by uncivil Civil War, not of 'good will' nor of 'peace on earth', turned many cultivated minds, heads and hearts away towards increasing fascination with practical discoveries. Natural Philosophy, Science, Galileo, Darwin, challenged Christian theologians to adapt. Dissociation of sensibility, thought and feeling, intellect and emotion, physical from spiritual followed through eighteenth century rationalism, 'enlightenment', nineteenth century revival of faith, twentieth century ideological horrors bequeath deep problems. Peace loving persons conscious of 'the higher dream', hope to bear witness to the faith and love experienced and trusted. The golden thread of *grace*: of ancient virtue, just and fair, temperate, courageous in humility and wisdom, enlivened and empowered by faith, in ***trust, hope*** and ***love***: is maintained, sustained and renewed.

Time is of the essence of opportunity to make patterns of regularity, efficiency and order but motive of **need**: practicalities: become tempered with faith, hope and love empowered by *grace* to face questions which are far more than tastes, preferences and surface 'choices' since they engage essences, substance, questions of value, and new freedom to discern and pursue virtue. In human currency of being and doing, we spend time wastefully, 'getting and spending', and sometimes wish 'we could buy' time. The island of individuality becomes less like a sad and lonely place, (albeit fine and private), when in company of Divinity. Presence, friends, poets, divines whose words express soul searing woes and ecstatic delight; watered by tears of agony and of joy, alive, within and around in universal heart of love, crucified, risen, redeeming. New perspective: realms of gold beyond hearts of darkness, see earth as though from heaven, beyond both *time* and *space*. Re-entry, back to earth, offers opportunity to explore and realise timeless virtue of what is just, just in time, moderate, brave and wise. (This mixing of metaphors of life and death inspires faith 'fast forward' towards eternity.) Metaphysicians who become mystics, realise need for **grace** in the present, here and now, to **save** and be saved in union with the wisdom and foresight of all ages.

VII

Judging

A young child cries: 'It isn't fair!'

Each word is prompted by one or more aspect of judging. Together, they make a *sentence*:

'**A**' is a preposition, indefinite, referring to an unnamed child who is conscious of something unfair.

'**Young**', an adjective about a 'child' (noun), who 'cries' (verb).

'**It**' does not identify what is unfair. The 'cry' may exclaim, accuse, appeal for recognition, sympathy, redress.

'**Isn't**' is present, active, negative.

'**Fair**' is a quality in virtue of being just, fair, an adjective of doing through being; being shown in doing. The cry accentuates, for it derives from and appeals to expectation of fairness. The child is sure that this something is unfair. A mistake? An accident? Anything you, I, any one, reacts to as unfair: minor provocation, maximum injustice, something to *cry* out about. Direct senses inform common sense (first level of judging), prompt feeling (second level), thought (third level) and evaluation expressed in the *cry* of *protest*.

Consciousness of fair or unfair is elemental. To claim and invoke fair play is regarded as norm of *order*. Over-reaction occurs in games and elsewhere. Taking unfair advantage is tempting when seen as 'getting your own back'. Consciousness of fair and unfair promote critical felt-thought; desire and need for evaluating and judging. Does the child cry for a good reason, rightly or wrongly, justifiably or not? Tension occurs in knowing right/wrong, good/evil, true/false. These opposites are essence and substance of the matter, of cry heard or unheard. **Donouns** are particularly frequent, useful, in games and in law: *start, call, order, catch, drop, run, race, pitch, stump, jump, stop, fault, let, point, love, game, set, match*; and many more.

Judge personifies function, capability, and responsibility of judging. *Judge*, a person, is a noun. What a *judge* does is performative, working to evaluate and conclude. The sentence about a child's *cry* indicates causing and judging, two participles. These connect the child's cry with what provoked it; something that 'isn't fair'. Possibly a trivial matter, perhaps imagined, perhaps an offence indicating favouritism and causing jealousy; perhaps unfair **blame** with danger of punishment, anxiety, *fear*. A child, a person of any age, may feel cheated, deceived, deprived, denied expectation of what is fair. Recognising fair and unfair (rightly or wrongly, truly or falsely) is primal capability of judging. Recognising *accident* or *intention* with evidence of responsibility, with or without ill *will*, malice, are crucial to fair and just judging.

Children have instincts. Discerning fair and unfair is innate human capability, to be cultivated inwardly, outwardly by others, throughout life. Subjective self-interest may mature to become objective. Concern for another person's well being, interests, points up what is essentially fair or not. Children learn to foresee and consider consequences, cause and effect, results, eventualities, possible endings. Stories, nursery rhymes, singing games, proverbs, fairy tales and fables illustrate aspirations with limits and boundaries for happy endings, calamities, tragedies. Verses and songs, particularly memorable, stimulate insight, assimilation and comprehension. Heard, enjoyed, considered, understood, they exemplify experience fancied and imagined. 'Once upon a time...' conventional opening, injects real possibility in experience of something happening, like the tale told with dream of living 'happily ever after'. (See **XIII I** and **II**.)

Playing a ball game encourages ways to enhance it with subtlety and skill; competing by matching, catching. A stick, bat, racquet adds hitting and alters the game of catch. Kicking a ball is another game. Games of catch, with and without bat or racquet, promote recognition of benefit of rules. Does the ball bounce? Is bouncing acceptable? If so, is it to be caught before and/or after the bounce? Do we agree? If so, we have a 'rule'. What about bouncing too high, too wide; throwing too fast? You can see where this has led. Bats, stumps, pitch of agreed length; sticks planted vertically, stumps, (two at first, now three) to bowl at, for the batsman to protect. Skill to hit or miss, field, catch, run and throw are practised, cultivated. Bowlers tease and tempt the batsman to get caught, run out, stumped, clean bowled. The game of cricket evolves. Ball and bat, pitch, field and boundary, wicket and wickets, crease, hitting, running, catching and stumping are among its refinements within the Laws of the game. Umpires, **judging**, are appealed to for decisions accepted as final until, unless technical precision, 'hawkeye' supplements them. The laws define details of play as it has developed. **The game came before the laws.** Size, materials, weight of balls and bats, 'overs', declarations, limited time, up to five days for Tests, 'limited over' matches are agreed. The skill, courage and fair play of individuals influence each other and determine the quality of the game. Any game is spoilt by cheating. Betting on aspects of cricket matches leads to international scandal. Enquiries are appointed. (See *The Little Book of Cricket*, Green Umbrella, 2005, page 60.) Playing in a team engages skill, control, cooperation, commitment and loyalty. Games flourish when manners, customs, limits and rules are respected. A fair contest enjoyed by skilled contestants who play wholeheartedly and well is more enjoyable for all concerned. Soccer risks ruin by over-inflated payments, cult of 'celebrity', performers who push rules, attempt to disguise fouls, rather than 'good sports' who 'play the game'. Pre-World Cup 2006 tension showed this. The skill, efficiency and goodwill of the German hosts were real winners. Wimbledon 2006, showed worrying tendency towards becoming a media event: too much theme park 'blaa' from some 'commentators' for those who remember the quiet, moderate eloquence: 'Oh, I say!' of Dan Maskell.

Awareness of fairness promotes thought about reasons and explanations. Inward consciousness of fair and unfair becomes concept then principle of just and unjust. Source, **innate principles, are not invented: they await recognition**; potential for fair play, civility, fair and free behaviour. Parameters, limits, boundaries make for optimum performance in the utterly serious business of work and pleasure, fun and games, joy in work, vocation and profession, exaltation and profundity. Suffering occurs — physical, emotional, mental and moral, unfair, unbearably hard to bear, usually unpredictable, often inescapable, surmountable in spirit. Tempted by bribes, acceptance causes more than personal shame, disgrace, remorse. No one is immune from danger, temptation, and their evil consequences.

Children from an early age tend to respond happily, carefully, with those who are consistently dependable. Good opinion becomes valued. Challenge comes early to some who test every limit. Serious criticism, warnings, are intended as steps towards self-control. Adult models of fairness include sibling rivalries: fair treatment as the expected norm. Cultivated to nourish capability of judging brings benefit of the virtue of being just; or perils of being unjust. Tempered with forbearance and generosity, justice is a balancing and redeeming feature of human experience from first to last; merciful and constructive rather than punitive. The quality of mercy is gentle, encouraging, forgiving as well as fair.

Childhood consciousness of fair and unfair starts this potentially civilising journey. Estimating and judging in mind engage evidence from different interests and points of view. Factors remembered, studied, worked out, on, in, then out again promote knowledge and understanding. Tracing cause and effect occurs in this process. What is valued provides criteria of conduct, realisation of possible *order*. Different cultures behave and enunciate different values (e.g. monogamy rather than polygamy, legitimate risk rather than ill-informed gamble).

Fair and unfair, like plants and weeds, coexist in human communities, societies, from the souls of individuals strong in spirit for good or ill. To be fair, to see principles and practicalities of fairness promotes wellbeing, personal and social health; good order.

Fair and just can be seen to emerge as natural justice. Balanced *form* and *order* increase perceptive ability of mind and spirit. The more they are cultivated the more is received. Geological evidence shows pre-human patterns of creating and destroying. Present stability, while it lasts, provides temporary stillness capable of change, of becoming unstable. Static and dynamic are evident in nature; in material, vegetable, animal and human form. Principles of cause, effect, balance, demonstrate ideas of balance recognised in natural justice. (See Philippa Foot: *Natural Goodness*, Oxford University Press, 2001.) Communal regard for discernment, wise to principles, seeks and finds methods of intervention for practical benefit, stability, improvement. At first, judging is instinctive, self-protective, momentary, immediate, transient. Is this true in other cultures? Later it is discovered to have social as well as personal consequences, objective, fair to others, beneficial even to all, but miscarriages happen and are shocking. Fanatics, terrorists occur in many cultures and endanger them.

Sun's creative energy and power continues to illuminate outward growth and experience, continuing life cycles; confirm continuing warmth, vitality and growth. First and last, these provide and reveal principle of light and dark, renewal despite decay, death; growth and parables of growth, life looking for and expecting to *find* what is fair and just. 'Perpetual light' (not conducive to necessary rest and peace in life on earth) hopes to dissolve fear and evil beyond emotional, moral and spiritual destruction caused; but not hopelessly beyond redemption.

Idea and expectation of 'a fair share' comes from comparison with others, people and things. Claims, needs, portions, divisions tempered in generosity, are intensified by greed. Success is stimulated and often measured by competition. Expectations, demands for affection, attention, time and talk, hunger for nourishment occur at every age and level. Some temperaments are far more excitable, competitive, aggressive, combative and demanding than others. Frustration leads to envy, criticism and quarrels. Angry words break out into **fight**. Another person attempts to see both sides; to ease the conflict, restore control, achieve peaceful resolution, reconciliation. A peacemaker sensitive to personalities as well as to causes is a diplomat who seeks harmony. Judging looks for motive, responsibility, *blame*. Sympathy and mercy: *will* to be fair, strengthen judging not as weakness but constructively; and with respect. Assertions, claims, litigation driven by demands for rights, less than the fruit of good will, cry for mitigation of something unfair.

Judge is performative (verdictive) and a **donoun**. The judge embodies, personifies, the function of judging. *Referee* and *umpire* see fair play, identify a foul, judge if a rule is broken. A *match* starts and ends with *watch* and *whistle*. Fair and just, vital ingredients in character of judge, umpire, referee, are not **donouns**. *Foul*, an unfair action against another player(s), is a **donoun**.

Fair treatment strengthens confidence and whets appetite for what is fair. Expectation of fair dealing, normal mark of civilised life can be diluted: lost, but unfairness breeds anger, resentment, disaffection, cynicism. Individuals, families, groups offer extremely varied experience, contradictory, paradoxical and confusing. To pre-suppose the value of being fair and just presents an ideal to be practiced as a primary foundation. The story of *Oliver Twist* illustrates extremes of experience. The orphan whose hunger caused him 'to ask for more' faced severe punishment. Oliver escapes from the orphanage, survives hazards, dangers, evil company, is re-discovered, then discovers and receives his true inheritance. Fagin organises a gang of boys to thieve. The Dodger, leader, teaches Oliver to pick pockets and Fagin receives stolen goods. Bill Sykes, cruel bully, supports but terrorises Fagin: fugitive from his own rages, from detection for violence and theft. After he had killed Nancy, who sought to protect Oliver, Sykes is captured and hanged. Dickens pictures innocence and wickedness, honesty and greed, kindness and cruelty, helplessness in the stranglehold of ruthless greed; then remarkable retribution among those encountered by Oliver. From orphanage via undertaker's shop, chimney sweeping and Fagin's den to the joy of welcome and well supplied benevolence of Mr Brownlow, Oliver learns who he is. He is known and knows confident security. His fortune changes.

VII i Just in Time

Tension between fair and unfair, feeling and judging fairly, spontaneity and control, liberty ordered, arise out of potential freedom for good; self-discipline as personal order, obedient to ideal of what is fair. *Time* enables timing, invaluable measure in living, being and doing.

What is the time? Is there time for this or that? Is there, will there be, time for you, for me, how much time have we got? How long will it take?

Asking the time does not ask what time is. We accept it as it is represented to us, and is experienced ourselves. Learning to 'tell the time' unites word and number. Time is experienced in union of light and space, sun and place. Greenwich Mean Time is measured at and from that place. The sun is at its zenith, noon, anywhere. Greenwich Mean Time occurs when sun transits there, taken as 0° degrees. Longitude has become time's tuning fork. An actual line on the path below the old Observatory enables a person to stand with a foot in both hemispheres, eastern and western. This line is drawn on maps and globes intersecting with the equator and its parallels. Lines of latitude and longitude, on scale of the map, provide co-ordinates drawn from these two. Celestial and terrestrial observation followed by calculations provide the co-ordinates. North, South, East and West are directions for judging direction, position in relation to Equator and Poles, with longitude. Time and Space, universal, integrate measure in hours, degrees, minutes and seconds. The lines drawn on maps do not begin as landmarks but connect them precisely; calculated from celestial sources, heaven to earth, 'dead reckoning' expected to be true. This interaction demonstrates metaphysical unity: integrated position.

Work is effort: *will*, energy and skill for a livelihood measurable in time. Employers, contractors, hire workers, 'buy' time, 'overtime', when work takes longer than agreed and planned.

Time is said to fly when we are taken up; thoroughly interested in present activity and enjoying ourselves in doing it. Time, then, is precious. In times of anxiety, confusion, fear, dread, waiting, grieving; time hangs heavily. Difficult times pass, since time passes; misery and joy, failures and successes pass into the past. (*Time*, and *pass*, **donouns**, share two natures with participles, timing and passing.) Occasional climactic moments when 'time stands still' are imperishable in mind and memory, head and heart, infinitely significant.

Much or nothing much may depend, or seem to depend, on being in time. To be just in time involves planning, punctuality, judging well in any sense and level, presupposing control within time. Time, our inescapable context, frees us if managed well. Time to tune into timeless energy and power, given and known in time and place, to 'recharge batteries', are holydays. Holidays, at first, emphasise relaxation, enjoyment, 'doing what you like'. Restoration, rest through change, is needed and hoped for: serious renewal at every level.

Routines provide pattern and regularity, ordered time, but initiative extends opportunity and rejuvenates plans, personal and public.

In public life, a prime minister is, was, judging and being judged, fairly and unfairly, in the time of being in power. Resort to country-house parties; clubs; a 'kitchen cabinet', gathers 'cronies'. All were beginners when first appointed and feel the urge to make changes, seen as improvements. One prompted a limerick:

> 'There was a P.M. who said "Damn
> I suddenly find that I am
> Just a creature that moves
> In predestined grooves:
> I'm not even a bus; I'm a tram."'

Self-confidence, characteristic for decision, can exaggerate, invent, inflate, disguise. 'Time will tell', as it tells, has been told, by witnesses, historians, on predecessors. 'Time will be the judge' but a voice needs words. Terms of reference for judging experienced in action are sifted from diaries and letters, memoirs, biography, autobiography to become fair and unfair verdicts; history just and unjust in time, authorised or not, revised in later studies. Actions may be ill-judged, misjudged, 'bowing to the inevitable', leading to fight and win, performed with or without principle and conscience.

Co-ordinates of time and place, interdependent and measurable, are context of bodily life on earth, here and now, past and future. Children discover memory and absorb sense of time scarcely realising processes, but consciousness of time develops to includes estimating and measuring it. To watch, use a watch; to keep, take and spend time, make opportunity for co-ordination. Known factors accumulate from experiences. Judging is enriched, overburdened sometimes, but focussed by immediacy. Sudden, unexpected change calls for instantaneous response, reaction to danger. Just in time or just too late may mean life or death. Responsibility includes initiative. Initiative involves responsibility. Both activate judging.

'Just in time' indicates constraint of time passing. Time and tide do not wait. Tides rising and falling move the waters of seas and oceans; refresh shores in rhythmic obedience to given principles of gravity and cosmic cycles, predictable. Human activities take place in time but are less predictable. Judging, short and long term, looks for what is fair in context, unique or repetitive, continuous, temporary or permanent, temporal and eternal. Capable of judging, human beings realise concepts of responsibility: need of all virtue, just in time.

VII ii Estimating, Inestimable

Estimates are made from anticipated ingredients and factors; time, place, materials, labour. They may be questioned, revised, withdrawn, accepted, rejected. Parties concerned want a fair deal for good work. Costs involve prices but purposes concern value. Inestimable value attached to a project does not immunise it from unforeseen or unforeseeable problems. Successes and failures, something done or left undone, possibly impossible, assists judging practical matters. Estimates for future possibilities are inseparable from the qualities of persons who may or may not 'measure up'. Materials, circumstances of time, place, wind and weather, favourable, fortunate, unfortunate, calamitous, call for continual appraisal until completion. Inward thinking and planning accompany outward doing, to direct, control and sustain effort to work.

Devices such as inspection and insurance protect vulnerability to accidents and frailty of guarantees. Estimating for repair, replacement, renewal, insurance cover claims against 'all risks'. This is expected to guarantee guarantor or claimant but, again, may miscarry. Practicalities and things are more measurable, tangible, than personalities responsible for insuring or underwriting them. Recommendations help in estimating and judging who to trust but are not accident-proof, fool-proof or cheat-proof. Intelligence and achievement, tested, are estimated by continuous assessment and by set examinations. Estimating qualities of character depends on personal recommendations, referees, testimonials to achievement, but use of words, composition, essays, communicate attitudes, need values, governing principles.

VII iii Valuing, Invaluable

Cost and price apply to practicalities bought and sold: changes and exchanges. Value includes the thing itself, perhaps an essential need. The principle, the spirit of the thing, is in what it is for: its function, meaning and significance, origin and purpose, for good or ill.

Valuing derives from experiencing value. Extreme disparity of fortune does not dissolve this personal capability. Sentiment may accompany need. Desire without sentiment challenges and is challenged by reason, competition, ultimate object and objectivity.

Valuing arises out of necessities for survival; indispensable practicalities: fresh water, food and shelter. Function and purpose are obvious. Discussion of judging began with being fair and just: qualities which emerge in experience, principles of behaviour, valued characteristics of character discerned among human beings, recognised, not invented; inimitable but imitated: cultivated rather than bought or sold.

Interdependence between people and things, people with each other, suggests relative value. Things measurable for quantity, estimable for quality, availability, tastes, range from general to particular, universal to personal. Parents transmit life instinctively, intended or unintended, and struggle, willingly or not, to provide for offspring to survive. Receiving and giving grows in consciousness of effort, responsibility and **will**. Value emerges in every level of experience and ascends with appreciation of what is fair and just, unfair and unjust. Parent and child, parents and children, affect each other and others for better and worse.

Control is necessary for civilised life. Fair and just foundation, virtues, require hope for will to control what threatens them. Practical projects emerge from advantages foreseen. Ideas, plans, estimates move concepts envisaged to be made real. The Channel Tunnel far exceeded original estimates of costs but the idea of it survived through confidence in its eventual value. Builders of cathedrals: Chartres, Canterbury, could look to the master-builder to estimate quantities and qualities of wood and stone, metal, glass, decorations. They built to express values believed invaluable among those who shared and found strength in their faith, their vision achieved, timeless in time. Artists, like monks, have profound, passionate, priorities to strive for, follow and express in their works. Power of patronage converges when qualities and resources determine and express vision. Military and political dominance enabled a

Chinese emperor to order the Great Wall, the terracotta army, memorials of dynamic ruthless effort of a determined ruler to protect, defend and guarantee memory.

An estimated price for insurance; a 'reserve' price at auction, relate to anticipated demand, difficult to predict. Unique work is not replaceable. Enrichment experienced is not measurable in that way but competition to acquire is measured, inflates, deflates. Ingredients of feeling, thought, inspiration and insight manifested in a work of art await response and appreciation; entered into and valued, beyond price, but artists need to survive and live. They need friends and patrons to support their work: appreciative listeners, readers, customers.

Value after valuing or valuation, estimate after estimating, require expertise. A person qualified to judge personifies that function. *Judge* is a personal **donoun**. To *judge* the *judge* is also to *judge* ourselves. Cost, sometimes used as a verb to equate estimate before and charge after, misleads since 'costing' is estimating until the final cost is known or paid for. 'To cost the cost' doesn't sound quite right. 'To count the cost' is familiar. *Count*, with *measure* and *number*, is a **donoun**. Genuine friends, benefactors, are generous, without counting. *Present* is a **donoun**, but gift is not. You *present* your *present*, make a presentation, but give a gift, bequeath a bequest, inherit an inheritance. The widow's 'mite', given out of her own need, values this generosity more than surplus 'largesse'.

VII iv Recognising: Taste? Choice? True?

Face, eyes, voice, fingerprints and signature are unique. Every person is identifiable. Even identical twins have distinguishing features, characteristics, known to those who know them very well. The Rogues Gallery at Scotland Yard assists identification of 'wanted' persons. The National Portrait Gallery includes likenesses of personalities, famous in their time and of continuing interest; a visual record of outstanding presences. Portrait photography, an art form, includes discernment portrayed in different technique and representation. Epstein's sculpted head of T. S. Eliot, photographed, engages two sorts of talent, techniques and skills, high quality reproduction: not imagined image.

Procedures in the mind, vision and skill of one who draws, paints, sculpts, photographs to make a portrait are unseen, inward, but revealed in the work. The artist may be unable to describe them in words. A photographer has equipment;

procedures to follow; technology plus personal technique more or less skilful, subtle. Capability of recognition is instantaneous when memory receives an imprint, caught, snapped through its lens, eyes. Camera pictures are filtered on sensitive film, like memory. Dark and *light* reverse: 'negative' to be developed: dark light and light dark. Printing restores to make a photograph. Reversed process is different from negative of denial. Seen in a looking glass, a mirror image reverses without need for technicalities of developing and printing. A second mirror restores to what others see. We see ourselves in a looking glass not as we are seen through other's eyes or in another mind and memory. Faces, normally symmetrical, have central singularity of head, nose, mouth, lips and chin; pairs of eyes and eyebrows, ears, nostrils, teeth lateral and vertical; infinitely variable combinations. Face, portrait, photograph offer interpretation.

Names identify things, people, feelings, functions, places, concepts, ideas, anything known of, named, known by name. Vocabulary develops in a 'fast breeder reactor'. Exploration adds resources and knowledge. Encyclopaedias and dictionaries need to be revised, supplemented. Hardware and software: Internet websites, 'search engines' supply information for those who discover how to seek it.

A proper *name* personifies identity and identifies a person. Premature identification may be mistaken; hypothesised, imagined, not yet surely known. A mysterious stranger captures interest. The Unknown, the Scarlet Pimpernel, 007: John Le Carré's spy sagas had compelling verisimilitude in their place and time. Burgess, Maclean, Philby, Blount were spies. Detection, intelligent guesswork looks for clues, information, knowledge. Intellect enables analysis, memory with hindsight looks with foresight, preceding and proceeding with reasonable expectation. Naming a baby concerns parents, grandparents, brothers and sisters, relations and friends. Why this name rather than that? The name identifies the person living with *need* and capability to do, to be doing, a life alive in *time*.

What name can be given to the original source energy, power and will of creation, unknown yet known of; realised 'prime mover' of created, creative order? Augustine of Hippo thought that 'that than which nothing higher can be thought' is expressed in the name of God. The Mogul Emperor, Akbar, searched for every known name of God: all the names by which God was then known, to be carved on his tomb. There are ninety-nine. It is near Agra. Augustine experienced and recognised One; One as three, Three in One: in being, knowing, willing; 'for I am, I know and I will'. (*Confessions*, Oxford University Press, 1991, page 279.) Augustine recognised men and himself like his maker, Creator, Father, Son, Spirit. Something realised to be beyond estimation, evaluation and judging is mysterious; surmised, guessed at, conjectured, perhaps affirmed. Approaching what is beyond horizons of knowledge and experience, explorers are gripped by expectation of imminent discovery. A missing link, an unsolved murder, an unidentified masterpiece: ultimate questions of life and death, meaning and significance. Whose was this body on the sea shore? Who was he, she? A mystery until identified. Doubt, disbelief, belief need verification.

Cognition precedes re-cognition. An 'incognito' is disguised. In *Twelfth Night*, Viola, twin to Sebastian, disguises herself as a boy, becomes page to the Duke and loves him but his heart is engaged elsewhere. The final scene brings revelations, recognition, self-disclosures and joy. Imagination, fantasy, fanciful and fancying are embroidered into dramatic revelations; faces and feelings voiced to reveal true identity.

VII v Conscience, Law

Con, to learn and know, prefixes science. Scientific method proceeds by observation, evidence and reason, experiment and test to answer questions asked. Mind distils essences and examines ingredients of a problem to discover solutions. Conscience identifies criteria for right action. Faculties of *control* are needed for conscientious willing and doing; forward in hope and retrospective in constructive hindsight. Recognising is not the same as concluding, but conscientious judging influences choice and action. Nor is judging the same as deciding although intricately connected when decisions are conscientious. (See **XI.**)

Three phases occur in doing: before, (considering in advance); during; and after (looking over what was done). From daily practicalities like food and clothes to complex personal and general questions, conscience reminds of responsibilities.

Since prejudice is pre-judgment, judging challenges and is challenged by prejudice. Pain and suffering, emotional and mental anguish, guilt and shame, crave mercy: relief. Conscience recognises causes; factors within infections, difficulties, problems.

Just, courageous, temperate, wise: the classic virtues offer criteria of value. For public purposes, circumstances, lead to customs, conventions and beliefs. Some become reinforced, enforced, when formulated into law. Diversity, dissent, deprivation lead to claims for fair treatment, redress of grievances. Demonstrations, marches, revolts in any, every century, *demand* improvement, *change*. Stability is generally preferred, desirable, norm. Respect for representation, talk, 'parlement' consent in parliament, avoids violent agitation, revolt; if change is accepted.

Actions brought to court: accusation, *charge* or *claim* are heard, with evidence, for judging. Quality of evidence is supported through procedures; taken on oath, a jury of ordinary people who hear: agree or fail to agree verdict; court officials and police to keep 'order in court'. The accused hears and must respond to accusation and plead guilty or not. Skilled defence against charge intends to enable the presiding judge to hear, acquit or sentence fairly. It is a scrupulous, generous and costly procedure, for the sake of individual and community. False evidence, lies and 'miscarriages of justice' nevertheless occur. Absence of conscience and human perfection, failure, necessitate procedures. Appeal may take years and years.

VII vi Resolving, Deciding

Deliberation leads to decision. Resolution minimises ambiguity, misunderstanding, further dispute with conscience, oneself, others and community.

In Parliament, the question becomes 'the motion before the House'; proposed, opposed, debated, amended, voted if not withdrawn. A motion carried becomes a Resolution; a Bill proposes legislation, and proceeds stage by stage to become an **Act**. A statute enacted may have far reaching consequences, personal, local, national and international, in policy and in law, but bad law makes more problems than it solves. Governments, past and present, intend new law to deter bad behaviour, but some legislate excessively.

Conventions, respected and kept, safeguard personal freedom more strongly than law. The jury of neighbours originally represented local expectation of peace for the common good: common law prior to proclamation, writ, legislation. Arrest and 'summary jurisdiction' tempt those who exercise them to abuse their authority unfairly. Immunity from arrest without charge became, is still, protected by Habeas Corpus writs and Acts. Belief in and desire for genuine liberty leads people to accept officers of the law, '**police**', to protect peace peacefully but empowered to *arrest, charge* and *summons* to court when disturbed or endangered. Individuals expect to be regarded as innocent until evidence sustains guilt. Monarchs no longer proclaim new law but delegate that function to Lords Commissioners who acknowledge ACTS.

Alfred the Great's governing principle was local justice, locally interpreted, locally enforced. Oliver Cromwell enacted adultery as illegal: not possible to enforce. Misty areas between offence, crime, wickedness and sin are not easy to differentiate. Freedom of speech is restrained by manners, conventions, and protected by laws of libel and slander. Legislators tempted to make bad law for good reasons abuse their power. Prohibition in the USA was repealed by amending the Constitution, but the powerful tradition among early settlers, puritans, continues in some localities and groups. Alcoholism, drug addiction, cause suffering.

When does personal behaviour in all its range and variety become a matter of public concern? Individuals resent interference but often need and appreciate sympathy and support. 'Mind your own business' applies in many contexts. Financial irregularities cause problems. Honest, voluntary, non-profit making public service encounters tension with need for solvency and appetite for prosperity. 'Sleaze' was coined for sweeteners, inducements to advance desired objects by discreet political 'bribery'. Intimate behaviour sometimes becomes subject of salacious gossip much publicised when difficulty, failure, infidelity, becomes scandalous. Normal conception by intercourse and fertilisation: is 'a fact of life'. Children listen, observe, learn from parents, others, books, teachers, and/or experimental experience. There are dangers. A girl, or boy, may be violated, raped, persistently abused. Prostitutes are paid for what is treated as 'commerce'. Contraception, increasingly simple and available, is promoted for health and profit. Many couples plan their families. Termination of pregnancy, 'legalised' by abortion, is nevertheless a matter of personal and public concern. It concerns value of life itself. Circumstances and situations vary very much. To lose an expected infant involves a woman in deep physical and emotional distress. When abortion was unlawful, problems concerned exceptions; health and survival; but statistics were undependable. Medical opinion, public and political perception have moved towards personal decision. Since the law was changed, abortion is 'on demand'. Resolving and deciding is up to the expectant mother; some regard it as an extension of contraception. Nevertheless abortion destroys a life conceived. This very personal responsibility seems private but includes public concerns: medical, educational, moral, ethical and welfare considerations.

A society where ingredients of stability, constancy, dynamic enterprise co-exist requires consensus, balance; risk of danger with control, prevention and cure, inspires others to do more, better, beyond expectation. Capability and determination are infectious but excess is repulsive, destructive. Achievements offer precedents, foundations, models to encourage and give confidence for greater effort, further achievement. Cautionary tales referred to, supply examples of failure. A prejudiced judge, corrupt policeman, dishonest trader, like rotten apples, spread rot. They occur on well established trees. Each tree needs inspection, disease diagnosed, pruned to encourage fruitfulness, to watch and spray against pests and blight.

VII vii Judging, Willing

Different fields of study have distinct vocabularies. Words used in a medical consulting room or operating theatre are firm, clear, other than those of commanders-in-chief, sergeant-major or ship's captain. Police on duty, on *beat*, charging, arresting, giving evidence in *court*, must use words precisely.

Personal domains preoccupy with subjective concerns until mind opens to enquire and explore, willing to learn from other, different experiences: life long education. Much of life, perhaps most, is lived in relation to other people in common activities, appointments and disappointments, prosperity and adversity, joy and sorrow. Aristotle thought that a solitary life was for beasts or saints. Slavery and servitude, accepted norms in antiquity, are known today. Disguised in many forms, subservience is compelled, denies willing will; suppresses and oppresses independent initiative; fails to liberate, to seek and achieve consent.

Individuals need resources to resist systematic humiliation, insult, degradation intended by inflicting physical, emotional, mental and moral torment. Extreme suffering can be survived; Primo Levi's account of his life in Auschwitz is a rare example of this capability. Dietrich Bonhoeffers's *Letters and Papers from Prison* express integrity sustained, continuity in memory, enduring faith and hope of resurrection. Nelson Mandela, militant leader, fighter for freedom from apartheid under white Nationalists, emerged from many years in prison with personal authority to negotiate, preside and rule with consent, deeply respected, beloved, dedicated to reconciliation.

Head and heart move mind for judging and willing, in practice, theory and principle, conscious of power to create and destroy life and things: to build and to civilise: or to confuse, corrupt, brutalise and ruin. *Will* is the *key*: to prison and to liberty: enslavement or freedom. Enduring conflict, inward and outward, personal, social, political, creative and destructive tension is experienced in these paradoxical opposites.

VIII

Willing

Linking Willing with Judging — Will the Key

'Will you, won't you, will you, won't you, will you join the dance?'
(Lewis Carroll, *Alice in Wonderland*, chapter 10)

You will. You will not. You — or I — could, may, may not, ought or oughtn't, might; or might not be willing to initiate, cooperate, consent, resist, refuse. Willing and unwilling are known in experience. Discussion with ourselves, with others, clarifies intention in mind to resolve and decide. Action, words, deeds may follow. Some 'keep their own counsel' until ready to speak, make a *move*, to *act*.

'Where there's a will there's a way' indicates willing as determination: purposive and resourceful. Uncertainty breeds hesitation, postponement. Reluctance suggests avoidance; avoidance and evasion eventuates as refusal by default. The schoolboy, 'creeping like snail, unwillingly to school', does get there. Staying away without leave is truancy. Unexpected distraction, a diversion on the way prevents arrival. Once done undetected, it seems so easy and is done again, probably habitually. A child who inhabits vacuums of indifference, imagined or real, at home or school, does not feel obliged to consult. Absence is a negative that seems positive, preferable independence. Willing participation is weakened, perhaps permanently, until a change of heart and attitude restores participation.

Willing co-operation co-ordinates common purpose into action. A majority may carry others along. Are you willing? Sometimes yes, sometimes no. Shall we? Shall I? In that moment, being and becoming willing is conscious liberty. Assessing, deliberating, evaluating and judging temper this freedom with responsibility. Without them, instinct and fear, desire and anger determine reactions and actions. One instinct challenges another; fear overcomes hunger; hunger overrides fear. Urge to survive motivates. Willing, beyond natural instinct towards order and virtue desired, is co-operative. Willing to search for better rather than worse, opportunity, is negotiation not negation, but 'no option, no alternative' is no choice. Waiting requires patience and control. Indifference is emptiness.

Instincts, repeatedly, supplement and are supplemented by intuition; sensibilities, feelings and thought in heads and hearts. Change of mind is not dictated by instinct but reasoned thinking and conscientious judging. Emotion may overwhelm rational analysis. *Mind* is focused by motive: *cause*: for, of, by, in which *will* becomes willing and priorities re-arrange towards fresh *purpose*; a new course. **Plan** may mean *will* as intention, judging and deciding; willing to *act*. Success justifies the effort of making up *mind*, overcoming reluctance, willing. **Donouns** expose this capability: integration of *mind* and *act*, being and doing, soul and body hinged together: fused, integrated.

Donouns *fuse* being, doing, *head* and heart together, e.g. *will* to *work*.

Willing is complicated by *conflict* between *desire, need, hope*, and *fear*. Familiar outward-inward-outward sequences intensify possibilities and alternatives. Judging helps to sift illusion from reality. Co-operation in communal and personal activities may *help* to overcome reluctance to subjugate self-interest for common good. Conflict involves paradox, opposite ideas, interests, purposes, motives.

The further an explorer searches, reaches, the more elusive and mysterious sources and resources become. A word processor is a collection of astonishing mechanisms capable of linking *mind* with memory. Hardware houses software that reproduces functions: writing, spelling, calculating, arranging, presenting, editing according to more and more ingenious programs. The genii, personification to this user, has no initiative, no imagination, no independence but projects solutions for user purposes. *Will* and *work* of the designer/engineer envisage needs for benefit of users. Many users begin by playing games. Judging contributes to deciding; willingness is ready to resolve and do. Instinct, desire, ideas, aspiration, intention move heart to respond and mind to consider action and to formulate plans. These survive as ideas if not realised in action and contribute to other projects, like a folder in the processor, ready to be called up. The genii, without initiate, accepts and enables *work* with *word*(s).

Metals melt under intense heat. Smelting refines metal from ore; steel from iron ore. Copper and tin smelted together *fuse* to become bronze. Alchemists longed to change base metal into gold. At Dresden and Meissen, making porcelain of high quality, beauty, strength was regarded as alchemy. English makers adopted practice from China. *Fuse* is associated with *conduct* of electricity, danger points connecting generator to user, wired for heat, light or sound. A *fuse*, then, is a safety device. 'Fuses', nouns, are set in a fuse box. As a verb, *fuse* includes blowing socket, plug, system; power lost. Fuses were frequent before plugs were individually fused. A hot-tempered person is said to have a short fuse. Confuse, infuse, defuse, refuse are significant in thought, in word processing, in emotional practicalities, in metaphor, metaphysics and alchemy. Refuse is decisive, conclusive, unwilling, performative. (See Appendix **B**.) Mending a fuse restores conduction; *current* of electric energy.

Conscious, known factors, personal and impersonal, can be appraised in mind. We know only a little, very little indeed, and are not custodians of others' willingness unless volunteered, obligated, dependent, enslaved. Personal escape from prejudice transcends limited self-interest; a high hope of human capability to be fair and just. *Mind* fed by intelligence needs *light* of what is good and true: cultivated *inteletto d'amore*, Dante's 'intellect of love'; head and heart fused. (See **X** and **XIII**.) Willing to serve these principles relieves a divided self beyond subjective limits towards vision of ultimate things: seeking and finding *light*, illumination, enlightenment. For what purpose; for whose sake do we seek perspective? Evaluation operates from what **is**: towards what might become in the widest, deepest, highest realisation, **beneficial**. Belief and reason, necessary for least and best, lead to further ultimate questions to be explored.

Willing search for what is true may sometimes opens unexpected, awkward, unprofitable and disturbing discoveries which distract motives for search. Eventual goal of this, of any journey, may *change*. To divine is to look further than obvious sources, even beyond known concepts and limits. To divine is not to invent since what is not there cannot be divined. Who and what is this it? Presence realised operates to and from; in different ways, directions, revealed and explored, explored and revealed, divined and disclosed. Willing to 'divine' and receive such disclosure brings responsibility; willing to become other than what one was; to renew and find our being in encountering and realising *will* beyond our own. This dimension of willing changes perspectives.

'Change of mind' dictated by instinct is a misnomer. Senses, common sense and intuitive sensibilities link sense perception with intelligence, thought with reason, theory and practice, and open ways to 'sensible', wise, action — if we are willing. 'Mind' focuses purpose to *plan*, willingly engaging '*will*'. Deciding what to do is 'making up your mind'. (See **II**.) Several people in agreement are said to be 'of one mind'.

Heart inclines mind to consider, *reason*, learn, inspect intentions and foresee consequences of acts. **Hope** unites feeling and thought, *desire* and *purpose*, possible and actual. The feelings of others whose interests coincide or differ from our own are influences. To become conscious of the idea of **will** divined, *'divine will'*, invites, invokes, powerful ways of being willing.

Willing varies with conscious aspirations in heart, and mind: desire and need in human being. The familiar outer-inward-outward sequence clarifies sources and alternatives. Possibilities involve conflicts, paradoxical. Judging helps to sift illusion from reality and, again and again, presents a one-way street. Courage to overcome fear prevents running away from frightening situations and eschews escapism. Willing to act involves **risk**, danger, courage, energy in virtue. Willing co-operation in communal and personal activities emerges, positive and negative. Purpose disguised represents a different view, differently willing other ways of accepting; disobedience subordinated to common good. Willing to think opens **will** to discover and explore. Consequences lead to responsibility in action. Thinking and planning ahead requires willingness to encounter different belief. This opens conflict, division between different beliefs: other purposes, attitudes, methods.

Achievements provide precedents, foundations, models to encourage and give confidence for greater effort, hope of further success. Cautionary tales, referred to, supply examples of failure as well as of success. Each person, community, culture, like a tree, needs regular re-appraisal: special care.

A leader inspires others to do more, better, beyond expectation. Capability and determination are infectious, although excess is repulsive and destructive. Military style authority includes disciplined obedience necessary to plan, co-ordinate and enforce reaction to evil action, singular, plural, systematic. Leaders raise morale, courage, loyalty, reliable co-operative willing obedience without undue compliance, submission. Authority injects confidence to command, expecting to be obeyed but leadership is tested by those who follow willingly if reluctantly. Need for efficiency, for effective **rule**, rules are respected. Leaders, rulers who lack authority of respect with consent are tempted to coerce, to compel, to abuse power and undo authentic leadership. Systems, constitutions, regimes fail when unwilling, unable to recognise and resist leaders who become autocrats, dictators, tyrants. *'L'Etat, c'est moi'*, is as dangerous in an inflated, vain, democratically elected leader as in a monarch.

Different spheres have distinct vocabularies for order and co-operation. Words used in a consulting room or operating theatre are not those of a commander-in-chief, sergeant-major, ship's captain. Police on duty, **beat**, law **court**, prison, use words with care. Councils range from voluntary organisations (NSPCC, Women's Institute, local clubs) to parish, cabinet, privy council sustained (or neglected) in willing recognition and acceptance of immediate, distant, indirect or direct, inward and outward authority derived from willing and judging. Self-constituted 'councils' run subversive terrorists organizations, quasi-military, repudiating law. 'Cabinet' ministers can find themselves excluded from consultation, collective responsibility, when 'kitchen cabinet' or 'special advisers' exercise power without them.

Being willing to be governed is expressed in voting, voluntary voice, representing majority opinion. Government, politics and education are intimately linked to cultural dynamics. Where belief is weak or absent, custom and convention dilute into shifting fashions, modish adaptations vulnerable to alternative personal worlds more compatible with anarchy than ordered reform. Traditional values persist in people loyal to a tradition valued with willing commitment; supported, respected and followed even when, sometimes, they would rather not. Reservations and disagreements, critical tensions have promoted constitutional reform such as extending the franchise. Change can be achieved peacefully, by evolution rather than revolution: persistent peaceful agitation of suffragists harnessed for war work, 1914-18, more persuasive than violent 'suffragettes'.

Head and heart move will to activate mind capable of judging and willing, practical and theoretical, in potential power to create and to destroy life and things; to order and to cultivate, build and to civilise; to confuse, corrupt, brutalise and destroy. *Will* is the *key*: to prison and to liberty; enslavement or freedom, chaos and civilisation. Conflict is inward and outward, personal (emotional and thoughtful) in social, political, theological questions at all levels. These conflicts engage creative and destructive tension; paradox sustained and inhabited until clarified, understood and resolved.

These processes recur between head and heart, and are repeatedly discussed in this exploration. Ingredients of stability, constancy, combined with dynamic relativity require consensus and balance; power to connect danger with *control*, prevention with eternally vigilant *care*.

IX

Will

Augustine: 'Let me ask you: have we a will?'

Evodius: 'I do not know.'

Augustine: 'Then do not ask me any more questions.'

Evodius.: 'Why?'

Augustine: 'Because I ought not to answer your questions unless you want to know what you ask...you cannot be my friend unless you desire my good. So far as you are concerned yourself, you will be able to see whether you have a will to the happy life for yourself'.

Evodius: 'I agree that it is impossible to deny that we have will. Go on and let us see what conclusion you draw from this.'

Augustine: 'So I shall. But first tell me whether you are conscious of having a good will.'

Evodius: 'What is a good will?'

(Augustine, *On Free Will*, 25, translated by John Burleigh, SCM Press, 1953)

IX 1 Consciousness

'Where there's a will there's a way' says the proverb and where there's a way, **will** intends and hopes to find it. Verbs identify **will** in action. Feeling, interest, curiosity move **will** to think, to *act*, to make and *mend*. **Will**, mysterious invisible essence in human being is experienced in thought, word and deed. Reactions and actions, conscious or subconscious, include automatic reflexes, intuition, impulsive, spontaneous. Infants cry when hungry or uncomfortable: too hot, too cold, in pain. Some soon cry for company, diversion, attention. Appetites and needs accelerate with growth. Demands satisfied draw appreciative response, conscious warmth of good **will**.

Will matures to activate, coordinate, co-operate, then initiate to construct and destruct. When conscious of another *will*, do you, I, follow, comply, obey like a slave, soldier, servant, disciple, friend? If so, for whose *will*? Does your own heart and/or that of another incline your *will*? Do you make up your own mind: consider, agree, disagree, initiate alternatives before going into action?

Is it possible to be sure of right action? *Will* aligns with intelligent perception of nature, physical common sense and memory as to how things *work*. Innovations: practical, emotional, thoughtful: medical/technical/political, modify instinctive reactions for better and worse. *Will* operates in distinctive areas, separable for description but co-ordinated in activity. Consciousness expands to identify, appreciate, and move us towards them. Undiscerned qualities emerge – of beauty, use, behaviour: each found to have its opposite: ugly, evil.

Consciousness of *will* awakens realisation of *desire* as motive to *do*. Heart symbolises emotion; thoughts and reasons. They interact, sometimes in unison, sometimes apparently at odds. *Will* is invisible, mysterious essence in human being, expressed in action, thinking, speaking, doing. Sub-conscious and unconscious instincts are not aware of motive. Conscious action includes reflexes, intuition, impulsive and spontaneous: motives clear or obscure, known or unknown.

Where does *will* originate? Like wind, moving air is active or still, inactive. Indispensable for breath, movement of breeze, gale, hurricane, are less or more powerful. The question then concerns origin of creative energy. Human *will*, like wind, experiences direction and strength though energy and purpose. Is *will* energised by belief as belief surely affects and directs *will*? Denial of motive in *will* confines human actions to what is instinctive, driven rather than envisaged, purposed, motivated, planned, controlled.

Consciousness stimulates *will* and *will* promotes consciousness; positive, negative, mixed, affirmed, denied: indicative of knowing; if only in part. These questions challenge head and heart to realise *will* for **commitment**. **Donouns** identify integration of head and heart by disclosing *will* to do, *will* to *act* requiring an *act* of *will*. To 'select all' future actions as words on the Word Processing screen to guarantee 'good-will' is not an available technique in life. Commitment to seek and find good-will is an approach. Faith, hope, love, affirm support for this formidable intention. Love may be love of good, but love exaggerated, unbalanced, distorted, abused, becomes evil; ill-will.

General and particular reflections follow four stages.

IX 1 i Dawning Consciousness

Con- is a frequent, con-structive prefix. Suffix '-ous' indicates characteristics such as monstrous, scrupulous, amorphous, magnanimous. Adding 'i', -ious intensifies experience: precious, delicious, fractious, serious persons, evident in actions. Consciousness is inwardly aware of self, others, external things. 'Nous', Greek in origin, is of mind, intellect. 'We', first person plural, suggests common mind, knowing and understanding.

Will: simple and complex, single, multiple — immediate and longer term — is tuned to and from consciousness; personal and collective need, taste, desire; stimulating recognition, intention, decision into action; actually doing.

Dawning consciousness, personal and self-conscious, moves, responds, awakens **will**, self-interest, to open towards hopes, aspirations, dreams, thinking of doing; intending to do, often with others. You or I may know little, very little, of others' consciousness and needs. Better, preferred to worse, but circumstances of life vary from conditions of prosperity, plenty, to privation, danger, constant fear, struggle for survival. Vitality, **will** to live, 'quickens' before birth and increases in healthy infants.

Consciousness leads to realise practicalities: alternatives, either/or, better or worse, good and evil, in different circumstances. Cause and effect, consequences, offer criteria for behaviour, evaluation in mind with matter; hope of co-operation, co-ordinating for good, not evil. None can avoid suffering. Physical pain is relieved by healing. Consciousness of emotional anguish, bewilderment, grief, spiritual agony continues. Drugs, alcohol, tempting escapist distractions, attempt to numb haunting, daunting, inescapable pain.

IX 1 ii Identity

Present tense, primal, *'I am'*, is, *of the verb 'to be'*. Now is the time: here and now. Consciousness precedes will to do; conscious sense of purpose, deliberately deliberated. 'I was' and 'I will be' are past and future. *Will has no past tense as such.* 'I would have' refers to what might have but did not happen. 'I **hope** to' may become promise: 'I will'.

Will to become, *will* to do, realises being in doing as *intention*; to *walk, run, swim, fight, work, act,* and so on, all **donouns**. To intend to do needs **will**, my own or obedience to another's. Consciousness engages *place* as well as *time*, where and when. Opportunity made or offered enables inclination and purpose to do, in thought, word and deed. Being, pre-condition of doing, is alive in living. Conceiving, creating, giving birth, require action with or without control. *Will* involves and confers identity.

Identity is nourished in presence. Fortunate infants become familiar with persons who nourish and look after them; whose feel, smell, faces and voices are recognised; who name, personal to themselves, intimates intimately. Who is this? Who are they? Who am I? I am named, identified. Consciousness expands in confident familiar, familial relationships when they communicate confidence, *trust*.

Originator/inventor overlap when an inventor is spoken of as originator. Name identifies and confers identity. Inventories list present contents. Checking reveals gain and loss, if any. Origin, known or unknown, is personalised as originator. A great originator is a continuing presence, recalled, remembered, appealed to. Divine presence; presence divined but mysterious, unknown but evident in created, creative, creating activity affirmed, is acknowledged, cultivated to become systematically, trusted, believed. This recognises the mystery of the original might and power of 'divine will'. First, the quest, then rumour, discovery, reality: or absence, vacuum, nothingness. You and I require *will*; best aligned to recognise and realise good and evil; to prefer good: identity confirmed for good. **Will** to 'select all' represents **will** to correct, make good as well as can be done. Categories assist identification but there is movement within them. Categorical recognitions, clarifying, may 'prove' perilous as well as reasonable.

IX 1 iii Volition

Consciousness of *will* over instinct raises questions of intention and control; voluntary, guided, misguided, free or compelled: the core of *will*.

Again, nouns name and identify people and things, animate and inanimate. Verbs are doing words. Motives clear or obscure, known or unknown, fair and unfair, outward and inward, formulate *will*. **WILL**, invisible, mysterious essence in human being, is expressed in action, doing. **WILL** is pre-eminent **donoun**. *Interest* and *help* indicate delightful, serious recognition: *laugh* and *cry, joke, weep, rage, cool* among many others. *Shed*, is *pun* **donoun**; *bin* and *trash* have become so.

Will responds, activates, co-ordinates, co-operates, initiates willingness, volition, to construct and destruct, responsibly or not, with or without another *will* to advise, *praise* or *blame*.

Consciousness moves *will* and *will* promotes consciousness; positive, negative, mixed, affirmed, denied: indicative of knowing if only in part. These questions challenge head and heart to realise *will* as commitment to act. **Donouns** identify capability of integration for they disclose **will** to do, **will** to act as an act of **will**. To 'select all' future actions in order to guarantee 'good-will' is not an available technique in life, but enduring commitment to seek and find goodwill hopes to estimate, evaluate, foresee, approach it. *Trust, hope* and *love* affirm energy to support such formidable intention. Love may be love of normal, natural good things and actions; done well; but if exaggerated, unbalanced, distorted, abused, these become distressing, wrong; opposite and opposed to good.

Evodius questioned Augustine about evil. Good and evil are co-ordinates of their dialogue. Cause and effect, principles of behaviour; of civility, law, education and order are considered. Augustine, born AD 354, at Thagaste, foothills of the Atlas mountains, grew and was educated in the Roman colony of Africa. Carthage, which, as elsewhere, had a Greek theatre. Tragedies and comedies performed there viewed mortality as under unarguable, ineluctable, cruel fate: inevitable but with a very funny side, comical and laughable. Augustine won prizes for verse speaking and rhetoric. He looked for happiness; sources of joy, delight, fulfilment in every area of experience. Conscious of goodwill, he was acutely aware of being disturbed, enslaved to self-centred ambition and, particularly, to insatiable, habitual urge for sexual pleasure. He longed for peace and freedom. *Confessions* describe his journey. Liberation into unity, body and soul together when, in a simple but dramatic act of will, he opens his heart and head to 'that which nothing higher can be thought', to God. Out of psychological depths and philosophical struggles, Augustine experienced reconciliation; his will freed in joy and peace, in harmony with that of his maker; his astonishing and astonished *mind* enlivened by increasingly faithful heart and *will*. He found assurance of mercy , forgiveness, **grace**.

Will, then, is not circumscribed, limited, but liberates individuals in personal contexts of expanding consciousness, knowing, deciding and doing. Conscience, close advisor to *will*, assists good-will, goodness and happiness, unique, mysterious, individual. Consciousness leads to realise practicalities of good and evil in any circumstances. Present tense is primary: 'I am' is, of the verb 'to be'. Now is the time: here and now. Consciousness in being precedes *will* to do, with conscious sense of purpose.

Will over instinct raises questions of intention and control. A volt is a leap and a sort of dance. In fencing it is sudden movement to avoid a *thrust*. It is also a measurement of electro-magnetic energy. 'Revolt' also involves action. Involuntary action is compelled, forced, without alternative. In extremity, refusal leads to torment and death.

To obey is to act obediently, as ordered. To order recognises volition. Those whose **will** is free may accept, desire and follow order for good; good order. Compliance mixes co-operation with obedience without agreement. Submission, permission, commission, remission, derive from distinctive expressions of volition. Per-, as in permit, perform, perfect, aspires to perfection.

Patriotism, fidelity, loyalty; sometimes mocked, satirised, are deep-seated capability of strength and power. Critics, not always constructive, resort to cynicism, mockery prompted by, sharp but shallow reactions, entertainingly comic, some rude, crude, seriously destructive.

IX 1 iv Contexts

Weather is a peculiarly English, British, obsession: too little or too much cloud or sunshine, wind and rain. Freak floods follow water shortages when heat waves in preceding summers dry and harden earth. Frosts and freeze-ups, gales, even a hurricane (as in Britain in 1987), any exceptional condition provides analogy of temperament and mood: storms of passion, fury, tempest, shipwreck: calm, pastoral peace; at worst, devastation, a wasteland. This is common experience. Pressure, like tension, affects consciousness, **will** and behaviour. Determination is tested, strained under pressure at any level; physical, emotional, intellectual and moral.

Vice coexists with virtue in contexts; situations when problems, difficulties and dangers occur and recur. Greed, envy, jealousy can be aroused by success and achievement, riches and power. Arrogance, pride, confidence, if they breed sense of superiority, lack humility. Conscious awe and wonder at great creative achievement invokes respect, regard, emulation. **Will** prompts consideration of intent and purpose in contexts of genuine experience.

IX 2 Consideration

Con- again, this time with original 'desiderare', desire, con-siderable, worth thinking about. 'Head-over-heart' is not quite 'mind-over-matter' but matter is material to, of, for and much else. Does it *matter*? Knowing and desiring *move need* towards informed preference. *Con*-centration centres interest. 'Paying attention' includes avoiding distraction, keen to learn, due habit of focus. Recipes for consideration vary but **will**, ever-present, offers alternatives, subject to essential duties and obligations realised.

These exceed choices, options, tastes without consideration of evaluation; of moral authorisation.

Consideration moves from consciousness into feeling and thinking: reasoning, evaluating, contemplating and reflecting. Do you *mind*? *MIND* is essence, diet and journal of philosophers, of philosophy, of 'moral science'. Frontiers of philosophy adjoin and enjoy common ground with natural sciences, practical and intellectual, practices and studies of experience including psychology and psychiatry. Law, ethics, politics, ideology, theology are kin with divinity. Creative and performing arts look across the world, from summits of Parnassus and Olympus, beyond Europe, to Mesopotamia and Sinai, Hindu Kush and Himalayas, Tien-shan, and China, Far East, to consider most ancient and most recent expressions of creative energy. The inhabitants of these islands were then in woad but 'earthworks', 'henges', stone, wood, show growing consideration: *will* to discover and develop.

Consideration of *will* beyond instinct and impulse, first consciousness, leads to initiative, determination, consent and decision. Influences before birth and throughout life, recur in discussing belief and education.

IX 2 i Of Initiative

Hope encourages initiative and formulates purpose; *will* to hope. Instinctive reaction to fear is self-protective, self-centred for survival, subjective self-absorption that impedes *will* beyond immediate situations. To look for implications of particular dangers envisage causes of what is fearful and dangerous, present and future. Hope with good-will rises to cultivate expertise: fire brigades, water shortages, flood and epidemic control, knowledge and skill in emergencies from natural or human causes. Self-preservation extends to common good and communal benefit. Memory, foresight and imagination contribute to initiative at every level of hope and fear, practical, emotional, thoughtful and evaluative.

IX 2 ii Of Consent

One will, singularly personal, may not seem to involve another, others. Danger and fear of danger is not first thought of as self-will, even by emphatic individualists.

Personal and communal reaction; what, if anything, to do alone or with another, others, requires *will*. *Consent*, singular and plural, ranges, arranges and rearranges *will* in present *need* and further eventuality; in any function and case. The meaning of consent, present and future, engages *will*.

> 'Con and sent consent to wed. Do they agree?
> If known intent is one, there is consent, content.'

Sent- is prefix (sentence, sentiment, sentry) and suffix (pre-sent, resent, assent, dissent as well as consent). All express *will*, not necessarily or exclusively your or my own. Content may mean acquiescence, with or without reservation, approval of what is present; content for which consent is required, given or withheld. These refinements are realised in persons and communities where liberty and freedom are valued and protected within good law; justice fairly and efficiently administered. These are high hopes, personal, social, communal and political. *Consent*, willing, requires (at best) leadership within a tradition of wisdom, knowledge and responsibility, conscience; weighty burdens to sustain light-heartening glorious liberty. Democratic systems are ships in need of navigation aids, direction-finders, rudders, controlled reaction to storms, cross-currents, perils of oceans. On land, these recognise danger: enemies, unseen terrorists, opposing values. At sea, principles of purpose, course, strategy, loyalty and skill test consent to decisions.

IX 2 iii Of Decision

Which comes first: *will* to decide or decision recognised as **will** experienced? Human potential to determine, decide and do seems obvious until uncertainty, indecision and lack of determination become bewildering hazards, postponements. Impulse can be compulsive; instinct irresistible. Some believe instinct is beyond control, impossible to resist. Consent appears irrelevant when a person feels compelled, 'driven', to do what conscience, and others, warn will lead to disaster, tragedy, remorse. Compulsion identified, is blamed for what was not a conscious intended decision. To be beguiled, enticed, coerced, inveigled; caught like a fly in a spider's web, is to be trapped. Ignorance and deceit are hazards. Lack of information hides caution as to risks, dangers, defences, personal and public. Being deterred or undeterred depend on being informed but, resolve, decision, determination to do or resist doing also depend on energy of *will*. 'Pressure' is mentioned now, more often than 'encouragement' or 'discouragement'. The idea that 'science' is sovereign; that 'genes' pre-determine; that inherent ingredients exempt from moral responsibility to decide is widely assumed, believed.

Decision requires determination, will-power, mental effort to learn, discern and balance ingredients and issues. Factors emerge in circumstances and contexts. Aggressive action differs from defensive reaction. Emotional tides, cross-currents, wind and turbulence are difficult to recognise exactly. Contradiction, paradox, confused priorities of purposes, are more substantial but harder to discern than motive of immediate gratification. Preferences, inclinations, options and opportunities experienced in childhood expand and change. Few are realised, fewer understood even by 'nearest and dearest'. If and when responses and hopes mature, pleasure is interrupted by pain, coexists with distress; happiness with misery, disappointment. Pleasure pursued sometimes proves transient, ephemeral; sometimes marvellous, enduring and profound. Gratified desire, when realised fruit of good-will, self-giving, brings joy; peace of soul. Effort to make the best of things pursues neither unrealistic aspirations nor hopeless, cynical pessimism, but encourages *will* to work, to strive for good, better and best: joy, delight with love.

Attitudes modify in processes of deliberation which affect decisions; changing 'mind' changing *'will'*. Challenging decisions weigh heavily, become difficult, even impossible; others are settled with light-hearted confidence. Habits of mind, systematic or scatty, affect actions and are affected by them. Effort to be punctual, polite, helpful, to listen and hear seriously promotes good-will. Expectation of common sense and courtesy, given and received, encourages good order. Keeping appointments promotes trust, avoids disappointment and being disappointed. ***Point*** and ***aim*** are **donouns**.

IX 2 iv Of Conflict

Head and heart in conflict causes personal distress. *Will* is more readily disabled when mind thinks what heart has no heart for. Unable to decide, determine, resolve, *will* finds difficulty to **move**, to **act**. Indecision can be influenced by temperamental inclination to observe rather than participate, to sustain balance from the sidelines; more referee than player, but inner conflict suppressed, denied, unsublimated, stresses nerves and tends to unbalance behaviour. Indifference is not mature detachment but may ease, disguise dangers of conflict.

The divided self is much studied. Schism, sharp irreconcilable division, resonates in schizo-, schizoid and schizophrenia. Delusions characteristic of paranoia reflect distressing inner conflict. Erratic behaviour was thought of as 'lunacy' associated with phases of the moon, beyond human control. Psychologists gather, study, case histories, evidence of experience in life and in literature. Psychotherapists, clinical psychologists, highly or moderately qualified, offer counselling, sometimes analysis, to treat and relieve distress.

Strike and **fight** enact open conflict. Opposing opinions and interests are intensified by gender, economic, racial, social, political and national rivalry. These escalate into enmity and hatred. Conflict faced is challenging. Realisation and resistance call for all virtues: courageous, temperate, just and prudent. Trust, good faith, empowers *will* for peace over conflict, war; love overcoming hate, grace relieving disgrace: good over evil.

IX 3 Will and Belief

Consideration promotes thought, discussion, debate: to make up mind and resolve *will* into action. Commonsense practicality and practicability are parameters of plans, realistic and realisable. Since *will* to do is what *will* intends and hopes to do in immediate or distant future, foresight is helpful, supported by experience. Vision of high purpose is pro-moted by belief. Pro- and con-, for and against: voices, opinions, votes. Con- , prefix of confidence to sail against con-trary currents, tides, waves, and to con-tradict, consider, confer, confide, confirm, conflict, conform, converse, convert adds many more attitudes and acts appertaining to *will*. Pro- is positively prolific. Per- aspires to per-fect per-formance: pre- to perfect.

IX 3 i Proverbial and Pragmatic

Proverbs, pro-verbal wise 'sayings', repeated, scripted, translated are powerful reflections of experience, cause and effect, **will** and mind. English outlook, language and life: colloquial, figurative and literary, abound with proverbs. Silk purses out of sows' ears; one man's meat as another's poison, a 'wise saw' enters 'a wooden head'. Mixing metaphor and paradox illustrate and add understanding. Warning not to 'be wise after the event'; nor 'reinvent the wheel' are cautions.

Nursery rhymes such as 'Rock-a-bye baby' connect young children with cause and effect. 'Poor Sally is a-weeping' is a singing game of the heart. Sally's hope to find a sweetheart depends on desire, expectation and circumstance, influencing her *will*. 'Oranges and Lemons' introduce debts and credits, owing and paying, in the City of London: church bells chiming trade, business, prosperity and adversity. Clerks in Orders met to drink at Inns and became specialist lawyers. Carey Street and the Old Bailey are not far apart. Lloyd's coffee house, congenial meeting place for men of property willing to underwrite risks, especially to ships, found profitable ways. The

Lutine bell, salvaged from a costly wreck, rings each disaster in 'the Room', rebuilt. 'Pragmatic' mixes busyness, business; affairs of state and commerce, personal and communal public experience and skill in dealing with them.

Leadership and management of organisations involves learning, knowing, deciding, finding and communicating *will*. 'The art of the possible' is proverb of pragmatism in politics and elsewhere. Search for criteria leads to discern generalities, governing principles suspect yet interesting to pragmatists. 'Sayings' remembered accumulate and are quoted: 'honesty is the best policy', 'my word is my bond'; 'who pay's the piper calls the tune', but 'proverbs lie on the lips of fools' and the essence of pragmatism is practical realities yielding proverbs: 'horses for courses', 'too many cooks...' although 'watched pots....'. Proverbs encourage or warn. Again, 'where there's a will, there's a way' but 'fools rush in where angels fear to tread': paradox.

Heart and head in conflict pull in different directions. *Will* requires and enables consideration and decision; what to do next, each possibility includes intention, evaluation, commitment beyond personal taste, preference, choice. **Consent** respects *will* since *will* gives or withholds consent. To agree or disagree, assent or dissent move to and from affirmation, positive belief, negative denial. A pragmatist who acknowledges principles realises that the 'exception proves the rule'. **Rule** is doing and being, a **donoun**, but principle is not.

IX 3 ii Foundations and Influences

Standing on firm ground, building on sure foundations are 'down to earth' clichés of experience. They are also parables of invisible strength. Upright posture implies *balance*; character that inspires confidence; trusted; known to be trustworthy. Expectations promote attitudes. Persons in context, sown, grown, are influenced by local conditions, grounding, among continuing practical factors; natural, environmental and human, *education* where cultivation begins and culture develops. Weeds and brambles grow, spread, choke growth unless restrained, controlled, uprooted. But brambles, wild or cultivated, have delicate flowers that yield delicious blackberries among thorny scratchy shoots. Myth and fairy tale link fear of danger in uncultivated nature, growth suffocated by malevolent **will**, but capable of renewal; wicked stepmother who poisons her rival; but 'sleeping beauty' responds to awakening love, reclaimed. 'Ground Zero' symbolises prosperity attacked, trade centre destroyed, remembered, reclaimed: acclaims prosperity renewable and renewed.

Foundations rest on practical experience, knowledge, and on moral principles that accord with what is true, objective, works well and promotes *will* to search for and know more of good, good-will, good work. Sure foundations tested by trial and error, are verified. Something unsure cannot provide sure, true foundation 'Sure', making sure, requires confidence to proceed, to experience and discover. Sure does not mean certain. Instability may occur if conditions change. A stable landscape, a good building, a dependable relationship may *change*, disturbed by earthquake. Accuracy, precise action such as for calculating numbers, is indispensable in Word Processing. Fascinating immediate interaction adds dimensions, unimagined until discovered, repeated, become available, even when limited to tiny parts of huge functions, varied, expanding, astonishing.

Will involves risks unless the outcome of action is certain. 'Fact' and 'principle', practice and theory, sense and reason concern and engage thoughtful people. Language development includes recognising, learning, using order and pattern, principles of grammar, foundations of eloquence: *might* and *power* to communicate. Super-natural and super-human energy evident in pre-human eras awaited such recognition, comprehension and discovery. Both are, were, and will continue while their order, *will*, continues to operate in time and place.

Whose *will*? For what purpose? How far, if at all, do foundations shift when beliefs change, when 'faith systems' conflict? The concept of the Enlightenment was said to be 'the age of reason' but cultural growth always needs reason. Reason exaggerated as be-all and end-all 'rationalism' limits imagination and tempts 'rationalists' to regard belief as superstition. A case, an opinion, a point of view dependent on 'reason' alone, is likely to overlook 'inspiration', 'revelation'; super-natural and super-human sources, but each ingredient of belief develops and benefits from reasoned investigation, analysis, understanding. Natural and moral science accompany philosophy and theology to consider fear and hope, war and peace, armaments and disarmaments, tragedy, comedy and glory. The 'fact' that alternatives are real, faced, recognised; and that words found for them reflects diversity of experience, insight, aim and *will*. Every area of study calls up new words with additions and subtractions by subsequent students who explore; search for foundations. Desire and duty, aspiration and *will*, heart and head, coexist: find *power* through **integration**.

Permanence provides continuity, dependable, stable, whereas *will* to move, initiate, develop, involves change. 'Static' and 'dynamic', referred to, are physical and metaphysical; mathematical moments and energetic transmissions: engagement with *power*, energy and *might*; **potential, manifest, realised**. Human search for consistent

129

foundation principles realises and accepts paradox as creative tension between bewildering alternatives. *Control*, **donoun** of *power* at every level of experience, concerns *will*.

'Will you — won't you?' is static at the moment of decision. 'Can you — can't you?' depends on forward looking purpose, plan, energy to follow through. 'Ought' and 'should' require respect for principles realised; exemplified in actual problems; include custom, convention, harmony and discord, better or worse, true not false, good to inspire, not evil to conspire. Desire with duty, joy with sorrow, laughter with tears, lightning with thunder, inspiration with revelation are common influences, differently combined, experience unique to each individual.

Fluent and affluent become influential. More or less effort of *will*, encouraged or discouraged, by influences that communicate effectively from seemingly impersonal sources, visible, invisible, timely and timeless, circumstantial, beyond individual range and control. To discern and find words seeks to encompass the un-encompassable, define the indefinable, seek to approach, consider, *divine* divinity. *Will* aspires, hoping to find and *make sense of experience*. Influences felt, identified, considered, are appreciated or repudiated, embraced or repelled. Conscious appraisal, self-critical, need criteria of value, virtue, principle to achieve 'success', acknowledge 'failure' which need long view.

Silent, unknown influences persist subconsciously. Pre-natal life is believed, increasingly thought and known to influence pre-birth growth; food, drink, sleep, exercise, attitudes during pregnancy. Infant communication, unspoken, unremembered, is significant. Words for things, places, doings are shared and relished. Hearing talk encourages fluency. 'Yes' and 'no', learned early, are evident response, inclination, intent, *will*.

Infants and children respond to music, talk, chatter, and conversation. Gardens, meadow, park and farm, woodland, pool, river, sea and seaside with indigenous life, birds, insects, awaken interest, observation, need of words and reasons. 'Why, why, why?' need answer and possible explanation. Pleasure and pain, friends and enemies, interest and boredom add emotion. Explanations offered promote thought. Positive and negative influences are received and felt, limits are challenged, tested, sometimes digested, imitated and adopted, together ignored.

IX 3 iii Ill-Will

How are you? Do you feel better? Why was the question asked? Friend, neighbour, doctor, employer, acquaintance, (a quaint word?) ask for your sake or for their own.

Health includes freedom from mild but inconvenient, uncomfortable ailments: a common cold or serious sickness, pain, dis-ease.

How is your heart? Does that question concern circulation, blood-pressure, blood-count or emotion: joy or heartbreak?

How is your head? If bumped or injured; inclined to suffer migraine, sinus, that is a normal enquiry. Are you 'off your head', or 'out of your mind', is not.

How is your will? Is it good or ill, well or sick? Not a question asked, faced, readily responded to among close relations, intimates. Difficulty with *will*, not quite 'ill-will', is not usually, willingly, discussed. Sickness of heart, mind, *will*, disturb balance of personality; distress of soul, psyche. Disturbances, like high and low pressure atmospherics, become evident. Sympathy, sought and received, is appreciated, but intrusive enquiry can alienate.

Ill-will and good-will show in attitudes and actions. Articulate, communicative people are more able to describe and discuss their feelings and reasons. Ill-will provokes anger and is provoked by it. Aggravation, aggravating upsets occur when surface calm is disturbed, control is tested, sometimes lost. Suspicion, fear of hostility, cause ill-feeling. Conditioned reflexes, unconscious, may be uncontrollable.

The gift, opportunity and responsibility of *will* is expressed in different intentions, purposes, plans. These depend on knowledge and *control*. Ill-will, unrealised, unconscious of causes and effects of frailty, unaware of need, causes difficulties, agonies. Gentle, tactful, unfailing good-will and concern offer healing. Self examination for 'motes and beams' is essential humility.

The very idea of 'ill-will', repugnant to some, is obvious to others. Frailty, failure, folly occur for good reasons. Attitudes will vary. Anarchic, manic, psychotic compulsions are other than measured, reasoned recognition of liberty and responsibility, freedom protected by *control* and enjoyed in health and wealth of good-will.

IX 3 iv Healing Confidence

Lack of appetite, inability to eat, to swallow, to digest nourishment are symptoms of upset system. Anorexia and bulimia are regarded as physical manifestations of emotional and nervous origin. Diabetes, bio-chemical imbalance, can be corrected by careful diet and insulin injection. Tests, such as blood-pressure, blood-count analysed, provide clinical evidence. Frustration, misery, grief, despair influence health of body, mind and will. Ill health enfeebles energy; weakens mind's ability to focus and clarify intention. Experience of tragedy inflames, quenches and deflates energy of *will*.

'Melancholy' now describes low spirits, sad, depressed for deep reasons. Robert Burton (1577-1640), anatomist/physician/philosopher/poet; literate-linguist/pastor/divine, investigated, and analysed interconnections, interactions. He collected and described his findings in *The Anatomy of Melancholy*, 1621, (revised and added to until he died; reprinted since, most recently, in paperback, 2001). The heart is 'the seat and fountain of life, of heat, of spirits, of pulse and respiration, the sun of our body, the king and sole commander of it, the seat and organ of all passions and affections. It lives first and dies last in all creatures'. (Pages 152-3.) Head includes brain 'seated within the skull or brain-pan; and it is the most noble organ under heaven, the dwelling house and seat of the soul, the habitation of wisdom, memory, judgment, reason...' (Page 153.)

Burton regarded 'humour' as juice of human equanimity, balance, health and happiness or their opposites: sanguine, phlegmatic, choleric, black (bile) in the guts. Diet and activity, exercise of body and brain, conscience and soul engage, ***integrate***, energise will for good and evil. Healing confidence is serious ***trust.*** Burton addresses the reader who employs his leisure 'ill'; warns not to employ wit in foolish disapproval or false accusation. 'For should Democritus Junior prove to be what he professes, it is all up with you; he will become both accuser and judge of you in his petulant spleen, will dissipate you in jests, pulverise you with witticisms, and sacrifice you, I can promise you, to the God of Mirth.' (Page 124.) Melancholy is no laughing matter but wit and humour, ever present, prevail.

For Burton, each 'partition', (section) has a synopsis. First includes causes, symptoms, prognostic tendencies: second, 'The Cure of Melancholy': third, 'Love-Melancholy', a riveting review of pleasant and honest objects of love; of charity, of love's power, of beauty, of artificial allurements, of cure of love-melancholy and finally, of religious melancholy.

Burton's words on 'cure of despair' refer to the healing power of faith: example, prayer; ***will*** 'to open himself to the advice of good physicians and divine...to hear them speak to whom the Lord hath given the tongue of the learned, to be able to minister a word to him that is weary, whose words are as flagons of wine. Let him not be obstinate, headstrong, peevish, wilful, self-conceited (as in this malady they are) but give ear to good advice,...and no doubt but such good counsel may prove as prosperous to his soul as the angel was to Peter, that opened the iron gates, loosed his bands, brought him out of prison, and delivered him from bodily thraldom...' (Page 432.)

Sir Thomas Browne, (1605-82) studied medicine at Montpelier, Padua and Leyden, settled in Norwich, 1637, and practiced as a physician. *Religio Medici* appeared in 1643. (G. Keynes collected edition, published by Faber & Faber, 1931.) Browne realised 'that here are not only diseases incurable in physic. But cases indissolvable in laws, vices incorrigible in divinity...I can cure the gout or stone in some, sooner than divinity, pride or avarice in others. I can cure vices by physic when they remain incurable by divinity; and they shall obey my pills when they contemn precepts. I boast nothing, but plainly say, we all labour against our own cure; for death is the cure of all diseases....Now for my life, it is a miracle of thirty years, which to relate, were not a history, but a piece of poetry, and would sound to common ears like a fable: for the world. I count it not an inn. But a hospital; and a place not to live, but to die in. The world that I regard is myself; it is the microcosm of my own frame that I cast mine eye on; for the other, I use it but like my globe, and turn it round sometimes for my recreation. Men that look upon my outside, perusing only my condition and fortunes, do err in my altitude; for I am above Atlas's shoulders. The earth is point not only in respect of the heavens above us, but of that heavenly and celestial part within us...'

Browne set out from and lives within contexts of faith: 'In philosophy, where truth seems double faced there is no man more paradoxical than myself: but in divinity I love to keep to the road; and though not in an implicit, yet an humble faith, follow the great wheel of the church, by which I move, not reserving any proper poles or motion from the epicycle of my own brain...' In colloquy with God, he takes his leave to 'sleep unto the resurrection'.

Burton and Browne, concerned to minister to ill people, were moved to compose poetry within their treatises. The times of their lives engaged conflicts and battles of ideas, belief, doctrine, civil war and its aftermaths. John Donne, Robert Herrick, George Herbert, Richard Crashaw, Thomas Traherne, Lancelot Andrewes, concerned with illness of will, passion, sickness of heart and soul, used words as healing metaphysicians. Faith and love, human and divine, offer resolution; self-knowledge of, and through suffering, compassion, pity, mercy. Despair, heartache, need consolation, healing, approached when *will* reaches for and finds confidence. Trust and fidelity, sustained by commitment, *will* to *trust* and continue loyal to that *trust*. Misplaced confidence, 'false' gods, hardens ideals into ideology, bigotry, a 'god that fails'.

Con-, that prefix again, and -fide is self-giving in trust to another who receives what is confided. Kindness between friends, families, 'kin', 'kindred spirits' shares and bears burdens, difficulties, problems, anguish, detect causes of illness and healing of ill-will. To confide is to **trust**. *Grace*, mysterious, amazing, sustains and strengthens the faithful. Loyalty and fidelity to opposing interpretations of faith and loyalty were strained to breaking point by civil war. Regicide did not solve the problem of power.

IX 3 v Learning and Believing

Sound travels, resounds in echo, is transmitted with and without wires and is received increasingly long distances away, often recorded. Words spoken and heard, communicate, inform truly or not, and are open to interpretation. Learning, knowing and understanding principles of sound enables techniques to make and maintain this communication. Open ears of willing listeners hear, receive and learn from immediate and remote sources.

Open hearts are affected and respond to interest(s) and influence(s). Open heads, open minds, receive and remember, learn to reason, appraise, consider, wonder and discover. **WILL**, positively and negatively, is engaged in these stages and tends to remain in 'neutral' before engaging forward or reverse gear, to decide and ACT. Different words are used for the moment of resolution: mind made up and action performed: performative. (See Appendix **B**). A **donoun** such as *need, desire, plan, project, urge, switch,* shows potential integration of being/doing. (See Appendix **C**.) **WILL** fuses, infuses, refuses energy to do.

To hope for the best implies good will. Evodius's question recurs: 'What is good-will?' How on earth do we, can we, know? As between 'sure' and 'certain', *doubt, risk* and difficulty are probable, possible, in any forward activity. To suppose, *reason*, conjecture, guess, affirm, are stages towards personal decision to do, be doing. **Inclination encourages commitment promoted by and promoting belief.**

External force, power, real or apparent, suggest inevitability and challenge each personal **will**. 'Evil' opposes 'good'. (See **X**.) Denial may be blind, ignorant, simple inability to recognise, trust and believe. Affirmation and confirmation strengthens faith towards systematic belief: the circle rotates, again and again, from 'suppose', pre-suppose, to become confident faith: belief.

IX 4 Will in Education

Will enlarges opportunities, in more ways than can de described, for education. Five areas emerge in present time, place, viewed within limited knowledge and experience from London. Each person's education is unique. First, individual in context: personal, social, political. Second, ability, innate and inclined. Third, cultivation in diversity, communal and universal. Fourth, cooperation. Fifth, slavery. Sixth, *will* to serve and to achieve. Seventh, *will* for good. These areas, particular and general, grow exponentially to educate. Pre-eminent question and perennial challenge within each is *will*. Eighth: *will in education, should be, needs to be, education of will*. Interaction of *will* with every inward and outward facet of personality is self-evident. Education cultivates consciousness of instinct, desire, reason and evaluation. Criteria as to value emerge, again, from customs, traditions, beliefs: resources of education willingly received.

IX 4 i Personal, Social, Political in Context

a. Personal. A map of the world represents the existence of that world, context of life. A map is made by combining motive with method, curiosity informed with knowledge and applied with skill to survey, measure, reproduce as accurately as possible, on scale. Material gathered is drawn on other material: parchment, vellum, paper, to projection on screen, IT, etc. Education transmitted encourages self-education: *will* to do, such as to map-read information mapped. Eye and mind learn to read, educated to understand, receive what is represented. Two maps of the world, one showing population, another of climate and vegetation, illustrate variety, extremes of hot and cold, wet and dry, where people live or cannot yet live. Generalisation of personal context began, continues, where you, I, others, exist, survive, thrive, in natural and developed ways of life. Study reveals extreme contrasts of range and variety, need and opportunity in ever increasing particularity.

b. Social. All births occur in their respective contexts, simple, complex and elaborate, but essentially the same. Human beings react to one another with love, hate, indifference. Social circumstances and conditions influence *will* in every direction, with, within and without other people, to realise their own identity. **Life is inherited, not chosen.** Individuality emerges in slavery and in liberty; in tribal villages and great polyglot cities, commercial, industrial and political systems. Dissidence, isolation, shyness, loneliness, alienation occur any- and every-where, accentuated by emigration to lands where cultural tradition are different, not at once understood.

c. Political. Social experience begins at birth, sustained in family, settlements, communities, tribes, formed and unformed groups, formal and informal societies. Nationality is a comparatively recent identification originates with language, natural frontiers, and circumstantial racial distinctiveness. Education is intended to nourish culture towards civility, civil society, civilisation. Confidence, trust and faith develop systematic belief. This nourishes characteristic basis of organised systems in long settled lands: near-, middle- and far-East: Europe, and Great Britain, and newer contexts.

Will is experienced differently between rulers and ruled, commanders and commanded, leaders and led. Compulsion differs from consent but order depends, at best, on willing agreement. Enforced acceptance, obedience, risks revolt, revolution if rejected.

Duties, obligations, responsibilities assumed are performed promptly or postponed. Lack of consultation denies expectation of cooperation and may disturb respect for continuity of custom. Enforcement challenged, resisted, causes battles of *will*. Sages, poets, scholars look for common ground before and during disputes. Soldiers, servants, slaves who, not expected to express independent critical thinking, are not free to dispute or disobey.

Looking back to the ancient Greek-speaking world mountains surrounding small fertile plains facing the sea encouraged city-states. The Polis, home of gods and men, could, would, debate anything, including notions, ideas, ideals of liberty, autonomy, autarchy. Athens enjoyed a strategic site above sheltered harbour and islands of the Bay of Salamis. Military and naval prowess resisted and overcame invaders. Independence of mind nurtured aspiration for continuing experience of liberty: freedom. *Order* required strong rule. Solon, wise and effective, formulated code of law. Pericles, incorruptible, inspired military and civic effectiveness. Citizenship was considered, analysed, discussed particularly in fifth to third centuries BC, led by Plato, Socrates, Aristotle. Citizens, few and privileged, excluded women and slaves. Modes of rule occasionally included *consent* but 'democracy', then as now, tended to break down through corruption and decadence. Dictatorship, tyranny, would follow until revolt, revolution hoped to restore *consent*.

Whose *will*, if any, was strong, eloquent, powerful to sustain good government? Plato's *Dialogues*, Aristotle's *Analytics, Physic, Metaphysic, Ethics, Politics* and *Poetics* continue to stimulate minds and influence practice when, wherever read. In Athens, Socrates drank hemlock, Plato was exiled. Discussions continued, speculative, rational among philosophers but power ebbed. The city of Rome, expansionist, militarist, prosperous, rich, increasingly powerful, faced problems of government. Over-extended, the Western Empire failed to repel invaders.

Constantine ruled from 'New Rome', Constantinople, (Byzantium), with new ingredient: belief in and vision of Christ whose Gospel, spread by disciples, apostles, percolated throughout the Roman Empire. Recognition of the Divine will known in Christ, Son and Word, 'on earth as in heaven' inspired conversion, transformation of priorities, 'beatitude' (*Matthew* 5-7), possible martyrdom. Life inside massive defensive walls involved struggles to determine 'orthodoxy', maintain positions, power, within vision of the City of God, waxing and waning, until Constantinople fell in 1454 to Islamic invasion, renamed Istanbul.

Good-will and ill-will occur in people wherever they live. Atlases include maps like snapshots of their time:generalised information to represent moments, stages, physical continuity. Exploration by navigation; distribution of ethnic characteristics, rise and fall of dynasties in China, mercantile trade; old and new powers and alliances. Reduction to scale limits detail but indicates highs and lows. Diversity in contexts, living and learning; hope of health and well-being; ever-present shadow of death. People in power, rulers, governments, enhance or spoil conditions of life, some do both. Sunrise, light, new day, illuminates afresh until sunset.

Political patronage includes key appointments: forming a government, the Cabinet; setting agendas at home and representing the country abroad. *Will* and energy for effective leadership need consistency and balance. Persons and plans get upset. A strong majority tempts a prime minister to pay less time and attention to the House of Commons, supposing that public opinion, wooed, will retain power at the next election. 'Spinning', presentation of attitudes and information, is no substitute for consistent policy and well tried constitutional convention and balance. Confidence erodes, ebbs, is forfeit. Personal qualities are tested by consistent responsibility; **trust**, trustworthy, trusted.

Trust nourishes *respect*, sympathy, understanding and personal good-will. Will-act can dissolve at the hyphen. Without *will*, we are automatons, incapable of autonomy, unable to transform ideas into intention and practice. Errors occur at critical moments. Concentration may lapse; anticipation fail, reaction over-reacts. *Will* needs consideration of purpose in action, balance, integration in public, political, personal life; inseparable to each other: integrated.

IX 4 ii Ability: Innate, Inclined

Consciousness of ability is realised in activities successfully performed. Experience and knowledge improves cultivation and releases potential to discover and do; to learn from and communicate, teach, what is effectively achieved. Urge to survive, curiosity to learn, to live and to live well are formative, formidable motives.

Immediate need prompts *will*. Inability to *will* at that moment is incapable. Disability infers loss. A person disabled has become unable to deal with some necessity. Rehabilitation refers to 'habitation', place occupied, inhabited. 'Habit' is a garment worn for a particular purpose, a nun's habit for vocation, a 'riding habit'. In behaviour, a good or bad habit is routine ability to live and work or fail to do so. Habitat refers to place; conditions where living creatures, plants and animals, are usually to be found: beavers, water-rats, dragonflies near ponds, lakes, rivers; snakes in grass, squirrels in or near trees, nut-trees; marsh-grass and marsh marigolds on marshes. Human personal habitat, occupancy, connects habit and ability with occupation, living and working, doing, often separated in many contemporary lives. Commuting to work, shop, study involves travel.

Ability, innate natural endowment, is waiting to be activated, realised, experienced, trained and educated. Wondering where ability comes from considers possible sources: 'natural endowment', inherited and developed. Personification of original **WILL**, source of energy, creative and destructive, invites nomination. To differentiate alternatives, better or worse, good and evil coexist in individuals and recognise *will* as essence of innate ability to do or not to do. Opposing *will*, positive or negative ill-will alternates with good, with innocent alternatives, virtuous decisions contingent on *will*.

Confidence, self-confidence in personal ability, encourages communication and **trust** in action and an open attitude to the outside world, to other people. Courage is nourished by encouragement, trust and good-will. Inability, sometimes inertia, may be uncertainty, lack of energy, absence of stimulus, support, encouragement. Ability cannot be liberated into action unless energy is available for dynamic activity. The language of applied mathematics and physics identifies impersonal sources of energy, *heat, light, sound; time* and *space*, infinite in astronomy and cosmology; microcosmic in structures of matter. Logos, nominated original, first word of creative, life giving, energising *power* begets, seeds, word, language. Logic, logistics, the-ologies of theology, are as it were 'logic' of 'theos', creator. Order and chaos, construction and destruction continue: light overcomes darkness, illuminates *will* to liberate ability. Dis-ease, discomfort, promote *desire* to be comfortable again. Receiving *comfort*, comforting, comforted revives well-being. Ability to comfort, to nourish, sustain, 'look after', is fundamental to good parents with children and promotes commitment, profession to *nurse*, to encourage learning in any direction indicated by need and conscious ability to *minister* to it.

A performative utterance is word/act: I will, I promise, swear, value, bequeath, give, deny, love. Without *will* to do, to perform, there is no true performative. To lie, betray, cheat are infelicities, unhappy. To avoid, be prevented, upsets *will* to do. Plausible persons 'play for time', deceive, sometimes with words.

Key, symbol, provide metaphor; metaphysical analogy and actual reality. The key of a *lock* enables its holder to *lock* and unlock, open and enter; lock up, lock out, lock in. Keys of maps show symbols of features mapped: colours for land, high and low, blue water; green, brown, usual for vegetation; many colours for rocks, geology. Coastlines show tide-lines, estuaries, rivers; cliffs, headlands, sandbanks, sand dunes. Lighthouses, buoys, underwater contours marking passages for vessels, guidance to navigators.

IX 4 iii Cultivation

Cultivation of plants, flowers, trees for wood, fruit, shade, beauty is *work* of gardener, domestic, commercial, and farmer for food: other motives. Experience increases knowledge, skilfully applied, to make the best of natural conditions with human ingenuity, practical then systematic, creative, artistic, dedicated energy to cultivate, *supply*, enjoy. Personal effort stimulates available ability, cultivated to cultivate, to increase fruitful knowledge, fruitful performance and pleasure flourishing together; *desire* and achievement for needs, desires, urges stimulated and supplied. Such fulfilment accumulates year after years, centuries, millennia of agriculture and horticulture: observation, experiment, trial and error success.

Cultivation: ground prepared and planted distinguishes specialist functions: sowing, hoeing, weeding, reaped in nursery, garden and farm; horticulture and agriculture: reaped and harvested. These translate into personal culture: common sense, customs, manners cultivated in behaviour. Speech and writing, literacy, accelerate mind towards intellectual development. Generalised subjects: Arts and Sciences, Classics and Mathematics, Natural and Moral Philosophy, recognised, diversify and specialise within themselves. Frontiers between specialist studies need not prevent or inhibit cross-fertilisation. Fellows of colleges with high table, 'combination', senior common room, hear and learn of others' work.

Competition for 'degree' courses, increasingly early specialisation, leads some schools to offer 'general studies' and some universities, 'foundation courses'. 'Thematic' studies, topics such as medicine, war, revolution, quasi-historical, are intended to cross-fertilise and 'integrate'. Double specialisation in mathematics and philosophy; triple such as philosophy, politics and economics, cultivate 'inter-disciplinary' understanding.

Diversity enhances unity: deep-seated tensions, enmities, are contained. Wider contexts of racial hatred, social and gender prejudice, intense and exaggerated religious differences, territorial disputes, cause distress, dissension, outbursts of violence. Appeal from local jurisdiction, law and judgment, to International Law and Courts is increasing. Administered at the Hague, this branch of the United Nations is universal in so far as it is accepted. The concept of the rule of law, far reaching, but disregarded by Basque separatists, Chechen rebels, the IRA, al-Qaeda: terrorists, violent dissidents, cultural differences, religious fanatics among them, fight for their rights, territorial claims, demands, by violent subversivion, not war as such, nor constitutional effort.

IX 4 iv Co-operation

The divinities, gods and goddesses of the Classical world were believed to co-operate with each other and with humanity, but recognised rivalry, jealousy and enmity. Heroic actions, deeds by a man or woman empowered by superhuman strength, were attributed to the god or goddess who personified that strength. A hero, such as Heracles, might be worshipped; regarded with collective reverence for exceptional strength; as an example that encouraged others. Zeus, father of gods, was not a human hero nor was Heracles a god. The goddess Nemesis, daughter of night, eluded pursuit by Zeus. Her name became associated with retribution. Apollo and Aphrodite, Mars and Venus inspired sculptures and paintings. Their cults did not stimulate doctrines and moral systems as such. Philosophical questions were considered among philosophers engaged in disputation rather than co-operation. Clear light of reason dispelled superstition but a common enemy, an invader, ignited will to repel, defend, fight to maintain independence by co-operation.

Will to serve, to co-operate, obey, 'fit in', engages *will* to be led, commanded, ordered. 'Forces' trained to defend and maintain peace are ready to be mobilised to fight in war. Volunteers are added to by conscripts when needed, but deeply rooted local regiments maintain their shire, county, regional connections: e.g. the Cheshires, the Black Watch.

Voluntary movements adopt rules to encourage order necessary for effective cooperation, such as the Red Cross and St John Ambulance, Women's Institutes, sports clubs. Trade unions, voluntary, soon became so powerful that governments legislated to restrict their activities. Thus, the Labour Representative Council: Unions, Fabian Socialists, 'Co-operatives' and 'Independents' determined to achieve representation in the House of Commons, 'Old Labour'. Police forces have rules and discipline procedures of their own. Borderline cases may reach beyond jurisdiction of British courts faced with terrorists. The USA, after 9/11, resorted to Guantanamo Bay, directly against principles of liberty and due process.

An organised co-operative, united in ideals and purposes, that become a politically effective party is likely to aim to achieve strict discipline, a 'one party' state. A dictatorial leader *will* impose conditions free cooperation: slavery in Mugabe's Zimbabwe. Heads and Hearts comply until misery, systematic failure, arouses oppressed persons to overthrow dictators, tyrants.

IX 4 v Slavery

WILL begins and ends with possibilities of liberty and freedom, bondage and slavery. Imprisonment fails to destroy this vision and capability. Privation, ignorance, obsession, addiction, vice, helpless despair challenge it. **Will** to co-operate is, by definition, more agreeable, productive and constructive than forced or coerced. A society that has cultivated and achieved expectation of liberty would be foolish to take it for granted. Each personal citadel of will flourishes with recognition and respect. Excessive interference, evident corruption, forfeit respect for constituted authority, power accountable. Call for *change* becomes insistent; peacefully, without violence.

Slavery was customary in antiquity. Freedom from burdensome necessities was enjoyed by the few who owned and depended on slaves. Leisure to cultivate interests, pleasures, delights, skills, abilities, to order cultivate, build; and enjoy time to think, philosophise, compose, govern, discover, *fight* and *find* interests which led to high achievement. Exceptional 'slaves' became trusted, trained, educated and powerful in serving their master. Prosperous Greek farmers who took to city life would leave a trusted slave in charge to '*run*' their estate. Joseph, son of Israel, sold into slavery, became surrogate Pharaoh, effective ruler of Egypt. (*Genesis* 39-40.)

A slave is subject to another's will having been bought, captured, inherited, compelled to accept enslavement. An 'owner' may delegate to a slave-master. A slave lives in personal, social, economic imprisonment without redress, without recourse to law. Culture of subservience, lack of education, persists for a time after abolition. Nevertheless, a person bought or sold into slavery does not always become a soul enslaved. Twentieth century prisons, labour and death camps, include accounts of survival despite cruelty, abuse, humiliation; every form of physical, emotional and moral suffering. Solzhenitsyn's novels of the Gulag, Primo Levi's autobiography of survival in a Nazi death-camp, Nelson Mandela, twenty-seven year's imprisoned on Robben Island, bear witness.

Personal bondage, body slavery, was taken for granted in ancient society. The Slavi were a tribe who lived on the banks of the Dneiper; 'slav' meant noble, illustrious, and they spread across Europe. The Romans made them captive servants, slaves. 'Angles' were late arrivals in Roman slave markets. There were 'slaves' in China, long before Israel, Greece and Rome.

Enslavement can be a condition of body, heart, mind, *will* and spirit; each and all levels of human experience, in or out of servitude but systematic slavery authorises 'ownership'. A disobedient slave could be compelled by physical subjection, force, torment, released by death.

Manufacturing tends to engender economic slavery, poverty exploited, 'sweat-shops'. Poverty makes any means of survival better than none. Political dictatorship without recourse to justice becomes tyranny. Nazi concentration camps, designed to liquidate opponents of any persuasion, became killing places; the 'ultimate solution' for those who resisted, usually Jewish or Christian, by race, tradition, belief; known, suspected and feared to oppose the 'new order'.

Persons enslaved can continue to think clearly, discern truly even when bodily life is confined by servitude. Faith, hope, love, remembered, sustain spirit of independence in mind, *will*, soul. Some survive with astonishing resilience and fortitude to become regarded as saints.

Ignorance and indifference, forms of enslavement, immunise *will* to act. Domination asserted as customary uses, abuses, power. Cruelty, meanness, ruthless use of force, reigns of terror, make regimes so feared that few find *will*, courage, to dare to resist.

Great enterprises: creative, defensive, include memorials to death and life: pyramids in Egypt; gardens, great gates, high structures in Assyria, Babylon, Persia; the Great Wall of China; Temples, Theatres, Sports stadia were built by slaves. Hadrian and the Antonine walls in north Britain under Roman occupation were built for defence. Armies under command did, still do, include conscripts in times of war.

Local labour, sometimes, is indented. **Will to work and conditions of employment have become an area of law as important as life, liberty and property; all are involved and dependent on *WORK*, free, ordered, compelled, enslaved.**

The abolition of Slavery in British territories, in 1833, came centuries after feudal bonds were dissolved. 'Manumission' derived from Roman slave-owners who gave a slave the hand of freedom. In the USA, states' rights to maintain or abolish slavery provoked civil war intended to maintain the Union from states willing to secede. A long, slow process towards genuine emancipation followed. Souls oppressed who know faith and hope make music, songs: 'Negro spirituals', hymns, folk songs of slaves with superb rhythmic melodies; words wrung out of misery; 'soul' music. Paul Robeson's profound, resonant voice; Michael Tippet's compositions and arrangements in 'A Child of our Time' communicate and maintain understanding. Martin Luther King, Rosa Park are heroic: Condaleeza Rice; a brilliant inheritor and beneficiary.

Slavery persists. Illegal immigrants in the UK, unprotected but for the conscience of employers and vigilant local inspectors, are enslaved although not 'owned'. Some domestic workers, often women, are 'prostituted' under conditions indistinguishable from slavery.

The British Constitution embodies custom, convention and law evolved during centuries since Roman occupation to safeguard people from abuse of power. John Philpot Curran, speaking on the election of the Lord Mayor of Dublin 1790: 'The condition upon which God hath given liberty to man is eternal vigilance; which condition if he break, servitude is at once the consequence of his crime, and the punishment of his guilt.' Often quoted as 'the price of liberty is eternal vigilance' this is an enduring principle. 'Rule Britannia' is more than militant nationalist jingo. Head and heart of Jesus Christ is liberty of **TRUST, HOPE, LOVE**.

Government by consent benefits from consensus, not easily achieved. Referenda test opinion but do not substitute for responsible representation and accountability to informed, critical debate. Power with responsibility is at the heart of personal *will*, public and private. Referenda assume every voter to be qualified and willing to decide. Slogans such as 'the people's decision', appropriate for popularity polls, shift and shelve responsibility away from representatives elected to contribute to and hear policy explained and debated. Regard and respect for well tried constitutional form; government by consent of Parliament: representatives in touch with their constituents and advised by impartial experts, civil servants, is weakened by referenda. Propaganda, ever an instrument of encouragement, propagates and cultivates serious thoughtful education stemming from scholarly erudition, is not superficial, partial presentation, notorious 'spin'. Monarchs, prime ministers, presidents, dictators, are tempted to confuse their personal will for power; as for the 'common good'. Having achieved and enjoyed power does not incline a ruler to withdraw willingly. Extension of the franchise and the rise of political parties enable peaceful change, usually the result of general elections, and guard against this danger. Some succumb to temptations of 'sleaze', especially if power of patronage disregards well tried conventions: principles of liberty and consent, damages collective responsibility for good government.

Inclination to dominate and exploit persists. The 1832 Reform Bill resulted in the election of a House of Commons ready to listen to the voice of William Wilberforce and others who were leading a cultural shift to regard people, including slaves, 'unskilled' workers, as able themselves and capable of good-will, kindness; ill-will, greed. Emancipation encouraged, as it continues to encourage, opportunity and quality of work not coerced with violence. Employment of young children; excessive hours of work became unlawful after the Factory Acts, and inspection of working conditions was introduced. Revival of faith, led by John and Charles Wesley, the 'Clapham Sect' (Wilberforce and others), Charles Simeon of Cambridge, the 'Oxford Apostles', Charles Kingsley, strengthened consciousness of conscience and increased concern for the evil of economic, emotional, intellectual and moral enslavement: poverty, misery, ignorance and much crime.

IX 4 vi Will to Serve and Achieve

Aladdin's magic lamp, when rubbed, summoned the genii to appear and say: 'What is your will, master?' Palaces and great wealth were Aladdin's until he lost the lamp. Midas, Gyges, Croesus, invoked power from gods to gather gold but were undone by their greed. Hercules' strength brought achievement through heroic courage, labour, not magical. Aesop's *Fables* and Ovid's *Metamorphoses* disclose parable and allegory experienced; animal, plant and human beings mixing wisdom and folly, desire, illusion, effort; destined to fail. Narcissus, exceptionally beautiful, fell in love with his own reflection seen in a still pool. He became a flower. Echo loved him but her words, unheard, returned to her, unanswered.

Liberty with responsibility presents opportunity for personal metamorphosis to genuine independence. The ideal of *will* to serve rather than to dominate, to give way, give away, for the sake of another person, cause, purpose, transcends limits of self-interest, self-will.

Early writers convey fear of unexpected metamorphosis. A snake turned to stone (*Iliad* 2. 319.) Moses staff becomes a serpent; then returns to its original form (*Exodus* 4. 1-4.) Power to cause such change was mysterious, awful, unaccountable, terrifying. Magic power might make sense of such occurrences. Magicians, witches were feared agents and could exploit that fear. Priest and priestesses suspected, sometimes respected, for powerful connection to super-human will, gods and goddesses capable of intervention. Rivalry among immortals vented on mortals could cause retribution. Persons of outstanding ability, virtue and strength were (are) challenged. Personal courage and skill led to heroic achievement assisted by super-human help: Perseus slayed Medusa to release Andromeda, daughter of Cassiopaeia. Stars and constellations commemorate heroic exploits; mortals endowed with immortality; but gods could be jealous.

Babylonian astronomy was known in neighbouring Mediterranean lands. Months, 'moonths' originated from the Hebrew calendar. Seed-time and harvest, spring sowing growth, reaping, repeating annually. Functions associated with life, necessities and living creatures were projected into the 'heavens' as twelve signs of the Zodiac, seasonally visible in the night sky, also came from Mesopotamia, but early Greek sense of destiny was not astrological. Homer's epics; classic poetic dramas (Euripides, Aeschylus, Sophocles); philosophy (Plato, Socrates, Aristotle) depict and reflect disaster: fear, terror, anguish, tragedy not as personal failure but as ineluctable destiny, inescapable, relieved by comedy to assist digestion, catharsis. Ovid's *Metamorphoses* disclose fatalism, suffering, inevitability. Consequences invite judgment: error seen as part of irredeemable destiny. Ceres lost her daughter Persephone to Pluto who released her each spring, for ploughing, sowing, growing, annual ritual, but Persephone had to return each year to Pluto: birth, death and rebirth re-enacted.

To propose a general theory of *will* pre-supposes bestowal of *will*, potential inner-freedom to enquire, discover, intend, resolve, decide and do, accompanies outward liberty to act in personal and communal contexts is universal human experience. When action achieves intended purpose it succeeds; if not, it fails. Both inward and outward potential of *will* are limited by constraints repeatedly discussed here: time and place, contexts, ability, energy and so on. Consequences are not always as intended, planned, hoped. Responsibility involves questions of value, criteria in purpose, conscience. What, if any, are secrets of success? Who and what does *will* serve? When and how does your, my, personal interest, purposes, objects, learn to see and to cultivate objective purposes, beyond our own?

*How may human nature, born and reared in natural experience, be moved to recognise higher purposes determined and **willed**?*

Education in and from nature was, is, foundation upon which survival, cultivation, propagation, grows, transmits remembered knowledge; skill and wisdom through persons who themselves contribute, cultivate, add and hand on to successors.

Plato considered the education of rulers as pre-eminently concerned for the good; for good government. *FORM* is formidable for *ORDER; MIND*, makes *SENSE* of SENSES: wisdom to *RULE* requires COURAGE and HUMILITY. **Donouns** integrate *ACT* at every level. Augustine describes himself divided between desire for self-gratification, ambition, and **will** for control. Paul, particularly wrote to Romans who, like Hebrews, were potent inheritors of Law. This letter was read, studied, and profoundly influential in Augustine's education. **Will** imprisoned, then liberated, is a recurring theme. Augustine learned that invitation to **trust** offers **grace** to accept what his own **will** could not itself achieve. Augustine's need for healing brought intense desire for forgiveness, mercy, grace. Vision of love, infinite divine love, showed him his helplessness. Humble, penitent, Augustine prayed for and found faith which brought mercy, forgiveness, deliverance, to his tormented heart, hungry mind, and helpless **WILL**. (*Confessions* VIII.) These two accounts of conversions, Saul baptised PAUL: AUGUSTINE, baptised by AMBROSE at Milan, continue to influence and educate **WILL**. To need, long to know, of and experience, **TRUST**, opens head and heart to **mercy**, forgiveness and liberty, the **grace** of God.

This New life involves dual citizenship: City of God and city of man. Vocation to serve the former engages **will**, effort to transform the latter: 'Thy kingdom come, on earth as it is in heaven'. Profession of faith engages **will**, good-will, in simple, personal ways, to serve. To grow, to experience **light** of **grace** unites head and heart, in ever present presence of the Comforter. Fresh words, true to new experience and knowledge, regenerate wisdom for good when heard, read, absorbed, digested: **will** responding to education.

IX 4 vii Will for Good

The prior question: 'is **will** educable?' continues to challenge you, me, anyone. Is it true to pre-suppose curiosity to mean desire for good?

Two stages: *first*, knowing good from evil and *second*, finding **will** for good. Without these, knowledge is detached from responsibility. Instructive training-courses in shooting communicate skill, 'know-how', without responsibility as to use. Ability to fire a gun, to shoot accurately, does not involve murder. Defence includes self-defence, warning shots, need for food, pest control: responsible use depends on intended purpose.

Education is intended to enable a student to reach a stage beyond which she or he can proceed themselves. *Will* is beginning, continuity and end. Few ever complete or perfect their education. 'Good' teaching, encouraging and constructive, leads pupils, students, to independent thought and responsible action. *Will* is tested in practicalities, in reality, not in fantasy, make-believe. Responsible action is up to you, to me in private and public, at, on, any stage. These words reflect consciousness of weakness, failures, folly, inadequacy.

If you, I, are conscious of *will* and sensitive to *will* other than our own, this question opens every level of experience and knowledge. Discovering what is true or false, good rather than evil, discerns mixtures, overlaps between them – paradox again. Intelligence informs mind and inclination of heart influences, moves **will**. Singly and together, assumptions are challenged and alternatives considered. INTELLECT functions through language, **WILL** to investigate ideas, insights, uses words, language, but words without knowing good and evil, true and false, lack sense, meaning, criteria of value, intention. (*Job.* 35 16.)

Inward and outward battles of *will* occur. Life tests *will*: parent and child, fraternal rivalry, friend and friend, competitors, foe to fight in dangers, rehearsed in games, contests; learning, preparing to support and defend purpose, commitment. Head and heart: doubt and faith; fear, despair and hope; hates and loves, *love itself moves will*. Knowing good and evil open questions, disclose problems, challenges, deepening realities, motive for willing obedience and disobedience, beyond 'choice'. Silent reflections; unspeakable until uttered, sung, voiced in words of prayer, emerge from deep seated needy *will*, fear, misery, beseeching; *hope*.

Discussion of *will* and belief, affirmed recognition of faith, confidence, trust as ground and inspiration of education: learning and believing. (See **IX 3 v.**) Fundamental (mental-funding) need not be or become inflexible, constricting 'fundamentalism'. **IX 4** approaches the prior question in four ways: first, motive; second, questions of control; third, indulgence; fourth, HELP.

IX 4 viii Motive

Why? What for? For what purpose? Motive prompts *will* to do, to consider how, where and when to *act*, to *plan* action. Is realisation of order peculiar to particular cultures or is it universal among humanity? Instinctive impulsive reactions, acts, may not be controlled or controllable. Conformity with or without conviction, apparent contentment, may *disguise dissent*: endangering peace.

Questions inwardly discussed often remain unspoken especially when subject to another *will*. To watch, wonder, consider, criticise, admire can prompt attempt to conform, imitate; to hope to succeed encouraged by seeing success while tempted to be discouraged by failure. Appetite for what is new, to learn and to do, is awakened by curiosity. Absence of interest, poverty, emptiness, makes survival a struggle.

Enslavement to good; service freely given is performed in liberty. Disease, ignorance, poverty, death continue; sufferers and observers of suffering *fight* for better conditions, less pain, greater opportunities, sufficiency, survival, simple enjoyment, *comfort*, happiness. This is formidable paradox: *Faith engenders opposite, opposing insights:* disagreement, conflict, bloodshed, bitter divisions often 'justified' by high motive: temptation to justify end to justify means. Motive releases unsuspected energy, new hope. Individual influence, negative and positive, stimulates development. **Delight** in simple things includes solving problems, easing difficulties. Opportunities are often uneven; extremely inequitable, make envy a powerful motive. The greater the privilege, the greater the burden of responsibility to offer, share and enjoy. Delight and pleasure are remembered together with misery, pain distress. Appeal to experiences stored in memory provides motives for good and ill. Personal memory is supplemented by family, larger groups, 'folk' memories over long periods among people who cherish their history.

The idea of liberty as responsibility offers opportunity for personal metamorphoses; trusted independence; to trust and be trusted, for good. This cannot be guaranteed. **WILL** and **TRUST** *fuse* unless *will* refuses, declines to engage in the agony of accepting responsibility.

One Deity whose voice, once heard, must be obeyed is central in Hebrew Scriptures. Creation 'in the beginning' formed and ordered light, water, celestial and terrestrial matter, time and seasons, vegetation, water creatures, birds and animals and human being, a man and a woman. Adam and Eve, archetype first pair, were not writing a diary of life in the Garden of Eden where peace, plenty and pleasure were enjoyed. Two trees were envisaged: the tree of life and the tree of the knowledge of good and evil whose fruit was forbidden. The serpent, alternate voice, 'evil one', told Eve that it was harmless. Eve tasted, and shared it with Adam. When they ate the apple of the tree of the knowledge of good and evil, they became burdened with responsibility and labour; mortal need to work to live, to tame the wilderness, know pain, sorrow, rage; fratricide between their sons, Cain and Abel. Catastrophic flood expressed the Creator's sorrow with disobedience of humankind; and determination to wash them away. Noah, one good man, was 'found faithful'; instructed to build a vessel, the Ark, to save his family plus pairs of every living creature from the flood: as punishment. (*Genesis* 6.5-8.22.) The flood abated; the dove sent out from the ark 'found no rest for the sole of her foot' and returned. Released again, she returned with an olive leaf and did not return the third time. Noah knew that the means of life were restored. The rainbow, manifestation of promise, bridged earth and heaven, sun through rain separating light in the exquisite beauty of the spectrum; enduring symbol, verification event. Noah understood the meaning without scientific explanation. Thought and research disclose how this miracle of creation is achieved.

Abraham, living in the flood-prone land of Chaldea, believed that a better land, space for progeny, awaited him in the north. He travelled, sure this inner voice was God's *promise*, was found faithful, obedient, even willing to sacrifice his only son, Isaac (*Genesis* 22), a shocking, archetypal test. Abraham believed God's *promise* that his 'seed' would 'multiply as the stars of heaven and as the sand on the sea shore' realised in descendents: Isaac, Jacob (Israel and sons). Joseph, the dreamer, particularly loved by his father, aroused his brothers' jealousy. They planned Joseph's death but were persuaded by Reuben, the eldest, to leave him in a pit, dressed in his coat of many colours given by their father. Passing traders found Joseph and sold him into slavery in Egypt. Interpretation of dreams raised him high at Pharaoh's court. He foresaw famine and received authority to *rule* and *plan* food supplies. Under Joseph the Hebrews multiplied, were hated and enslaved; their sons killed at birth. Saved by one: Moses, brought up at court, who led them out after the final plague, first Passover, to return to the 'promised land'. Discontent led to quarrels and doubts as they journeyed. Moses had to *judge* but needed criteria. Jethro, his father-in-law, advised him to pray for guidance. (*Exodus* 13. 18.)

The account of law revealed on Mount Sinai is powerful formulation of God's (Jehovah's) *WILL*. (*Exodus* 22.) A 'tabernacle' containing these Ten Commandments engraved on tablets of stone was carried during return to the 'promised land'. Judges could not ensure good behaviour, according to the law of Moses, and called for a King.

Saul was anointed King, but envied and hated David, popular hero, poet, skilled in war, but vulnerable to Bathsheba. Their son Solomon, wise judge, famed ruler, built the Temple to hold the 'Ark of the Covenant' containing the written Law. (*1 Kings* 8. 1-9.) God's presence and **WILL** expressed in the commandments led to high priestly ritual, earlier and different from Athenians honouring Athena at the Parthenon. Saul was succeeded by David, then Solomon, undone by excess (300 wives, 700 concubines). Prophets such as Elijah, remembered Call and Promise, Covenant, demanded rededication supported by drama on Mount Carmel. Solomon's Kingdom split. Enemies attacked, conquered, and Hebrews were exiled 'by the waters of Babylon'. Their return inspired effort to rediscover divine purpose: the *will* of Jehovah. The walls of Jerusalem, the Temple, were rebuilt. Scribes, schooled, searched texts to rediscover the law and the history of the Patriarchs.

Hebrew literature, study and scholarship, central in foundation and continuity of Christianity, envisages and promotes unshakeable commitment to *promise, trust;* response of those 'chosen'. Christ's call, universal, inclusive to all who believe: whose faith and work seeks and realises the new Kingdom, 'in' but not 'of' this world. Israel's history, exclusive, encompasses experience of obedience and disobedience; exile, persecution, diaspora of people determined to survive, maintain identity in tightly knit communities, self-protective, unreceptive to persons of different race and faith: 'gentiles'. Marrying 'out' meant expulsion from the family. 'Ghettos' did not obviate common ground of 'Judeo/Christian' culture but led many to deny and repudiate it. In Israel, as in Greece, earlier memory, and history, is in thousands rather than hundreds of years: millennia.

The impact and spread of the gospel, good news of Jesus Christ, includes epic journeys, controversies, extremes of glorious and appalling behaviour; blazing bitter rows, schisms, persecutions, violations of the gospel of love and peace co-existing with gentle, virtuous, saintly, heroic martyrdoms. Realisation of failure, inadequacy, *shame* recognised in mind, deep need, lead to penitence. Mercy, forgiveness, *grace* for renewal brings peace of soul out of anguish, anger, *shame*, to look for, find, believe and accept God's *will*. Personal vocation: apostolic, evangelistic (evangel as good news) reconciliation, new birth; sacramental, pastoral care, healing and teaching, continue among Christians who celebrate together and support one another. Foundations of vocation and profession empowered and sustained by faith, hope and love; good over evil. Acknowledging need begins with recognising personal fault: calling, praying, beseeching help. Language of faith experience includes absorptions and adaptations of Hebrew, Greek and Latin words. **Sin**, more a moral and theological concept than crime, (illegal), continues in 'sin-bin'. 'Episcopal', 'diaconate', 'apostolic', 'eschatology', continue from Greek. 'Wicked', serious, is used for an amusing way out. Good and evil, dialogue in mind and tension in **will**, feature everywhere, every day, in moral consciousness. Psalms, verses, poems become hymns. 'Guide me, oh thou Great Jehovah' (*Cwm Rhonnda*), Bunyan's Pilgrim's song: sees life as a hazardous journey across Jordan into Promised Land. Early Christian Latin verse, *Veni Creator Spiritus*, calls for inspiration, mystical energy and power; indwelling presence of the Holy Spirit, as in St Patrick's Breastplate. The shield of faith quenches fiery darts, temptations, to wickedness. Lovers hunger for the beloved presence. Christ promises the Comforter, healing power, ever-present. Faith brings this experience: knows this reality.

'Chrism', Greek word for 'anointing' (usually with olive oil mixed with balsam) signified exceptional favour, blessing, 'chosen one'. Followers, disciples, friends, heard Christ's words and witnessed sick persons healed. Peter, James and John, the three closest, were asked: 'Who do men say that I am?' and 'Who do you say that I am?' (*Mark* 8. 27-29.) Peter's answered: 'Thou are the Christ'. What did, does, this mean? Son of Mary? Son of David? Son of Man? Son of God? Anointed, chosen one? Heart and mind voice belief. Simon Peter, first to affirm, later denied knowing Jesus. (*Matthew* 26. 69-76). Peter, the 'ROCK', led the early church from Jerusalem to Rome, and was martyred there.

John records Jesus' saying 'I and my Father are One' (*John* 10. 30), continuing presence the Holy Ghost, the Comforter, **grace** with them, faithful for ever. (*John* 14. 16.) Jewish conviction that God is One (*Exodus* 20. 2-6) follows the first commandment given, received, by Moses. At Athens, Paul was asked to explain 'new doctrine'. (*Acts* 17. 19.) Looking at statues, imagined images, there on Mars Hill, he sees one 'to the unknown God'. This he says, is the One 'in whom we live and move and have our being; as certain of your own poets have said'. (*Acts* 17. 23-28.) Resurrection of Christ, the Son, is met with scepticism, but they agree to hear Paul again. Christian scholars in the second and third centuries in Alexandria, led by Clement and Origen, who had already gathered texts into the New Testament: Gospels, Acts, Letters, faced the question: could one Divine person be three? Father, Son, Holy Ghost, equal, one in Trinity? Who was precedent, who dependent? Arius doubted the concept and doctrine of the Trinity. Search proceeded towards consensus agreement; common mind; an enduring controversy.

IX 4 ix Control

Search for a general theory of *will* includes recognising inner freedom to *trust*, believe, decide; and outward liberty to *act*; implosive and explosive dynamics. **Control** needed may be exercised in personal and communal contexts. Respect for others' liberty enjoins consultation. Upward reference, if available, authorises and shares responsibility for decisions made and done. Downward directions, 'directors', expect and are expected to direct, may add controllers intended to control, 'executives', chains of persons who manage and/or are managed. Manage is NOT a **donoun**.

Traditions of responsible liberty look for agreement; *consent*, not 'dictat'. This distinguishes 'democratic' from 'autocratic' systems. Looking far back for sources of belief and early views of power shows superstition, inspiration, and systemisation into constitutions searching for effective *control*. Military victory is a well-trodden path to power, ancient and modern. Divine authority, believed or not, is invoked, used — abused — to enhance the *will* of rulers, governments, in the eyes of the people governed. This present world of high-tech communications assists social, economic, political systems which have contrasting methods of order. Different wars to *rule* and *control* conflict or promote them. Nevertheless, problems of organisation in communities continue to need personal moral decisions. Matters of life and death, danger and survival, lawlessness and law, oscillate between ignorance, superstition, *fear*, need illumination of reasoning belief. (See **XIII I i.**)

A ship's captain accepts information, advice, support and gives orders. Command directly disobeyed, is mutiny. The chief pilot controls an aeroplane; a driver controls the vehicle driven. Error or failures cause accidents. Stalin, ruler of Soviet Russia, developed networks of agents, KGB, to secure his power in the name of communist 'orthodoxy', conformity and obedience. Soviet espionage and western counter espionage extended under *'Control'*, ringmaster of 'the Circus' in John Le Carré's language. British MPs are expected to conform to their party 'whip', the 'party line'. A paper 'requests attendance' at debates, particularly at 'divisions', and is called a whip. 'Withdrawal of the whip' suspends membership from a parliamentary party, not from the House itself, when an MP habitually disregards the Whip. A 'free' vote accepts MPs vote from personal opinion, persuasion, belief and conscience. The 'age of consent' for behaviour with social, economic, legal and moral consequences has called for a 'free' vote, without a 'whip'. Conflict continues on elemental questions: abortion, euthanasia, limits of welfare, law, order, health and education.

IX 4 x Indulgence

To act indulgently requires personal freedom to indulge. Free to do what is expected, hoped, believed to be delightful, perhaps for the first time, pleasure desired and fulfilled in experience, is likely to be sought, indulged in, repeatedly. *Will* finds energy for instinctive needs; appetites demand necessities. Pleasure experienced inclines *will* to repeat, to indulge for enjoyment. Appetites of need are enjoyable. Hunger in infants is necessity, not indulgence, but conscious enjoyment grows, develops with experience.

Pleasure enhanced with knowledge and understanding, cultivated, refines. Deprivation, frustration, suppression, inhibition complicate spontaneity. Over-indulgence, surfeit, can spoil pleasure and destroy *will* to *control*. Uninhibited, insensitive indulgence loosens capability for self-restraint so that unbridled instinct becomes self-destructive and dangerous to others. An 'indulgent attitude', at best, is pleasing, courteous, kindly, complaisant, inclined to favour, able and willing to enjoy. To 'humour' someone suggests to play along; to yield without restraint or control. *Will*: self-will, *will* for others, positive and negative; is the perennial human dilemma.

Education for good is affirmative, encouraged, cultivated knowledge and experience of joy and delight. *LIGHT*, physical, mental, emotional and moral disclosure; eyes open to vision, *purpose*, meaning and *hope*. Easier written than realised and received. Enthusiasm communicates confidence; love of 'whatsoever things are good...' wary of dangers: not so good, evil. To recognise and appreciate value is *light* of knowing good; essential realised good; value in every *sense*. *Will* to act: to *desire*, prefer, indulge, with *control* is experienced in, for and from knowing good or ill; valuing; preferring good.

Practicalities express principles: musical and mathematical, discovered in natural and in moral sciences; not good or evil in themselves but used or abused in action. Education aims to cultivate understanding, evaluation, preservation, necessary destruction. Paradoxes of life and death, nature and civility, offer opportunity for use or abuse. Generous love may disguise self-indulgence and express profound sacrifice. Some seek and find refuge in extreme alternatives: isolation, devotion, seclusion, or dedicated 'socialising', 'net-working', to pursue riches and power. Material prosperity, peace and plenty in moderation, are achievements of culture and civilisation, but greed, lust indulged, is not good.

Good fortune with good-will relieves, assists people in adversity, poverty. To indulge includes gratifying, enjoying, appreciating simple and subtle pleasure, unspoiled, intensified when shared: happiness unexpected rather than pursued;

recognised here and now. It is illusion and delusion of materialism that money 'buys' happiness. Hearts and heads, desires and thoughts, must distinguish superficial satisfaction of appetite from original balance of deep-seated **need**. Failure to **integrate** causes confusion. Free to do right for wrong reasons or wrong for good reason bewilders, undermines confidence, causes difficulty to see clearly and truly. Ideas of perfection, harnessed to real possibility, promote effort evaluate, decide, act wisely and well. Inescapable compromise may limit the best. Uncontrolled demand, greed confused with need, appears to justify entitlement as of right. Affluence and indulgence do not overcome dissatisfaction and a culture of complaining develops.

Pleasure given and received in love changes when believed beyond material liability; immeasurable. 'Love' seen as subject to and limited by material contract is a business arrangement. Wedding, freely agreed, presupposes hopes for glad co-operation, reciprocal pleasure, responsibly procreated at every level, advantage mutually enjoyed. Commitment, with love, fidelity, lifelong, may or may not be believed and promised. Marital discord is commonly caused by tension, conflict of **will**, about material matters: physical indulgence, gratification, money. These represent and express **will**, trust, emotional harmony in prosperity and adversity but intentions, good-will, may conflict. Promises made may or may not be regarded as breakable. If so, they are likely to be broken and marriage to be regarded as failing.

To say that something cannot be had 'for love or money' recognises common ground of desire and ingredients of achieving. Charity begins at home but does not end there. Charity covers 'a multitude of sins'. 'Sin' is a theological concept derived from evil, opposed to highest good. Hurt and offence, dis-ease and dis-comfort are social and personal, but principles of good and evil, evident and real, are sources of law. Crime may not be sin. Many sins are not crimes. An accused person found guilty is sentenced. Punishment differs from retribution, inward suffering, remorse of conscience. Statistics of charges, accusation, conviction, crime and punishment, imprisonment, do not measure motive, intention or virtue. It is difficult to assess moral progress, possibly unwise, undesirable. Students of 'sociology' prefer not to think in such terms. Can human society, 'civilised', dare to discard them as did More in *Utopia* or Butler in *Erewhon*?

Indulge is intended to please, gratify, enjoy, appreciate. Indulgent describes one who indulges. An 'indulgence', noun, objectifies indulging as indulgent action, possibly dangerous, culpable. Unknowns, uncertainties, disruptions, make guarantees unreal. Blame may be attributed as to a debt unpaid. Resort to law, to litigation, increases when societies depend on rights, contract rather than on trust. Attempt to foresee and pre-empt loss due to conflict leads to 'plea bargain': indemnity claimed, paid, intended to restore balance and reopen possibility of good faith; equitable. Plea-bargains are agreed between lawyers, quasi judges, whose judgment accords with law. Without law, judgment lacks authority, authenticity 'Settled out of Court' is agreement to resolve a dispute, the particular case. Plea-bargaining attempts to circumnavigate between prior settlement and uncertain verdict concerning property measured in money, not punishment in purgatory, although suffering occurs.

A word applied to a creditable action for reason other than motive of the act itself includes *shift*, deception, potential bribery, *'fine'* as payment to escape blame. An 'offender' charged may escape through 'false witness'; 'sworn evidence' untrue. Falsification on oath involves 'perjury'; evidence needs proof 'beyond reasonable doubt'. Genuine intention, motive, may be impossible to establish.

Explaining difficulty, failure, requires ingredients discerned. Detectives look for evidence; doctors examine for symptoms; psychotherapists listen for recognitions, motives acknowledged; moralists moralise; confessors hear confessions: stringent self-examination, deep therapy. These functions intertwine, interact. Lawyers endeavour to defend their clients before judges whose function and intention is to administer justice according to law. Attempt to pre-fix judgment is likely to lead to undesirable, dangerous consequences.

Thomas Aquinas (1225-74) entered Benedict's Abbey at Monte Cassino (founded AD 525) aged five, for life. His *Summa Theologica*, systematised reason and faith, philosophical theology for study and instruction, at a time when monasteries were multiplying, cathedrals were being built and crusades embarked on. Moral authority, vital ingredient, of power if government is to advance from tyranny to consent. The question of energising and sustaining goodness concerned Aquinas. Can personal virtue be achieved? Where may head and heart find *integrity*; unity? Thoughtful love, reasoned loving moves towards the light of Divine **grace** believed and experienced sacramentally. Faith links effort with **grace**: pastoral and moral, responsibility with the clergy, the priesthood; but the golden thread of disclosure before Christ is evident in experience of **trust**: known to Hebrew patriarchs, prophets, priests, poets. 'The sacrifices of God are a broken spirit: a broken and contrite heart, O God, thou will not despise'. (*Psalms* 51. 17.) Yearning for **GRACE**; hunger in head and heart, seek nourishment in action, devotion, virtue, beatitude.

Aquinas, 'angelic doctor' and Dante, 'philosophical poet', offer dichotomy between classic and romantic inspiration; divine revelation and human love; **will** transformed through regular practice of faithful vocation, mended, healed, redeemed. Suffering is counterbalanced in joy and mirth, throughout delight experienced. Christ's thinkers digest events and interpret the gospel, 'peace on earth, good will'. Old scholarship renewed through physic, physical, metaphysical expansion engaging theological, philosophic, poetic and musical transports of delight. After having experienced temptation, suffering, alienation, overwhelming at the time; martyrdom for some, deliverance from evil is ultimate, confident hope.

Dante (1265-1321), born in Florence, was energised by reason and love outside monastic life; deeply aware of liberating inspiration revealed in Christ, and intensely cultivated in secluded devotion. *The Divine Comedy*, the title itself a relief after ineluctable tragedy of Greek drama, was completed in exile at Ravenna where Dante died. Hell, purgatory, paradise are envisaged as states, conditions experienced in time and place, among those whose destruction, redemption and hope is described. Accompanied by Virgil, classic personification of Reason, they travel together, descending to lower and lower regions of ever deeper torment. Hell is experienced: witnessed in allegorical landscapes as vivid as John Bunyan's Doubting Castle, Giant Despair, Slough of Despond, House Beautiful whose ruin still stands above the road from Bedford to London. Virgil departs when Dante, crowned and mitred over himself, is ready to ascend the cleansing terraces of Mount Purgatory. Self-examination is assisted by singing angels of virtue appropriate to each terrace of vice. At last, human love is chastened, freed, and Dante is fit to meet Beatrice, in person, at the summit. In Paradise, they ascend together through angelic orders: the Divine Imperium.

Who on earth are true custodians of virtue, goodness, personal and social moral excellence? Who, if anyone, can claim to 'guarantee' forgiveness? Questions asked, answers proposed, believed, accepted, may be found fallible, doubted, discarded. Ignorance and denial often focus on self-absorbed self-interest. Visions of ultimate perfection; objective, aiming for quintessential virtue, affirm sovereignty of good personified as 'almighty God': singular, unique — than which nothing higher can be thought — in monotheistic systems of faith. To offend, be offended, by neighbour, society, self, indicates need for forgiveness. Absent recognition of sovereign good reduces failures to mere shortcomings. No significant person or principle is offended. Penitence reduces to 'apology'. 'Hurt', 'upset', 'inconvenience' lack substance of 'offence' against law, natural, human, divine: but *'Sin'* is deliberate offence, known when considered. 'Error' often occurs in ignorance. Offence offends; subjectively and/or in principle. Extensive knowledge and opportunity multiply the likelihood of ignorance and of error. 'Moral' education adapts when relative, conveniently permissive, less regulative. The other extremity, 'prohibitive', tends to subjugate *will*, suffocate initiative, liberty of love and hate. But 'permissive' implies, requires, 'permission'; from someone, somewhere. Reduced moral responsibility substitutes 'choice' (personal *taste*, convenience) for recognition of right and wrong, good or evil.

Indulgence includes vital ingredient of freedom and at least — perhaps at best — retains rein and harness of virtue, discarded at peril. On a beautiful sunny morning my godfather would rub his hands together and say 'It's a lovely day for the race!' 'Which race?' 'The human race'. Competitive sports: organised athletics, horses, cars, ball games entertain by high performance to *win*. Spectators sublimate personal loyalty and ambition to *support* these efforts and enjoy them vicariously, wholeheartedly.

Fines and inducements, 'sweeteners', are used and abused to strengthen will to succeed, to win. Buying and selling 'Indulgences', pieces of paper promising *pardon*, forgiveness, relief from punishment, have been justified as raising money for good purposes and condemned for treating forgiveness as if can be bought or sold, traded like a commodity. Chaucer's Pardoner summarised his business. (See Appendix **D**.)

Aquinas followed Benedict's *rule* of prayer, thought and work: accepted, obeyed, dedicated, devoted to God's *will* as sovereign good in disciplined habit of life. Dante lived in the City of Florence, rich in monasteries and churches endowed by prosperous merchants, rulers, citizens; a flourishing culture, earthly and heavenly, where Augustine's City of God and Benedict's Rule were well known. Prince and Bishop, guardians of prosperity, law and conscience experienced tension between body and soul, heart and head, earth and heaven.

Vows of poverty, chastity and obedience were, are, intended for life by monks and nuns who accept the *rule* of the *order* joined. Monastic life may look like a refuge from temptation; from impulsive, instinctive passions. Practicalities regulated with prayer, study (indoor work in library, scriptorium) and outdoor work, cultivation, joined to nourish soul and body in chapel and refectory. Need for sustenance, fear of inner instability, hope for peace, usefulness, **control** are reasons for accepting monastic vocation: **vow**. Superior authority, Abbot or Abbess, confessors, spiritual directors, encourage self examination cultivated, observed with intensity, a moral laboratory.

Chaucer's pilgrims tell their tales as they travel. First by function (knight, miller, reeve, cook), later by vocation (prioress, monk) and profession (physician, clerk). Chaucer weaves their patterns of life, individual, communal; into a tapestry of pilgrimage together to Canterbury. The Pardoner's Tale displays systematic avarice from which he lives in luxury. Fear of punishment, here, hereafter in hellfire, is played upon to extort funds from credulous victims: 'But let me briefly make my purpose plain; I preach for nothing but for greed and gain'.

Common motive, in action in the City of London, Wall Street, defunct Bank of Credit and Commerce, Enron, anyone, anywhere, anytime, is tempted to greed; to believe it good. Loss by swindle, confidence trick, lie, cheating, occurs on any scale. **Fear** tempts some to believe they can buy immunity. 'Mis-selling' continues. 'Fool's gold' deceives but the folly is ignorance; the wickedness is in exploiting it. Fear of retribution for guilt, of hell, torment, damnation, terrifies. 'Terror' claims vengeance, retribution. Chaucer's Merchant and Man of Law reflect wide experience, vividly applicable today. The Parson, an enduring presence (evoked by Oliver Goldsmith's country vicar), is described in the Prologue:

> 'I think there never was a better priest...
> Christ and His Twelve Apostles and their lore
> He taught, but followed it himself before.'

The Parson tells no tale about himself but, at Canterbury, he is persuaded to speak. His 'prose-sermon' helps listeners to prepare for confession; to examine themselves for **sin** and for virtue to help and save. (See appendix **D**.) Chaucer examined his own life and writings in 'Retractions', as did Augustine of Hippo.

IX 4 xi Help

Donoun, *help*, checks integrity of **will** in action. This *help* is present, unnoticed, not guaranteed. Realisation is contingent on context, concentration and intention. Genuine motive: ***need, will, cry*** for ***help*** look for and invoke responsive ***will*** to heed that *cry*. Either may fail, be untrue; make listener deaf or indifferent. Aesop's shepherd boy, in sole charge of the sheep, was told to cry 'wolf' when needing help. He cried 'wolf' when frightened, although none was there. When a wolf did appear his cry was ignored. '999' calls are directed to fire brigade, ambulance, police in order for fast *HELP*. *COST* is met from resources, voluntary for sea rescue, lifeboats; compulsory taxation for police, the NHS, not always perfect.

Help **donouns**: *call, cry, need, save, rescue* are uttered in immediate danger. Few activities are without *risk*. Escape from danger occurs with or without help.

Capture, torture, poison, murder are deliberate acts, intentionally performed. They may or may not be crimes, sins. *Sin* is a **donoun**; crime and offence are not. *Call* for *help*, if heard, may or may not be answered effectively, if at all.

Will to help, to save, to *rescue* from danger faced, may mean, in extremity, destroying an enemy, an evil genius: Sherlock Holmes versus Moriarty. *Rescue* offers and provides escape when someone cannot help themselves. SOS calls 'Save Our Souls' from enemy or friend. Courage accompanies risks and dangers, shared.

When, where, how is danger realised? Common sense knowledge emerges from practical experience, outward/inward, warning, encouraging, informing. Learning to *look*, listen, learn, needs encouragement. Signals become recognised, natural and physical, noise, thirst, pain etc prompt initiative. *Smoke* may *alarm; lock* secure; *light* illuminate. Each has positive and negative function. Some risks can be 'underwritten'; fire, floods, burglary but personal betrayal, deceit, is harder to realise and cope with. Expertise and skill develop with training, practice, engaging hands and heads. Values and virtues are vital criteria.

Why is not heart a **donoun**? Obviously it is not a verb, but each life depends on heart beat. Personal *will* does not initiate this. It is given, received, at birth. Heart health understood is promoted by increasingly remarkable medical techniques, 'by-pass', even 'replacement'. *Will* can be encouraged, assisted by healing medicine and devoted, skilful care. Physicians need help when they themselves need mending. Speculation concerning resources of soul, psyche, approaches metaphysics; sources and resources known of but unknown, beyond reason; even beyond imagination. *GRACE* is in-exhaustible unfailing good, found and known in faith, hope and love; needed in ever present conflict with their opposites.

X

Evil

'You're an attorney. It's your duty to lie, conceal and distort everything, and slander everybody.'

(Jean Giradoux, *The Mad Woman of Chaillot*, II 1945)

'What? Shall we receive good at the hand of God, and shall we not receive evil?'

(*Job* 2.10)

'Deliver us from evil.'

(*Luke* 11. 4 and *The Book of Common Prayer*)

X 1 In General

X 1 i Light, Darkness; Fear, Nerve

Good and evil are opposite realities, powerful in experience, known in intent, expression and purpose at every level; witnessed, recognised, received, celebrated or suffered. They are nouns, and adjectives of quality, dynamic and personal. **Purpose** moves **will** to act. In *light* and darkness of events we recognise evil and good. Shadows of evil cloud good-will and blur distinctions between them. Visibility changes. **Light** enables **sight** to see more clearly, further, higher. Perspectives alter appearances.

When does a bad deed, a wrong decision, a wicked plan, involve evil? Extreme evil is 'absolute', but where and when practical, pragmatic, bad behaviour occurs in every day life, often circumstantial, subjective and relative, it is normal, perhaps charitable, to soften the concept of evil.

Ignorance of evil precludes identifying it as such. Life in sheltered, fortunate circumstances make it seem possible, convenient, even enlightened, kind, to explain it away.

'Judge not that ye be not judged'; 'Evil be to him that evil thinks' — encourage compassion, not condemnation. A romantic imagination finds 'absolute evil' indigestible, repulsive. To liberal situational ethicists evil appears naïve until unmistakeable.

Fear of evil is itself the evil of *fear*. In face of evil, courage needs confidence to strengthen **will**. **Nerve** means courage; confident **will** ready to *risk*, to *act*. Nerve, a noun, is substantive, self-existent. *Nerve* as a verb strengthens heart and *mind*. Courage is a virtue. **Good**, substantive, is adjective and adverb. **Evil**, also substantive, adjective, is not an adverb.

Evil is confronted in natural events, disasters; behaviour of others, animosity, enmity; and in ourselves when intemperate; tempted to disregard virtue. Courage is needed to recognise and face up to temptation. The Japanese carve three 'wise' monkeys: hands cover eyes to 'see no evil', ears to 'hear no evil' and mouth to 'speak no evil'. These near human faces reflect attempt to exclude evil when encompassed or challenged by it. Their folly, if monkeys are capable of human 'folly', is offered as wisdom. Eyes and ears covered or closed, shut out sight and sound of danger, evil influences, temptation. Mouth, covered, shut, cannot speak good or evil. These monkeys are presumed to know evil from good. Without such knowledge, evil would be unknown, hidden. Why, then, raise their hands to protect themselves?

Lust for possession, domination, over-riding power, gratification, are temptations human beings are prey to. Tempered through conscious virtue of temperance, moderation: capability to **control**, strengthens **will** to become systematically, responsible, civil. People are also capable of amoral, immoral cunning and wickedness. *Fear* is common to all living beings. *Fear* of danger, *pain*, destruction, warns but does not necessarily distinguish intrinsic good from evil in experience. Who is not prone to folly, weakness, failure to recognise and resist temptation?

X 1 ii Ideal, Idealism

Idealists imagine and pursue their best models. Concepts of the ideal are envisaged with *sight* and insight. Open eyes, balanced minds enable good intention; **will** lives in hope, in commitment to find the best rather than worst; to overcome evil with good. A false or exaggerated ideal upsets balance; a particular imperative becomes obsessive. Idealists may distort, fantasise, thrive on illusion: antithesis of ideal.

Idealism systematises what is believed to be ideal, but constrains as well as liberates motives to feel, think, speak, do. Purposes **move will** to *act*, to make and contribute to events for good and evil, excellent or ruinous interpreted as they serve the system, the creed, the '-ism': utilitarianism, socialism, conservatism, communism etc: any **fundamentalism**.

In light and darkness of events: natural, accidental, intentional; through things, situations, other people become recognised. Visibility changes: seasons, times; light and energy of morning, afternoon and evening modify and intensify vision, daydreams, night dreams. Inward sight promotes further, deeper, higher vision. Different points of *view* offer perspectives. Perspectives alter appearances but not substance, essence, innate presence, intrinsic quality. Evaluation concerns appraisal of *function*: good challenges evil in personal judging, willing to see; willingness to overcome; not to ignore, succumb to or pretend that evil is not real. Insecurity, need for confidence, assurance, may promote artificial responses. Ideas of superiority lead to forms of evil: to pride and arrogance. Political idealism tends to fantasise, to distort vision and criteria into illusions, antitheses of ideals: extremists: left and right; wrong rather than right, affirm ideals, sometimes systemic idealism.

X 1 iii Power for Good and Evil

'Mind sets' include moral blindness, deep enough to become characteristic in personal and general culture. Excessive self-confidence tends to become arrogant. Racism, masculinism, deteriorate into assumptions, pretensions of power that engender oppression: social, economic, domestic violence and cruelty. 'Ethnic cleansing', an appalling euphemism deludes into an 'ultimate solution'. Ancestry, blood, education engender constructive confidence, but assumed superiority engenders bigotry, intolerance, lacking the virtue of humility.

Misfortune is not intended evil. Accidental death is not murder. A murderer at large is thought dangerous but 'time' may offer opportunity for amendment of life. Infectious or contagious sickness, epidemics, typhoid, influenza, plague are increasingly prevented by immunisation. Knowing evil requires response, personal *will* not to harm, injure, torment and *torture*; to deceive, betray, or *kill*: all these impose evil, but inclination to return evil for evil intensifies. In practice, **force** is needed to maintain **order** for the common good. The statue of Justice surmounting the Old Bailey, Central Criminal Court, holds scales in one hand to weigh and balance the sword of Justice pointing upwards in the other. Effective rule of law depends on enforcement. Belief that evil is overcome with good hopes for a general theory of *will*, good-will by virtue of justice: scales of mercy and the sword.

Two radio journalists, Richard Dimbleby for the BBC and Ed Murrow, freelance for US networks, reported the final stages of the war with Germany, 1945. They accompanied soldiers into **Belsen, Buchenwald and Auschwitz. The presence of evil in those places was, they said, palpable.** What they saw was beyond words. When they recovered themselves sufficiently to speak, they broadcast what they saw: death camps to exterminate living persons; gas chambers, crematoria, mass graves, grim remains when the camps were abandoned in the face of allied armies' advance. Devised by the Third Reich to destroy suspected enemies of their regime: citizens blamed, hated, for refusing to assimilate National Socialism were identified by SS and Gestapo. Racial characteristics with cultural hegemony, Jewish, is easier to identify than individual faith confessed. Six million were killed in circumstances that verify evil.

The 'nuclear deterrent', atom and hydrogen bombs, undoubtedly deterred. 'Cold War', apparently quiescent, had good and evil consequences 'Terrorism', not new, but differently dangerous is a very present evil. Terrorists possessed by 'idealism' determine to destroy: to undermine by violence, a regime or system they hate.

X 2 Dynamics of Evil

X 2 i Natural and Supernatural, Chaos, Error, Fault

Principles of **order** and pattern are evident in nature, in physical life. Inclination and *will*, much discussed, distinctive human behaviour, may reflect, be modified by and be determined by evaluation, values recognised in virtues sometimes referred to as **moral**; open to interpretation, acceptance or rejection, decision.

We experience evil in two ways: the evil we do and the evil we suffer. Good and evil coexist as desires and dreads, attractive and repulsive, hopes and fears. Hatred grows like briars among good fruit bushes. To disentangle good and evil is itself an **act** of *will*, a necessary prelude to deliberation, resolution and action, liberation without self-deception. Earth is endowed with **light** and life, nourishment for well-being, until eventual exhaustion requires **rest, sleep**; weariness, readiness, to perish and die. Learning to survive and live with joy and sorrow includes discovering *power* to *test* limits, positive and negative, strength and weakness in things, people, ideas, plans and purposes: to spoil, poison and destroy: or cultivate for good.

Chaos, recognised, theoretically systematised, can be created. Confusion leads to error, commonplace in misjudgment. Genuine mistakes include forgetfulness, 'absent mind'. Consciousness of quality in things and of virtues in behaviour, character, raises questions of fault, guilt, blame. (See **XI**.)

X 2 ii Gravity, Cycles, Negation

Gravity is experienced as falling: landslides, raindrops, slipping, not up but down, loss of balance, 'down-to-earth', from high to low, but pressure systems rotate: cyclones and anti-cyclones, cyclical.

The 'demon of the absolute' beckons to and from opposite extremes. Evil causes suffering. We prefer not to *suffer*, try to avoid but cannot escape suffering. Goodness in being, being good, is sometimes called 'angelic'. Suffering thought to be caused deliberately, could also be accidental, incidental, unintentional, even super-sensitively imagined. Parameters occur at every level and interact into cycles of action, reaction, sometimes of paralysis, negation. Spoiling, destroying occur relentlessly in the natural world of things and creatures: in life and death. Originating, making, growing, building, creating and recreating are primal for survival. Cycles begin, continue, end and begin again: birth, growth, wear and tear, levels and degrees of maturity, death. **New concepts of being: second birth, rebirth, resurrection affirm dimensions of soul in continuity.** Individual capability to respond or repress, enquire or ignore is present at each level of consciousness. To discern and enjoy; to make and create, cherish and encourage, **share**, necessities, supply needs for things and doings valued, requires knowing, active, responsible response with good-will. To **harm**, injure, **torment**, torture; to deceive, betray, kill, impose evil.

X 2 iii Personification and Responsibility

Stars, winds, volcanoes, identified by name, personify energy and characteristics. Moral qualities are often personified as angels or devils. A wicked, poisonous, cruel, virulent malevolent individual is personified as a tormentor, a fiend. This seems to indict a human person as beyond *hope*; a fatal sentence for an extreme case, judicial rather than pastoral. Absolute personal evil is indigestible and repulsive to imaginative romantics and to liberal situational ethicists naïve in the face of evil. Eyes closed are blind, but shock can ignite *will* to open them, to look again. Direct encounter with personal evil scars memory, disturbs balance, sometimes lifelong. Hobgoblins and foul-fiends, witches and wizards of evil intent in different forms at different times and places have names. Evil as malevolent power: personal danger, tempter, Satan is known also as Beelzebub, Lucifer, Mephistopheles, Screwtape and Wormwood: out to corrupt and destroy.

Dante envisaged hell as imprisonment in infernal torment, the consequences of moral destruction observed, but survived with *reason*, in company of the poet Virgil, and inspired by vision of personal love: Beatrice: real person, known to poet.

Just and fair, virtuous, heed free speech, toleration: ideals aimed at and cultivated, not universally admired, practiced by fragile ambivalent human beings. Aesop's *Fables* disclose moral experience in the tale told. Enduring cultures have moral bases: the Ten Commandments revealed to Moses; Buddha's discourses; Mohammed's prescriptions in the Koran (Qur'an believed divine authority of Allah); systematised, intensify debate. Speculative thought increases critical exploration of far-reaching problems, revisions, reconsiderations: collisions are difficult to avoid.

Dilemmas, mutually exclusive alternatives, make wise decisions difficult.

Moral philosophy engages recognition of virtue as personal liberty, but discipline of **WILL** is necessary, indispensable, for communal well-being, civil order, jurisprudence in dynamic experience of, people, citizens caught in dilemmas. Complex webs of evil where paths of virtue are hard to **find** and still harder to follow expose gaps between principle and practice, prosperity and adversity, intervention, direction and *laissez faire*. Rulers do well to lead, to exercise **power** wisely and responsibly. British government has evolved during centuries of trial and error.

Civil strife, stimulated by discoveries, economic development, theological conflict, religious bigotry caused revolution in seventeenth century England. These tensions were not new. Elizabeth I reigned, ruled, strengthened by adventurous initiative, exploration, naval exploits contrived to contain them. The Elizabethan Settlement contributed to enduring experience, powerful influence of good faith in practice, exemplified by Alfred the Great; relevant in Doomsday Book, Magna Carta, by Thomas à Beckett, Simon de Montfort versus Crown; 'Model Parliament' of Edward I, instability of fights for the Crown until the marriage of Henry VII united claims of York and Lancaster into Tudor ascendancy, Gloriana. Stuart problems included succession: Charles II without legitimate heir, James II, William and Mary. George of Hanover became King George I but spoke little English, did not chair Cabinet Council meetings and could go back to Hanover. His First Minister, Walpole, First Lord of the Treasury, achieved constitutional renewal turning back and looking forward: to revive representation, accountability; Cabinet Government responsible to Parliament, usually achieving peaceful change. British experience reverberated elsewhere, not always successfully, and the principles on which it is based need respect and constant vigilant fidelity to avoid the evil of revolt, civil war.

Revolution in France reflected changed beliefs, different ideas of authority, and reappraisal of social order. Constitutional Monarchy had not developed. Separation, more like divorce, of State and Church (Catholic but not Reformed) was observed by those who framed a new Constitution for the 'United States'. Alexis de Tocqueville crossed the Atlantic and, after a six month visit wrote his classic *Democracy in America*, and *On Revolution*; classics. Walter Bagehot's essays on the 'English Constitution' (unwritten) affirmed the Crown as safeguard from the 'evil consequences of revolution'.

Post-revolution study of society in France, became sociology, soon cultivated in London at the School of Economics and Political Science, financed by George Bernard Shaw (dramatist and author of *The Intelligent Woman's Guide to Socialism and Capitalism*) and his wife. Beatrice and Sydney Webb, students of Trade Unions, USSR; Clement Attlee, Harold Laski, strengthened the growing Labour Party increasingly represented in Parliament. Christian socialists: Charles Kingsley, F. D. Maurice, William Beveridge, R. H. Tawney, George Bell, William Temple, not 'secularists', advocated reform for compassionate reasons.

Political and economic aims to redistribute wealth, promote welfare, require efficient administration. Social sciences, academic off-shoots of moral philosophy, distinguish sociology from 'social administration'. Further change, the New Labour project, *mix* 'public service' with 'private enterprise': government organisation (including the distinct, distinguished, objective tradition of the civil service) confuse motive and intention, believed advantageous but, without principal aim, become unclear, muddled, inefficient. Selling off 'agencies' such as weather forecasting, Ordnance Survey, welfare services, prisons, disengage ministers from their responsibility: enrich the exchequer with stealth taxes but diminish public trust and respect.

The momentum of media growth promotes presenters and commentators, critics, some more ambitious than principled, as powerful influences outside Parliament, capable of challenging constitutional principle (e.g. the Hutton Report).

Sociology, logic of society and theology, logic of God, explore different areas and levels of experience, beliefs and attitudes. Good faith, public, depends on leaders, rulers, able to see and encourage the best rather than the worst, good rather than evil, experienced in British tradition.

Momentum of **change**, alters balance, tending to disguises what is worse although hoped to be better. Constitutional upheaval pushed through without careful considerate regard for long term consequences breeds cynicism, political apathy: evil consequences of spin and sleaze. The independence of judges; of police forces whose leaders, better not known by name, wear wigs or helmets to signify function, need impartial responsibility exercised with **integrity**.

Head and heart, mind and soul acting together strengthen individuals to recognise and resist evil.

C. S. Lewis nominated Screwtape and Wormwood, personal devils, to attack human frailty. Their task is to find subtle ways to **tempt**, to lead astray, to do what ought not to be done — or *neglect* what ought to be done. Screwtape trains Wormwood to capture converts to new life of faith, grace and joy. Devilish concentration on surfaces of things: appearances, superficial appetites, transitory pleasures confuse issues, disguise and conceal true *function*, meaning and right use. Natural appetites trivialised or exaggerated lead to bewilderment and *waste*. The victim is reduced to vacillating ineffectiveness by anxiety and *fear*; until confidence is regained: renewed dependence on 'the Enemy' whose *grace* empowers: whose 'strength is made perfect in weakness'. This, says Screwtape, must be avoided at all costs. Personal problems, temptations, recur and test virtue all through life. Set aside as 'private', secret not public, challenges towards increasing maturity.

The ideal of good *order* envisaged in *Utopia* depends on 'right reason' for personal control. In practice, *force* is needed to maintain order: common good, for survival, self-defence, personal and communal. Necessary, minimal, controlled use of force is not intended evil. Motive is key. Errors need correction. Lies kill trust, poison relationships with invalid evidence, false witness. If admitted, owned-up-to, understood, forgiveness and healing become possible. A bad tooth, cleaned of decay and rebuilt is restored to health. Gums heal when a bad tooth beyond repair is extracted. Evil influences destroy a person who lacks knowledge, strength and *will* to resist them. Rioting intoxicates rioters. Individuals collectively inflamed, lose control and become dangerous. Passionate commitment for good or for evil needs evaluation, the filter of thoughtful conscience, meditation, the agony of assuming responsibility. To '*fight* the good *fight*' is not flight but response to evil; fancies flee away with fears which challenge courage.

X 3 Heart and Soul

X 3 i Death, Spirit, Conflict, Tension, Morale

Ending and meaning, ends and means, means and ends are often beyond comprehension.

Continuity of life beyond death is a matter of ***trust, promise*** believed, personal faith. Suffering is associated with every level of personal passion and agony. If fear of death is transformed by belief in resurrection, this is new **hope**, good news indeed.

Can suffering be avoided, escaped from, arrested, limited, cured? Physical pain, disease, caused by simple and complex factors is fierce, hard to bear, even when alleviated.

Emotional reactions 'move', motivate, set in motion. Thought needs information, knowledge, intelligence for scrupulous evaluation. The learned professions: clerical, medical, judicial, pastoral, educational, pursue and promote temporal wisdom beyond temporality. Good and evil are adjectives applied to actions, verbs, and to nouns: to ideas, thoughts, feeling, notions as to actions and things. Motive in doing; reasons, use of things, and things themselves made, is good or evil. These stark statements affirm what is often denied, cloaked, rejected but **paradox** sharpens and clarifies contradictions.

Violence accelerates towards deliberate terror. Evil acts are feared and hated. Are those who order such acts more culpable than those who obey them? Silent witnesses, bystanders, feel helpless, turn away, remember and bide their time. Inescapably evil actions cause suffering, agony of body, mind and soul, heart and head together, grievous. In vortex of evil, death may become deliverance. To die with courage, dignity, concern for others, is the final challenge, eased by recognition of good and evil; known, remembered and understood.

X 3 ii Thought, Faith, Work

Asking 'how' concerns process and the principles of process. Asking 'why' ponders origin, ***will***, motive, purpose. The theory of the evolution of living organisms soon became replicated in theoretical, philosophical, political and moral spheres. Evolution seemed to offer a universal key to unlock understanding of ***progress***: essential **donoun**. Natural Selection applied to human behaviour suggests conditional inevitability that limits individual **motive**, initiative and responsibility. The idea that moral improvement is pre-determined by evolving circumstances; that *progress* is inevitable; is not yet demonstrably convincingly connected with personal goodness. Human beings have not evolved beyond reality of evil.

Will, thought naturally innocent, looses that innocence when alternatives, good and evil, are denied. Self-gratifying, indulgent motives distort personal judgment. Hearts, easily beguiled, entangled, are lead astray. Thinking heads are tempted to exaggerate rationality in belief that *reason*, clear thought, is sufficient to *control will*; that *reason* is all that is needed to *change* the *mind* and *will*: to redirect determination and resolution. Confronting our own fragility, **temper**, failures, calls for more than knowledge of good and evil. Strength to overcome evil needs *power*, special, even super-natural energy: *grace* available and received; infinitely divined 'divinity'. Moral calculations assess, weigh good and evil and are contradictory: paradox again. Casuists accept qualified evil for the sake of greater good; a worrying argument in theory but tested in practice by diplomatic effort for peace and prosperity: *trust* and *hope* with Chaucer's Abbess: *'amor vincit omnia'*, *'love* conquers all'.

Like *wind*, spirit is invisible, but moves, inspires in spirit of good and encourages spiritual virtues: **faith**, *hope* and *love*. When these enter consciousness they become characteristic of an individual soul and influence behaviour. Words thought, spoken, written and received are influenced by the spirit which blows, breathes, communicates for evil or good.

Souls grow with spirit. Does the soul enable people to do and to make as well as to be? If so, it **works** and enfolds *will*. An evil spirit veils good purpose: confuses *form* with substance, appearance with reality. 'Soul' and 'heart', as if interchange, identify the core of feeling, but 'soul' includes spiritual needs, good to overcome evil. Soul moves mind to reach for good and true purpose; universal, objective. This adds dedication of *will* to devotion of heart. A 'soul-searching' 'soul-mate' supplies human need to share delight, to participate, and be understood. Inspiration received and given, being healed and healing, is not sickening wickedness, destructive. It can be, if evil.

Language, mathematics, philosophy offer foundation principles of grammar and vocabulary, accuracy and shape, logic and reason, embedded in the soul of man. Aristotle wrote of the soul as that which animates. This essence of life animates all living and is the dynamic of existence. If the soul is embodied, then principles of order and pattern (as Aristotle himself recognised as expressed and found in nature) are understood in practice and united through it. Plato thought of the soul as being somewhere between spirit and flesh, their junction and conjunction. The spirit, first principle of life-giving animation, becomes conditional and variable in experience because of the gradual development of human consciousness and *will*. At this point, spirit and soul do not always find union, and if they do, the union may resemble marriage; not always harmonious. Augustine referred to memory 'as it were, like the stomach of the mind, whereas gladness and sadness are like sweet and bitter food' (*Confessions* X, xiv, 21.) But his translator notes that 'Augustine deliberately refused to express a firm opinion on the question of how the soul is united to the embryo, whether by heredity from the parents....or by special creative act by God, or because pre-existent...' Despite fierce criticism for his suspense of judgment, Augustine to the last, refused to decide.' (Note 34, *Confessions*, page 178.)

The categories of philosophers may guide us towards spirit but soul embodied prompts and needs analogy, allegory, imagery, metamorphosis for spiritual discernment. Looking for experience of **spirit** suggests heightening aspiration and intensity. To climb with sure *purpose*, with *hope*, is quite different from ascending the same path in **fear** and misery. Christian souls envisage evil as hellish, good as heavenly. Dante's vision of *The Divine Comedy* saw souls as 'shades' in infernal regions of experience, suffering torment, until drawn by *light* upwards, purged, alight, as 'flames' in paradise. Dante survived hell in presence and guidance of Virgil (manifest reason expressed in poetry) but is inspired by vision of the figure of Beatrice, magnetic embodiment of human love. Beatrice leads his ascent in Paradise. Once again, *'amor vincit'*.

Attempts to unravel tangled webs of deceit expose knotted, broken threads of uncertain origin. Direct evidence of wickedness has planned and unplanned results, but incomplete, is open to interpretation. Calamities occur, intended or not. Good as well as evil purposes go wrong, sometimes reproduced as comical. What a clown does with a bucket of whitewash appears unintentional, is watched with apprehension of accident, mess, folly, tragi-comedy. Spectators may laugh until tears flow, not at the clown but with sympathy for the human condition exposed by good-humoured clumsiness, amusing, pitiful, innocent. Genuine accidents, mishaps, mistakes, are not promoted by ill-will with intention to harm. If they were, they would not be accidental. Evil is no joke.

Thought of good offers encouragement towards better, greater good. Generosity promotes generosity. A magnificent vocabulary of finite and infinite good: comforting, helping, encouraging, understanding, edifying, healing. These are gloriously beneficent; magnificently joyfully saving. In being forgiven, we are delivered from evil. Forgiveness, mercifully, overcomes evil with good. (*Matthew* 5.)

Difficulties and frustrations in childhood intensify during adolescence. Unless realised, healed, these crystallise into habits, attitudes, mind-sets that cause suffering.

Unhealed wounds, injuries, are handicaps of continuing pain accompanied by danger of perversion.

Suffering caused deliberately, intentionally can, some think should, be blameworthy. Done deliberately, to accept **blame** needs humility as well as honesty. Self-justification: 'it wasn't my fault', 'don't blame me', asserts innocence, or is deceitful. Competition, stimulating, aims to succeed; to win, not lose, but right and wrong, true or false, good and evil co-exist. Undetected cheating may affect result, unjustly. Acknowledging fault appears weak. A child or adult who has lied, tends to stick to the lie to 'get away with it', even when another is blamed, perhaps punished. Lies shelve responsibility and if habitual, masquerade as self-confidence. 'Giving' reduces to self-gratification, bribery, without generosity. The confidence-trickster's trick is to convince a victim to trust in order to exploit that confidence.

Do ends ever justify means? Sophists and casuists beget situational ethicists, circumstantial, casual, incidental. Children who discern adult motives distinguish just punishment from unjust 'persecution'. Foretastes of fair and unfair, true and false, good and evil prepare **hope** and expectation of justice and injustice. Warm affection promotes spontaneity, beneficial response, but over indulgence, 'spoiling', causes later suffering. Favouritism breeds jealousy, grudges remembered, resented, festering if unexpiated; visited on unarmed, unsuspecting victims through no fault of their own. Sequences of behaviour emerge when deep-seated, suppressed resentments explode on close, intimate friends. A trivial irritation becomes disagreement, an angry quarrel becomes a *fight*. Ethics of non-violence (thought, word, deed) are suspended, disregarded; relationships are damaged, severed, in domestic and other spheres of life.

Wars of words degenerate when lying and cheating protect or advance their interest by pretending, by falsifying. Deceit, fraud, tip an iceberg when what is true is submerged, frozen by *will*, ill-will to deceive. *Trust* is enfeebled, open co-operation closed and opportunities dependent on it are lost. Loss endangers relationships of potential benefit and strength, individual and communal. Hot-blooded anger becomes cold, calculating enmity, punitive vengeance. Anger, envy, jealousy are passions known to poison motives, actions, unless bridled, controlled: goodness melts *will* to deceive.

X 4 Ethos and Ethics

Ethics, guidelines, are recognised from behaviour compared, preferred, in different communities and contexts. They emanate from practical experience, from customs and manners which influence behaviour. A community with accepted ethics acquires an ethos. Ethos derives from ethics and strengthens communities to function together, formally and informally. A village, a tribe, a school, a ship's company, a constabulary may develop an ethos, not always for good. Envy, jealously, bullying have evil consequences. Ethos in a community, character in a person, sets standards of behaviour. Habit and custom at least, at best, fall and rise, diminish or raise expectations. Communities, large or small, family, neighbours, school club, gang, team, work, develop with need, common cause, interest, companionship. Appeal to 'family values' means nothing without experience of families who value family life. 'Esprit de corps' exists in a 'corps' with 'esprit': morale, tone, loyalty, effort and solidarity; discipline beyond the limits of self-interest. Mercenaries 'worked up' are paid, but comradeship engages people in common cause, together.

Ordered, orderly living, is best maintained freely, not enforced or posited. Good **order** derives from intrinsic values; stronger, deeper, higher than ethics. Natural law fuses into and from principal: moral and practical. Endeavour to read the mind and will of fate, of gods, of God, hopes to divine ultimate order; good and evil. Concepts of pleasure, responsibility, obedience, include freedom to agree or disagree. To do or not to do raises questions of evaluation. **Power** to act according to principles, rules, laws, depends on initiative and control; personal discipline. Spontaneous conformity flourishes with agreement. Obedience, obligatory, is wiser than ineffective rebellion. Rejection of particular ethics, customs, manners, if any, is usual during adolescent exploration. Fairness and justice, toleration and free speech are close to ideals. Ethicists regard ethical principles as rational, scientific, political, economic and so on; relative and situational rather than intrinsic. Debate intensifies when ethicists challenge belief suspected to be 'beyond reason'.

Moral principle, believed divine in origin is trusted. *Challenge* intensifies *debate*. Speculative thought: far ranging, encounters problems considered critically, revised, reconsidered, while interest is sustained by maintaining relevance. Faith strengthens and is strengthened by commitment, devotion. Migrating believers often maintain their ethical, cultural traditions. Comparison stimulate comparison; discussion and studies need toleration, not always present or reciprocated. E-mail, wireless communication, websites add pace to availability and recruit support.

Moral: noun, precept, recognises virtue. Moral philosophy appertains to discussion of personal liberty; of discipline necessary for communal well-being, civil order, jurisprudence. People are caught in dilemmas, sometimes in complex webs of evil where paths of virtue are hard to find and still harder to follow. Gaps between principle and practice are bewildering. Moral principle regarded as ethical concepts has moved from divines and philosophers to sociologists. Academics wrestling with esoteric details, (important as these are) hope to apprehend, know and understand and follow them to and from practicalities. Ethical precepts, situational and circumstantial, are studied for definition, not invitation to engage **wholehearted commitment to the good**. Grammar of language assists clarity without commitment. Inspiration engages energy convinced of having something to say but dogmatism stimulates dissent, revolt, disruptive behaviour; violence intended to undermine and destroy the order of its source. Honour, energy of good-will, volunteers for good. 'His order rooted in disorder stood, and faith unfaithful kept him falsely true' is paradox of these dilemmas. Faith and honour are less acclaimed since Tennyson's time.

Consensus ethics, prevailing customs, become conventional: 'done' or 'not done', thought right or wrong, rightly or wrongly. Communal cohesion is sustained while customs continue to work well; assumed, accepted, respected and maintained as simple decencies; clean, clothed, kind, courteous, fair, appointments and promises kept. Sworn evidence, oaths of allegiance, loyalty, fidelity solemnly made, reflect and strengthen lasting commitment. Celebrations: joy at birth, at wedding; grief at tragedy, death, mark exceptional events, sacred as of the essence of life. Customary ceremonies, genuinely felt, strengthen participants in common experience; serious, genuine feeling not switched on and off. Affectation of solemnity appears shallow, even hypocritical, but reticence protects this inner personal sanctuary. When feelings are raw, vulnerable, exposed, embarrassing 'scenes' occur; occasionally inappropriate, bad manners, sometimes very funny, but 'beyond a joke'.

Ethics recognise courtesy, customary for different people, in different ways. The deeper the differences, the lower the common denominators of *form*. Genuine *form*, even if shallow; thought hypocritical, refines behaviour. Conviction: balance, dignity and sincerity; is seen for what it is and does. Appearance of *form*, to recite rather than **promise**, uses words without intention of keeping the **promise** stated, is worn like a mask to conceal **indifference**. Manners smooth social life, cover insincerity but feigned courtesy and civility becomes hypocrisy. Avoiding offence is not always sustainable. Manners springing from gentle civility include ***control*** and toleration. These qualities are like crystal formations from liquid good-will. Good and evil in direct conflict make hard dilemmas for excitable temperaments.

Courses of action call up precedents. What did others do in comparable circumstances? Parent, brother, sister, mentor, known example? Generations of naval strategists since Trafalgar, facing an enemy, wondered what Nelson would have done. Proverbs suggest simple, sensible advice. 'Discretion is the better part of valour'; 'be not wise in your own conceits'; 'nothing venture, nothing gain'. Success may be vital, but knowing virtue does not guarantee discretion, valour, humility, wisdom. Valour is courage, primary virtue with prudence, temperance and justice. Engagement with evil takes place in heads and hearts. Duty is expected, not only at sea.

Ethics expose contradictions about priorities including control of information. Freedom to disclose, restrained by obligations of secrecy, confidentiality, requires tact and diplomacy. Is 'economy' with what is true deliberate deception? Ethics are entangled by conflicting obligations in personal and political areas to confuse loyalties. Refusal to speak may be 'to hold one's peace'. Suspicions of duplicity by persons with public responsibilities call for investigation, in case of illegal, even criminal conduct. Evidence, found, expects action to follow: integrity verified.

Ethics are not confined to one culture. 'Environmental ethics', call for the welfare of the planet across cultural and political frontiers faced with 'global warming', frightening climate change. Feminist ethics derive from reactions to male chauvinism, masculinist, but ethics and manners melt in the fires of personal and political passion. Political ideologists; Marxist, National Socialist (Nazi) overpowered familiar customary ethics and rewrote norms of behaviour as well as history. The 'cultural revolution' intended to reinvigorate Chinese Marxist-Maoist socialism. Terrorists, Irgun, IRA, al-Qaeda, Hezbollah, are fundamentalists who ***fight*** for their ***purpose***, not by convention of war 'declared', but by inciting **fear** of terror.

Knowing good and evil generates morality. Ethics are 'fall out', not origin. Self-interest and convenience refine experience rarely beyond our own. All decisions need **sense**, intelligence, thought and judgment, with practical consciousness. Promises kept, obligations respected, duty done, debits and credits reckoned fairly. Knowing good and evil is moral consciousness. Ethicists, sometimes refugees from morality and divinity, imply them to be hard-liners rather than persons aware of primary reality of good and evil. Moralists may react by regarding ethics as circumstantial dilutions of morality, enlightened self-interest whose notions of right and wrong are convenient.

Customary behaviour alters when momentum of change modifies accepted norms. Unconventional behaviour is not necessarily unethical or immoral since customs wane and dissolve. Genuine reasons to value first principles rediscovers and renews them not as 'situational' but in Plato's awakening of the 'Good'.

Civility and civilisation emerge out of *order*: **respect**, devotion, obedience to sources that *command* them: and promote pursuit of virtue, goodness, erudition, wisdom, justice. Power persuaded for its own sake makes these fade; darkness returns: revives bewilderment, despair. Fanatics and zealots, anarchic gangs led by spellbinding individuals appear. Some lead armies and move in, like vandals at the gates, to take the city. Other inward dangers emerge: corruption, decay, decadence when principles of good and evil are forgotten, disregarded, denied. Ethics have little chance of survival if mainstream affirmative culture loses its dynamic. Treasuries of learning are neglected, destroyed, lost. Seclusion, possibly monastic, attracts individuals who strive to preserve, maintain, renew orderly ways of life. Devotees themselves are not immunised from temptation, corruption, evil, **disintegration**. Heads and hearts, thought and feeling, are individual citadels, integrated to resist decay. Persecution makes victims into refugees desperate to escape evil. Some carry their culture and transplant successfully, elsewhere.

Gradual reform of outdated institutions protects society from extreme disturbance: evils of revolution, civil war. Continuing principles of critical accountability and representation, access to justice, literacy, education, honest prosperity are for good. Public opinion, informed debate, needs virtues maintained, affirmed, incomparably more enduring than fashion. New technology offers immediate, worldwide communication, as transforming as were sound and TV in the twentieth century.

Radio and TV stations offer striking examples of attitudes, methods and manners. In Britain, the BBC was established to 'inform, educate and entertain'. The Royal Charter distanced corporate life from direct government intervention, (political) and the licence fee safeguarded from commercial dominance. These principles, faithfully practiced, were not found wanting. Programme makers, editors, producers, directors were expected to exercise conscientious judgment; personal and corporate responsibility. The Royal Charter, agreed by Parliament, required renewal. BBC activities, reports and accounts are reported annually. Licence fee income is reviewed at intervals sufficient for stability, intended exempt from commercial competitiveness. Commissions, committees of enquiry proposed change. The Board of Governors of the BBC was designed to maintain arms-length independence of Government: to appoint, support (or criticise) senior directors and the Board of Management. Pressure, political, commercial, sectarian, idiosyncratic is constantly exerted and only resistible when genuine impartiality and independent responsibility prevails. Trustees differ from Governors, as will become apparent.

Thereby hang many tales, crises, accusations, enquiries from and of Yesterday's Men; hopes for Tomorrow's World. Melt down in attitudes, behaviour, limits unlimited by individuals determined to break ground, **escape** restraint. Nevertheless, freedom to think, report, debate and criticise, survive, continue to offer occasional highest quality programmes. The twin principles: arms length from government and secure finance of licence fee income are recognisable, although frequently threatened, outwardly and from within.

Revolutionary regimes act very quickly to control broadcasting. Top level political appointments and intervention by Wilson, Thatcher, Blair; ruthless spin by Blair and Campbell upset balanced reaction and decision. The suicide of David Kelly scorched the consciences of MPs, BBC executives schooled to expect upward reference by reporters, and by some in Downing Street: customary channels of consultation no longer there.

Soviet revolutionaries hated the old Russian regime blamed for poverty, misery, inequitable privilege. Tsar, family, courtiers, were assassinated, slaughtered. Marxist idealists believed they could destroy negative exploitation, overthrow the old regime and replace it with comradeship, equality, redistributed wealth, a classless society. Private property in finance, commerce, land they regarded as evil. Evil is not destroyed by evil but extreme situations invite extreme methods.

X 5 Cultivating

X 5 i Plants and Weeds

EVIL is LIVE reversed.

Gardens are, by definition, cultivated. A garden may be a place of pleasure and tranquillity, beauty, order, benefit and fruitfulness. Spoilers and destroyers are ever present. Pests appear, and weeds.

Debate with a botanist friend as to the difference between weeds and plants led to considering if a weed is 'a **plant** in the wrong **place**'. Is there a 'right' **place**? Is 'plant' defined by intention: the act of planting? Is a natural growth a weed, because not deliberately planted? Wheat and barley originate from wild grasses, cross-bred, cultivated for improved seeds, cereals. Peas are planted for food, sweet-peas for their delicate multicoloured beauty and fragrance. Both appear not too distantly related to convolvulus, 'bindweed', that entwines and strangles. Cultivation brings experience, knowledge, skill, **success in plant culture**. The loveliest and most fruitful garden reverts to wilderness when neglected, uncultivated. With no one to miss its pleasure and **produce**, none mourn its passing, or suffers loss. **Donouns** flourish in the cultivated garden of words.

To know a good thing: seed as food, a beautiful and nourishing apple, a nut; a good deed, a good idea, needs evaluation, qualities appreciated, enjoyed. Taste involves likes and dislikes. Comparison clarifies preferences; like, unlike, dislike; better or worse. Food deliberately poisoned needs words to describe the *will* of who poisons: worse than bad: evil.

Horticulture, cultivation for growth and beauty, is scientific art. Gardeners' vocabularies grow to match their expertise and specialities. Methods, techniques and tools; benefit of light and shade, warmth and coolness, dangerous extremes; soil conditions, fertility; all promote knowledge, system, experiment, science; plans, experienced skill in artistic designs. Care and culture for growth require ceaseless vigilance. Learning, experimenting, adds to well being of plants to live, bloom, bear fruit, reproduce and multiply.

'Pastoral care' from conception to birth, nursery to fruitful maturity, describes work of gardeners, of shepherds, applies to ministers who suffer, as all do, weeds of ignorance, disease, confusion between right and wrong, good and evil.

Natural processes are neither good nor evil unless people benefit or suffer from them. Forces in tension *change*, build and destroy. Natural processes were left to themselves until human ingenuity learnt to use and *control; work* to promote growth, guard against danger, establish and maintain ways to live. The Nile river flows through desert, forms a delta and reaches the Mediterranean. Early inhabitants learnt to take advantage of seasonal high and low water, by irrigating. Alexandria, great city in antiquity, whose harbour was flooded, is now being explored by divers. Dutch people reclaim incursions from the North Sea by building flood defences and draining 'polders'. Desalinated land becomes fertile for intensive agriculture and horticulture in the Netherlands where crops flourish: tulips and cereals in Flanders.

Natural symbols encourage understanding. Poppies bloom among ripening corn. The poppies were not sown. Weeding during growth would damage young grain-bearing corn shoots. They grow together until harvest. In Flanders, such fields were battlegrounds in the 1914-18 war. Poppies symbolise those who died, each life spent in face of appalling suffering and attrition of trench warfare. Poppies are cultivated elsewhere for opium. Green stem, blood red petals, black centre, seed capsules which, crushed unripe, provide opiate that sedates suffering, calms nerves and relieves tension. A poppy is a complete symbol of the life of a soldier, wounded, bleeding, dead: brief beauty, until blood-red petals fall. Opium suppresses and relieves pain but becomes habit-forming, deadly addiction. Poppies flower annually in renewal of life, harvest, death. Dying and living, they are worn in remembrance. Wreaths are laid on war memorials: the Cenotaph in Whitehall, and in cities, towns and villages thankful for their liberty, by descendents of those who fought and died. Another war is being fought in Afghanistan where opium poppies are very profitably cultivated.

Great rivers personify elemental natural power; hopes and fears of persons who live by and on it. Songs: 'Ol' Man River'; profoundly memorable in bass voice of Paul Robeson; 'Old Father Thames', a temperate river; the Lorelei rock whose enchantress endangers navigators of that fast flowing passage of the Rhine; the Volga boatmen rowing against powerful currents; songs and poems of Jordan, Ganges, Tiber. T. S. Eliot, child of St Louis, Missouri, witnessed the river in spate and thought of it as 'a strong brown god'. The people of New Orleans suffered in 2005.

Renewal of life, cycles of continuity in times and seasons recur for fresh growth, fruitful, terrifying, beautiful. Effort and skill in cultivation enhances life. **Will** to prefer and pursue the good involves resisting weakness (conscious temptation) to establish and **control**. Beneficial practices are noted, remembered, codified like ethics. Principles discerned, conceptualised, are perennials like moral principles: virtues. Heads and hearts are not made of stone. Face to face encounter with reality of evil includes **fear** of suffering and the suffering of **fear**. Deliverance is needed.

X 5 ii Immunities and Guarantees

Alfred Nobel pioneered industrial processes for making, using, explosives, highly dangerous **power** for good or evil. Constructive in mining, quarrying, building, defending; but destructive in aggression, bombardment, **attack**, causing *fear*. Nobel's enterprise proved profitable. He endowed prizes for original work in science, medicine, literary achievement, peace-making. Virtue, its own reward, makes good use of knowledge. George Bernard Shaw satirised Nobel and Christianity in *Major Barbara*: blood and fire: 'what price salvation?'

Natural selection applied to human behaviour suggests conditional inevitability. This reduces and limits recognition of individual motive, *will*, initiative and responsibility. A clever, ingenious thinker, Dr Faustus, made 'friends' with Mephistopheles to explore evil himself. Marlowe and Goethe dramatised the legend. Faced with the rise of Hitler, the Nazi party, Thomas Mann portrays a brilliantly gifted musician-theologian, Leverkuhn, whose life moves to cruelty, vice, eventually personifies evil. He called the novel *Dr Faustus*.

Wondering, believing, about life beyond death has led to building great tombs, pyramids, mausoleums.

Noah, believing that he heard God's voice, accepted warning of *flood*, built the Ark and *saved* his family plus pairs of all living creatures from drowning. The concept of protection, safe from disaster, repeats in the 'ark of the covenant' containing tablets of stone engraved with the Commandments, representing the Law, continuity of Divine Will for good. Built to be carried with the people until they reached Mount Zion, Jerusalem, where a place was built: sanctified to hold it: the first Temple. Such words reflect faith in supernatural presence and power.

Church, cathedral, library, places of wonder, learning, worship, celebrate in music, word(s), decorative glory, prayer and sacrament. **Power** to live the living life of faith, nurtures practice of divine presence, maintained. Loss of purpose in life, particularly 'religious' in Augustine's understanding, is loss of soul. Protective systems do not guarantee immunity from loss.

Umberto Eco's novel *The Name of the Rose* depicts evil in a monastic community; the librarian's destructive fanaticism. A senior cleric is sent to enquire. He discovers raw, unsublimated sexual appetite, degrading failure to maintain original elevating vision, the soul-enhancing capability of the monastery's founders.

The University of Pittsburgh, USA has a tower resembling that of a gothic cathedral. It houses most classics of the Humanities, is called 'the cathedral of learning', and can be seen for many miles from the city. (See Franklin Toker: *Pittsburgh, An Urban Portrait*, published 1986, by the Pennsylvania State and University Press, pages 83-90.)

If no harm is intended, is there blame? 'It isn't fair' calls for redress. If good was intended, where did it go wrong and why? Whose fault, if any? Ill-natured action deserves no praise. Praise tempts to vanity. These commonplaces pre-suppose self-awareness, ability to **purpose** and to **control**. To cultivate good rather than evil, constructive and reasonable, cannot be guaranteed or taken for granted. Casuists accept qualified evil for the sake of greater good. Love involves suffering borne by one, some, for the sake of others.

An adventurous young person needs challenging opportunities: **risk** such as speed, but has no car. One says: 'It's fun driving fast. Why shouldn't I? I help myself; take the best I can get into and **drive** away, so fast they won't **catch** me: I don't care whose car it is. Better than doing nothing, hanging about the street while others do the driving. My mates think you're nothing if you daren't try things yourself. So I mess up the car? So it's insured? So I may injure some fool who gets in my way? That's life, a **chase**...why should I be left out of it? I want action...Call me a joy-rider...I certainly enjoy a ride...accidents are not my fault...what do you mean by good and evil? There's life and death. I'm alive'. (Sex-encounters are spoken of as 'joy-rides', self-gratification without responsibility.)

Appetites demand nourishment and control. **Control** does not suppress **desire**. Sublimation, if known of, seems unattractive. Frustration adds anger. Flat-earth perspective is low level. Anything seems better than nothing. **Control** in the **face** of temptation needs knowing good and evil in things, feeling, thought, evaluation, intention. Good and evil regarded as obsolete seem unreal, old fashioned, irrelevant. To behave as though they were unheard of, unknown, is amoral. Immoral relates to accepted morals. Unethical may mean absence or ignorance of particular ethics, or disregard of them. Behaviour beyond exclusive self-interest is where ethics began but morality may demand more than personal convenience.

'I love', 'I hate' activate object with subject. Needs excite appetite, ideas, things, experiences. To project, reject, object, subject, inject, deject show potent common suffix. Reaching towards completeness includes function, meaning and purpose: the principle of the thing, the spirit of the person to enact the whole. Short or long term concern, self-interest, enlarges with altruism for the sake of another; motive emotive to purposes greater than our own. Per- , prefix of perfect, perform, perchance, perimeter, perish, reaches for absolutes.

Negation is not necessarily indifference. Illness, weariness, inertia, indolence, weaken **will**, postpone action. Enthusiasm, encouragement, persuasion sometimes helps to overcome such difficulty. To like to do what you (or I) ought not to do; to dislike doing what ought, should, could, must, be done are perennial dilemmas. Duty recognised as obligation presents itself. Can I? Should I? May I? Ought I? What happens if, when, I fail? Implications refine, confine, sometimes define possibilities. Negative reactions dissolve motive to will but determined purpose, conscious sensibility, strengthen intention. Forbearance, direction, *control*, effort for another's sake, clarify objectives and motivate for good.

Impulse as immature purpose and behaviour may become informative, controllable, in maturity. **Good-will transforms reluctance into renewed opportunity to become wholehearted, single-minded, unified in devotion to good purpose. A vision, an ideal, a *hope*, calls for devotion, steadfastness, integrity.** Heroine and hero are models of endurance and bravery in their generation and beyond. Florence Nightingale nursing soldiers in Crimea led her to train and educate nurses; Marie Curie's discovery of radium, radioactivity, advanced cancer treatment; Alexander Fleming recognised healing power of penicillin; Eglantine Jebb founded the Save the Children Fund. Black-hearted villains who persist in evil purposes are remembered too.

This minimal exploration of good and evil motives regards hearts as centre of living feelings, heads and minds to **reason, plan** and direct *will* with grace, energy of SOUL to sustain action. Every enterprise proposed, opposed, suggests and invokes alternatives. Questions, doubts, disagreement, denial, conflict, enmity, negation raise criticism in mind and feeling: for or against, in heart. It is from hearts stimulated by senses that passions ferment. Thinking debate urges need to recognise good and evil. Physical, emotional, intellectual and moral passion throb together, capable of integration in *love*, in heart and soul. Good and evil are often expressed inconsistently, erratically. *Love* promotes good but perverted love is evil; passionately obsessive, destructive, aggressive *hate*.

Material things in immovable places are evident, their origin known or unknown. Building, finding somewhere to live; shared, rented, bought involves needs; ties, commitments, expenses, obligations concluded at death. Liabilities and benefits, evil and good, may be passed on. Some people during life find their burdens excessive, objectionable, intolerable. To 'move on' makes a virtue of untying ties. Single or plural occupants leave a place empty, vacant, deserted, dispossessed, nobody's home. Unoccupied buildings decay, exposed to nature's depredations. Conservationists attempt to revive memory, re-invent, but cannot re-embody soul. Re-occupied, repaired, furnished, refurbished for use, a place with scope for health and wellbeing: fear, evil and misery, becomes a home again.

Heart, mind (head) and *will*, distinctive to feel, think, resolve and do, interact with each other. Finding *will* to do, in harmony or not, dependent and independent, is not a clinical linguistic affair. To realise and articulate frontiers; to discern powers, mysteries, mysterious energy of action, is beyond words. Creative permutations and combinations occur in music; are rumoured, evoked, caught in great poetry, in divinity.

Characteristic patterns of behaviour reflect temperament; quiescent or volatile: sweet and foul moods, words; systematic, capable, energetic, methodical in style, achievement, or their opposites. Contradictions, conflicts, disturb concentration necessary for increasingly profound thought. Tensions inhibit, qualities inhabit, habitually trusted to strengthen and refine dynamics of spirit. Like atmospheric pressure, high and low, stillness, wind and hurricane, clear and cloudy skies influence **body**, (senses and nerves, nourished, replenished and transmitted to mind). **Heart** (organic) responds in feeling, emotion: **Mind** (cognition, recognition, reason, analysis, memory, wondering, imagining, thinking) unites with heart for felt-thought towards objectivity. *Will* (fed by desire, purpose, thought, resolve, intent) stirs all four together into potential union, integrity, balanced inner being, growth of **soul**.

Soul, personalised spirit embodied, is expressed in behaviour, conduct, doings, journeying through life guided with *reason* and beckoned by *love*. Evil distracts, causes suffering and is suffered. Mistakes, accidents, disasters, faults (our own and others), involve blame. Consciousness of good enables soul to learn and grow. Since body, heart, mind and will interact with speed and subtlety, it is seldom clear exactly where movement originates. A clear impulse; an emanation of power occurs beyond personal consciousness, feeling and practicalities, to operate within them.

Looking for experience of **spirit** suggests heightening aspiration; inspiriting, spirited, inspired. Physically manifestation of spiritual energy and power is expressed in a tall, tapered point, a **spire**. Inspire, suspire, perspire, aspire, conspire, respire and, ultimately, expire are ups and downs on one suffix. Spiral stairs lead up to a look-out tower, a long view for observation or warning, a lighthouse. Models of DNA, the double helix of identity, identification, elemental inner structure, ascent and descent, down and up and up and down. Telescopic photographs of spiral nebulae suggest these patterns. A spire of inadequate design built with inferior material will prove unstable. Spiritual quality, at best, promotes and is associated with material integrity, but spirit is intangible, untouchable, invisible power of evil or good. Personal thought, buildings, governments, need inspiration, quality of spirit for good, but are spoiled, damaged and damaging in weakness, in evil. Manifestations of spirit are recognised in the soul of an individual; each 'receiver' receives, not always consciously and knowingly. *Will* accepts, rejects, (switches off) or ignores, indifferent. **Phone** is a **donoun**.

Spirit is evident in soul when sources of **power** combine energy with **purpose** into action in a 'high-spirited' person, not 'high-souled'. Comparing electric generators, the energy of electricity and its use, distinguishes them. Lightning disclosed existence of electricity. Observation, study, experiment, tests find knowledge; ability to replicate, captivate potential power; to promote and use it. Lightning was, is, not human invention. Sight (recognition when repeated, perhaps to strike again) led to identification, identity, name. Questions concerning nature, function, potential use, eventually answered, *spark* others. What might electricity do and what could be done by electricity? What are its properties? What purposes, good or evil, can we, shall we, may we, use it for? Generating electric power is achieved through generators, often huge, in 'power stations'. Habitations, factories, street lights are wired to them. Some hospitals, farms, remote dwellings, boats, ship, aeroplanes, have their own generators. Heat, light and sound: theoretical and practical physics, invite and invoke metaphysics, analogies, soulful and spiritual. 'Chips' used in computers, mobile phones, are too small for uninitiated eyes to see. Soul is personal transformer of energy from source to user, connected, enabling instant integration, switched on to *work*. Soul, essence of personality, energised, inspirited with good and evil motive, **purpose** transmitted into action behaves with *will*, willing or unwilling and develops characteristics of character, capable of development; memorable, stronger than death. Spiritual power shares energy, to animate; **LIGHT** to enlighten soul. Affirmation or denial of *will* have exponential consequences in culture of spiritual energy since **'spirituality' is not realisable in a vacuum but manifest in action, in evidence of human experience.**

Distinction between being and doing is active analogy of spirit and flesh with soul, *hinge* at the interchange, embodied in the flesh, astonishing structure of bones, organs, blood, veins, nerves, senses. We are and we do: sometimes, even when we seem to be doing nothing, or say, perhaps think that there is nothing doing, nothing to do.

Spirit, first principle of life-giving quality of animation, original, becomes conditional and variable in experience because of the **gradual** development of human consciousness and *will*. Sometimes we refuse to develop, deny the idea of any such opportunity and ignore responsibility. High spirits and low, good or evil, strong or weak, open being endowed with the essence of life; in tensions of opposites, paradox and contradictions. The positives initiate. War between opinions, beliefs, precedents, possible co-ordination of spirit and flesh, body and soul; of love and of perverted love, is unceasing until moments of balance, peace, truce. What is true? **The last, final judgment is not our own. Another *will* that will know who you are: who I am, each need integrity.**

Vitality; distinct and interactive is duo of outward-inward experience, flesh and spirit, body and soul to perform together. Alternated to inward-outward, their order changes: spirit and flesh, soul in body, spirit qualifying *will* for good or ill intent. Plato thought of soul as being somewhere between spirit and flesh, junction, conjunction. Electricity was unknown to him as to Aristotle, but *light* and dark and shadows, *time* and *space*, music, provided them with rich analogy, as now.

Weather, already discussed, suggests frames of mind, outlook, mood, particularly in northwest Europe. High and low pressure, 'set fair', lows, depressions. Calm, stormy, register on faces of friends and barometers. Fog, drizzle, downpour, deluge, brilliant sunshine represent mood, morale. All permeate poetry, drama, music. The poet, dramatist, philosopher: all three together find exceptional wealth of words, local to England of their *time, place* and history. Local and worldwide weather patterns suggest characteristic climates determined by latitude, altitude, distance from the sea. **Light** and dark, **heat** and absence of heat are primarily due to relative position of earth and sun. Personal existence receives, absorbs, then gives. In this way, too, soul differs from spirit. **Principle differs from quality; being is distinct from doing; soul animates body, invokes motive and motor co-ordination beyond instinct when integrated with heart and mind for good and, and, or, evil spirit energy, fuel of *will* to love and hate.**

Is evil generic? Is it relative to good as necessary opposition, known in contrast to evil? Can we learn to recognise evil? These questions assume, presuppose, reality of evil as more than contingent like and dislike; taste and preference. Evil as cause of suffering and as opposed to good is dangerous beyond the gestures of the three wise monkeys who hope for protective immunity. We cannot **control** what is to be seen and heard, although we can look away, deny, and attempt to insulate, to isolate ourselves. Insensible is not sensible nor lacking sensibility. Responsibility encourages care. Interest encourages listening, hearing. Speaking and doing are personal. Words, spoken words, are difficult to control as immediate reaction overcomes restraint; some think too fast to 'bite your tongue'. Actions, conscious, may or may not be controlled; controllable. Jung listened, studied, counselled and analysed his insights, observations and insights throughout his life.

Life of the mind, when *sensibility has become dissociated*, is not expected to co-ordinate with characteristic behaviour, character. Ingenuity, inventive intelligence to murder, rape, plan and carry out robberies demonstrate talent detached from good purpose. Evil assumes many forms: false 'facts', (not facts) misconceived, wicked ideas, ignorance, denial. Mental and moral blindness and deafness delude into actions which cause others to suffer, and are experienced as wicked, as evil. Open eyes, ears, all agents of a questioning mind, test *sense* and encourage pursuit of what is true, good, wise and beautiful. Freedom from deception, illusion, folly, deep evils of actions in spirit of hatred, cruelty, destruction; grows with understanding. Empathy exceeds sympathy with intuitive insight: paradox recurs.

Will to survive, to find *order* and learn from it, brings freedom, as good water liberates from thirst, and cleanses by washing. Conflicts arise when obstacles frustrate purpose and prevent achievement. *Will* for **common good** can enlist greater purpose than self-centred, self-serving intention. This fifth level of commitment engages devotion; soul searching. Conscience assists and is cultivable. Access through faith, light over darkness, overcomes evil with good. Faith encourages thought, engenders hope, prayers. Evil is hellish; good is heavenly. (See also **XIII**.)

XI

Conscience

'Know thyself. Nothing too much. Moderation in all things.'
(Translation of inscriptions at Delphi)

'The Kingdom of God is within you.'
(*Luke* 17.21)

'Know then thyself; presume not God to scan.
The proper study of mankind is man.'
(Alexander Pope, 1688-1744)

'In a word — trust that man in nothing, who has not a CONSCIENCE in everything. And in your own case, remember this plain distinction, a mistake which has ruined thousands — that your conscience is not a law: NO, God and reason made the law, and have placed conscience within you to determine; not...according to the ebbs and flows of your own passions, but like a British judge in this land of liberty and good sense...'
(Laurence Sterne, *The Life and Opinions of Tristram Shandy*, Book II, Chapter XVII, London, 1760)

'That part of the personality which is soluble in alcohol.'
(Henry Chadwick, *Some Reflections on Conscience*.
Lecture to the Society of Christians and Jews, 1968)

XI 1 In General

Conscience, cultivated, becomes *will's* intimate, inward counsellor. Critical of norms, conscience differentiates qualities in things, feelings, thoughts, intentions, encourages, advises and warns what to do or not do. Intent and purpose need this sensibility for guidance: criteria concerning virtue. Conscience accentuates consciousness of better or worse, right and wrong, wise and foolish, good or evil.

CONSCIENCE unites CON- with -SCIENCE. To con is to learn, in general and in particular cases. Con- , abundant prefix, to –clude, –duct, -fide, -firm, -flict, -front, -form, -fuse, -join, -junction, -substantial, -tent, -vent, -vey. Science, infrequent suffix, includes pre-science and omni-science: **integrated sensibility**.

'Scientific method' observes, explores and tests evidence. Knowledge, with reason, extends confident action. *Fire* burns, consumes, refines. *Water* waters, refreshes, extinguishes *fire*, falls, flows downwards, floods when unable to *drain* away. Conscience stimulates considering consequences of action. 'Conscientious method' evaluates experience, personal and from others. **WILL** fires when ignited; inflamed or extinguished; water irrigates and quenches.

Head and heart have innate consciousness of pleasure and pain, pleasant/ unpleasant reactions, alternatives, without knowing and naming conscience. ***Conduct*** reflects attitudes and intent. Good manners, civility, beyond instinctive reaction, engage purpose, decision and control. Sensibility and responsibility, essential ingredients of conscience, discern alternatives and encourage will to control.

Opinions and beliefs differ concerning human capability for control: of self and of others. ***Will*** may or may not attend to conscience and follow its advice. 'Behaviourist' theories have modified opinions of responsible conduct: 'He/she can't help it!' Does this show sympathy, or pity? Constructive concern affirms *will* capable to accept responsibility, to decide and do. Subconscious motives may be suppressed: conscience promotes recognition.

Manners protect, and irritate, people in social contexts and situations. Instinctive intuitive impulsive actions disregard conscious constraints, but manners realise and respect the sensibilities of others and operate towards careful foresight and control. Good manners are considerate, more courteous than rude or aggressive, kind than unkind, perceptive of needs and feelings, civility within customs, ethics, laws and principles. Spontaneity challenges and is challenged by conventional expectations.

Manners not moved by genuine sensibility, untutored by conscience, are 'mannered'. Convention formalises patterns of association between generations and relationships in almost all walks of life.

Courtesy and diplomacy assist personal, social, political relations in 'polite society', but conscience is unconfined by artificial limits. Virtue includes humility, not arrogance or pride; temperate, not intemperate; courage not cowardice. Conscience polarises tension between self, and others who have different, sometimes opposing interests; tenderises concerns and feelings; sharpens perception, encourages effort, responsibility, reappraised purpose. Absence of genuine sensibility makes manners imitative; tending to dissemble, mislead, deceive. A *promise* made with no intention to perform is untrue and unhappy. Pretensions leads to hypocrisy. Feelings and thoughts, hearts and heads need cohesion: felt/thought and thinking/feeling fused constructively.

Appetites and desires express natural needs. Excessive, perverted, disordered appetites upset balance and weaken *control*. Conscience warns of dangers; risks, perils of unbridled urges, passions destructive to self and to others. Brakes are as essential as accelerator in a healthy vehicle with well-fuelled engine: fit, energetic, under control.

Senses also mislead. Conscience becomes aware of every conscious, relevant resource that is capable of cultivation. Circumstances, environment, inherited contexts and gifts need and offer criteria caught, taught, learned, renewed, reappraised inwardly. Debate seeks to resolve. Resolution becomes tuned to the tuning fork of conscientious action. Characteristics peculiar to family, community, culture, nurture individuals to discover, accept or deny the liberty and obligations of responsibility.

The diagram of CONSCIENCE hopes to clarify some of these connections, good and evil, individual and universal. Opinion and belief about conscience are far from unanimous. Is it innate in every individual? How far do circumstances and conditions modify cases? The concept of conscience develops when **WILL** is affirmed and accepted. Some go no further than to acknowledge 'choice'.

Conscience identifies virtues through experience. Just, moderate, humble, prudent (wise), each challenges and is challenged by injustice, greed (lust), pride, folly. Opposing beliefs intensify conviction but conscience promotes balance. Intemperate anger rages and causes wars. War may be just? Civility, control (dependent on *will*) promote negotiation, diplomacy, toleration and peace.

Three spheres are considered: **XI 2** In Particular; **X 3** Judgment; **XI** Illumination. These recur again and again. The diagram shows ascending order, 1, 2, 3, 4: practical, emotional, thoughtful, moral, (evaluation) reverses when illumination brings confident resolution, cyclical as well as vertical. Examples of personal goodness encourage those who know their *need* of conscience. (See also Figure 2.)

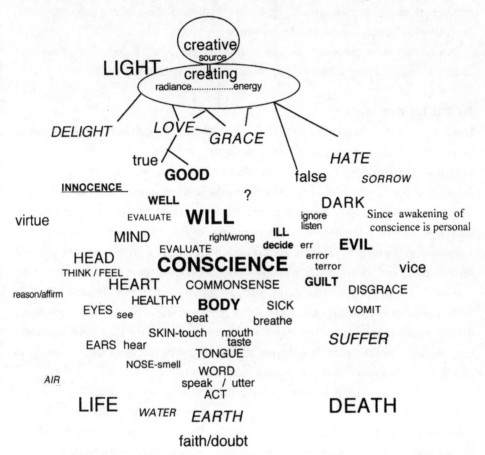

XI 2 In Particular

XI i Guilt

Guilty or not guilty? Accusation of having offended is met by admission of guilt, by silence or by affirming, pleading, innocence. Who accuses? Parent, sibling, friend, neighbour, teacher, employer, police officer, barrister: whoever charges, witnessed, alleged offence. An act innocently conceived, performed, may offend someone. The doer is accused and blamed. Admitting guilt involves self-accusation. Conscience, if consulted at the time, is remembered. Cause, motive and reason, are not always simple.

Regret, remorse, are forms of suffering, not physical but often have physical effects: sleeplessness, weeping, emotional, mental and moral misery. When these accelerate into acute pain of soul; grief, similar in effect, it is depressing. Folly and wickedness due to aggression and ignorance, cause isolation, alienation, loneliness, depression although reason may be elsewhere.

Actions done in ignorance do not realise responsibility, liability, but Courts of Justice do not accept ignorance of law as excuse or justification.

XI 2 ii Ignorance

Did you, I, we, they, know that an action, innocent in some contexts, involves guilt in others? Could, should, ought we to have known?

The substance of guilt is in intended offence. The cause, reason and responsibility for what is done or left undone, by and to others, to ourselves, is motive of an *act* performed. Guilt involves *blame*. Feelings move, up/down, down/up, in and out, in known situations remembered. Daydreams invoke feelings; inventions rather than authentic recognitions, informed, explainable. Threads within events include uncertainties and unknowns. People sometimes pretend ignorance; *disguise, mask,* shameful, disgraceful, actions done. Silence can mislead. *Trust*: trusted steadfast loyalty overcomes suspicion and encourages understanding. When things go wrong, disenchantment and betrayal are experienced. 'To the best of my knowledge' appeases my conscience but is incomplete. Appeal to 'what everyone else does' is plausible norm in manners, convention but not personal responsibility.

Regulations benefit practicalities. Ethicists construe codes to guide behaviour. Principles, universal, apply in situations; are stronger than ethics, relative, or desires, subjective. Some ethical insights echo principles. Enduring principle recognised and known overcomes ignorance; first time discovery engages experience, understanding, intended commitment. Discernment becomes regarded as revealed when belief proves to be true. Conscience at the highest level concerns matters of principle, beyond taste, ethics, manners, even beyond unlawful and illegal acts. The Ten Commandments are a recognised statement of principles. Some are positive, others negative. The consequence of disregard encourages regard and acceptance. Nietzsche did not see it. Origen (c. A D 185-245) said that *'there is no discord between the Gospel and the natural ethics of all informed and educated men'*. (*Contre Celsus* III, 40.)

Conscience promotes diagnosis of error. *'Help'* and *'search'* intend to offer workable alternatives, rescue from ignorance: that helpless feeling of not knowing what to do next. Head and heart, behaviour assisted by conscience to offer *help, search, save,* reminders of dangers on departing from paths of common sense, goodness, virtue, honour and fidelity. What a programme! *Need* and *desire*, the more powerful they are, the greater the temptations and the higher the stakes to overcome them. Sinners now need to learn, to overcome ignorance, listen to conscience with *grace* to resist temptation.

Is temptation resistible? Does your or my answer depend on what we *believe*: what becomes *known* through experience, our own, or assured by others? Without resistance, 'go with the flow', 'do what comes naturally', ignore conscientious criteria for personal control. Expectation of freedom encourages doing what we like. Genuine freedom reaches for and accepts constraints necessary for common good: principles of virtue for healthy well-being. Is ignorance ever bliss? Perhaps in perfect unimpeded innocence. Augustine, neither innocent nor ignorant: 'Love, and do what you will' expressed union with the divine **WILL**: love of the highest whose *will* he ever willed to follow.

Since evil is experienced in *fear* and in suffering, guilt derives from harm, damage, injury, misery: fear and suffering caused by known, intended, culpable action, not imagined but performed. Guilt, then, is more than remorse for actions done in ignorance.

XI 2 iii Responsibility

Responsibility involves accepting consequences of opportunities and actions, not always predictable. To assume responsibility includes *hope* for success and *fear* of failure; credit and blame. Conscience encourages people to lead, initiate, accept responsibility. Egos tend to inflate, tempted to think they know best. All are accountable in the event. Some become managing, controlling, inclined to order, in short, to assume power.

Innate curiosity as to 'facts of life' starts early. Innocence protects but curiosity invites activity. Cause and effect, naturally inseparable but increasingly separated, have long-term personal and social consequences. Something new has origins but no exact precedent; no directly related experience, custom, principle to refer to. Massive changes in custom, belief, information, inclines individuals to think of personal taste, preferences, choice as only for themselves, private. If conscience is numbed or dumbed, indulgence becomes habit and habit addictive. Codes, 'guidelines', law do not provide will-power to challenge and resist local 'culture': exaggerated 'hype', 'clubbing' and 'drugging', anything enjoyable, delightful and in original, normal and natural. The contraceptive pill appears to exempt from natural responsibility, but does not terminate appetite for pleasure. There is no contra-conscience pill to prevent addiction; no anti-conscience patch; but personal goodness and happiness are in danger without conscience.

Addicts have become unable to control addiction. **Will** discovers and experiences freedom through responsibility. Loss of **will**, addiction, becomes destructive, eventually life threatening. Knowledge, responsibility and conscience support resolve; hope for commitment of **will** with **power** to sustain it.

XI 2 iv Greed and Corruption

Money suggests prosperity, 'good fortune', luck, fruitful work. Success opens opportunities for generosity: Nobel, Nuffield, Harkness, Rockefeller, Cadbury, Gates, Buffett and many unknowns. Some pursue bigger business opportunities, greater riches. Some are ambitious for political power. Temptation to suppress scruples, conscience, seems justified by longer aim.

Time in a London prison employed to encourage study among victims of misfortune, weakens guilt among men on remand, exposed to confused expectations. Some believed they had been cheated by the 'system'. Support failed, was often blamed, but being caught, 'found out', was a form of self-blame for foolishness rather than due to irresponsible or wicked behaviour. Conscience becomes suppressed by cynicism. A 'white knight' personality was a confidence-trickster convinced by his eloquent interpretations of undeserved prosecution; persecuted rather than guilty. A highly intelligent public school Oxbridge graduate, was 'in' for having floated no less than a hundred and eighty companies to outwit the Inland Revenue. A middle-aged Teddy-boy retained styles of speech and dress of his once 'fashionable' identity; a bobby-dazzler, bowler-over of 'chicks' who had 'lived for thrills' and been betrayed. Most would talk about their exploits and/or their sufferings. Some responded to encouragement to read and to write; others found relief in art classes. Many had felt more rejection than encouragement and trust; were needy rather than wicked. A few had a mind-set of criminality but could foresee, admit, how difficult it was, would be, to 'go straight', to disentangle from the 'underworld' net with which they had become 'entangled'. Few were 'East Enders'. Watching that TV 'soap' for time to appraise characterisations was far more lowering than encountering prisoners on remand. Most were conscious of alternative worlds not dominated by greed and corruption. Some hoped for genuine liberty, even within the walls.

XI 2 v Terrorism

What is new to say about terrorism? Extending contexts, global: immediate communications, mobile phones, e-mail; huge funds from oil-rich supporters: 'suicide' killers who die to kill others.

What makes a terrorist? Is it ancestral hatred, resentment of past 'exploitation, of untapped resources such as oil gone elsewhere? Poverty, cruelty, privation, misery, injustice, power resented and abused, provoking suffering, resentment; anger into violence? Early rivalries, gangs, bullies, street and playground anarchy, exclusion, alienation, ineffectual or wicked adult behaviour causes disaffection, misery, fury and overwhelming urge for revenge. That is a worrying catalogue.

Truancy expresses rebellion, will for independence. Unemployment nourishes boredom, resentment. Disenchantment begets cynicism, appetite for revolt. Nihilism is indifferent to suffering of others but gratified by **will** to power, dangerous, destructive fundamentalist 'idealism'. Comparatively new factor among terrorists is deliberate suicide: choosing death for their cause. It is not martyrdom. 'Suicide terrorists' take advantage of the protection of ordered life and of law by disregarding them. Instead of a bullet proof vest worn to protect, an explosive garment is detonated to destroy wearer and victims together. A terrorist is trained to accept orders, enforced with ruthless totalitarian severity based on agreed **will** to die.

'Rule of law' depends on *respect* for *power*, fear for punishment and conscience and consent to abide by law. Offences, crimes are tried and, if law has been broken, **sentence** pronounced is enforced. 'Treason' was the traditional name for political terrorists such as the Gunpowder Plotters, conspirators. Murder, arson, robbery with violence, grievous bodily harm, are not usually or necessarily political. War 'breaks out' or is 'declared' by nations or groups of nations when aggression has occurred or treaties violated. 'Terrorism' is neither personal nor territorial although both are involved. Its roots are 'territorial', its participants aggrieved, become unscrupulous, subversive. Conscience approves counter-terrorism to uphold the value of principles of law: the virtues of being (hoping to be) temperate, fair and just. Hesbollah, reportedly funded by oil rich Iran and Syria, claims the land of Israel in an ancient and undying fight.

The IRA claim now to have surrendered their aims or arms. Power-sharing, 'peaceful co-existence, was for long personal rule by a nominee of the Prime Minister in London. Less violence is reported and 'power-sharing' has been announced to recommence in May 2007. Citizens of the USA inherited revolution, terrorist activity in their War of Independence. Idealists continue to pursue perfection by subversion and formidable courage.

XI 2 vi Decision

What could, should, ought, might you 'choose ' to do? Genuine alternatives often become 'one-way' streets. Instinct, irresistible, predetermines animal actions. Human beings conscious of flesh and spirit, body and soul, discover potential ability, *will* to *control*: to prefer, select, resolve, decide. *Power* to *act: grace* and strength are needed.

XI 2 vii Opportunity

Children who desire to please begin to experience conscience. Sub-conscious awareness of pattern, arrangements, sequences enjoyed are followed. The three R's of infancy — Rest, Regularity, Routine — promote stable well-being. Sensibility for good and evil becomes known in positives and negatives: pleasure/pain, joy/sorrow; delight/misery, success /failure, like/dislike, love/hate received and given.

Cultivated sensibility awakens when opportunities open. Seeking approval, appreciation, affection, above and beyond self-interest avoids offending and enjoys benefit. Levels of experience, unrealised but coordinated in childhood, may survive and mature. Denial of conscience suffocates its voice and upsets balanced well-being. Opportunities to give and take, be generous or mean, invite use, misuse, abuse, invoked by need, subconscious until experienced. Simple practicalities provide models for ultimate matters.

XI 2 viii Commitment

Activity provides opportunity to look for the best; to test, evaluate, decide and do. Discussion, direct, borrowed, overheard, benefits or damages transition from impulse to thoughtful resolution and decision: commitment. Knowing who to please, or displease, powers motive for good or ill; parent, neighbour, friend. Conscience promotes conscious *will* to unite quality with virtue: the best we know and hope to achieve.

Commitment engages consistent *purpose* in intention to do: an undertaking to be relied on; a responsibility promised to be performed, followed through, completed once, repeatedly, dependably, to and for the dearest and best.

Commitment involves time and date. Now, later today, tomorrow but it may not be possible until next week, month, year. Is this commitment to be trusted? Commitment is personal. Is this person trustworthy? How can you know? Do you believe that the concept of *trust* is realisable; that individuals, you yourself: people you know, are capable of fulfilling their commitment? Is he or she to be trusted? Am I considered trustworthy? No one can be quite sure of their own *integrity*. These questions challenge us to affirm or deny. Conscience advises, clarifies, cautions. To *trust* or not to *trust* is the watershed between commitment and withdrawal, affirmation and denial. Children know it and say 'You **promised**; can we do it **now**?' *Trust* is experienced early, easily lost, difficult to re-establish. Commitment depends, again, on *will*: and intention.

XI 2 ix Dogma

Conscience is often thought to voice nothing more than rules to be obeyed. Dogma enunciates guiding rules, parameters, indicators, derived from principles known to exemplify living needs for virtue and compassion. Such principles are sources of right judgment, good manners, order and law within which freedom is realised and enjoyed in sovereignty of good.

Plato observed that it may pay to do wrong, to steal, to act unjustly in secret. (*Republic*, 358-361). Gyges the Lydian found a ring that made him invisible. This he reckoned freed him to do what he liked. Gyges murdered the king and took the crown and the queen for himself. Could he rule unseen? What was the queen's situation, opinion, conscience, *will*? Was her experience relevant? Was she in Shakespeare's mind as Hamlet's mother?

Shakespeare's clowns relieve tension: tragedy with comedy. Wise fools draw off malignant evil with wit and humour while they dig Hamlet's grave. Touchstone, the 'fool in the forest' jokes with 'melancholy Jacques' about heart-ache. Malvolio, whose vanity is flattered into folly, becomes pitiable and darkens comedy with tragedy, madness, a joke too far until the tricksters laughter bursts out into a happy ending, but not for Malvolio.

Launcelot Gobbo, Shylock's servant, has a problem. He wants to work for Lorenzo, loved and beloved of Jessica, Shylock's daughter. Lorenzo and Jessica plan to elope. Lancelot has carried messages between them and cares for their happiness. He would far rather work for them than for Shylock, mean and severe, although a doting father who will be outraged to loose Jessica. Lancelot's position will become impossible if his part is known to Shylock.

Lorenzo and Jessica, exquisitely happy, invite Lancelot to work for them. He is overheard debating with his conscience in a street in Venice: 'Well, my conscience, hanging about the neck of my heart, says very wisely to me...'

'Lancelot, budge not
Budge says the fiend.
Budge not says my conscience.
Conscience, say I, you counsel well.
Fiend say I, you counsel well;
The fiend gives me more friendly counsel:
I will **run**, fiend; my heels are at your commandment;
I will **run**.'

(Shakespeare, *The Merchant of Venice*, II. 2)

Lancelot Gobbo is a man of conscience. If not, there would be no alternative to consider, no voice to disregard. He is torn between obligation, inclination, changing circumstances. Shylock was a hard taskmaster. Lancelot was neither slave, serf nor bond-servant. He was free to leave.

XI 3 Judgment

Two people who live on different sides of a street, quarrel constantly, their voices raised, often from upstairs windows. A neighbour exclaims: 'They will never agree. They have opposite premises.'

Final judgment occurs afterwards; a 'post mortem' of action, event, experience. Pre-judging looks to foresee, anticipate, but cannot *judge* what has not happened. The inward faculty of critical scrutiny, essential for making judgments, continues before, during and after action but is in suspense to consider decisions: to connect conscience with priorities.

What has been done cannot be undone. Consequences follow. Ultimate judgment does not rest with an individual, a court, a jury, a judge, however fair. If disastrous, old voices mutter 'There were warning signals'; 'I told you so'. Being wise after an event does not quell the pain of self-accusation, the remorse of conscience unrealised or disregarded.

The beauty of beatitude is realised vision of better than worse, good or evil, even perfection over imperfection. Failures recalled, guilt remembered are judgments of experience. Progress and improvement include effort to redress grievances, to right wrongs, to overcome evil with good. Crisis, itself a form of judgment, provokes need to *act*. Cause, evaluated from available evidence; concluded, leads to decisions, some premature, pre-judged. Judgment is not always of action intended, planned. Evaluations, estimates, may prove inconclusive. Judgment concludes with **sentence**, decision. **Judge** is a primary **donoun**, before, during and after judgment concluded, subjective, objective.

XI 3 i Evidence

Investigating actions done and motive for doing them attempts to ascertain information described in words. Tests verify verbal evidence: true, partly, or false. Conscience, consciousness of guilt and innocence, of responsibility and possible *control*, uses reason to recognise criteria and to devise ways of testing authenticity of evidence.

Procedures and processes, simple and complex, need 'material evidence', 'facts'. Measuring time, distance, temperature, quantity enables comparisons and cross-checks. Forensic, pathological, circumstantial, link sequences of conscientious investigation. Motives emerge with reasons; but are often fuelled by emotional, psychological, mental energy from prior damage, anger, guilt, revenge; elusive, unknown or suppressed, but relevant in heart, head, memory. Evidence suggests reconstruction of motive but some actions occur without restraint of conscience or consistent reason. Unconscious, and conscious, tendency to deceive masks knowing, realising truly, and obscures recognition of evidence.

XI 3 ii Understanding

Facts, like food, need to be digested. Apprehension and comprehension, digestive juices, render information more understandable. Interpretations contradict each other, even when evidence is verified and sworn. Opposite points of view expose paradox. A building looks quite different from different sides, sunny south, shadowy north; elevations viewed east, west, by eyes seeing different things: different eyes viewing the same building.

Dogmatic assertions, less than comprehensive, contradict different interpretation of evidence. Conscience recommends possibility of error; humility as well as commitment. Self-accusation of exaggeration, limited view acknowledged (confessed) relieves guilt. This requires objectivity beyond subjective limits. Learning, believing, knowing, contribute to understanding enlarged in ceaseless re-appraisal. Pleasurable experience, sensual, emotional, excites appetite for more; greed for gratification. Excess upsets digestion, perspective; reduces fitness, sensibility of conscience. A person becomes 'fed up'. Some long for music, 'food of love', to relieve surfeit of appetite, kill it with excess; disenchanted rather than fulfilled.

XI 3 iii Conviction

A *convict* is a person convicted, judged. To *convict* is verdict of jury and/or judgment pronounced by the *judge*. A Court hearing includes evidence intended to enable fair, just judgment. 'Should' and 'ought' are words that may pre-judge listeners, but are needed by conscience: conscientiously advising *will*.

Conviction depends on confident belief. 'Beyond reasonable doubt', affirms this (or that) is true. Is the prisoner guilty or not guilty? This is considered by jurors, expected to be persons of conscience. Convicting should carry conviction. Evidence heard, admissible or dismissed, discussed, promotes knowledge and understanding of the *conduct* of the accused, believed or disbelieved true. Guilt leads to *blame*, to *sentence*. Conscience moves among those present at the hearing. Is the verdict, announced by the Jury, just? New evidence, unheard, perjured, is ground for appeal. *Search* for a fair and just verdict is well 'tried' procedure, sometimes very long and increasingly expensive but the governing principles are safeguards.

> Nevertheless, Lewis Carroll, in *Alice in Wonderland*:
> > 'I'll be judge, I'll be jury, said cunning old Fury...
> > I'll try the whole cause, and condemn you to death.'

Conscience, elsewhere, guides hope for innocent enjoyment and equitable distribution. Sudden reversals of fortune, loss or gain not necessarily deserved or earned, feature in many of Charles Dickens' novels. Nicholas Nickleby encounters extremes of vicious and virtuous behaviour, recognised at the time with commonsense misery and/or appreciation. The systematic avarice and foul, uncontrolled temper of Mr Squeers led him to treat boys in his 'care', who were his sources of income, with cruel violence. Smike was singled out for peculiarly unjust punishment. Nicholas's uncle Ralph Nickleby sent Nicholas to work for Squeers at Dotheboys Hall, in a network of extortion that made him rich. Nicholas, a young man of conscience, was hated, feared, despised, by Squeers. He escaped with Smike. Nicholas encounters the prosperity and glad charity of the Cheerybles in happy contrast; generous benevolence, abundant solvency of pocket and soul. Dickens portrays judgment in action: thoughts, words and works of persons of conscience, uncommon among those who breathed hot, polluted air of Westminster and trod devious slippery paths among lawyers of his day. Dickens' sympathetic understanding of poverty, corruption, injustice continues a powerful influence on the consciences of his readers, dramatic film and TV producers, and viewers.

Effort to insure against poverty, sickness, unemployment, by systematic 'welfare', has not eradicated corruption. State and personal charity relieves need. Is this an entitlement, guaranteed by law, more or less fairly administered? Convictions reflect policies of governments who come and go.

Effort, energy, skill, thought are hired, bought and sold. Work (see **XII**) as labour includes means of production, distribution and exchange: root and fruit of sources and resources for health, wealth and happiness. Different points of view, conflicts of interest, purpose, belief, cause alternative plans of action conscientiously proposed and opposed.

XI 3 iv Just with Mercy

Love and *hate* empower *will*. Excess of either perverts. Victims cry for mercy, hope for and seek justice, compensation. Judgment is often difficult, suspended, postponed. Judges and juries are capable of ignorance, prejudice and subjectivity, arrogance without mercy.

Litany, Common Prayer, sets out sentences wrung out of human frailty and failure. Each pleads for deliverance, positive forgiveness, for misery experienced: 'Lord have mercy upon us and incline our hearts to keep this law.' Said or sung, these words affirm and recognise high, divine, super-human law. Associated with severities, prohibitions, 'thou shalt not', these seem to contradict the liberty and mercy of love. Miscarriages of justice, unjust decisions, unfair thoughts, words, actions are more common than prayer, but prayer reflects extreme need. 'We *beseech* Thee to hear us' *pleads need of mercy* when conscience is guilty. Guilt is felt in heart and known in head. They need to be at peace.

XI 4 Illumination

LIGHT, elemental, primary and in every category of **donoun**, illuminating, as *FIRE*. 'Artificial light' imitates and supplements natural *light*. Alarm clocks are urban substitutes for cock-crow. Dawn precedes sunrise and sunlight illuminates day. Moon and stars relieve night from total darkness but life continues to depend on heat and light of the sun and alternating diurnal, monthly, annual rhythm known through experience, observation, measurement and analysis. They are believed to have continued since the beginning of time although no human being was present at that unrecorded day. Guesswork, reconstruction, astronomical and geological evidence, pre-historic and historic; assist detecting and discovering. 'Getting to know' leads to knowing. 'Knowledge' illuminates mind as light illuminates things: feeling, thought, value; *recurring theme of this exploration.*

Artificial light supplements sun light and illuminates differently. Rooms without windows sometimes 'borrow light'. Open eyelids admit light; closing excludes it. 'Inner light' is not borrowed from elsewhere, but received, acquired, through good fortune of parents, teachers, friends, who communicate wisdom in actions, in spoken and written words. Educated, cultivated persons are occasionally described as 'enlightened'. Conscience offers illumination, inherent recognitions from senses and common-sense, which, if cultivated, illuminate to high levels of sensibility.

XI 4 i Temptation

Individuals face temptation at any time, anywhere. Conscious 'choice', simplistic, pragmatic, develops into recognition, preference, between what is harmless or harmful: to ourselves, to another, others, on small or large scale. Resistance or failure to resist temptation has consequences. Each strength and weakness, success or failure, leads to more as appetites grow by what they feed on. What we do the first time is particularly significant. Any guiding principles, codes, laws, customs evoked by memory and conscience, are challenged when opportunity tempts. It becomes tempting to contrive opportunity.

Conscience illuminates alternatives and what is significant about them. Lancelot Gobbo personified the 'fiend' who tempted him from 'duty' to Shylock, anchored by conscience. With perspective, this fiend was not a devil tempting him to evil but an advocate in conscientious debate between an old and a new loyalty. There is particular danger in failure to recognise temptation when tired, frustrated, feeling low, lacking energy to resist moodiness.

'Begone dull care! I prithee begone from me!

Why be difficult when, with a little more effort, you can be impossible?'

Such simple slogans illustrates how common is the condition. Weighty volumes of moral and pastoral erudition hope to relieve individual need. 'Lighten our darkness', personal prayer of heart and head, is felt and thought.

XI 4 ii Solvency and Solutions

Guilt can be regarded as debt; something to be paid for if not forgiven or settled, possibly by a benefactor. Estimating and measuring costs, debits and credits, is evident in practicalities. It becomes increasingly complex in questions of feeling, of joy and of suffering, life and death. These are inestimable. Temptation to suppose that love can be bought results in disappointment, darkness.

Solve and absolve, solution and absolution, resolve and resolution, dissolve and dissolution are interactive. Accounts are calculated in figures that represent, symbolise, transactions; buying and selling. Inability to pay causes insolvency. Refusal to *pay* can be called to *account, demand* for unsettled debt. NOTE the **donouns**. Inaccuracy occurs. Accounts 'massaged' are represented deceptively, spun. Assets and liabilities are enumerated on balance sheets. Some are tempted to apply commercial criteria to personal dilemmas.

Directors of businesses need to achieve solvency. Conscientious decisions, honest, well judged economy, neither mean nor greedy. Companies and traders are trusted by customers when they deal fairly with orders, products, 'goods', invoices and bills. Capital, for this it is, makes opportunities for employment, research, development, improvement. Conscience requires accountability; consciousness of temptation to subterfuge greed, resisted. 'Ethical' investment includes scrutiny of business practices and purposes. Intoxicating drink, dangerous drugs, abortion clinics, brothels: all challenge levels of behaviour conducted with reference to values far from enforceable. Conscientious objection, disapproval, is personal, essential responsibility in any sphere, shady or illuminating.

XI 4 iii Power

Liberty: freedom from oppression, dictatorship, slavery; systems control which abuses of power are difficult to resist. Rulers, elected or not, are tempted to confuse office with power, and power with authority to assume personal sovereignty over those ruled.

Self-government, personal, essential in ruler and ruled, needs conscience and responsibility to discern and distinguish good and evil projected on small screens of family, neighbourhood, local community; enlarged for countries, nation states, and increasingly extended to international, worldwide spheres of global consciousness and organisation. Conspiracy theories may or may not be justified. 'Knowledge is power' but interpretations depend on what is believed as to motive and intention. This mystery is considered by philosophers past and present. Intersection of belief and reason occurs in heart and head together. To contemplate 'that than which nothing higher can be thought': Augustine's and Anselm's recognition of Divinity, Deity is ever present, all-powerful; to liberate revelation by inviting human response in faith *(trust)*, *hope* (expectation) and *love*. These are means of *grace* for true freedom.

Power to decide and do is of *will*. Conscience is relevant to *will* when known, regarded and consulted. Individualism in rulers, like most 'isms', tempts to become exaggerated; inflated into mania. Interest in and concern for wellbeing, prosperity and peace identifies conscientious rulers who promote them. Conscience promotes conscious knowledge of good and evil intentions and aims, purposes, methods are systematic, (–ocracies), including autocracies. To formulate purpose and exercise power accountable to elected parliaments, to voters whose vote has power to change leaders, rulers, peacefully, by consent, without violence, characterises democratic systems which, above all, refer to highest source of good and evil.

XI 4 iv Identity

Self-consciousness, self-awareness, self-knowledge, self-determination, self-fulfilment, all these are often discussed as things in themselves, without reference to conscience and self-control. Can responsible conscientious behaviour be achieved and depended on without them? Societies become civilised and flourish through affirming what is true. Form and order discovered are sustained, communicated, maintained through promoting order: in order, by order, ordered in law for liberty and freedom. Use of force becomes necessary if social order breaks down and, in individual cases, when personal discipline fails; self-control is, at that time, lost. Restoration is needed, personal metamorphosis.

'Property' implies propriety, properties of things, properly organised and arranged, visible and invisible, as of body and mind, heart and head, soul — not quite the same as spirit. All contribute to identity assisted by conscience. Becoming trustworthy is encouraged by *trust*. *Trust* nurtures confidence, self-confidence. Simple activities, collecting, arranging and rearranging need encouragement, appreciation at home and school. *Fear*, failure, suffering, feeling inadequate are inescapable to people of sensibility at any *age* and *stage*. Identity panic is a danger not only to Hamlet. Temptation to blame others fuels helplessness without relieving it. It is difficult to know and unsafe to guess motives, intentions, of those who make others suffer. Hamlet's sensibility, torment, agonies, are extreme personal misery. His soliloquies communicate tortuous labyrinths of *doubt*, self-doubt; indecision between action and inaction; provoked and unprovoked suffering, the haunting question: 'to be or not to be'. Not 'to do or not to do' for he realises that his anguish in being concerns not knowing what to do, failing to do. His position is unbearable. Complexities so intricate, so inexplicable, bewilder this Prince. Any action is open to doubt, misconstruction, suspicion of and exposure of guilt, unrelieved pain. To shrug it off, to abandon any notion of moral ingredient, conscience, in such a dilemma tempts him to wait on events. Illumination does not come.

XII

Work

WORK serves purposes for necessities, desires and pleasures. *Work* finished, if ever, is 'over and done with' but can finish the worker. After-thoughts, improvements, occur to doer, maker, worker, user, beneficiary, and to critics. Forethoughts, planning, preparing, intends to promote quality and efficiency. Complete satisfaction also is rare. Motive affects, determines, **will** to **work**. Appraisals: subjective/objective, personal/impersonal, influence learning through working towards increasing satisfaction. Consciousness and conscience endow intention, purpose, effort.

Work such as manual digging, preparing ground, is menial, repetitive, obedient to intrinsic order, understood and ordered by nature, another, by divinity discerned. A gravedigger may not know for whom he digs. It may matter who dug to those who mourn, bury, are buried. Death the leveller is eventual, climactic, conclusive: the one certain end of bodily life.

Epitaphs use words. William Kent's gravestone is inscribed:
> 'As I was so are
> Ye, and as I am
> So shall ye bee.'
> (William Kent; died 4.9.1640, Islip St Nicholas, Oxon.)

Robert Louis Stevenson composed his personal *Requiem*:
> 'Under the wide and starry sky
> Dig the grave and let me lie.
> Glad did I live and gladly die.
> And I laid me down with a will.
> This be the verse you grave for me:
> Here he lies where he longed to be;
> Home is the sailor, home from the sea,
> And the hunter home from the hill.'

Patriarchs and prophets, heroines and heroes, sinners, saints, kings, queens, princesses, princes, presiding persons, arouse peculiarly passionate interest in death as in life. Shakespeare's grave-diggers exchange sympathy, deep and shallow as the graves they dig for victims of jealousy, ambition, lust, murder, at the Danish court. They dig for Hamlet, heir to the throne. Words of soul anguish accompany exchanges of exquisite wit; comedy relieving overwhelming tragedy. One grave after another will be filled, Hamlet's last. Horatio, Hamlet's friend, says:

> 'Now cracks a noble heart. Good night, sweet prince,
> And flights of angels sing thee to thy rest!'
> (Shakespeare, *Hamlet* V. 2, line 370)

Work with words, unending, continuing, inexhaustible, becomes increasingly specialised. Exploration, motive of this work, is effort of an indigenous inhabitant, slightly literate, on Prospero's Island. Desert islanders, invited to select music, 'discs', were assumed to take the Bible and Shakespeare's works 'without saying', two volumes encompassing heights and depths, millennia experience in hearts and *heads*.

Insularity, personal, singular, accompanies isolation but words communicate, journeys in thoughts, feelings, ideas, beliefs that transform human experience, towards culture and civilisation. High risks are faced in challenging, strenuous *work* with words.

Insulated, isolated persons need contact. Defoe's story of Robinson Crusoe, (based on the experience of Alexander Selkirk), years alone on an uninhabited island, see a footprint in the sand, witness cannibals; rescues and teaches 'Man Friday' and benefits from his companionship. Deliver becomes deliverance, *save* salvation, restore restoration, redeem redemption.

Work is done singly and together at different levels, (see Appendix **A**), inwardly and outwardly, intimately connected, potentially **integrated**, consciously directed. *Will* includes imperatives: indicative, interactive, paradoxical, tense, frustrating, stimulating, metaphysical, and mysterious glimpses of glory; promise of eternity. Four discussions of work emerge: within this synthesis; repetition persists: assisted by cross references:

WORK 1: Feet on the ground, earthed, natural for good and evil, invoke 'I' words: identity *work* defined, identified, indicative, identity, individuality, ideas, investigation, drawn together, integrated.

WORK 2: Organised, ordered, communal, collective activity, enterprise; purposes practical, felt/thought, moral, civil and civic, 'political'.

WORK 3: Faith and work: practicality discovers principle; natural recognising supernatural; human to superhuman, *divined* divinity where rational limits and expectations respond to intangibles: magnetic *sound, heat light*, ultimate power. *Work* led by belief in *purpose* and *plan*; intention and initiative discloses priorities, norms, possible balance.

WORK 4: *Need* and *Fear*: a literary excursion.

XII 1 First Words

XII 1 i Ground Level

WORK, donoun, engages original activity in being, doing, creating. First word uttered: **IS**, in **being**, with ***will: will*** to ***work***, who may or may not be acknowledged, believed and known '**I AM**'.

Work of nature, natural cycles making and creating, destroying and renewing, selecting, and evolving preceded human living being. Visions of paradise include resources enjoyed; plenty, harmony, peace; *rest* and recreation, joy, *play* in archetype of simple infancy of innocent humanity. Consciousness of given *order*, of disorder arouses questions of alternatives, experienced as dissatisfaction, loss, alienation, exile. Words for experience of emotion and, of pleasure and pain, modesty and exposure, innocence, shame and guilt, remorse are followed by longing, in head and heart for mercy, forgiveness, restoration. Sense, feeling and thought; body, mind and soul are *identified*, consciously *differentiated*.

Archetypal memory persists; backward looking to recall and forward looking to recapture and *plan*. *Work* engages effort to supply basic necessities, essential needs. We ***work*** to live and live by ***work***, our own or of others, with benefit of natural resources endowed that nourish instinctive appetite, ***desire*** with ***reason***. Thought and action need ***purpose***: *intent*. Discovery benefits and/or harms people with one another and with things. Discovery works with techniques that require accuracy, discipline and balance unless, as the Sorcerer's Apprentice discovered, powers unleashed become uncontrollable. Words packed too tightly together bewilder rather than clarify as Moth and Costard discovered. Re-reading helps. Editing engages economy with words: too severe?

Work to do, waiting to be done, prompts negative and positive reactions. To gain, defend, secure, maintain, explore, is to work towards recovery and improvement. All work requires energy. Fulfilment emerges, encourages, from believing and knowing, that assist being in doing; doing well as in well-being; in *work*, at *work*, achieved ascends at best through every level. Words are found, 'coined' to join natural with supernatural, discerning origins recognised and understood in the laboratory of life itself: living and partly living. To live and learn, learn to live, is personal in *time* and *place*, responding to who and what is encountered.

XII 1 ii Identity and Name: Work Defined?

Identity in work is closest when work is a way of life strengthened with willing wholehearted commitment. Doing and being reflect ***will*** in action; identifiable act named, personified: to ***plant, farm, fight, nurse, judge***.

Active work is activity, occupation, employment in making, inheriting, earning a living. Some physical characteristics, genes, features, names, are inherited. Talent needs cultivation of mind and memory to improve, to work well. Training adds skill to commonsense. Experience and knowledge communicable in education promote virtues: scrupulously, fair, courage and loyalty, objectivity, wisdom. Character affects performance. Health and fitness, self-discipline, informed *mind*, clear *head* and kind heart determined to work well. Qualities, values valued, are easier to say than do: said than done, glimpsed in others, good examples. Mechanical and technical work require competence and perseverance. Machine-minders need sustained concentration and accuracy. Dependable minders may become supervisors. Success and failure reflect responsibility: quality of character.

Hunter, Farmer, Miller, Smith; Forest, Sawyer, Carver, Wood, Tree, Carpenter name families whose descendents may have become something other, such as machine operative, trader, publican, doctor by circumstance, necessity, opportunity. Diversity, variety, plurality, multiplicity reflect individuality, unique in varied context: family, tribe, locality, country, city, faith. Attitudes, outlook, casts of mind are nurtured to mature in the nature of work. **Donouns** abound: *farm, milk, sail, cook, fight, deal, bank, trade, nurse; work* itself. The suffixes, -er, -or, change 'do' into 'doer' but ***cook***, like ***fire***, is sovereign; cooking is a process; cooker a processor. **Nurse** embodies work of ***care***: expert, informed, methodical, directed by 'doctor' with the benefit of experience. Consciousness of conscience and responsibility, innate, increased when cultivated, ***find*** principles of ***order*** that direct and develop thinking: skill for good — or evil.

The Oxford Dictionary lists thirty-nine uses of **work**, transitive verb; purposeful activity for impersonal and personal cause, reason; practical, theoretical, artistic, more and less essential.

Work in doing, making, is action: *work* for *work* to be achieved, seen or unseen, visible and invisible. Yours, mine, another's *work*, is keen or reluctant, voluntary, involuntary, compelled, necessarily derived from purpose not always known or understood by worker but connected if and when realised. Rising standards of living transform concepts of necessity but *work* is resourced by what is already known, worked out, worked in, with, by and from *work* done, and developed, best connected with essential origin and purpose.

Work may promote perfect *delight*, pleasure and enjoyment; also *strain, pain*, boredom, *dread*, loathing, misery, resentment, detestation. Feeling, thought and imagination stimulate and are stimulated by work. **Will**, wherever, whoever **will** to work comes from, moves, urges, causes and requires a person to work for themselves, for another, others, both. Co-operation advances individual and common purposes; constructive, destructive; good and evil.

Motive, (discussed with **will**), is voluntary, obligatory, inescapable when enforced. Being obliged is not quite being compelled. An obligation accepted determines courage and effort to work without regard to preferences, danger, enjoyment or ambition. Obligation injects 'ought': responsibility expected by custom, virtue and duty accepted, more or less willingly.

Levels of physical, emotional, thoughtful and evaluative *work* include *work* done by hand, heart and *head* (in *mind*) are discussed with Judging (**VII**), Will (**IX**) Evil (**X**) and Conscience (**XI**). Particular work, tasks, require vitality, union of mind and matter, mind over matter, **will** to do. Good-will initiates, evaluates effort of *will* to work beyond hand to mouth urgencies of primitive existence and emergencies. Anticipating danger makes work to prevent and cure. Insurance and medicine are described as industries. High capability works out purpose, function and use; methods to unravel, interpret, applied in getting on with the *work*. Specialisation segregates work of initiators, discoverers, inventors from that of planners, managers, directors, who think of themselves as employers. Wise to ideas that occur at 'ground level', workshop practicalities, workers are dependent and interdependent; in danger of separation. 'Old' Labour knew and drew on this to find ways, not always peaceful, of co-operation to maintain *work*. Wise employers and employees know it.

Yours, mine, another's *work* is keen or reluctant, involuntary, voluntary, compulsory, necessary and/or for pleasure. *Will* (wherever and whoever it comes from) moves, urges, causes and requires work. Will to work: instinctive, inspired, includes hope to understand the nature of things, of the *work* and of ourselves. Need to generalise in mind accepts specialisation in practice. Time and motion, material and place, need, energy and skill; all are involved in *work*, simple or complex. Focusing on one ingredient includes others, in interdependence.

XII 1 iii Functions, Simple and Complex

Machines are valued when they save time, effort of labour. They work with superhuman speed, intricacy, strength, but success or failure includes, depends on, design and engineering, human skill and responsibility. Marx's syllogism that 'those who work acquire nothing and those who acquire anything do not work' predates 'workaholic' and 'work-shy'. Those imprisoned by material necessities and economic conditions respond(ed) to Marx.

Hats and helmets symbolise function. 'Hood' implies maturity of mind, head; manhood and womanhood; motherhood, fatherhood, degrees of learning, priesthood. 'Hood' is also cover, a secret agent, detective, spy disguised, and a poisonous snake, the hooded cobra; the wolf who deceived Red Riding-Hood. 'Hoodies' are possibly more shy than intending wickedness: incognito.

Work follows motive; positive, negative, desired or opposed. Constructive creative *work* is spoiled, wiped out, by destructive contrary activity. *Work* is invalidated by inaccuracy, mistake, error. Deliberate mistakes turn *work* in wrong directions. Bad *work* requires correction, revision, perhaps demolition. Good *work*, well done, deeply enjoyable, fascinating and satisfying gives pleasure; communicates dedication and joy. Performing arts: acting, dancing, making music is *work* as *play*, practiced with great effort, intense dedication, precision, interpretation.

Production differs from promotion and persuasion. *Work* in advertising, selling, public relations, aims to popularise, to make or break reputations rather than produce essentials: things and policies of substance: thoughts, words, works. Fast communication multiples news and has spawned this sort of *work*.

Working continues to strengthen and be strengthened by character of worker and quality of *work*. Managers sharpen and fortify broad and narrow views of employment. Unemployment, idleness, lack of occupation tempt into the evil of boredom; of having nothing to do. Inability to be active seems to 'enforce idleness'. Solutions are needed for wellbeing in head and heart.

Work undertaken willingly, gladly and freely is deeply satisfying when achieved. *Work* done reluctantly, with difficulty, perhaps painfully, subject to another *will*, is eased by fair and reasonable expectations, encouragement, but blighted by coercion in domestic, economic and political contexts. Forced labour and slavery are extremes; people working without protection or redress; compelled to endure cruelty, torment, enslaved.

Mathematical language: integral and differential, static and dynamic, focuses metaphysical consciousness through work. Addition and subtraction; multiplication and division, co-ordinates, series, move from simple to increasingly complex functions. Applied to practical work, static and dynamic concepts of, balance demonstrated and measurable, require fulcrum, moment, weight, force and resolution of forces, products, divisions, gradient, acceleration, active *work*, gravity at every level, in every *sense*.

XII 1 iv Energy: Work and Play: Wit and Humour

Work to do and *will* to do it need energy but lack of energy is not always weakness of *will*.

Will and energy reciprocate. Appetite, desire and need motivate *work*, constructive, destructive: energy expended, spent, dissipated. Physical injury, sickness, disease incapacitate some but need not destroy effort of *will* to achieve in others. Energy of *will* may diminish, suffocate, lost by many means. Constructive *will* to survive may resist dependence. Living on frontiers of severe physical, emotional, nervous, psychological stress stimulates, dissolves or resolves energy. Each personal generator of energy is unique, mysterious, unique but has much in common with others. Motive will generate search for resources according to demands made on them but illness, disease, physical and psychological imbalance, lack of energy and of confidence bewilder and disable *will*. *Work* to do and energy to do it are stimulated by personal and impersonal factors, ours, and those of others. Continuing responsibility responds to pre-emptive hazards of life itself and draws energy from them.

Work includes practical doings together with thoughtful searching, learning, striving to know, hoping to understand: presupposing possibility of understanding. A finished object, 'work', is open to criticism, subjective and objective. Initiating, making; responding, repeating, processing, starting and completing, whatever the material, whoever the people: intention and aim includes and is determined by quality of commitment, self-giving. The origin of all things, species discovered, known, developed and enjoyed includes evolution, adaptations, strategies for survival, functions and processes that unfold and extend. Advance occurs through natural and personal energy, *will* to do, make, appraise and maintain *will* to work.

Growth is sustained by using and imitating energy discerned in nature. *Water* falls, is used to irrigate by devising ditches, tanks, reservoirs. Wind, gravity, animal power, were harnessed by early people. Sails, pumps, ships, steam engines are very recent in history. In time as in due course, but beyond time as now measured, it is necessary and possible to realise *change*, altered perspectives, metamorphoses through attempts to contemplate great distances of time beyond measurement:

> 'Time no longer; no more time to search for that elusive rhyme...
> Yet here is rhythm, music: pined, opined; word still, in mind.
> Then linger, long enough, to find
> Form, order, pattern: that first word for world.
> Bird song, water dripping: songs of work, sublime.'

Time in our lives passes: ineluctable, finite measure of mortality drawn, marked, from cosmological pattern and order, applied and applicable in practicalities of life and *work*, each *watch* watching and watched, preparing for 'dead' line; postponing until tomorrow, doing and enjoying now this minute, maintaining, preserving, enduring to each end.

Time derives from light and distance. Stars, galaxies, planets, comets have energy, motion and rhythms on time-scales of unearthly, extra-terrestrials extent. Their order becomes memorable; known from sun and moon. The energy of **WORK** in making them is immeasurable, inexhaustible, immortal energy of creation beyond time-scale of present human measurement. The 'time of our lives' means particularly memorable.

Measuring time has proceeded on since parameters discerned, measured; sunrise and sunset. Knowing how time works and how to work it does not identify its origin. Aristotle regarded time as sixth of his categories or predicaments. Augustine wrote that providing no one asked him what time is, he knew. We speak of spending time, of arranging a time, of time lost or gained. Umpteen proverbs and metaphors reflect experience of and in time. Augustine, intensely conscious of his physical body, was a man of huge energy, vitality, intelligence, virility whose appetites tempted and tried his *will*. He experienced *grace*; that which transformed control of uncontrollable desires, sublimated inwardly. Continually responsive to external, outward and inward sensibility, Augustine knew his *mind*, his intelligence nourished in *power* to know, remember and **will** to do. Memory, expanding personal treasury of direct and indirect experience he found capable of infinite expansion and profundity: provided limitless riches; known and unknown: access to and from universals; his soul alive to realms and realities disclosed within time; to, from, and beyond it.

Classic classifications such as Aristotle's categories, Augustine's in *Confessions*, Newton's laws of motion, Einstein's discernment of relativity, are terms of reference in words and figures. The architects of Egypt, Greece and Rome did not think in those terms, but they experienced and respected gravity and devised systematic structures. Shakespeare drew from Ovid and Plutarch; from the English Bible translated from Hebrew, Greek and Latin and from anyone, anywhere, his absorbent psyche encountered: soaked up, and metamorphosised. Every thread, rewoven into living drama, inimitably worked, re-worked, in a life lived in energy, power and the mysteries of creation, infinite extremities, intensities of experience of *work* as *play*, expressing the 'divinity which shapes our ends'.

Work contrasts with play; is relieved with wit and humour, a song in the heart.

'What is an epigram?
a dwarfish whole
its body brevity, and wit its soul.'
(Samuel Taylor Coleridge)

An artist needs talent, time, inspiration and intense effort to create or perform a *work* of art. Someone who appreciates, empathises, sympathises, provides crucial encouragement. Tragic/comic, consequential/trivial amusement makes laughter; tears of grief and of joy, spontaneous, deeply felt. The performing artist becomes utterly absorbed in a particular performance and transports audiences into participants. Appreciation makes devotees kin to worshippers. 'Fans' *fan* flame, inflame talent, ablaze with appreciation of achievement.

In the sixteenth and seventeenth centuries, 'humour' meant fluid. The four body fluids: blood, phlegm, choler and melanc were characterised as sanguine, phlegmatic, choleric, melancholic. (See Ben Jonson, *Every Man in his Humour*, 1598 and Robert Burton's *Anatomy of Melancholy*, 1621.) Blood and phlegm make appearances, choler and melanc, unseen, are manifest in 'moods'; all four affect behaviour. Uneven supplies upset balance and balance is upset if supplies are uneven. Contemporary understanding of humour is closer to mood, good or bad, as a swinging feature in personality, soothed or stimulated externally. Sympathetic recognition of inner balance, internal 'chemistry', is renewed area of research for chemical medicines, pills, intended to redress balance disturbed.

To appreciate and make jokes, to laugh and promote laughter need *wit*, good *humour*; but ironical, satirical reactions sometimes become sick, dirty, black. Blood as 'humour' suggests good and bad blood. Is this inherited tendency: pre-determined *will*? 'Bloody-mindedness' persists. Cool and hot blooded, temperate and intemperate, thick and thin, represent devotion; pale indifference, degrees of heated passion, love and hate, raw, un-sublimated, unless controlled, civilised, sublime. A bleeding heart identifies blood with humour; wounds renewed; perennial suffering. Phlegm, normal mucus, inflames and distresses nose, throat and lungs. Sneezing, wheezing, difficulty in breathing, are associated with spitting, expectorating. Bringing it up, 'spitting out words' is phlegmatic reaction. Choler, bile, is a digestive fluid. Excess disturbs and causes inability to stomach food undigested in a 'bilious attack', vomit, sickness, 'throwing up'. Impure water causes infection, epidemic, cholera. A choleric person gets angry, and anger is infectious. Melancholy was regarded as a morbid condition due to excessive black bile fluid making a person ill tempered, sad, depressed. Humour and temper continue to be connected with moods. Deep melancholy is baffling, variously regarded as physiological, temperamental, circumstantial, psychological; treated with whatever specialist, counsellor, consultant consulted, believes will help to heal; to restore balance.

Attitudes to work, to performances in life, affect and are profoundly affected by wit, humour and temper. To laugh at ourselves, with and without others, during deeply serious activity relieves, restores perspective and balance as Shakespeare knew. Emotions emanate from heart, custodian of blood, vitality of body. The temple of personality, the **soul**, is where will, energy of mind and body, interact and integrate together, hinged into action; affected by and affecting thoughts, words, *work*. Soul, seat of well-being, is where humour and temper nourish virtue and courage: high-hearted happiness, low deceit of wickedness, evil, to and from *will* to *work*, all are empowered by energy, confidence, *grace* for sustenance, nourishment. Hope to heal dis-ease: maladie, melancholia, depression, stretch every therapist, school of therapy, friend, teacher, counsellor, pastor, minister who hopes to nurture well-being.

A word game devised for Jessica Mitford's eightieth birthday party invited players to choose the title of a book or poem and, by altering one letter, alter its meaning: e.g. 'Black Beauty' into 'Block Beauty'; 'A Sale of Two Cities'; 'The Taste Land'.

A newspaper reported that her favourites were 'Alice in Ponderland' and 'The Now Testament'.

XII 1 v Integrity of Work: Profession, Vocation, Confession

Work, verb and noun, (**donoun**) is metaphysical without poetic conceit or fancy. *Work* encourages, and at first depends on, sense to develop and establish habit: receive and receipt; deceive and deceit; conceive as concept, conception, conceit, distinct but connected to poetic 'conceit'.

Excellence achieved might seem to justify conceit but tempts to self-satisfaction. WORK changes material into something else made with energy, skill and effort: a log into a canoe, clay into pots and jars, blocks of snow into igloo. An idea conceived looks for materials to make it. The idea is born, becomes a *form*, a concept; then a *material manifestation*, product of energy, *will* to *work*; to *change* something into another thing. Even when processes are familiar, deliberate, repeated, the mystery of transformation is not completely captured, de-mystified, explained and expressed in words. Poets, intensely perceptive, approach appreciation with exceptional insight and emotional intensity, but explanation is elusive without the language and vocabulary of transforming faith. Incarnation and epiphany, resurrection and eternity, which recognise and acknowledge *super-natural manifestation*.

Inward transformation, 'second birth', is change of heart led by *will* surrendered to another, a lover in love, a soul hungry to recognise the highest and best; which transform mind and rearranges intention, determination, *will* itself. Response to words, heard or read, remembered, digested, may *move* your or my *will* to positive or negative response. Change of heart affects, *mind*, transforms thoughts and attitudes. Priorities are rearranged. Saul, called Paul after 'conversion', describes himself as a 'new creature: old things are passed away; behold, all things are become new.' (*2 Corinthians* 5. 17.)

Augustine experienced conversion, transformation, in the garden at Milan, described in *Confessions*, and central theme interwoven throughout this and all his subsequent works. Metamorphosis of conversion enabled Augustine to experience release from enslavement to 'sexual habit', *desire* beyond *control*.

Will surrendered is transformed through **GRACE**: word for power and comfort of super-human energy. (*Ephesians* 1. 17; 2. 5-8 etc.) Augustine knew his ability to remember and recognised in his *mind, will* to do; but was in desperate need of strength beyond his own. Memory, expanding treasury of direct and indirect experience, showed his capability of infinite range and profundity; limitless riches, known and unknown, access from and to universals; his soul increasingly alive to realms and realities disclosed within *time*, yet beyond it.

Ordinary life, original, natural, ordinary normal development, challenges us to find ways and means to understand, prove and improve, contribute to and enjoy happiness. From necessary essential routines new work emerges, believed to be worth doing, likely to involve *toil, risk*. To investigate and discern what is and is not present, alterable or not, capable of growth, hope of improvement, does not always work out as hoped. *Work* of *mind*, theory aided and transformed with high technique, practicalities, assists in cracking codes and discerning mysteries. Technology promotes speed to *produce*, but has unforeseen, uncontrolled consequences; endangering ozone layer, icecaps, fertility itself. Investigations move from level to level, from sense to thought, evaluation, quality, purpose, meaning and enjoyment, to return to everyday practicalities concerning primary, intimate and ultimate attitudes to life and work, first and last things.

We know what *work* is when doing it. Knowledge emerges in *work* observed, done well or not. Thinking, wondering, what went wrong; could be improved. Unlike motives, intentions, consequences experienced, practical actions are seen. Why dig there? What are they digging for? Is it to plant, to bury, to cover, uncover, recover, find water, prepare foundations? Is the digger a planter, undertaker, archaeologist, well-builder? Planning permission, now required for trimming trees, building new, and modification of old buildings, generates publicity, protests, occasional formal enquiry. Reasoned conclusions thought unreasonable, are sometimes obstructed. Directors of operations work for those who decide, plan, financed from public funds.

Reciprocal respect for purpose and method, of service and task, includes quality of materials used and of work done. Carpenters inspect, feel, examine wood used to work, work on. *Work* engages material with purpose, intention with concentrated skill. Conscientious good-will, ordered virtue are among qualities of character, of *personal integrity*. A diamond cutter needs knowledge and skill before and after cutting. A cutter is constrained, skilled, to make the best of each stone. Dealers need honesty and judgment.

Information technology transforms organisation. Telephone, modem, fax and e-mail, to *order, record*, calculate, *account*, speed transactions. Financial skills, estimates, book-keeping, debts, loans, profit or loss can be computed very fast with artificial intelligence. Needs, materials used, skill and expertise, produced, achieved, return to motive, effort, purpose and *will*, subject and object. No *work* is exempt from poor quality performance, of subversion or fraud, hackers and viruses.

The Paradise garden where water flowed, food grew, animals were friendly and people were without shame or blame is archetypal memory. The cunning serpent deceived, tempted Adam's wife Eve to disobedience. This garden, millennia earlier than Robinson Crusoe, shipwrecked sailor, worked to survive; or twentieth century cannibal isle of Sweeny and Doris; he and his island girl possessed, possessing, she 'done in' (T. S. Eliot, *Sweeny Agonistes*, CPP, page 125.)

Exploration for the source of the Nile, for the origin of species; engages wondering and considering first breath, utterance, word, movement of wind, breathing, to create. A brief history of anything varies with mind, language, knowledge, experience, theories and belief known to the writer. To geographer and historian, a river is a river in any land and language, water flowing from wherever it rises. Architects of Athens and Rome worked without Newton's laws as such. Threads woven into living drama, re-worked inimitably, in awe of life lived in the power and mysteries of creation, infinite extremities, intensities of experience: works expressing the 'divinity which shapes our ends'.

Word thought, said, done integrates in action, *work*. Actually, that is to say 'in practice', we learn and continue to learn through doing. Words are found for what is discovered and done. Words, present and available, for a running commentary if appropriate, multiply in work. Language itself, spoken, written, increases.

As an *act* being done, *work* is a verb. *Work* is also the name for an act, the object of a particular act, a noun: *dig, rake, hoe, plant, cook*. When you work, your *work* is the *work* you do. The two make sense together, performed by performer in performance. Coincidentally, *thirst*, *water* and *drink* are also **donouns**. *Produce, work* to *produce*, is good, authentic, genuine. If not, it fails, like an 'unhappy performative'.

To order and name expresses confidence of an existence: in being from creative substance, energy of origin. Creation is what was and is, what is and will be. To identify the mystery of **energy** and *will*, cause and effect in the created, given world; continually working, renewing, modifying, evolving, is **identified by name**, different names in different cultures. Unutterable Hebrew 'Jehovah', 'Jahwey'; Aristotle's *De Anima*, Mohammed's 'Allah', William Blake's *Old Nobodaddy*; Augustine's 'that than which nothing higher can be thought', 'Our Father' known in Christ the Son, present in the Holy Ghost the Comforter: three in one, one in three.

Existentialism derives from being and thinking about existing. 'I think, therefore

I am' follows 'I feel, therefore I am' — but I live, **work, will, wonder,** feel, think, and am capable of all sorts of other activities in being alive, living, doing; working in necessity, *fear*, obligation, good and ill-will. An '-ism' possesses us for the time being but 'enthusiasm', (from en-theo), continues to sustain energy and power in enthusiastic persons, susceptible to but not necessarily 'possessed' by them. (c.f. –isms with –asms.)

To think, feel, and wonder about life, single and communal; about purposes and ends of life, looks for sources and resources precedent to existence. Infinitely greater than a derivative microcosm yet a life in need of them all. I have a name, as you have. 'I am', a name some believe too solemn to speak, identifies that which is; the substance, essence, energy of creative power. Moses heard a voice from a bush on fire, burning but not consumed. 'Who are you?' The answer: 'I AM THAT I AM'. (*Genesis* 3. 1-14.)

The Emperor Akbar (1542-1605), as mentioned before, ordered that all known names for the Creator (whose work he hugely enjoyed) be carved on his tomb. There are ninety-nine names on its exterior, near Agra, inside a superbly designed and constructed edifice, earlier but less exquisite than that built by his grandson, Shah Jehan, in memory of his beloved wife, mourned, remembered and intended as beautiful as she: the Taj Mahal.

Id (Latin idem, the 'the same one'), identical, is used for a unit of germ-plasm, biological. Id distinguishes an ingredient of personality, distinct from ego. Id- is in idea, idol, idle, idiot and idiosyncrasy. Ego is personal sense of individuality, the irreducible self, yours, mine, anyone else's, a common factor with others but itself unique. Strong egos, egotists, egotistical, are particularly conscious of themselves and of other egos. A frail and tentative ego, an unconfident self, needs and may draw strength, support, from resources outside itself. When 'conscience' looses currency, consciousness of soul dwindles. Those two words, conscience and soul, continue vital in personality and character. Their absence leaves a vacuum. Self-esteem, self-worth, intended substitutes, reflect subjective, self-preoccupation: known to oneself rather than becoming known, as we are known, with and through others whose confidence confirms.

Vocation is Calling. Confession acknowledges *need*. Profession responds to vocation and is fruit of confession.

Common words develop shades of meanings. People are not always able to understand each other. Appearance; face, actions, functions, *work*, play, friends and foes are outward, visible. Inward apprehension: sense, wonder, emotion, thought, spoken, written, *work* as best we can; seems, and appears, as 'self-expression'. Seeing, watching and hearing others working, doing, speaking; some with **love**, much valued if not rejected, others with indifference, apathy, emptiness; some with **hate**, failure, despair; harsh negatives destructive of balance, peace and happiness. Most, almost all live and work with conflicts, ambiguities. Inhabiting paradox contributes to creative tensions. Crises of confidence occur. *Work* may become constructive, positively relieving, confidence sustaining even to perfectionist standards; panacea. Organisation is needed.

XII 2 Work Organised

Physical organs, internal, invisible, work to maintain bodily functions: lungs breathing air to ventilate heart; heart beat to circulate blood, pulsing through veins, arteries, to fuel senses, nerves, brain; stomach receiving nourishment digested, transformed into energy; brain to serve mind, memory, wondering, thinking, spontaneously, deliberating *will* to *work*.

Organs, wind instruments, reproduce many sounds, as of an orchestra. Organists play, perform, make music: eyes reading, ears listening, mind/*will* ordering fingers, hands and feet; manual keyboards; pedals, 'stops' to modify, exemplify music composed, read, or improvised by exceptional exponents. Simultaneous co-operation and control make music. Organised work involves EMPLOYMENT and ENTERPRISE. Government, increasingly centralised, directs organised work to maintain ordered life: provide frames, patterns: aims not aimlessness, hope rather than hopelessness in heads and hearts.

XII 2 i Employment

Persons are not always 'employed' by what 'occupies' or 'pre-occupies' them. Some work for another, others; some employ themselves, (self-employed), some find another to oversee *work*. Employers watch, keep an eye on workers or find an agent to see work done and done well. *Work* for another accepts that *will*; at least, obediently; at best wholeheartedly, engages commitment, concentration, skill, enjoyment. Domestic prosperity (household, locality, business, industry, nation) proliferates work. Lateral and vertical relationships, levels, interact in time and/or money, for prosperity.

Labour is 'costed' when *work* is understood to mean what a person is paid to do; for doing, employed to do; organised within an 'organisation'. Earning; getting and spending, working, playing, leisure, pleasure, are increasingly equated with *work*.

Games and sports commercialised, join the 'entertainment industry'. Being paid to play alters motive and purpose of any 'game'. Greed sharpens **will** to win; tempts to unfair advantage. Some cannot resist temptation to foul, cheat; against fair, true competition. Speed; high skill, fine style, find delight to play and be seen playing. Real value, productive and enjoyed, provides genuine benefit achieved: the good of producing, building, learning, healthy happiness of good work.

Working 'for love, not money', calls for freely given effort. *Work* readily reckoned in 'kind' exchanged needs. 'One good deed deserves another' occurs without price or contract but 'mass production' employs workers on bare 'nexus' of money earned. Minimum wage without concern or generosity tempts employers to think first about bigger profits and, if there are investors, shareholders, higher dividends. Priority of greed was called the 'unacceptable face of capitalism' by Conservative Prime Minister Edward Heath.

Improved machinery, higher technology, continue interdependent. Co-operation, includes familiar routines, 'conveyor belt' skills, as do fishermen, nurserymen. Singular writer, computer operator who generate *work* need equipment, customers, 'employers'. Specialists are 'consulted' for advice. Medical, legal, educational head and heart problems need resolution. 'Professional partnerships'; medical practitioners into group practices and hospitals; teachers in school, college, university; clergy in parishes, deaneries, dioceses, minister support and encouragement, improvement: lifelong experience to learn the tradition of good-will to serve: concern which needs and benefits from costly equipment, qualifications and administrative expense.

Public services depend on good-will, personal conscience, willing co-operation, which challenge governments to realise that teachers, nurses, police, many others need recognition as nurseries of courtesy, civility, learning, for good health and order. The voluntary principle in action is the true root of freedom. Devotion and good-will among those who work, overwork, serve, not for riches, but for fulfilment. Material needs are undeniable, not denied vocation, professionally motivated in charity; pre-eminent virtue is its own reward.

Organising thrives with continuity of expectation: virtues transmitted for good. Criteria of value; success rather than failure; motive and ambition mature when fresh demands accompany promotion, advancing ability to achieve. Business enterprise depends on profitable initiatives: making, producing, buying and selling, transporting and distributing goods. Successful enterprise requires good *work* at every level. The functions of employment, *work*, overlap in all spheres. Many professionals employed in private enterprises and in public service work with efficiency, skill, unstinting effort which develops ability, improves quality without waste; prosperity, enjoyment and benefit for common good.

Motive, singular, gains strength from encouragement and communal well-being, shared effort, interest, appreciation. **MOVE** and *work* accept personal pronouns. He and she, singular; and they, more than one, of either gender or both. who is worked for, moved to serve, work with, can be as important as the *work* itself. Practical, technical, political, economic, legal under and overtones of life occur as societies grow. To apprehend, comprehend and understand what occurs in *work* includes disputes. Communal *work*, collective and social, gathers to and from individual doing. *Work*, doing and making, is essence of function in every activity. **Words overlap**, instantaneously distinguished in *mind*, to interact and combine practicalities for conscious, deliberate repetition.

Words for *work, work* with words involve listening, learning to use and read a language. Talk, discuss, recollect and strive to set down words from sounds, signs, symbols, numbers and letters, ideas and hopes. Sounds have shapes, absence and presence, 0 and 1, zero and one, O: I for example, and SOS; others make music: drum, flute, piccolo, euphonium, trumpet, string, organ. Words in sequence form sentences to make communication effective; subject and verb in statement, *work* and the object or purpose of the *work* as of a sower who sows seeds. Colour, shape, pattern add character, quality.

To activate is to get going. Activity continues until stopped, ended, finished, by *will*, accident, intervention; by energy exhausted, power failure, inward or outward. Human activity, *will* and effort, effort with *will* is sometimes invisible, impersonal, unavoidable, instinctive, involuntary sneeze, swallow vomit, weep. Original work includes volition and with it, responsibility. To act is to do, to take action, once or repeatedly, at any level. A difficult decision, simple or agonising, is to *act*. An act enacted, deed done, business transacted, plural or multiple activity, doings, are caused, understood, misunderstood, or mysterious. Considered as performance, acting is *work*. **ACT** multiplies with prefixes and suffixes of motive and achievement. To re-act can be positive and negative; for, against, or double negative become positive or destructive. *Work* involves acts, singular, plural and processional (processes). *Work* to please, to play, to amuse may be serious, light-hearted, frivolous, but criteria of failure and success, partial, imperfect, perfect; incomplete, complete; all involve effort.

Work tested for quality provides models, offers examples indicative through reason, taste, evaluation. To prove or disprove, approve or disapprove, follows practice tested to accord with *governing principle*. Exceptions and extremes require recognition. Heart response warms head to consider, to try to see how to resolve, needs *will* to determine, direct, mobilise into action; able and willing for effort, effective *work*.

Work 'for the sake of' a person, commitment, purpose, friend, family, quality, is positive.

Work is operative (opera): for nurture, sustenance, strength but includes, risks, failure, error, deliberate wickedness. These realities need recognition, acknowledgment. Forgiveness reclaims, renews and restores: redeems from evil, from sickness to health. Well-being, pleasure, happiness, peace and plenty are profit which sustain heart and soul, mind and body, since responsibility is accountability in life to life itself, for health and wealth. Restored when lost; balanced, not a balance sheet or weighing machine of material but, parallel engagement at every level, paradigm and parable of *work*. A parasite depends on *work* of others.

Dynamic activity demands times of stillness, reflection. Memorable moments caught in a photograph, snapped, are instants between movements. Quiet times, contemplative, receptive, reflective, purposive or incidental, occur with particular intensity immediately before or after sleep. Study of statics precede and succeed dynamics; weight in balance without motion. Statistics are gathered, measurements organised to inform; compared for trends in *time* and *place*, offer perspectives. Movement promotes *change* in things, situations and people. People generate *change*, sudden, dramatic, with wise foresight; but also, sometimes, to damage, to destroy other's *work*; intended evil.

XII 2 ii Enterprise, Control, Intelligence, News

Natural growth, productive, is imitated and encouraged by cultivation. Reproduction occurs by instinct, awakening consciousness, of actions, to make, create, pro-create, and to reproduce. Energy for pleasure is supplemented by ingenious techniques, power generated, but human survival continues to involves much drudgery. Leisure, (outside vision of paradise), is momentary (brief) or nonexistent but prosperity moves people to celebrate, to feast and enjoy. Systematic leisure, privilege of few increasingly enjoyed by many, depends on enterprise to succeed and *control* and continue. To lead, rule, exercise power includes ability to delegate *work*. Responsibility assumed becomes authority exercised; relieved when shared. Traditions of personal trust are not sustained when ambition and the rewards of power loosen obligations of loyalty.

Interdependence arises from necessity, practical co-operation, skilful routines. Exchange has practical advantages. Levels of civility, mutual trust, enhance good living. Illness, ill-will, upset motive to **work**. Enterprise, success, prosperity are positive, constructive motives but envy, resentment, threaten their cultivation and endangers freedom to do well. Greed, excess, cheating, lies, threatens 'free' enterprise and undermine confident prosperity. Conflict, ever on or near the surface, engenders intimidation, violence, cruelty, war.

Cure of bodies and souls through study and learning developed early in Europe and elsewhere.The Romans absorbed much from Greek culture and became an extensive empire. Christians preached, encouraged, endeavoured to practice **trust**: faith, **hope**, and charity, never easy. Persecution led to growth of monastic and convent communities. Health and education, now much funded from taxation, continue to include work of volunteers. Pastoral help, specialised such as Samaritans for those in despair who contemplate suicide, Cruse counselling in bereavement, social and sports clubs, Churches, faith communities for all ages inspire, maintain voluntary, willing support, often cooperating with 'statutory' social services.

Words for work overlap, circulate in mind, interact to combine and focus in practicalities. This is an apology for deliberate repetition in these generalisations. When we do nothing, have nothing to do, we appear unoccupied, unemployed. Internal routines are working away, pulsating, digesting, replenishing, not always geared into conscious will to work. Withdrawal, occasional soul weariness, apathy, reluctance, absence of **will**, cause inertia. Support from friends, family, therapy (medical and other) hopes to assist, to revive confidence, re-ignite **will** and renew energy: recover energy to invigorate **will**.

Work becomes an art form if critical, self-critical worker imitates, follows and challenges frontiers for something new, fresh, different, excellent, transforming. Artifice surrendered to artificiality looses authenticity. Imagined images, appearances, fancies, disguise and mislead. Interdependence of surface and substance ignored in ignorance, fail to transform. Imagined pictures, invented images distort with incomplete, insubstantial perception although cartoon and caricature communicate. Confidence to discover essential **hinge** between appearance and reality, **surface** and substance, grows and reaches beyond first level practicalities. Law, intended to protect, includes libel, slander, defamation, obscenity, but such laws are changed when conservative or liberal protagonists determine to change them. Broadcasts are particularly vulnerable since words and pictures are not documents as such.

Responsibility: in conscious discretion, loyalty and trust led by Governors, 'Trustees', appoint senior executives accountable to them for programmes. Exceptional concern for contents (often political) and costs leads to public enquiries who examine and report, e.g. the Committee on Broadcasting (Pilkington) 1960. Weakness, deceit are not unlawful, criminal or sinful but reflect the range and change in human behaviour. How do programme makers achieve worthwhile, interesting, entertaining work which is not dull? T. S. Eliot, giving evidence to the Pilkington committee, banged on the table saying that pursuit of popularity 'begins by underestimating public taste, continues by insulting it, and ends by debauching it'.

IT, e-mail, Internet, websites, etc are transforming broadcasting with advertising and with reciprocal communication between programme makers, producers, presenters, and listener/viewers. The Hutton enquiry into the death of David Kelly, 2004, was neutered. Responsible control, to be effective, needs follow through.

XII 2 iii Government: Practical, Political, Lawful

Great cities and nations include all sorts and conditions of people; workers, idlers, parasites, crooks, enterprising newcomers, aliens, 'illegal' immigrants hoping for assimilation, 'naturalisation'. A government department which fails to regulate, know, record and control that for which it is responsible endangers public wellbeing and destroys confidence. Citizens are of cities. Sovereign governments expects order among those subject to them, including cities: London and others, whatever their race, faith, creed, at home in common wealth, the idea and reality of Commonwealth.

Politics, 'the art of the possible', becomes 'democratic' with government by consent expressed in votes. Hope that support of a well-informed majority, wise leadership, brings and maintains good order over disorder. Voters have consented to being governed. Access to information is needed for informed criticism and understanding. Information distorted before being communicated abuses power. Press hostility intensifies; 'exposure' displaces news of constructive activity and lowers the tone of public interest and debate. Apathy increases. Personal conscience, critical responsibility, is challenged in new ways for old familiar dangers.

Justice is intended to protect liberty, fair to all; hoping for consensus, for common good, stability, prosperity. **This powerful vision engages high ideals of personal conscience, quality and integrity, accepts dissent, but is vulnerable to persons who intend to destroy it.**

Stability is maintained unless, until, it is upset beyond repair. New sources of prosperity and wealth stimulate enjoyment and benefit. Struggle to survive changes with welfare provisions. **Work** to manage, control, maintain, develop and grow engages development and foresight. Signs of rot, decay, corruption grow worse unless recognised and repaired. Indifference, neglect, absence of responsibility, signal decadence. Individuals infect groups, negatively and positively. Peace and plenty; glad, reasonable, willing co-operation is only possible with vigilance to overcome different interests in open conflict, injustice resented, resort to violence. Haunting spectres of poverty, danger of return to slavery, servitude, forced labour, without redress, occur. Lawlessness, anarchy, disintegration open opportunities for powerful leaders such as Lenin in Russia, Hitler in Germany, Mao tse Tung's China, others unnamed, until the tyrant is overthrown, rejected by consent or counter-revolution': sudden or slow. Underlying culture: great, enduring tradition of literature and music in Russia, enables independent minded individuals vulnerable to fear of rulers and to ruler's fears; to be vigilant, maintain their own unrelenting work and sustain an 'underground' intelligentsia as did Pasternak, Solzhenitsyn, Shostakovich, which renews the soul of oppressed and suffering people: under regimes of cruelty which can happen anywhere.

Mass production tends to threaten individuality at **work** but good management opens opportunities and fosters loyalty to employer. Robert Owen at New Lanark, Cadbury's at Bourneville, engaged vertical responsibility for those employed while respecting lateral solidarity, co-operatives, unions. 'Class-consciousness' includes constructive interdependence with respect and responsibility, not necessarily oppressive, subservient, resentful. Masses of people employed to work with little skill, minimum wages and no satisfaction get together knowing that they sustain prosperity without sharing enjoyment of it. The trade union movement sought and achieved representation in Parliament as the Labour Party but Socialist principles, confused by leaders of New Labour, need clarification.

Dissent, violence, seventeenth century Civil War, Regicide, these are tattooed in memory, revived by revolting colonies in North America, revolution in France, distress after Napoleonic wars. These led to extending franchise, now universal. Acts of Toleration, Cabinet government, Constitutional Monarchy generally stable; particular the personal quality during long reigns of Victoria and Elizabeth II, which maintain continuity in times of great change. Political parties depend on votes: rivalry and conflict; they do not guarantee wise judgment and integrity among leaders. Some are tempted to allow the ship of state to veer with winds of populist reaction rather than to steer with confident knowledge of significant constitutional form, principles, inherited but adaptable.

Finance, personal and political, includes parameters of debits and credits plus confidence to challenge 'inevitability'. Bankers and traders promote prosperity, *risk* gain and loss. Bankers in Florence, Venice, lent to merchants; Bruges developed the first stock exchange; the Hanseatic league promoted trade and commerce among European ports. Overseas exploration, maritime communication, mercantilism, colonisation brought prosperity and sea-power to Great Britain. Habitués of Lloyd's coffee house underwrote risks and shared profits. Identifying markets, trades, fair dealing brought, brings wealth. Success enables benevolence, philanthropy, charity. 'Good works' continue tradition among City companies, Goldsmiths, Mercers, and exceptional individuals such as Gresham, Thomas Coram. In the USA, increasing scales of opportunity, wealth, enabled international generosity of Carnegie, Ford Foundation, Harkness, Gates and Buffett; and of Leverhulme, Nuffield, Cadbury in England. Inherited wealth confers privilege with responsibility; freedom to cultivate interests, tastes, activities, innovations; from archaeology to ocean racing. Ashmole, Soane, Fitzwilliam, Smith, Tate, and great Royal collectors: queens, kings, princesses, princes and consorts; patrons, collectors who bequeathe.

Inflexible social privilege and wealth tempt to arrogance, oppression and expectation of subservience. Escape, emigration, outlawry are safety valves in folklore and history. Revolt, revolution, may be anticipated by reform; sensible peaceful change safeguard against anarchy. New prosperity makes fresh fortunes, but economic opportunities are uneven, inequitable, variably appreciated and differently exploited. Equality attracts people with nothing to lose; who long for better circumstances. Excellence is highest aim but notions of superiority, pretensions tempt to abuse power. Inherited privilege offers opportunities: reputable tutors, books, buildings, equipment, sports. Pride may beget prejudice. Commitment to work; conscientious habits, discipline, cultivated in monastic orders; and by persons ordained to communicate faith and *work*, belief, confidence and effort shared with pupils, students, regardless of background, setting examples, patterns, opportunities, influences still evident in educational communities and open to systematic renewal.

Economic and social deprivation, unless regarded as inevitable, call for thoughtful, urgent, constructive solutions. Post revolutionary France studied society itself, the republic of equality and fraternity, as new entity. Comte, Saint Simon, developed the concept of 'sociology', believing that political and social behaviour could be regarded and investigated as 'science'; statistical, rational, capable of showing trends and envisaging consequences; politically manageable for improvement; cultivated in England at the London School of Economics and Political Science, itself founded by benefactors, including George Bernard Shaw.

Not all thinkers, past, present, accept separation of economics from *will*; moral responsibility, nor believe material wealth to be primary criteria of good life. R. H. Tawney, professor of Economic History at the L.S.E, researched land use, enclosures, city development, acquisitiveness in pre- and post-manufacturing economies and recognised inspiration rooted in faith and belief; enduring motives in changing contexts of cultural balance. *Religion and the Rise of Capitalism*, and *The Acquisitive Society* are classics of their time. Adam Smith had discussed wealth from manufacturing industry and consequent poverty as inevitable, challenged by Jeremy Bentham, J. S. Mill, Robert Owen. Political and economic upheavals in post Napoleonic Europe were witnessed by Marx who proposed radical revolution. The Fabian Socialists favoured representation in Parliament, as did Kingsley, F. D. Maurice, Tawney, William Temple; Christians.

Marx observed poverty as consequence of explosive increase of private wealth. Capital, beneficial to few from labour of many, he saw as materialist, dynamic since money from owners to workers, minimal wages, promoted more and more capital for themselves. Marx prescribed abolition of private property, common ownership, communal effort, comradeship of *work*.

'Dialectical materialism', influenced by Hegel's idealism, became ideology, quasi-religious but different from National Socialism. Marx believed redistribution of wealth essential since 'property' meant privilege, inequality, sources of classes and of class hatreds, root evils of social injustice. *Will* to work for communal common prosperity would sustain individuals and benefit all, the whole. Abolition of private property would end its harmful consequences. That 'those who work acquire nothing and those who acquire anything do not work' seemed true when earners of wages, minimal, knew no minimum wage; no protection for safety at work, grim working conditions, arbitrary dismissal without redress. Belief that class differences depended on property seemed obvious when wealth alone brought position and power. Lenin absorbed Marxist ideology and led revolution in Russia. Marxism was systematically and ruthlessly imposed in what became the Soviet Union. Dictators, rulers who become tyrants, use and keep power; with violence; some are racist, 'fundamentalist', aggressive,'militarist'. Communist regimes have collapsed or been modified. Hard-left socialist economies, disenchanted with consequences of doctrinaire Marxist authoritarianism, have changed political and economic landscapes, even in post Mao China. Marxist idealism and practice were dictatorial, oppressive and extremely vulnerable to corruption: as are others.

XII 3 Faith and Work

Work, outside visions of Paradise, is indispensable for human survival. This does not constrain or qualify what, when, how it is done and where, why, who does it. Ways and means increase well-being and prosperity unevenly enjoyed and differently experienced. Prosperity, for the fortunate, appears to disguise necessity, poverty. Much is 'taken for granted' in absence of thought or faith. Argument is customary, usual, necessary, in pragmatic, open, accountable cultures. Faith concerns the future, learns from the past and looks to reason for guidance towards unknowns glimpsed, sought and hoped for. *Conflict*, and paradox continue to challenge. (See also **XIII I**.)

XII 3 i Natural and Supernatural

Work of nature proceeds without human aid. Life depends on natural cycles to create, grow and destroy. Animals adapt to survive or become extinct. Human life, evolved from natural origin, has become highly skilful in learning from nature and understanding and imitating natural processes.

Human beings sometimes claim and are claimed to enjoy 'supernatural' capabilities. This distinguishes people from other animals. Attitudes to work, hopes and fears of individuals and groups are led by thinkers who believe, believers who reason: speakers, orators, writers with practical natural common sense to initiate change. Social, economic and political circumstances, contexts of *work*, wealth and power, range from slavery, military, monastic obedience, to willing service with *consent* and responsibility. Good-will, recognised by philosophers, emerges as desirable. Ideas proposed are doubted, questioned, tried out, and when successful, believed. Faith opens possibilities, reasons to believe. Constructive persons who carry conviction are vindicated, or not, in the long term.

Natural processes observed are imitated, repeated, developed to sustain life; things produced, reproduced, distributed, exchanged. At the coalface, work is direct although indirectly directed through employer, manager, whose work is to decide, arrange, order what is to be done. Specialist geologists and mining engineers, help.

227

Seashore coal suggests coal seams eroded, free as fish. Inland, land owners assert need for permission, permit, licence, franchise, perhaps disputed. Work changes from natural practicalities to questions arising from custom, principal, theoretical: the first sense of super-natural.

Nature, hard taskmaster in disaster, is amazingly generous in stable conditions of peace and plenty. Fertility, fertilisation, growth is observed, reproduced, cultivated and enhanced. **Work** to nurture requires **will** to make necessary effort. Conservation and renewal are ever present urgent responsibilities. Water to **drink, wash,** irrigate is primary. Wise use includes transport and energy. Direct and derived use need effort, care and skill; **work** that makes or mars quality and quantity of water and organised supply.

Plentiful water, on tap, drawn from good supply as needed, becomes dependent on builders, particularly plumbers. Effort to use water wisely, and well, needs **will**. Incalculable resources of emotion promote motion, devotion, **will** to **work**. Supernatural **light**, energy, may be found. SUN shines naturally with 'supernatural' energy and power. Its heat absorbs moisture from oceans, moves rain-bearing clouds to supply naturally distilled **water**; supernatural?

XII 3 ii Human and Superhuman

Mathematical work measures, calculates from practicalities: size, shape, number, quantity, added, subtracted, multiplied, divided. Theory discovers theorems of size, shape, series; proceeds into areas of higher mathematical analysis, probability, intellectual **work**. Applicable to static and dynamic states, stillness and movement to make and maintain **work** includes **change**; energy to **change**, to recognise of laws of motion. From careful preparation to completion, **work** is initiated to do, be done, to complete and finish. More **work** is promoted in doing: potential and actual.

Reading, including Euclid, is *outside-in* work, recognising, absorbing another person's ideas, shapes, words into mind, remembered and understood. Listening and hearing, words enter through ears. Responses to readings and hearing is modified by inward expectation, ways of comprehending. Writing, like speaking, is from inside-out, using words to describe, exclaim, discuss, reason, exemplify in hope that they make sense if read; worked out into words, worked in **order** to communicate. That which is beyond human grasp, knowledge, comprehension, is thought of as superhuman: intended to clarify, not to confuse.

XII 3 iii Divinity Divined

Reflection and contemplation are quiet, invisible, inward concentrated **work** to absorb direct and indirect experience: to listen, remember, connect, recollect, **order**, digest, make **sense** of, interpret and **hope** to comprehend.

To describe the indescribable, speak the unspeakable, mutate the immutable, includes words that intensify 'to and from', undisclosed into disclosure, germs germinating; sounds as music: into poetry, words drawing on and formulated through rhythms; able to **hum**, sing; melody and harmony, patterns out of noise, discord finding unsuspected order. Conception becomes gestation sustained with devotion; research, meditation, contemplation, quest and request, beseeching search for what is and is not; **work** to discern what is beautiful, good, true, wise.

Metaphysical insight is present, potent, potentially expressible in words of **form**, **shape, colour** and **sound**; discovered to disclose theory, aspects of divinity divined, realised. Music moves to motivate with dynamic rhythms, melodies, tunes to **dance** and **march**: bands brisk, in the mood in eloquent inventive spontaneous jazz. Compositions composed engage patterns of co-ordinated sounds; eloquent chorus, orchestrated orchestra, each detail of individual voice and instrument supported and enhanced by orchestration, heard solo, in concerto, all kinds of music. Majesty, solemnity, depths and heights sound and resound in exceptionally balanced acoustic resonance of grief and exaltation, mourning and sorrow; praise, celebration and thanksgiving; words into works of appreciation, emotion, inspiration and aspiration beyond words. Fantasies invented **move** away from reality. Faith and **work** **integrate** what is true. Discovery of what is true proceeds from question to conjecture to possibility of confident faith, **affirmed**, then verified in experience. Disaster occurs when attempt to verify is disproved and 'proves' disastrous.

At last, just and last, is the question: 'is it true?' Curiosity, attitude, expectation, need confidence; you and my personal capability to affirm or deny, and proceed accordingly. (See **XIII I** and **II**.)

XII 3 iv Energy and Power

Energy invigorates vitality, mobility, reason, thought, faith, every level of existence. Energetic beings, creatures, all life are enlivened; able to work until exhaustion demands rest, renewal, until death. Physical energy; distinct in heat, light and sound holds together in substance, matter, in gravity and relativity; chaos, order, pattern become understood and utilised, personal energy; **work** in any vital activity.

Interchanges occur, **synergy**, one sort of energy into another. Theoretical abstraction learned, expressed in head and heart felt at heart: is physical **manifestation**. Not only in rest and sleep but invigorating feeling, thinking, evaluating, deciding: being willing to work. Energy is generated and regenerated in generosity, new every morning, day, week, month, year and so on from strength to strength, *power* to *power*, health and wealth.

Energy includes power to change. Sun's energy promotes cohesion: interchangeable heat, light, sound in space/time: realised organics; studied as moments of stillness, statics, moving as dynamics: 'mechanics'. Harnessed to work for human purposes, energy derives from and is supplemented by and through *light, heat, sound,* into wind and *water*, making weather and climate. To derive energy from these sources shares their energy without knowing why it is there and works that way. Discovering *how* something works offers opportunity to imitate natural method and to produce and reproduce energy. 'Power-sharing' implies cooperation for common good, energy differently generated, willing working for common purpose; humanity sharing combining energy and power.

Emotion, response of feeling generates interest, switches between, into, to and from outward cause and inward energy of heart for power and effort of mind. *Need, fear, desire,* anger, all forms of passion, are personal dynamos of action and inaction: energy to work and to refuse to work. Civility, obligation and duty follow when *control* subdues, polishes rough into smooth, wild into gentle doing. *Will* engages physical, emotional and mental energy motives, motivated to sublimate energy of *will*; work for necessities and pleasures gained, received, shared. **WELL** is a happy pun. Good *water*, clean and accessible, makes a happy **well**.

The range and variety of work is communicated in verbs. Every practical, physical act: to eat and drink, to look and see; plant, water, weed, harvest all require effort, *work*, to supply *need*, to sustain, conserve, expend, extend and expand energy and make more to spend. *Fall* derives from gravity. Movement of *water* to its own level offers waterpower. A person who falls has lost balance and no longer stands or sits upright. To *rise, climb, lift* require effort, energy, *work*.

Judgment (see **VII**) filters purpose, decision, *will* with *energy to do*. Motive, requires virtue, quality of mercy; appreciation of mercy. Every level: one, two and three, unite in finding the fourth: common time, being in *will to do*. Thus, *work* is interactive, desire and need transformed like *fire* to *heat*, to *light*, to *sound*. Body/mind; felt/thought, need/*will, fuse* in living SOUL, expressing in nature, purpose, quality of actions, *work* for survival; yours, mine, or for someone else. Mind sees motive as *reason* for *will* to do together: *desire* heated for what will be done. **Work** itself is powered by energy, synergy, unified to reflect and enhance in *function*: recognised to be as it is for what it is, living and life-giving, potential for what it could *will*, with *power* and *grace*, become, what is to come.

Resources of life in heart and head emanate, to and fro, throughout each life. Earth, world, universe, cosmos engage every aspect of intimate personal being, intimating processes, as we *process, claim* and reclaim potential energy in doing, sometimes intimidating. Each soul cultivated grows in culture, interaction between abstract and actual, spiritual and physical, soul and body conjoined, begotten to integrate fruitfully. The glory appears to be in things but *substance derives from source*, the belief, *will* and energy that is promoted and promotes them, the power that gives glory, recognisable, true glory.

Pleasure incidental to *work* is joy in fulfilment, fundamental harmony not so much by choice and taste as by response to the call, a destination destined: destiny. This is fulfilment of a different order, so powerful as to be experienced as vocation, recognised, felt, and thought to be predestined, that for which we were and are truly made. Longing changes into belonging, the explorer finds and enters into what was searched for. Hat changes to hood, womanhood and manhood, fatherhood and motherhood, priesthood: enhanced, liberated effort.

XII 3 v Function, Identity, Name

Guessing, speculating, are practised in games. **Work**, as function, is mimed, enacted without things: material 'properties'. Ambiguities flourish: is this an embalmer or masseuse, shoemaker or chiropodist, stoker or undertaker? Naming by function identifies unity of being and doing: e.g. Fisher, Farmer, Miller, Smith. Families retain such names long after at work as the function identifies.

'Official' functions include Clark or Clerk, Sergeant. Vocation, 'clerk in holy orders' (clergy, parson, vicar), Priest, Priestly, Dean, Monk, Nun, Abbot, Bishop, King. Practical functions: Cook, Skinner, Brewer, Palmer, were, are, processes. A Turner made wheels or barrels; Thatcher made reed roofs. Some nouns become names: Tree, Wood, Forest, Fish, Rose, Worm, Crab, from primal life. Colours such as Green, Brown and Black; valuables like Gold, Diamond and Jewel; but not alloys or artificial things, yet. Living creatures, species, specified: Bird, Swallow, Nightingale. Lamb but not chicken or hen, dog or cat, snake or crocodile except as 'nicknames' or epithets. Bull but not cow; neither pony nor horse, stallion, mare, colt, foal. Father to son: Peterson,

Davidson, Jameson, Johnson, are 'sir' names, daughters 'maiden' names. When families join and retain 'jointure', both names express connection.

Individuals need a name. Memorable rulers receive acclaim: Alfred the Great, Duncan the Meek, Richard the Lionheart, William the Conqueror, Henry the Navigator. Many Christian names given at baptism are of Hebrew origin and inspiration; Adam, first man, named Eve, his wife, 'mother of all living'. Sarah, Isaac, Rachel, Jacob and Benjamin, Joshua, Samuel, Solomon, Esther, Naomi and Ruth continue. Greek and Latin heroes and heroines: Aphrodite, Venus; Philip and Alexander. Literary echoes resonate: Marina and Miranda but not Goneril. Orlando but not Othello or Iago. Rosalind, Jessica, Ophelia, Juliet, Portia, James and Jacques, Sebastian, Ferdinand and Olivia, Cecil and Cecily. Charlotte, Emily and Jane, Emma and Elizabeth: Jane Austen's heroines. Association between name and character persists. Emigration and immigration have added names of different cultural origin: race. faith, religion, region which enrich and are enriched in English usage.

Work, singular, holds us together. Plural cooperation integrates with others. A workshop, a school, a hospital, a company, team, regiment, ship, office promote, at best, comradeship, innovation and loyalty: common cause and shared vocation. A *chain* is no stronger than its weakest link. *Work*, noun, is **link** in *chain* of *work* to be done; human **need** supplied by doing the work. *Work* can be possessive; your work rather than mine, but interdependence connects, sometimes glues us together. Concluded, it is a 'finished *work*'; a meal prepared and eaten; an idea, system, work of art, things of beauty bringing joy forever, permanent. Phrases echo: in work, out of work, making short work, going like clock-work, work-bag, workshop, workhorse; and sombre paradox of the old workhouse for those no longer capable of *work*.

Work is versatile: a verb to do and make, an adjective as in workshop and a noun, this work, your work, now and then, from time to time, wondering, watching willing, thinking, reading, up and down the levels, feeling and doing.

Unity of working at work integrates when work is well and truly done, successfully achieved. Conditional qualifiers, ills and cross-accidents, may intervene to upset worker and work. Desired functional unity is potential within us as we work with purpose and control. *Work* in heads and hearts: **hand, mind,** conscience and **will**, maintains responsibility, real and realised. Weaknesses, **fear** of failure are identified and overcome. An experienced, skilled and confident carpenter checks wood and tools, detects faults and accidents for what they are and proceeds with purpose, plan, procedures known to overcome them. Wood and Carpenter, Post and Chair, nouns and functions are names. Saw, chisel, screws and nails are not.

The object, the **work**, and the objectivity of the worker, unite deed and doer; personal engagement, commitment, integrity invested in **work**. Objectivity may reach for and attain a personal detachment which cares only for the **work**. The fully professional servant acts with selfless devotion; to help, heal, teach, advise, minister. An artist works with every personal resource available to make, to perform at the highest level of cultivated talent or gift. Opposite is indifference; automatic repetitive routine without care beyond minimum; to 'get by'. This **paradox** is presence and absence of commitment, wholehearted or half hearted realisation of vocation. Human individuality and resources are variable, self-contradictory, sometimes infinite. Comparisons, generalisations illumine differences, exceptions, motive, ability, energy and **will** to **work**.

XII 4 Need and Fear: A Literary Excursion

Consciousness, through senses and nerves, head and heart, psyche and soul intensify responses: personal, collective, communal. Capability to react, consider, accept or reject, digest, respond and ponder is discussed in these exploratory essays. Failure to feel, learn, understand, face, leads to deny danger of need and fear, unseeing, unhearing, unacknowledged. Mind, memory and imagination (not fancy) enlighten feelings and thoughts. **Will** to face, to manage and overcome are not always effective but **need** initiates. Consciousness of normal appetites does not eradicate their power. Conscience advises effort to control, manage and balance them. Positive and negative dangers: drought and flood, earthquake, epidemic, aggression, unjustified violence such as terrorism multiply suffering. Shared misery, unless overwhelming, promotes common response: courage to bear, forbear, overcome. **Need** and **fear** concern inner and outer danger; both take courage to control.

'-eed', not a suffix as such, makes words for actions, motives, concepts. N-eed, deed, feed, heed, greed, bleed, speed, seed, weed, creed, freed are words that challenge **capability to integrate**, invigorates vitality in action , animating: anima and animus. Ear, one of a **pair** of organs which h-ear, receive sound, preferably cl -ear-ly.

NEED and FEAR, **donouns**, are portrayed in creative and performing art forms which imitate and reproduce experience of danger, suffering, shock/horror. When identified, synthesised, each is expressed, portrayed, recalled, reflected in word, dress, music to digest what is identified. Extreme examples comprehend every level from immediate *need* to survive, to *fear* as terror. A moment, a 'snapshot', catches context, contrasts, similarities and opposites, constructive and destructive, dramatic and powerful. War and peace, peace and plenty, plenty and poverty, poverty and suffering, suffering as pain, pain from deprivation, disease, remorse, grief, emotional and moral anguish, agony. Cruelty and suffering threaten personal balance. This threatens survival. Endurance, poise, courage require courage. Confidence opens and promotes opportunity, means and ends, give and take, recovery, generous health, wealth, well-being restored. Again, 'balancing' measures, 'accounts', cannot guarantee other than practical calculations but unpredictable, unpredicted misfortune complicates them.

Words woven with warp of consciousness and woof of comprehension explore tragic and comic experience. Urge to realise and explain; to perceive patterns, attempt to understand, digest and tell the story. Such 'stories', prosaic, poetic, are digested, remembered, told; often embroidered, elaborated, enhanced in imagination. Each teller, writer, invests the story with such levels of insight as they attain, apprehend, believe and know.

A good 'novel' is more than invented fiction. The 'novelist' assumes licence to personify and 'characterise'. Disclaimed resemblance to 'any living person' does not dissolve knowledge and experience 'embodied' in the story told. Writers of historical novels deliberately reflect and dramatise past contexts. *The Cloister and the Hearth, The Children of the New Forest, The Three Musketeers, The Scarlet Pimpernel, A Tale of Two Cities, Gone with the Wind* portray characters in their contemporary settings without risk of slander, defamation. The reader encounters persons in **need**, in **fear**; heroic, vulnerable, fragile; virtuous and vicious, simple and complex, with enduring appeal. Behaviour expresses character. Fantasy, unreal, escapist, 'unearthed', becomes realised. Strange areas: *Narnia*, Hogwarts, are imagined places where very old conflicts are renewed. The novels mentioned are set as if in real places where fierce need and fear were experienced.

'Real life' letters, diaries, biography, autobiography, written material of history, may be partial, subjective, objective. A 'case history' speaks for itself. A tale 'told by an idiot', a gossip, a raconteur, a poet, a prophet, are deepened with analogy, personification at every level. Ultimate 'good news' is forward looking, sustaining, to meet every *need*; to overcome *fear* through redeeming power of love over hate through grace empowering, *hope, trust, love*. Mercy; whole hearted compassion in action, cultivates responsible, just, redemptive living. (See *Humanitas* 4, 2. April, 2003.)

Fiction writers intend to capture interest; to fascinate, possess, in un-putdownable stories: fearful, shocking, tantalising, appalling, marvellous: ultimately satisfying or not. 'Pure fiction', fictitious, is not 'pure' meaning, 'virtuous'. Vice co-exists with virtue. A great novel is constructed in terms of it's author's consciousness, knowledge and experience, direct and indirect. 'Plot' is story peopled, enriched and impoverished, with whatever background. Fables and metamorphoses, parable and allegory enrich observation and experience. Sympathy is engaged by portraying need and fear, tragic and comic to enlarge, extend, amplify, moderate and temper extremes. Distortion disturbs, upsets balance, which may or may not be sustained, restored, but a 'good' read is not always an 'easy' read. Tastes raised and lowered, heightened and debased, are influenced. Un-, sub-conscious recognitions promote insight and thought, capable of moulding and remoulding inclination and *will* of a receptive reader.

Limits of reticence were exceeded by D. H. Lawrence's *Lady Chatterley's Lover*. Publication in Britain, 1960, of the hitherto forbidden, unexpurgated edition claimed freedom of expression, constructive and destructive authenticity of human experience. (See *Mr Apollinax*, TSE, CPP page 31.) Attitudes to behaviour, modest, immodest; inhibited and uninhibited, differ, develop and change but fundamental needs and fears continue. Reserve need not suffocate or pretend. 'Inhibit', in fifteenth century Ecclesiastical Law, meant 'interdict': to forbid. The Latin stem *'inhebere'* meant to hold on to, or to hinder, relating to 'habit'. Sublimation, safety valve of passion, energy expressed in other forms, original, creative, imaginative work, invigorates human behaviour. Matters of conscience and control, intimate, secret, have outward consequences. Control of vital instincts in such matters are not readily restrained by law; divine, ecclesiastical, statutory, natural. (See also Willing **VIII**, Will **IX**, Conscience, **XII**.)

If all novels are 'stories', not all stories are 'novels'. Saga, history, legend, myth are tales told, retold, sometimes in novel form, long or short, of mystery and imagination. Qualifying terms: comic, historic, romantic, realistic, tragic include *need* and *fear*, suspense, peril, detection, disclosure. Novelists conscious of political, philosophical, moral over- and under-tones reach and engage distinctive levels of experience. 'Romance' and 'science fiction' are on, or beyond different fringes. A contemporary novel may last and become 'historical' if appreciation continues. Earlier writings, far older than England and English, become accessible through translation. Prosperity and leisure enable reading for pleasure. Cultivating, sharing interest and curiosity for education, personal edification in living, ruling, failing to rule; open questions of governing as tyranny, dictatorship, oppression, liberty within and without law: order, revolution. From copying to printing; from recording, radio and TV transmission, video, IT, circulation grows. Adaptations of writings: of drama, poems, stories, wisdom old and new, increases demand for original texts, books. Internet is not quite, as yet, readable any and every where. Young and old, particularly, enjoy listening to reading aloud.

Reputations of novelists come and go. A popular volume now, past, may endure to be though a 'classic'. Characters characterise what is unique yet common features in personality, in needs and fears, head and heart, loves and hates.

Novels named for places: *Northanger Abbey, The Mill on the Floss*; for persons: *Tristram Shandy, Emma, David Copperfield, Jude the Obscure, Anna Karenina, Ivan Denisovich*, 'a Day in whose Life' now reads as an historical 'documentary' of the Soviet Gulag. Solzhenitsyn's record of need and fear, forced labour, is authentic history. Political ideology imposes economic and social conditions which licence to oppress, force conformity, suffocate dissent rather than enhance and liberate. No government is perfect but anarchy is sometimes worse than bad government. Comparative peace and stability of England after 1815 encouraged expanding industry, prosperity over poverty, post-enlightenment roads from serfdom. Need and fear are ever present. Faith, idealism, conscience are reflected in education, medical innovation, constitutional reform, critical journals and novels. Appetite for books was nourished by the novels of Charles Dickens (1812-70), Anthony Trollope (1815-82) and George Eliot, (1819-80). Readers enter the lives and worlds of Nicholas Nickleby; of The Warden, the Barchester of Josiah Crawley, Obadiah Slope and Mrs Proudie. Intimate personal tensions, **need** and **fear**, good and evil, poverty and wealth, greed and generosity, hunger for power rather than to serve, recur; reflected from life in literature.

George Eliot, born Mary Ann Cross to a Warwickshire land 'agent', knew rural and urban life. Parish as hamlet and village, market town were her childhood context. William Blake's 'satanic mills' intensified prosperity and poverty, commerce, but land has enduring economic, political and social consequence. Fascinated by cultivation at every level, practical, emotional, commercial, intellectual and moral, George Eliot's novels comprehend human existence and condition; rural, urban, in garden, farm, family feeling, thinking and believing. Social, philosophical, economic and political attitudes, aspirations, are rooted in personal beliefs, situations, then and since.

Silas Marner, skilled weaver, is overtaken by personal tragedy in an unnamed town. He is falsely accused, 'framed', by his most 'trusted' friend who poisons the mind and destroys the trust of Silas's fiancé. They belong to a close-knit brotherhood of

Christian believers who meet in 'Lantern. Yard' for worship, study and fellowship. Silas Marner's beloved Sarah marries treacherous William Dane. Silas leaves the town. Despair changes his character when faith in the God of Love turns against 'a God of lies'. Carrying his few possessions, including his loom, he walks and finds a former stone-cutter's cottage by a disused quarry near the village of Raveloe. There he works compulsively, reduced to 'the unquestioning activity of a spinning insect'. His high quality weaving sells locally. Silas does not drink at the Rainbow, nor is seen at Church, nor accepts or shares anything. Commercial transactions are strictly limited. One evening, he beholds five hard-earned golden guineas and worships them. He has become a miser. His gold, hidden in small leather bags under the cottage floor is taken out and counted nightly before sleep. He subsists on small change, silver, and makes no contribution to neighbours; is feared, reviled as mean, rumoured to possess dangerous powers; suspect.

Raveloe and its inhabitants appear in the third chapter. Strong and weak personalities, more or less prosperous, energetic, idle, working, playing; open and secretive. Among them is a family experiencing deceit: fratricidal strife. Silas is robbed. One evening, the bags of gold are gone. Distress drives him to the Rainbow where surprise is stronger than sympathy. Silas feels the loss of his gold as bereavement. Christmas is coming, and some incline to show kindness. Dolly Winthrop emerges, a modest and convincing heroine. She 'was in all respects a woman of scrupulous conscience, so eager for duties that life seemed to offer them too scantily'; she was a very mild, patient woman, whose nature it was to seek out all the sadder and more serious elements in life and pasture her mind upon them.

Dolly was the person always first thought of in Raveloe when there was 'illness or death in a family'. She was 'a comfortable woman...good looking, fresh complexioned...never whimpering, no one had ever seen her shed tears; simply grave...inclined to shake her head and sigh almost imperceptibly like a funeral mourner who is not a relation'. It seemed surprising that Ben Winthrop, who loved his quart pot and his joke, got along so well with Dolly; but she took her husband's jokes and joviality as patiently as everything else, considering that *men would be so,* and viewing the stronger sex in the light of 'animals whom it had pleased Heaven to make naturally troublesome, like bulls and turkey-cocks'.

Dolly heard of the robbery, feels concern for Silas Marner and calls at his cottage one Sunday afternoon with young son Aaron and some fresh baked lardy-cakes. Dolly becomes a central figure in subsequent events. Deception, ***need, fear,*** injustice and guilt unravel at Raveloe. A very sick, drug addicted mother dies in the snow near Silas's cottage leaving her child, a golden headed toddler, who is attracted by light and enters the cottage; and Silas warms to her. Dolly, kind, generous, warm hearted counsellor, assists with small garments, gentle encouragement, wise advice as Silas emerges as adoptive father, generous and good; good as gold, invaluable, beyond price. This authentic account of love, betrayal, hate, loss and recovery, grief and restoration affirms goodness of love, not as divisive property or status, real as they are, but in generosity experienced then and there, with mercy. Eppie stayed with Silas who 'reared her in almost inseparable companionship to himself'. 'Perfect love has a breath of poetry which can exalt the least instructed human beings...'

George Eliot's *Middlemarch* is a county town, a wider community than Raveloe. Characterisations reflect personal tensions in larger social, economic and political context. Belief and personal character grow with reforming ideas, to improve and change. One man's self-deception leaves a disintegrating chasm between appearance of rectitude and reality of greed for power: money and property to **control**. A solitary scholar/theologian without responsibility in parish or college community, is a different archetype, dangerous mismatch between devotion to divinity, convinced of his rightness, but surprised by **need** and **desire** for human expression, for a wife. He magnetises the idealism, energy and devotion of Dorothea. Marriage to him, despite her every effort to maintain and express her love, struggles with his insensitive, systematic, cruel oppression. In the last resort, she cannot accept his domination.

Projects to improve housing, build a hospital, extend the railway are issues of the day for people and voters of Middlemarch. The general election battle for the 1867 Reform Bill is background. George Eliot had no vote. The personality and longevity of Queen Victoria disguised change during sixty transforming years: from Chartists to Suffragettes, from Robert Owen to William Beveridge, Walter Bagehot to Karl Marx, Bryce, Dicey, Tawney and Temple: Prime Ministers from Melbourne, Wellington, Peel, Russell, Grey, Gladstone, Disraeli, Salisbury, Rosebery reach into the twentieth century. Widening franchise required development of political parties. New sources of prosperity and power challenged patronage of land; social inertia benevolent and/or corrupt. Organised Trade Unions, quickened by Socialist ideals, democratic and Marxist, developed into the Labour Party. Christian vision, Church of England ('the Tory party at prayer') encountered dissent: the 'Non-Conformist conscience' closer to earlier puritan, 'leveller' faith. Common ground for the sake of extending the franchise and for educational opportunity was, nevertheless, achieved. Later novelists,

Trollope, Galsworthy, envisaged characters different from Nickleby or Silas Marner. Novels reflect **need** and **fear**, achievement and hope, among characters observed, constructed, to face life in their contexts and circumstance. Resources and systems, ideas, ideals, beliefs incidental to experience are depicted in story and plot. In Russia, Tolstoy, Chekhov, Dostoyevsky, Solzhenitsyn, communicate times where existing social, economic, political systems, idealism and belief were being challenged. Lenin's revolution there differed from Cromwell's in England nearly three centuries earlier, but revolution, fight for change, even Regicide, characterised both.

Essayists tend to discussion of problems, situations, circumstance, ideas and aspirations without personification and story of a novel or the individual history of biography. Hope for prosperity to alleviate need, to overcome fear is sought and expressed in critical analysis, review, comment on present conditions of discontent and danger. With liberty of expression, critiques appear in papers, pamphlets, periodicals such as *Spectator, Economist, New Statesman* among others; occasionally into book form: e.g. Bagehot's essays *The English Constitution*, Adam Smith's *Wealth of Nations*, Marx/Engels *Communist Manifesto* and Capital, Matthew Arnold's *Culture and Anarchy*, R.H Tawney's *The Acquisitive Society*.

Lectures have performing power of direct delivery plus urgency of date and place and, at best, enduring impact. The Gifford lectures at Edinburgh: William James on *The Varieties of Religious Experience*, Owen Chadwick on *The Secularisation of the European Mind in the 19th Century* consider changes in belief, attitude and behaviour as roots of cultural dynamics, energy, synergy. T. S. Eliot's *The Idea of a Christian Society* (three Boutwood Foundation lectures, Corpus Christi College, Cambridge) delivered under shadow of war with Nazi Germany, (published by Faber, 1939, repeatedly since) followed by *Notes Towards a Definition of Culture*, (1948, The BBC Reith lectures) occasioned Radcliffe's *The Problem of Power*, 1951 (O'Nora O'Neill's 2002 series *Trust*), deserve continuing study.

George Orwell's *Animal Farm* is a political text of direct, simple impact; a compelling allegory of revolution: 'one party' state with the seeds of its own destruction, prophetic. Consciousness of ignorance and omission plague this aging generalist. Ordinary observers and informed political theorists strive to clarify patterns of ideas and tendencies of their age by comparing with others. Upheaval, dissent, may culminate in civil war and violent revolution at any time. Strife in mid seventeenth century England drove philosophers, poets, preachers, to intense effort. *Need* for stability and *fear* of anarchy are characteristic of civic disorder, danger of anarchy.

Leviathan, Thomas Hobbes (1589-1679) great treatise, was printed in 1651. He had met Galileo, Descartes, in Europe and in England, leading thinkers who became the nucleus of the Royal Society. Leviathan, originally Hebrew, was a large aquatic animal, real or imagined, dangerous to human beings. In English, Leviathan is a giant; of will-to-rule, power of government difficult to resist, personal, but able to become institutional with a life of its own **personified** by Leviathan. British maritime experience suggests the State as a great ship sailed purposefully in conscious, realised knowledge of tides, currents, weather, enemies and unknown dangerous monsters. Commanded with authority, direct and delegated, setting sail to navigate, helm, maintain order by summary jurisdiction if necessary: mutineers would be despatched. The ship's company know *need* and *fear*; peril on the sea. Obedience enforced causes physical, emotional, mental, moral and psychological strains and stresses. Personality clashes; circumstances of storm and tempest, fire and foe, but fair weather balances fear and restores well-being. Command is exercised by admirals, flag officers, flotillas, and sailors of the fleet in which they serve. Suppose such a ship claims autonomy in defiance of shore authority? Leviathan, then, would be no mere underwater threat, but power to endanger reason, order, sanity of command. Demanding requires obedience, loyalty: commitment involves fearful personal 'abuse', miscarriages of justice, occasional, temporary or permanent.

On-shore revolution, Leviathan personified causes, bewildering change, uncertain rule, social and civic distress. At sea, it is called mutiny.

Hobbes's land-based Leviathan emerged from witnessing a **disintegrating** society: the State he had known. Balance between Crown and Parliament was lost. Conflict between ruler and ruled; opposed beliefs; culminate in civil war. What next? Could he identify and reaffirm fundamental foundations of English society and culture? Hobbes was a mathematician, friend of Galileo and Descartes. Practice reflects principle; principle is reflected in practice. Theorem in geometry, shapes, have common properties: squares, triangles and circles: but dynamics of power, *will* and energy like heat, light and sound operate in living being. Leviathan, the State, is alive. What if it is beyond *control*? Surely *need* for *order: fear* of tyranny and chaos, will revive when re-examined, refreshed, re-stated. Hobbes examined sources, forms, principles of energy of power.

The *Leviathan, or the matter, form and power of a Commonwealth, Ecclesiastical and Civil,* is an enduring work concerning elements and fundamentals of government. Four parts: of Man, of Commonwealth, of a Christian Commonwealth, of the Kingdom of

Darkness. Each includes chapters discussing particular themes. Part IV, chapter 46, concerns philosophy as such , and the darkness of vain and 'fabulous' traditions. In conclusion, Hobbes reviews his work and refers to sovereignty and tyranny, zeal and idolatry, good manners and public tranquillity. Leviathan, intended to protect liberty, may suffocate it: hold or fail to hold balanced order, justice and peace. Three and a half centuries since 1651, of ups and downs in growth, prosperity, manufacturing methods, population increase have changed and enlarged British government to function, intervene, in ever increasing areas of personal responsibility. Hobbes' text has been variously interpreted, admired and vilified. Occasionally forbidden reading, burned: more often a set text for study. 'Conscience', 'consecrate', 'allegiance' occur in considering the Kingdom of Darkness. 'There ought to be no Power over the Consciences of men...' (IV. 47.) Virtue is presupposed, and acquired. 'Wisdom, Humility, Clearness of Doctrine and sincerity of Conversation....' Mathematical thinking discourages illusions, delusions. Hobbes is scathing 'of Fairies, fancied', and of Ecclesiastics whose superimposed doctrines are not dissimilar in use, and abuse. He accepts poetic personification under 'King Oberon', (reference to *Leviathan*: in Shakespeare's *A Midsummer Night's Dream*, II. 1, lines 174-5). Scripture, Hobbes' compelling authority, recognises Beelzebub, Prince of Daemons and he accepts that Ecclesiastics are 'Spiritual men, and Ghostly Fathers'. His Fairies are Spirits and Ghosts. Hobbes' Fairies and Ghosts inhabit darkness, solitudes and graves: Ecclesiastics who walk in the obscurity of doctrine, in monasteries, churches, churchyards...(op cit.).

While Robert Burton gathers encyclopaedic experience of heart and soul distress in *The Anatomy of Melancholy*, Thomas Browne offers clinical experience from his general practice in *Religio Medici*; Jeremy Taylor, imprisoned by Cromwell, considers *The Liberty of Prophesying*. Sheltered exile in South Wales he writes *Holy Living* and *Holy Dying*. After the Restoration, Jeremy Taylor is consecrated Bishop of Down, Connor and Dromore. His ministry of reconciliation, grace, forgiveness, peace is deeply sacramental.. He dies in 1667, the year when Milton's *Paradise Lost* is printed.

The 'fall-out' of civil war has not ended. How has the Ship of State becomes thought again to be a monster: Leviathan: alive? This question continues suspended, as it were , among Metaphysicians. Jeremy Taylor prays, celebrates sacrament, knows, lives, and communicates the Gospel, endures prison and maintains unequivocal golden thread of personal salvation in Christ with all the social and political responsibility required. His work offered inspiration to Coleridge, to Bishop Heber who edits his works, fifteen volumes, (1822) and others since.

Search for a 'general theory' of **will** moves towards faith systematised: heart and head, felt/thought **integrated** as outlined in the contents of this exploration. Advancing towards the work of experts, specialists, 'schools of thought' and belief, emerge. Some claim and, if believed, are regarded as authoritative in their sphere be it sociological, ethical, political, economic, psychological, theological. Authority in power requires conformity, commitment, obedience, loyalty. Freedom, the liberty of prophesying, engage critical thought. Paradox is seen to be inescapable. Different readings lead to different conclusions.

Thomas Hobbes' *Leviathan*, (like Charles Darwin's *Origin of Species*), can be read in ways that lead to mutually exclusive interpretations. Is he a revolutionary? A ground-breaking analyst of the human comedy, divinely practical, realistic, de-constructed to re-construct into 'liberal enlightenment' or a traditionalist who adapts cultural foundations of faith and order in the face of civil war, strife, and the perils of anarchy? Does Leviathan come alive in any system of government necessary to reduce, preferably avoid, chaos?

Leviathan continues to haunt. A strange, huge, hitherto unknown sea monster beached on the shore of Chile, July, 2003, an enormous mound of disintegrating flesh, was a recent manifestation.

William Blake, (1757-1827), artist, engraver, illustrator, poet of genius comparable with Dante (less systematic), bestrode the watershed between eighteenth century complacency, post seventeenth century revolution, and nineteenth century realism. Dramatic expansion was accompanied by **fear**. Blake's vision, sympathy and imagination soared between earthbound, down-drafts of materialism, greed, dark satanic mills, and heavenly updrafts of sublime beauty, transforming glory and greatness. 'Bring me my bow of burning gold; Bring me my arrows of desire...'

Ancient legends of Laocoon, Behemoth, Beelzebub, Leviathan resurface when self-evident evil challenges illusion that romanticism; 'Panglossian' optimism, saw progress and 'enlightenment' as inevitable. Blake's simple verses express good and evil coexisting. Head and heart know **need** and **fear** in 'Songs of Innocence' and 'Songs of Experience'. His poems: 'The French Revolution' and 'Visions of the Daughters of Albion' include meditations, forewarnings, mystic consciousness of Urizen, Old Nobodaddy, Jehovah. Women's Institutes and Old Labour embrace in singing 'Jerusalem'. 'For the Sexes; the Gates of Paradise' are verse and illustration of finite infinitude and integrity.' (See Blake, *Complete Writings*, edited by Geoffrey Keynes, pages 760-771. Oxford University Press, 1966.) His poem 'The Everlasting Gospel', written circa 1818, (Keynes page 748) is a deep, dramatic exemplification of paradox.

Political manifestos propose policies and promise programmes to win votes. Circulated: hand written, printed, handed out, broadcasted, e-mailed, a manifesto propagates a view. True, un-spun from heart and mind of the person who wrote it, with and without help, a manifesto needs 'party' approval: adopted to promote voters support at an election.

Parliament had been emerging and evolving for millennium by seventeenth century civil war. The franchise then was limited. Political parties and general elections have evolved, and continue to evolve since. Potential voters must register presence and place to exercise their vote and then decide who to vote for. Names of candidates are distributed by active party people. Occasionally, a slogan from a manifesto captures interest and support. Voter apathy, a sense of helplessness, follows large majorities. A strong leader will be effective, ruthless, then divisive. Lloyd George, after 1918, proposed 'a land fit for heroes to live in'; Margaret Thatcher with large majorities from1979, was 'a lady not for turning'; Prime Minister for eleven years.

The Binding of Leviathan by William Waldegrave (Hamish Hamilton, 1977) is subtitled 'Conservatism and the Future'. His object was not 'to attempt to write a long Manifesto for the Conservative Party nor to write a history of the Conservative tradition' (Chapter XI) but to explore underlying ideas that are 'the common currency of a political culture at any time' (Chapter XII). He is indebted to Aristotle, Augustine, Langland, Hobbes.

Born 1946, Waldegrave was privileged, gifted, rewarded; he matched opportunity with responsibility. Newcastle scholar at Eton, open scholar at Corpus Christi College, Oxford, President of the Union and of the University Conservative Association, 1st Class Lit. Hum.1969; Kennedy Fellow at Harvard, elected a fellow of All Souls 1971, appointed to the Central Policy Review Staff, Cabinet Office, 1971-73, Justice of the Peace for Inner London Juvenile court, 1975-79, elected M.P. for Bristol West in 1979.

The Conservative Party, out of power in 1945, had emerged with fresh thoughts and zest for effective leadership influenced by R. A. Butler. Macmillan became leader and PM. After the 1950s and 1960s, Quintin Hogg, Lord Chancellor, hoped to follow Macmillan to Downing Street, 1970, and disclaimed his inherited Viscountcy. Out of office, he continued to think, speak, judge, believe and care for human well-being in thoughtful, provocative, words and, since 1972, edited the fourth edition of *Halsbury's Laws of England*. His Dimbleby Lecture, 1976, described British Government as 'Elective Dictatorship'. In retrospect, prophetic of New Labour: Leviathan again.

Waldegrave's *The Binding of Leviathan* has an epigraph from Aristotle's *Politics*, (1263b, 13-14):

'Socrates's mistake derives from a fallacy in his basic assumption. Certainly unity is necessary to some extent in both a household and a State. But it does not need to be total. There is a point at which increased unity destroys the State, and also a point, short of that, where a State remains, but in a worse condition. It is as if you were to reduce a harmony to a unison, or a complex rhythm to a march.'

Leviathan, Hobbes' personification of government, is less amenable to leadership than a ship commanded; command of a fleet of ships; or an army led by persons qualified, able, to command and delegate with consent and loyalty, to co-ordinate constructive co-operation but not at war as Royalists and Roundheads were or as the United Kingdom was united in war against Hitler's Nazi regime in Germany. An orchestra, already mentioned, has music composed, scored for performance. Instruments, instrumentalists distinctly led, are conducted together to interpret a composition. Head, hand and heart-felt skill, vitality and quality do their best. There is no sound when they are silent. The State, personified as Leviathan, is bound when its system confines, controls, oppresses, effectively dictates and can only be challenged with violence. Liberty, personal and communal, is not protected. Growth of Parties accompanied extension of franchise, eventually universal for qualified registered voters. A big parliamentary majority tends to become compliant.

Waldegrave considers Britain's 'special problem'; 'the growth of government'; 'countervailing forces' and 'political possibilities'. These, common to government of any, either party, continue. Need for prosperity, fear of bureaucracy, corporatism, party roots in Socialism versus Capitalsm; Unions versus Big Business were ingredients of post-Second World War economics and politics but **'no one knows how to run bureaucracies. Bureaucracies are increasing. No wonder the public thinks something is wrong'** (Page 28.)

Marx offered his blueprint, an ideology claiming authenticity: progress through common ownership, equality and justice. Waldegrave writes that:

'Intellectually disreputable as the concept of historical inevitability may seem to many — and morally and governmentally quite useless as it certainly is —

believers are not confined to Marxists or to the Left. Thus, it is not the concept of historical inevitability as such which puts Marxist Socialism into conflict with Conservative thinking since it is possible for many such theorists to leave a place for the individual's apparent consciousness of free-will, while meaning that the theory gives little or no help in day to day life, and leaves open to argument all the old questions of morality and personal action'. (Page 53.)

Waldegrave continues:

'What was, and is, objectionable to Conservatives is the use of the concept of historical inevitability to give believers greater rights over their fellow men than non-believers. Like some austere Calvinists or Inquisitional Catholics, those who understand the direction of the cycle have a duty further to advance it...Thus by one jump — the identical jump made by Hegel's fascist descendents — the believers find themselves equipped with a philosophy which enables them to make no difference between those who disagree with them and those who are delaying the progress of all mankind towards the promised land. Materialism prevents them from saying, like some Christians in the past, that the soul of the tortured individual is actually benefited in another world; but the cry that millions unborn will benefit from the present slaughter of dissenters opens the gates to the torture chamber just as effectively.' (Page 53 continued.) 'Marx gave a fatal impulse to the concept that classes, not people, are interesting'. (Page 56.)

Post-war nineteenth century changes have been occurring here and worldwide: economic, political and social. Thatcherism, at first regenerative, but inclining from and to protracted forms of materialism, was displaced by 'New Labour', refreshing, beguiling, but lacking integrity. The post-Second World War Capitalist/Communist paradox: Iron Curtain to Cold War: thawed when Hungary, Poland, Czechoslovakia simmered against Marxist domination in and from Soviet Russia, hastened by Chernobyl, grasped by Gorbachov, aided by Thatcher and Reagan, dissolved. Adenauer's Germany, De Gaulle's France had forged new Europe; NATO giving way to development of the UN within American wealth and idiosyncratic leadership. British tradition of Commonwealth, good-will to cooperate, is caught between European scepticism, militant Islam and vapid or angry criticism.

New forms of **terror** speed 'global' consciousness, *fear*, all under the shadow of nuclear capability, the 'ultimate deterrent', danger of annihilation. *Need* and *fear*, poverty suffering, conflict, injustice continue. Each powerful challenge, confronted or circumnavigated, awaits another; earthquakes, floods, starvation recur from natural disaster, from indifference, or cruelty, or both. Voluntary effort; generosity, good-will, is frequent, heart warming but inadequate for Darfur, Ruanda, Ethiopia, Somalia. Consistent, courageous leadership is called for in political, public life as in domestic and personal experience. China thrives between one Party rule and crackling, money-making industry: **WORK**, trade, capital orientated 'outsourcing', even Government finance, Banks, IT, increase the prosperity of English speaking peoples.

Waldegrave was appointed to lead the Department of the Environment under Thatcher but was harassed by 'animal rights' fanatics and 'mad-cow disease' hysteria. He lost his seat (as did Chris Patten) to 'New Labour' in 1997.

Part III of Waldegrave's *The Binding of Leviathan* considers 'Conservatism, Community and The Future':

'People must belong somewhere: if the State destroys communities which are benign and can coexist with it, then communities will arise which are not benign... The State should fear inflation like the plague...second, it should beware of the casual clearance of landmarks without which communities cannot live.' (Pages 109 and 117.)

'New Labour', receptive to many of Waldegrave insights, has shown scant regard for landmarks of convention, wigs, Woolsack, local participatory/control of education and police, inherited wisdom. Nevertheless, market place, well and clock; pub sign, church tower, spire, bells; war memorials, cenotaph, are among built landmarks, recalling and commemorating high achievers, leaders, heroes, saints, martyrs, whose lives make landmarks, manifest and personify their work.

Waldegrave foresees the 'beginnings of a return to a barter economy'. (Page 110.) These few extracts suggest perennial philosophical, political problems. He concludes that Keynesian conservatism is declining and that Liberalism and Marxism are both flawed. (Page 124.) He proposes no definitive theory, but hopes 'so to bind Leviathan that communities may once again find in the world the predictability and the stability they need for growth and survival'. (Page 124.)

He continues:

'The conservatives understand that the basic moral values are assumptions lying behind any social or political propositions, and not derivable from the latter. Some would say they are God given; others that they inhere in the nature of man, and that though they may change slowly over millennia, and though few will agree exactly on any exhaustive catalogue of things which are right and wrong without question, few would argue about a central list which turns up regularly wherever civilised life lasts.' (Page 149.)

XIII I

True?

Figure 1 *Plato's Line: Four Stages of Cognition*

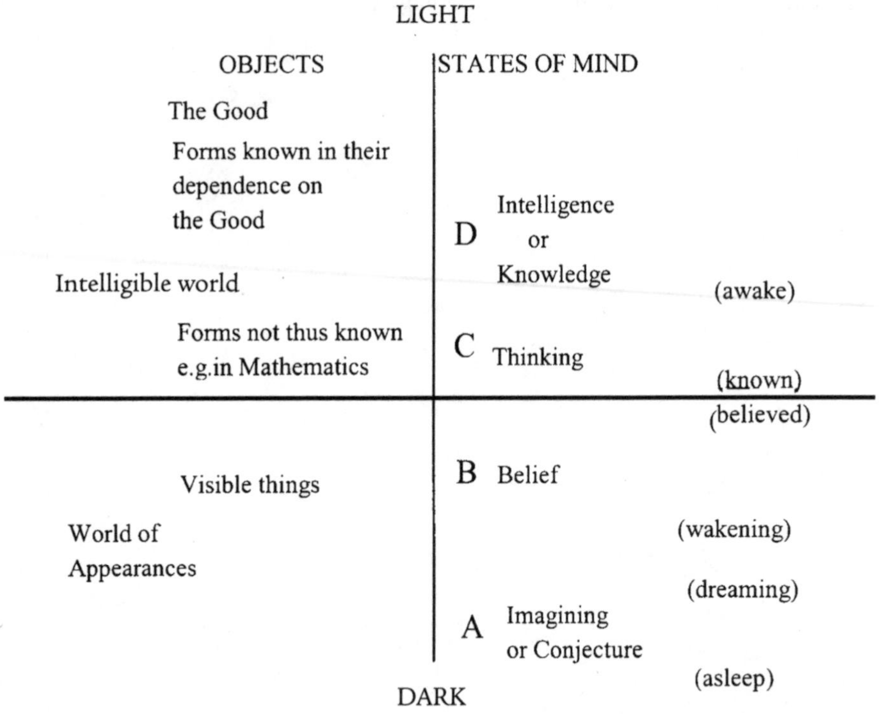

LIGHT

OBJECTS	STATES OF MIND

The Good

Forms known in their
dependence on
the Good

D   Intelligence
  or
  Knowledge   (awake)

Intelligible world

Forms not thus known
e.g.in Mathematics

C   Thinking   (known)

(believed)

Visible things

B   Belief

World of
Appearances

(wakening)

(dreaming)

A   Imagining
  or Conjecture

DARK   (asleep)

Plato's stages of consciousness and transformation ascend from dark to *light*, asleep awakened.

Head, heart, MIND seek illumination, disclosure, creative energy to recognise what is good and true.

Light itself is *resource* of infinite energy, change, origin of species. Divinity *reveals*, is being revealed, in hearts and minds reaching for light.

Plato's exploration of the Good is unending.

Evil is not good, dark is not light. Light shines in darkness. Darkness is overcome by light.

Hearts, illuminated, are warmed to believe and see. (1 *John* 1). Spirits of good and evil conflict in each soul. Inseparable until distinguished; separation needed is sought in real experience. The Good, explored through wondering and believing, becomes known, restores to true reality, redeemed through suffering, freed and healed from evil.

Figure 2. *Circulation of light and heat, rising, spirals, towards definition:* what was, is, will be: good and true unified.

Plato's Levels: A, B, C, D, or 1, 2, 3, 4 show upward awakening; **inspired; changed through disclosure; revealed in** light of the good and true; stronger than evil, untrue, deceptive, false.

WILL, inward, human, looks for Divine *will* revealed. **LIGHT** illuminates towards the true and good. Inward disclosure, healing, restoration, ill to well: mended.

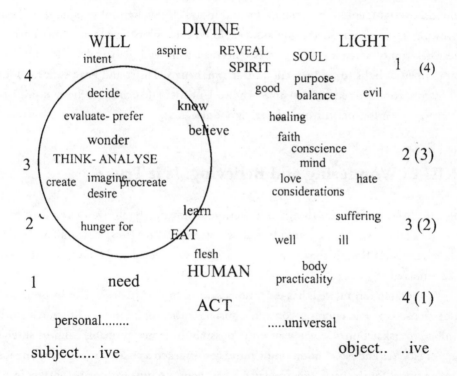

Figure 2: Illustrates first upward movement, drawn towards *light* for transformation.

Light is given, life-giving reality, overcoming darkness; revealing origin; divined, not invented.

Measure, rhythm, discovered in, of, time and space discloses inherent *order*, discerned, realised: repeating, proceeding, changing and unchanging, towards concepts of permanence, visions of eternity.

The levels, 1-4, Plato's stages of consciousness and transformation, emerge out of first darkness. Light shares and sheds light of light drawing upwards to wonder, enquire, believe, reveal, know. (Figure 1.) Hungry heart and enquiring head, mind, seek to.

N.B.: The closed circle, mind in head, receives light; gathered by and through open eyes in mind from body, practicalities, seen in, with, light. Confusion, dark, needs *light* to illuminate *order*, to apprehend wholeness, unified, regenerate creative energy, disclosure of the good and true. *Light* provides, offers, infinite energy for life, growth, realisation of 'beauty so old and so new'. Appetites, hunger, passionate curiosity to realise original 'Divinity', source energy in being becoming known in hearts and minds. Eyesight, emotional insight, mental moral clarity; light of good and evil; *will* growing in each soul. Sovereign Good, explored through believing, becomes known; restores reality. Passion, suffering, is redeemed from evil. Personal world, mind in head open to light to wonder, enquire, affirm, believe. Heart and head seek food for thought: to learn, know, become whole. Unbelief, disbelief, at best, stimulate constructive criticism; at worst, denial, ignorance, loss.

XIII I i Wondering and Believing: Is it True?

Practicalities known in things and actions: moving, fetching, carrying; direct, mechanically assisted, are found to follow patterns. Water flows downhill and finds its level: vessels float if they hold air. Principles, discovered and known, are trusted, remembered.

A principle formulated, has exceptions said to 'prove' the *rule*. Doubt promotes questions. Do you enquire, consult, consider other opinions, inclinations, until willing to risk action? Do you wait until 'possibly' becomes 'probably', almost surely? Yes or No? Yes and No. A questioning mind continues to *wonder*. Urgent spontaneous action hopes for the best. '*Jump* and you'll get there', no time to 'look before you *leap*.'

Appraisals and purposes, ends and means, means and ends, take *time* if *time* is available. People, things, incidents occur in their contexts. Human reactions, instincts, are at first, self-interest but beyond self, become objective. Response becomes responsible.

Good and evil sharpen discernment of intention in, head, heart and mind. Conscience promotes conscientious sensibility; confident strength to see and know what is good and true: practicable and wise.

Codes, rules, laws, are criticised, believed or not, respected, retained or discarded by later generations. Belief, Plato illustrated, is more than sense-recognition rationalised. He distinguishes wondering from believing, and sees believing as a stage towards knowing.

Belief engages commitment to another, an other: a person, purpose, principle, principal, person, purpose, project with objectives **beyond self-interest**. 'Unhappy' performances occur from insincerity and self-deception. (See Appendix **B**.) Without *doubt*, there is no hesitation, no *reason* to hesitate. Plato illustrates belief to be more than sense-recognition rationalised. Knowledge remembered, absorbed, inherited, learned, is considered and accepted; or rejected. Commitment is powered by confidence and tested in the laboratory of living experience. Loyalty and devotion, personal awakening, engage *change*.

Qualities of personality and character emerge in behaviour. Adjectives for material things apply to actions: strong or weak, fresh or rotten: trees, teams, friends, ideas, rulers; but judgment, fair or unfair, sound or unsound, is not confined by things. Trees live and die, *judge, trust,* engage **WILL**: knowing and willing. *Trust* and trustworthiness assist *search* for what is true. Honesty and integrity emerge through trust; tested qualities of character, behaviour. Things and processes provide analogies recognisable and recognised by people who become aware of them.

Names identify particular and general things: an oak is a tree, a dog of any breed is an animal, a telephone an instrument, a computer a machine. Proper names apply to individuals and to places whose existence is believed, accepted, from heard or written evidence. A living person embodied, well- or ill-met, named or 'known as', is encountered in words, their own or from others, and may become a presence in mind, memory and feeling (head and heart) who influences feeling, thinking, willing act for good and ill. A disturbed and disturbing person may have an 'evil spirit'. Othello was disturbed by Iago. (See **III iii**.) Faust determined to meet the Devil in person: to experience evil for himself. These and others are encountered in literature, legend, history.

The temptations of Jesus concern body, mind and soul. First, bread for desperately hungry body, sufficient. Second, tempted by power of mind to wrong use of things; the evil of false ideas. Third, tempted to worship power itself; not of God but in rebellion; evil in the soul, not good. (See *Matthew* 4. 1-11.)

Proverbs, precepts, may mislead until authenticated. Feeling, thought, evaluation, intent, determine action in different ways. Instinctive reaction may be modified, controlled. Speech and action respond to others who also wonder what is true in word and deed, practicalities. Time and opportunity limit appraisal but critical questions return, sometimes urgently. Plato's horizontal line is crossed, intersected, by the vertical illustrating transition from wondering to believing, ascent towards the Good. Responsibility engages more than exercise of mind, head, of intellect, academic, since evil engages suffering *pain* and grief: heartfelt *hope*: belief that evil be overcome with good.

Divinity experienced is power in heart and head; felt, thought, open to who will 'feel after and find', as Greek poets sensed, believed, knew. Finding is experienced as being found. (Paul at Athens, *Acts* 26. 19-34.)

Can we ever be sure that something is (whatever it is) without qualification and in all circumstances, true? Is this 'Demon of the Absolute' (Paul Elmer More (1864-1937)) comparable to Absolute Zero where fusion occurs, unseen but real in concept and in matter? 'Facts' become known, 'established, confirmed in acceptance, conviction, or dissolved in doubt, disbelief, rejection when illusory, untrue. Disillusion, sudden or gradual, follows realisation that expert, experienced, trusted voices are fallible. Words of others, living and dead, heard and read, form the common mind, but commitment, (yes, no, perhaps) is personal to individual *will*. Influences derived from others, something, and, or, from elsewhere, soak in communally, as it were, 'in the blood'. Doubt leads to questions which arouse doubts until answered satisfactorily. Thinking promotes independence; independence encourages thought, discussion with ourselves. Ideas and belief, spoken and written, occur in any sphere of life. Between credulity and disbelief, illusion and disillusion, naivety and cynicism, *light* opens and clears vision, response of commitment, action willed and willingly done. Various, sometimes contradictory interpretations are discussed. 'Beyond reasonable doubt' and 'an established fact' are familiar phrases for conclusions believed true. Belief is the fruit of commitment conceived out of curiosity, fertilised by confidence and delivered in trust. This circulation in heart and mind, heads and hearts together is dynamic. Human beings are capable of response to *will* other than their own. 'Doctor's orders' are believed, hoped, to enable healing. The Good expresses Divine *Will*; able to *mend*, restore, heal what is known to be broken, sick, dis-eased, of evil. Human response is not imposed but is response of *trust*.

Life, a birth, a death, are practicalities, events. What is their meaning, purpose, significance? Assisted by knowledge, interpretation, backward and forward looking, head and heart seek to understand and wonder what to believe. Elements and substance, sought, recognised, are enlightening. Infinite variation in heads and hearts, in personal inclination and *will*, seek *order*, orders and patterns of order. Concepts arouse critical questions. Critical challenge invites dissent in *hope* to *find* meaning and purpose. Fear of change, of instability, can endanger enquiry.

Motive, emotion, purpose, intention, resolution, responsibility and *Will* recur again and again in this exploration; warp and weft of patterns of life whatever the material. The stuff of the cloth, scale of the loom, where, when and how patterns are determined, preferred, woven; whatever quality, colour, strength, weakness, beauty, ugliness: of thought, word, deed. Climate, weather; all conditions contribute to contexts of function and work. A weaver alone intensifies isolation; independent although interdependence is inescapable. Freedom realised is valued and variously interpreted. Patterns and examples, rather than precepts, are respected, followed, or ignored. Absence of patterns, models, examples, leave nothing to be guided by; no terms of reference.

A decision made in mind is a commitment to intended action, verifiable when performed. 'Performatives' unite decision in action. To promise, bet, assess, bequeath are done by saying so. A 'performative' states intention in action. (See Introduction and Appendix **B**.) The *promise* is realised when kept, enacted, performed to, eventuates as an event. A gift given, a debt paid, a partnership agreed, maintained, promised in good faith is faithfully fulfilled. Intervention, prevention, from any source; persons, reasons, can distract intention and disturb its fulfilment Failure, weakness, broken bones and hearts, inadequacies, are experienced and recognisable, poignant to observers who share sorrow in tragic events close to them. Witnesses are touched and moved by events witnessed, intensified by photographs, TV radio, written reports. The reality of royalty extends consciousness of inheritance as succession, birth and death, continuity and history. Present joy and sorrow, duty, delight and misery are exposed to unrelenting publicity. The searchlight of interest in exceptional common experience is felt in uncommon degree. Critical appreciation of character and quality attracts, deserves, sensible appreciation and those who diminish it diminish themselves. Feelings arise to deepen love and hate, hope and fear, joy and grief, plenitude and deprivation. Grandeur and high style are life enhancing; not intrinsically corrupting unless excess tempts and becomes decadent. True? Promises made are not always kept. Appointment becomes disappointment, unhappy.

'Material fact', relevant information, is not necessarily a measurable material thing. 'Scientific fact' usually means something evident, 'proved' through observation, critical reasoning assisted by experiment, tests tested, monitored. This process is as old as human sense intelligence, curiosity and *will*. More and more detail is revealed, 'light years' beyond earlier imagination.

The concept of 'material fact' works from practicalities, *first level of things* that *are* as and what they are: given, identified, recognised, named and known. From elements to compounds and derivatives their quality, purity, function and use become known. Modification occurs with and without human effort. Alchemists sought secrets of material *change* in order to apply them, hoping to make gold from base metal. Metaphysicians realise metaphor and analogy to disclose meaning that *makes 'sense' of experience*. Some things, actual and factual, are significant in themselves: an eye, a key, a switch. Symbol and analogy open head and heart, when invisible realities emerge from elemental facts, practicalities.

Search for what is true realises *change*; what was and *will* be beyond what it is now. Surfaces and appearances lead to sources, depths and heights, changing perceptions. Something to do, to be done, engages performer to perform: *will* to *act*, in fact. Intelligence, memory, skill, effort operate first level of senses through feeling, thought, evaluation and intention to return with purpose, intended doing. (See Figures 1 and 2, above.) Discussion of fact; of the nature, meaning and significance of things, events, ideas emerges from essence, substance, with meaning, value and purpose. What is called 'fact' is itself discussed in seeking what is true. 'Material fact' pertains to a particular investigation, fact that matters, material to, as well as material of.

Animals inspire allegory: Aesop's *Fables, Animal Farm, Watership Down*. Does animal survival exceed instinct? Human responsibility includes forethought, deliberation, plan, decision to act. Recognition of good and evil accompanies will to do, to act for good. Some animals, naturally clean in habit and habitat, adapt to human expectations and become dependable, but not all.

Trees provide wood, shade, shelter. Birds frequent their branches, up and down, heard, watched, named, classified by ornithologists. Some are valued for their eggs, flesh, bones, feathers; some for personality, appearance, company. Birds are survivors: flying, perching, feeding, nesting, singing. In England, robins are favourites. Who killed Cock Robin? The death of this distinctive, friendly red-breast concerns pain and lamentation. Who did it? Sparrows can be aggressive, fight over food, jealous and threatened by robins. 'Moral' instincts? The nursery rhyme, said or sung, is a saga of loss. The questioner leads the chorus for all, the sparrow having confessed.

"'I, said the sparrow, with my bow and arrow, I killed Cock Robin."
Who saw him die? "I", said the fly, "with my little eye. I saw him die."
Who caught his blood? "I" said the fish, "with my little dish."
Who'll make his shroud? "I" said the beetle, "with my thread and needle".
"I'll make the shroud."
Who'll sing a psalm? "I" said the thrush, as she sat on a bush.
Who'll be the Parson? "I" said the rook, "with my bell and book."
Who'll bear the pall? "We" said the wren, both the cock and the hen,
"We'll bear the pall.'"

And the refrain repeats:

'All the birds of the air were a-sobbing and a-sighing,
When they heard of the death of poor Cock Robin.'

This nursery rhyme imputes human sensibility and *will* to each bird They enact funeral rites of those times, some undertaken today.

Wondering about death links living with believing. Facts as to cause of death are not always known or clearly established. Between body and *will* is an area referred to as soul. (See **XIII II 4**.) Weakness in sickness, dwindling energy, frailty of age signal approaching death. Inward reconciliation promotes peace. Death of body does not extinguish soul. Life beyond death is of great interest, wonder and belief.

Observation and reliable testimony assist detection and diagnosis in human experience. Patterns emerge, questions follow in orderly procedure: medical examination and in court hearings. Justice requires scrupulous care, but the most careful code cannot guarantee accused or accusers to speak only what they are sure is true. Witnesses willing to testify are themselves examined, cross-questioned, for reliability. Were you there? (Time and place.) Who, when, what did you see?

Under oath to tell 'the truth, the whole truth and nothing but the truth' requires direct evidence, but 'the whole truth' is too formidable in demand and expectation. Each witness is asked, told to testify to first-hand evidence, recognised as true. To deceive, mislead, is perjury. Can those who hear evidence be sure it is true? Unconvincing evidence does not carry conviction. Juridical and medical investigators may consult and consider 'case histories'.

Thinking and hoping derive from wondering and believing. Confidence fuses into expectation; mind sure that, whatever **it** is, *IS* so. Suppose this was already in being before anyone knew? Whatever this **IS**, implies, means, promotes wondering what to do with, about, or for, **this; the** ORIGINAL: first cause if you like, explored through tracing its presence expressed in created things, creative *work*: evident in what has been, was, is being, done. The joke of IT being IS, **IT**, is inescapable.

ET, brilliantly contrived Extra Terrestrial, is not, does not, live as a human being, but human expectation suggests continuity in what follows, what next. Co-operating with event and process stimulates examining, exploring what is already in being and may develop, evolve. Being and doing unite in a moment. Change transforms, is transforming and will further transform when discoveries extend and processes are imitated as if invented. Watering and irrigation imitate rain and overflow. Practical analogy, parable and metaphor are clues , keys, to transformation. (See **VI ii** and **XIII II 4**.)

Retracing origin follows hints, guesses, sometimes evidence as to what and how **IT** happened.

Why? For what purpose? Wonder, conjecture, hypothesis, reasons to believe? Fruit to seed, seed to fruit, seedling to tree are evidence of life in event and process; confidence to solve problems; to answer questions that challenge individuals to affirm or deny. Collective affirmation becomes common belief towards communal culture. Vision and purpose, sustained in confident practice, encourage and sustain a culture that civilises and may become a civilisation. People and trees flourish in beauty, stature, fruitfulness, confidently conscious of common good. Knowledge and appreciation of nature; natural roots, trees, seed-time and harvest, earth's health and fruitfulness replenish faith to look ahead, to overcome pessimism. Ignorance of cultivation, inability to sustain growth, reduces will and energy. Their culture becomes enervated, artificial, ineffective, unsustainable. Mechanisation and technology, hugely beneficial for production, separate individuals from naturally creative resources of life. Many find joy, and renewed effort in cultivating plants in window boxes, pots, grow-bags, allotments and gardens.

Questions in ordinary life move people to wonder, ponder, become philosophers: to look for reasons and develop systematic methods of thought, pattern, *order*, criteria of value, possibilities within appearances. Doubts, questions, proposition, supposition, presupposition discussed in mind and with others go where they lead. To wonder what is true; why what actually happens, what is significant, what it means and what, if anything, follows, requires confidence to recognise and understand to that end. What could, should, might, ought or ought not to be thought, felt, said and done? These require inclination and intent, reasoned but beyond reason. Belief, fundamental in Plato's discussions, includes hypotheses, intuitions, allegories and adventures with ideas. Reason encouraged Plato to consider and learn. Reason amplifies and is amplified by belief towards the Good. The Good, the goal, depends on pursuit of what is true. (See **XII 2**.) Belief yields knowledge: believing leads to knowing.

Sense impulse and appetite are immediate but problems prompt personal questions. Individual action is increasingly isolated in many contemporary lives. Spontaneity overtakes, overcomes, premeditated purpose. Need for collective response resorts to substitute momentum: 'raves', football matches, rallies, marches. Liberating and complicating consequence raises questions beyond limited self-interest: quests requiring commitment. Hopes and fears, beliefs and doubts, need personal embarkation with courage, fortitude. To integrate new vision, good or evil, with ordinary daily life challenges inclination to prefer familiar routines, minimal risk, sitting on an available fence. To follow a vision, involves risks and changes. Plato defined, 'divined' vision of the Good: sought, believed, the Good itself is source and ideal. (See Figure 1, above.)

Mind, will, work, are capable of purposive objective or subjective activity, in head and heart, of human being. Heart and soul are not **donouns**. *Face* portrays individuality, recognisable identity. Integration of brain and *mind* occurs in *work*. Paying attention in head, heart and will, being and doing, is action. This integration benefits the work; with characteristics of the character of the worker, the doer. Conversely, lack of concentration, limits integration. *Work* is incidental, not systemic action.

Is this true? Is this where soul formation and growth occurs?

The concept of normality suggests that 'healthy' persons enjoy integrated activities, 'know-how', with little knowledge of 'why' beyond immediate motive. Practicalities and priorities are absorbed before 'head' knowledge, understanding memory, is known of, known or available. Intuitive action, imitative behaviour, challenges those taught to learn, think, communicate and cultivate mind through tutored 'academic' study. Commitment, devotion, is of the heart. Teaching, learning 'by rote', without belief, lacks conviction. Knowing the rules of a game is not taking part, playing, but prepares for participation and enhances watching.

Search to discern the seat of character, if successful, assists its cultivation. Learning rules without playing the game separates theory from practice: 'spectator' from participant. Natural goodness is experienced in healthy pleasure but disapproval, rejection, conditions, outlook of puritan, censorious not constructive, priggish. In games, rules emerge to refine enjoyment. Controlled skill intensifies competition. The game analogy, 'game plan', is pushed to represent hope and purpose of life, personal achievement and success. To pre-suppose that life is a game, revives comparison with Shakespeare's idea that 'all the world's a stage', but sees players as contestants rather than performers, actors. Both analogies apply to games players, actors and spectators. Shakespeare, poet, dramatist, surpassing composer of poetic drama, theatre director, actor manager combined composing with performing. This conjunction of head and heart in action enabled soul growth as when music, voice, instrument and poetry communicate divine inspiration integrated. Vocabularies of insights are irrelevant without inspired, coordinated disciplines. What is true is lost sight of until revived. The culture, the civilisation that depended on access through belief, is impoverished, reduced, until belief is reborn, recovered.

Words become meaningless without essence, their oneness with the source that begat them: the manifest reality.

Adjectives describe and inform e.g. of colour, clarity, quality. Verbs, doing, act at one or more, some at all, levels of meaning. *Shiver, shake, sneeze, spit, laugh* are physical, spontaneous or deliberate; some offer analogy and metaphor: blush with excitement, shiver with fear, shake and spit with rage. Subjective and sovereign activity: appetite, response, emotion, passion, become adjectives e.g. appetising, responsive, emotional, passionate. Verbs that are nouns (**donouns**): *need, thirst, hunger, desire, want,* are of inward and outward being, subjective and objective, potential of potent unity: the ***need*** met, ***thirst*** quenched, ***hunger*** fed. In contrast, to yearn, aspire, loathe, reject, detest are not nouns. Persons experience yearning, aspiring, loathing: for or against a person, object, method, idea..

Words for ideas and thoughts, dreams, visions, beliefs, appear to, and do emerge out of physical activities and appetites. Some occur inexplicably, from unconscious, unknown sources and need practical words to transpose, as it were, from superhuman to human sight and insight. This restores union of divine and human. ***Dream*** is unique. Concept verbs unite condition with reaction e.g. ***need*** with emotion; ***desire*** with ***wonder*** and thought. *Wonder* is felt, aroused by one or more of the senses that awaken curiosity in mind and need evaluation. ***Wonder*** may become ***awe***, inspiration to aspire beyond physical limits, known norms and limited horizons.

Numbers are learned from fingers, beans, counters, beads. Signs and symbols become familiar, remembered learning grammar of mathematics. Simple terms and processes, shapes and patterns develop into series and sets. Notions of equivalence, of equating, of congruence, **differentiation and integration** are words whose meaning is essence of math-theme-atical knowledge. Numeracy needs literacy to speak and write. Minds endowed with particular mathematical ability move faster than speech. To observe, listen, hear, describe illustrate, assists estimates and calculations: a span, a foot, a yard arm. Hands are extraordinarily practical, and mathematical: two sets of five digits make ten. Analogies make sense of counting, measuring, sizing and calculating in abstracted figures. Innumerable quantities cannot by definition be quantified. Oceans challenge explorers. Navigation at sea needs east and west as well as north and south. Dawn and sunset, longitude distances travelled were transformed when exact calculation was achieved. Mr Harrison's fourth chronometer proved good and true: beyond sight of land, on seas and oceans for accurate positioning. Radio and Radar provide subsequent technology. Light, sun, time and season are continuing natural endowment.

Mathematics, like ethics, derive from practicalities. Principles are recognised; defined. Strait lines, verticals, perpendiculars provide steps, literal and theoretical. Early builders of pyramids and temples discerned and used principles of shape, size, weight, strength and gravity. Theorems and formulae worked out by Euclid, Pythagoras, continue true, clear and communicable. Not all teachers of mathematics resist temptation to exploit the mystique of theoretical ingenuity. Language of specialist culture needs sympathetic introduction; delight in shared exploration rather than abstruse initiation, likely to bewilder. Connections unite mathematical and physical recognition, analysis, with sound in music, scale, tone, octave, key: and add delight to wonder. Mathematics, in turn, enhances practicalities. Distances, shapes, levels are surveyed and measured to make maps. Routes are recorded, engineers measure levels to plan, dam, pump and construct waterways, drains, foundations for roads and railways, airports. Architects conceive designs for building.

Human beings wonder, awaken, feel, think, evaluate, believe and act, but ground level is common to all.

Outside-in and inside-out, lives are lived from external contexts internalised, reacting, responding learning: partly understood. **Donouns** express potential interactivity. Universal and personal, personal and also universal, interaction moves from and to direct *sense*, ground level. *Practice* enhances *speed* of *mind* and memory. A *mark* on sand, clay, papyrus, vellum, slate and paper becomes 'writing'. *Work, save,* and *record* use *mind* to absorb, remember and comprehend. Before the days of calculators, books of tables, logarithms, featured in classrooms, often dog-eared and ink blotted. Text and exercise books written, are not yet entirely superseded by worksheets, print outs, e-mail.

Words and figures, shapes, sounds together make music, speech and language captured by eyes and ears, sense; inward orchestration resonant in *mind*, remembered with *reason* and imagination plus *hope*, in heart and **will**, effort to understand personally, not 'parrot-fashion'. Outward to inward, expressed outwardly again, scrutinised, criticised, corrected until confidently, surely known, a *gain* gained. **Gain** is a **donoun**, but lose, loss, lost, are not. *WORK, SHAPE, FORM, SIZE, FIGURE* as well as *WORK, SAVE, MARK, RECORD* are emphatic **donouns**.

The origin of life, the first cause, is personified as Prime Mover. Singular anonymity invites nominated identity. Plurality appears with multiplicity; imaginative flights of fancy in exploration. Early Greek, Norse, Indic culture personified and named god or goddess into language of thought and speech, being(s), doing(s) increasing vocabulary. Speculation extends, multiplies, accelerates. What is believed and thought true at one time as far as we know may alter thereafter. Sudden, dramatic *change* challenges confidence in continuity. Unsubstantiated speculation, untested belief, invites superstition. 'Rationalists' who depend only on reason believe that belief is resort of the superstitious, not on positive affirmative attitude of reasonable people. Sensible **guess** encourages belief where there is little evidence and no proof. **Guess** affirmed and verified becomes knowledge. 'Belief' is believed because believers have found that it makes sense of experience. Wondering leads to something known through faith. Comprehension of past and present, 'learning from experience' is invaluable for the future. Danger of 'dogma' recurs.

Knowledge is cited, used, by people who act in accordance with what they interpret and believe it to mean. In discussion, debate, dispute, information is quoted to support different points of view and belief. Minds aware of doubt continue to wonder what is false or true beyond material limits. Vision inspired, released, becomes constrained by reason and evidence. Social-economic-political ideologies, quasi religious, have been and are believed to be true. People who follow gods that fail cause and experienced devastation. **Temptation to suppose that because something *could* be done it *must* be done is dangerous in any sphere of power.**

Pursuit of what is true involves recognising pretence, disguise, deception. Children enjoy 'pretending' and 'dressing up'. Disguise continues in adult life. Make-belief includes intention with *purpose* to *present* **change**. Theatrical conventions on *stage* dramatise performances performed. 'Fancy dress' at carnivals and parties disguises to amuse, for good or evil purpose. To make the best of oneself, to put on clean clothes, a fitting outfit, personal in style, *taste* and quality resembles a brave *face*. *Control,* partly acquired, is partly absorbed through example in family, education where there are decent, civilising habits. Sometimes a *face* is a *mask*, concealing more than nervous uncertainty. Need to appear confident, to inspire confidence at difficult or testing times, helps to stabilise situations but eyes weep from the heart, spontaneous as laughter from voice, throat, mouth. Emotions of grief and joy intensify in thought, head. Carelessness, neglect, ignorance, weakness, fear, anger, despair, conscious or not, feature in human experience. Is it true?

The four levels (see Figure 2) operate outwardly and inwardly. Life-threatening dangers: bleeding, inability to breathe, extreme hunger and thirst, are urgent and undeniable. Conscientious reflection is telescoped in immediate physical necessity. To refuse help or rescue may be death: possibly martyrdom.

Belief that appetites and instincts cannot be trained, restrained, controlled, continues to be debated and disputed. (See **XIII I vii**.)

XII I ii Verifying

You are offered an apple. How does it look? Where did it come from? What is known of the tree, grower, provider, seller, giver? Will you try it, 'taste, and see' if you like it? Might it be harmful? You wonder; *trust*; take it, *bite, taste* and eat, or *spit* it out.

The apple itself: is it ripe, fresh, sweet, sour, rotten; does its quality show in appearance, condition, reputation? You cannot tell without trusting someone else or trying it yourself. Your eyes and nose report. Could it be poisoned or poisonous? Is it an apple of discord? Apples crop up in folk stories, myth, nursery, scientific and literary memories. Were you warned against it? Are you taking a risk in eating it? It looks good.

What does acceptance signify? Is personal taste and appetite sufficient? Cautions: warnings that it was stolen or forbidden: would you believe them and refrain? Knowledge and conscience might influence you against eating, or be disregarded. Is this apple a symbol as well as a fruit? Snow White was offered an apple poisoned by her stepmother, jealous of her beauty, to kill her.

Consequences emerge from eating. If enjoyed, you learn that you like that sort of apple. If it made you sick, you will not want to eat another.

Suppose someone you trust forbade eating the fruit of that tree with reasons, would you believe their warning? Would you rather appraise the appearance of the apple yourself? If the warning was justified but ignored, you experience consequences and can only blame yourself. You were told that the apple is fruit of the tree of the knowledge of good and evil. The apple, apparently a good apple, is '**forbidden fruit**' The burden of your decision is inescapable but knowing good and evil is not always supported by *power* of *will* for good.

The apple is a symbol. If poisoned, the eater sickens. If of discord, two want it and refuse to share. What I eat becomes me. No other person can eat what you or I have eaten. An innocent bite is expected to nourish, not harm. To bite in ignorance is risky; to bite in disobedience is foolish. It is not apples in general that are to blame.

The temptation of forbidden fruit is not that the fruit is bad but that an act of disobedience rebels against known *will* for good. Your or my appetite for an apple, for any fruit, is personal responsibility. Who says otherwise? Belief changed to disbelief has consequences. Paradise lost follows rebellion against known good. An 'own-goal', a 'self-inflicted wound', but the apple analogy concerns temptation. Human capability to think ahead has limitless implications: freedom, responsibility, conscience and law: natural, human, divine.

Curiosity promotes enquiry. What 'fuels' powers, good-will in action? Light is needed. Without light, it is dark inside each personal cave. Sight and judgment require illumination; inner light. Emergence from Plato's shadow world into direct light involved, involves, curiosity, effort of mind and *will*. Courage and confidence are not instinctive, automatic. Emotions, real rather than imagined, encourage resolution in thought to form personality and character in action. Opportunities and difficulties challenge each person to recognise true and false, good and evil, in mind, into action or inaction. Is this so because those who have thought about it believe it to be so? Do explorers, speculators, depend on unverified rumour, evidence, believed or not? Denial and affirmation determine *will*. 'How do you know?' 'Is it true?' 'Are you sure?' 'I believe so'.

Awakening consciousness opens wonder, interest to learn, seek, to understand. *Hope* to make sense of experience is assisted when order, pattern, process in natural and personal functions emerge. To know what we have done, are doing, intend, *hope* to do includes realising what is or is not best left undone. Belief fuels and is fuelled by commitment, but freedom includes critical capability for dissent, *conflict*.

XIII I iii Paradox

'If the conclusions are prescribed, the study is precluded.'
(Frederick Temple)

Paradox expresses co-existing opposites, contradictory, mutually exclusive, both true. Recognition accepts opposite incompatible extremes.

Opposite poles, north and south, day and night, light and dark, white and black are in contrast: opposite, alternating, coexisting. Different opinions, contradictory statements are familiar in experience, evident. Logic and reason encourage habits of mind, either/or, that impede recognition of paradox. Contradictions difficult to reconcile in thought and action appear mutually exclusive; either/or, not both. To verify is to search for and find what is genuine. Confident that an idea is true is a destination achieved, verified.

The notion of paradox as contrary to received opinion depends on opinion having been received. An opinion is not a fact, but encourages clarification and realisation, so far as it goes. Medical 'opinion' acted on is itself tested by results of treatment prescribed. Schools of thought differ; some oppose each other with mutually exclusive ideas, opinions, policies, plans, and practices. Paradox occurs when convictions push and pull in opposite directions. Unsustainable tension causes *break*; an anchor drags, debate becomes enmity, argument a *fight*, stability destabilised. Discipline, necessary to promote efficiency, seeks to impose conformity but suffocates creative spontaneity, initiative and originality. Mutually exclusive opposites, both true, make paradox. Protagonists sharpen arguments and intensify disagreement. Wars in words become wars with weapons. Diplomats propose practical, minimal co-operation to relieve tension. Policies of interest to opposed parties open ways forward. Conviction, like a perfect crystal, develops when quality, material ideas, disclose clarity and space. Balance and gravity hold things together. Recognition of paradox assists respect for those whose convictions differ.

Light itself is continuing reality, predictable, dispelling and overcoming darkness. Dark evil exposed by light of good overcomes evil.

The principle of non-violence coexists with that of *force*. Physical and moral order violated was answered with 'an eye for an eye' retribution. Law has developed to authorise and legitimise arrest, apprehension until brought to court for a fair hearing, acquittal or sentence. Opposing principles collide when 'non-violent' demonstrators trespass and refuse to leave. Law appeals to *reason*, principle and precedent, prosecution defended, innocent until proved guilty with evidence.

Paradoxical contradictions sustained in balance may stabilise understanding of opposing interests and different points of view. When drama intensifies misunderstanding; communication lines are overloaded, an earthquake occurs along a fault line. Diplomacy and control, negotiation and toleration, seek to restore balance and stability. Collision of forces, policies, principles, coexist within limits until upset, sometimes deliberately.

Toleration is not indifference. Vice and virtue, like dark and light, co-exist within individuals, families and communities: elemental opposites includes faith and doubt, good and evil, hope and despair, love and hate, life and death. The dilemma of paradox occurs when one clear, true view coexists with another. Different views, appreciations, opinions collide to endanger responsible action and peace.

Paradoxes appear to be, sometimes are, unreasonable contradictions. Reasoning moves along frontiers, sure and unsure, speculative, possible, probable at the time. The more complex the question, the greater the need for comprehensive intelligence: a long view, clear definition, realistic perspectives. Recollection, sympathy, imagination and an open mind encourage tolerant interpretation. The core practicalities of everyday life depend on what is true. It is dark. It is impossible to see without light, natural or artificial. Gradations of twilight, sources of light, quality of sight, illumination and vision vary. The first level of practical sight is known ability to see. Light illuminates outward sight and assists inward illumination, knowing and understanding. Blind eyes cannot discern if it is light but light helps them through other eyes. Paradox occurs when eyes and mind, heads and hearts, feeling and thought, see differently. Failing, or refusing to see, hardens into intolerance. *Light* exposes, darkness conceals. Inner vision intensifies when blind eyes are undistracted.

XIII I iv Learning through Believing

Centrifugal force flees from the centre; core of this explorer's enquiry. Navigators at sea use compass; surface magnetism. Sun, stars, sextant, time chronometers, calculate latitude and longitude, enable charts and maps, available from earlier voyages. Nevertheless, ships and navigators, people, get thrown off course, at sea, on land. Natural analogy of whirlwind or tornado, whirlpool, vortex, are destructive but survivors tell their tale.

The signposts of reason and precedent patterns go to their, our, limits. In absence of signpost or pattern, presupposition begins as an intelligent guess to be explored. Imagination and vision suggest a conclusion, more or less confident. We are living on the surface of a sphere in a state of perpetual revolution hurtling through space on a path, an orbit, knowable, known, predictable relative to the master sphere, the Sun. This is contrary to appearances and, when suspected, verified, believed, caused an almighty upset.. Galileo's observations, carried forward from those of Copernicus and earlier suppositions, seemed to defy received opinion and challenge deeply held beliefs.

XIII I v Apples, Galileo, Newton, Darwin

Here is a repeating sequence of practicalities: taste, function, possible significance again from an apple. First, an apple is fruit of an apple bearing tree, known in England; English, and elsewhere. Second, the apple itself: has been considered. You cannot know or tell without trying it yourself. Your eyes and nose report. Third, the apple is offered. Fourth, in obedience to warning, knowledge and conscience influence you against eating. Snow White did not suspect that the delicious apple offered by her step-mother, jealous of her beauty, was poisoned and intended to kill her. The voice of parent, guardian, trusted friend is believed and expected to be good. 'Playing with fire' is self evidently dangerous.

Newton, convalescing in his orchard, observed apples falling to the ground. He timed, measured, found consistency which enabled him to recognise the force of gravity. Further observation, measurement, calculation showed principles of movement and stillness, states of rest. These showed 'laws of motion'. The principle that every action has an equal and opposite reaction includes recognition of balance, equilibrium, static, momentary status until *change*.

Force, power to *move*, is dynamic. A body continues in a state of rest or of uniform motion until compelled by another force to change that state. Mechanisms devised to harness *power* follow Newton's principles, laws. See-saws, pulleys, gears depend on them. Engines, steam, are engaged to drive pumps; locomotion follows. Water and wind power imitated nature millennia before Newton lived, but his clear, measured observations, insights and definitions were and are transforming.

Liberation and control, human dynamism, energy used positively and negatively; emotional and moral energy for use and abuse is realised although less measurable or calculable. Pressure exerted with or without respect for consent can support or destroy. (See **IX**.) *Will* can find power to defy torture and imprisonment intended to break it. Newton was restless for further exploration. His mathematical and scientific genius led to **dissociation of sensibility** between his formidable intellectual power of reason and his encounters with faith, 'orthodox' belief, among contemporaries. Disputes, frustrations, led him to experiment with alchemy.

Motive to resist is immeasurable. Will-power and courage are incalculable. Balance can be disturbed. The apple challenge represents responsible decision as moral: obedient or disobedient, for good and evil, true or false. To wonder, observe, test, affirm, verify, is available in practicalities. Balanced energy, control of feelings, thoughts, evaluations, are supplemented by conscience, judgment and *will*. These equip but do not always empower. Cultivating moral capabilities, not easy or pleasurable, makes us persons rather than creatures. Magnificent creaturely instincts are enhanced in knowledge and understanding in three phases of consciousness: *being, knowing and willing*. These three co-ordinate and unify search for what is true; looking for the spirit of the thing; integrating head and heart.

Each personal sphere, soul, grows in knowing and believing; believing, knowing and understanding. *Will* confers possibility to act responsibly and to *control* to discern sovereign good: freed to seek, *find* and follow the good in humility, courage, *will* to do. Liberty, independence, is experienced through wonder, enquiry, questioning, seeking as best we can, what we can, for what is true. Willing acceptance of what is discovered envisages paradise regained: newborn joy and delight in the good and true. Passionate curiosity frustrated by limits, failures, conflicts, disturbs peace of mind: distressing but stimulating.

Curiosity promotes enquiry. Light is needed. Without light, it is dark inside personal cave seeing and judging only from shadows. Sight and judgment require movement out into light, generating inner light to see truly.

Darwin's recognition of evolution and concept of natural selection were differently disturbing to him and to critics who understood and applauded or who failed and condemned. *Will* to re-think; test, qualify, modify needs confidence. Conclusions depend on apprehension of principle from accurate evidence believed, verified, accepted. To alter a 'mind-set' disturbs, shocks. Debate of detail, only partly understood by non-specialists, does not preclude recognition of new theory and principle. Darwin's work, closer in time to the twentieth century than Galileo's, or Newton's, is personal. Ape ancestry caused shock.

Similarity and difference between animal and human nature; of instinct, emotion, mind and will, determination and control are crucial to what is believed to determine behaviour in personal, tribal, and collective culture. (See **XIII II**.)

XIII 1 vi Shakespeare, Diamonds, Crown

English voices: poets, philosophers, translators: Chaucer, Langland, Tyndale, Shakespeare, Milton, Lancelot Andrews, Pope, T. S. Eliot among others, renew and extend the language. The common tongue is refreshed, reinvigorated. Range, confidence, eloquence grow through cultivating the gift of words. Shakespeare, poet and musician, wrote plays: dramatic histories, tragedies and comedies, mixing characters with characteristics old and new, repeatedly performed and appreciated. Essential reality of character assists understanding and cultivation of it. We see ourselves, but may develop spectator censoriousness without joy or pain of playing the game. Rules emerge when games are played. Some push the game analogy to represent hope and purpose of life, personal achievement and success. Shakespeare's 'all the world's a stage' is relevant again: to presuppose that life is a game, a play: but players are again contestants rather than performers. Shakespeare combined composition and production with performance. This conjunction of head and heart in action nurtures soul. Music, voice, instrument, depend on inspired sensibility, attuned to meet increasingly profound response, over and over again, words in music: food of love.

Words become meaningless when disconnected from their original, given, reality. Shakespeare encompassed encyclopaedic sources of information, references, worlds told and re-told, universal, biblical and classical, continental, insular, pre-eminently local. Critics write volumes of interpretation, appreciation of his work. Dictionaries quote his phrases to illustrate usage. Comic, tragic, classic, romantic, practical and magical: his plays translate and are performed, drawing laughter and tears wherever their universal artistry transmits. **Power** interested him, for good and evil. Personal passion, love, envy, rivalry. Jealous hatred between Iago and Othello; ambition in Macbeth; parental power, love and love abused by King Lear; and Hamlet. Rivalry personal, and dynastic; red and white roses fight for the **Crown**, for political power symbolised by circlets of gold, settings for diamonds; rich symbols.

Diamond is pure carbon, hardest element known, perfect in crystal form and cleavage. Cutting and polishing brings out multifaceted refracted light in all colours of the rainbow, the spectrum. Diamond is outstanding for beauty, quality, rarity, and endurance. First, the stones themselves, found in 'pipes' of rock where intense heat, pressure and space provide conditions for crystallisation. Surface rock, eroded and washed out as river gravel, alluvial, sometimes carries gold and diamond. Second, qualities of shape, crystal form and cleavage enhance their beauty to sparkle and delight. Third, function adds to pleasure and pleasure to function: a single stone set in a ring; an eloquent brooch, bracelet, necklace, tiara.

Crowns speak for themselves and identify the functions of the wearer. The Crown Jewels of England express sovereignty of service personified; personal power evolved within constitutional limits, conscience and law. Abused, doubted, challenged, forcibly overthrown but restored again, when recognised as invaluable; irreplaceable. Symbols of majesty represent the good of *order*, of constitutional authority worn to personify duty and service after having delegated powers of government to representatives of communities, elected by constituents.

The Upper House is being modified but retains a revising function. The Lords Temporal, traditionally inheritors of property and title of Peer, affirm ingredients valued in upbringing, education, expectation of public service, vulnerable to temptation, private, public. The greater the privilege, the higher the opportunity and expectation of responsibility and the deeper the fall. Simple honesty: the difference between a loan and a gift: money for a peerage, a seat in the Upper House, compromises 'patron' and 'patronised' political opportunists. Selective or elective, surrenders primary ingredient of inherited security. Plausible talk of 'heritage', trust in buildings but failing to trust and respect those persons who value and exemplify fidelity to their inheritance, is meaningless. The Office of Lord Chancellor, 'keeper of the King's Conscience', cost the head of Beckett and of Thomas More. Judicial, executive and administrative functions of government unified in the holder of this great office, next in precedence to the Archbishop of Canterbury who follows the Sovereign. The Lords of Appeal, Archbishops and Bishops, life peers, (and life peers unwilling to bind their descendents), benefit from those whose families have connections and political experience over generations of service and leadership but are not obliged to attend and contribute. It is remarkable how successive generations follow professions, vocation and interest: clergy, legal, medical, naval, military, agricultural, financial and land. A wealth of experience more to be cherished than resented, despised, cast aside.

Opening Parliament is formal expression of continuity. Newly elected and re-elected MPs are reminded that the State, larger than party, community of constituencies, is the representative nation. They are summoned to attend the Queen who wears the Crown, symbol of sovereignty as service. Worthy and unworthy monarchs have worn it. The function of the Crown Jewels exemplifies this sovereign purpose; *will*, consent and accountability; worn beauty and splendour to magnify the State occasion, grand opening of parliament whose purposes are to criticise and consent to government, including taxation and legislation. The Crown synthesises authority authorised. Wearers are constrained by convention and statute, likely to be disregarded by 'elective dictators' who take power, cling to office, but rarely outlive the occupants of the Throne.

Walter Bagehot (1826-1877), in essays on *The English Constitution*, distinguished functions of the Sovereign as 'dignified' and 'business'. Opening Parliament, robed, attended, the Queen wears the Crown, reads the Speech which unites the Royal Will with that of her Government. Royal Presence widely recognised, now televised, adds significance, style and dignity, and makes occasions memorable, valued, appreciated. The Crown as fount of justice; of honour for outstanding service. Critics who deny ideals of loyalty, courage, obligation to serve country and commonwealth 'above and beyond the call of duty' reduce to personal, political ambition. Dignity overlaps with business and 'business enjoys benefit of dignity', as different as gifts are from loans.

Privy Council meetings, formal but convenient for 'Orders in Council', remind ministers, secretaries of state, overworked, whose office includes attendance, that the monarch is less 'powerful' but more important than those who come and go. Royal experience is continuous and, Bagehot observed, 'offers a splendid career to an able monarch', who is above party, always informed by the 'boxes' regularly received, well read. To be *consulted* (informed), to *encourage* and to *warn*: enables enduring influence, through regular 'audiences' for prime ministers and others who recognise lengthening experience and continuity of the Crown. Traditions of courtesy, good faith, devotion endow immediate practicalities that benefit families, schools, communities: national and international; for common wealth.

Royal presence, life and behaviour, strengthen for good, and sadly, tragically sometimes, for ill, but the good is stronger. Human beings born or wedded into royal life, enjoy exceptional opportunities and privilege but are circumscribed by limits of social and constitutional restraint. Public curiosity, indiscriminant, prurient, populist, brings unrelenting publicity but need not destroy opportunities for outstanding public service. Crowned heads, princesses and princes, have opportunities for unusual careers. First-hand experience, unencumbered by personal ambition for fame or fortune and the partisan political posturing, competing, of politicians disfigured by ambition.

XIII I vii Control? Aristotle, Personal, Political

To think clearly is the aim of philosophers. To intellectualise is to define, but gaps open between intelligence and virtue. Is it true? Is it good? Socrates (BC 469-399), Plato (427-347), Aristotle (384-322) considered each, both questions, in lives, deaths, actions and thoughts, their discussions studied since.

Belief taught as 'rules' seldom nourishes a soul with joy or empowers *will* to obey.

Paul at Athens (circa A D 51) addressed philosophers: Epicurean, Stoic, on Mars Hill. They were unimpressed, but willing to hear him again. (*Acts* 17 15-18.) The impact of Christianity, the Gospel, affirmed faith in transforming *grace*. Saul of Tarsus, Roman citizen by birth, Pharisee by education in Hebrew promise, law, prophecy, was a man of passionate convictions. He persecuted Christians, witnessed the martyrdom of Stephen and set out for Damascus to stamp out 'believers' there. On that road, vision and voice of the living Christ spoke, called, blinded him. Led to those he had intended to destroy, Saul was baptised: Paul: his sight restored protected by Roman law, travelled to teach **and** preach.

Greek thought, reasoned, encountered vibrant faith, commitment. Debate, disagreement, effort to define faith, Creed, developed Christian thought: Justin Martyr from Samaria (circa 100-165); Irenaeus (circa 130-200); Clement of Alexandria (150-215); Tertullian from Carthage (circa 180-225); Origen of Alexandria (185-254): early believers, became acknowledged 'Fathers': Augustine of Hippo (354-430) whose faithful heart and thinking faith clarified vision of Christendom Empire, describes his conversion in *Confessions*. Devotion, study, faithful heart and thinking faith enabled him to clarify vision of Christendom: '*De Civitate Dei*': City of God.

Disputes, schisms, continued, elucidated, fortified by Thomas Aquinas. 'Scholastic' theology was challenged, shaken by protesters. Independent thought was reclaimed when new continents, new scientific discoveries; rising 'nationalism' to which Rome did not adapt to renewed biblical study or to desire for 'scientific' 'proof' rather than to divine disclosure. Such a sweeping summary exaggerates by generalisation, which risk balanced perspectives. *HOPE* for deeper wisdom, moral responsibility and goodness is enduring goal of faith and *LOVE*.

Simple need learns to look beyond appearance. Appearances explored from outward objects, still and moving, enter inward experience. Natural curiosity intensifies hunger to discover, to discern where a question may lead. Five agents, (William Blake's 'five windows of the soul'): eyes and ears above nose, which is above mouth, communicate to and from brain, organ of mind. Skin, with sensitive nerves inside and out, responds to pleasure and pain; touch and being touched inform mind immediately. Senses, capable of responding together, are distinct from one another, sensitive to direct, deliberate, stimulants and to perceptions discerned. **Touch** is emotional as well as sensual. To be moved in heart is to respond with feeling, reaction, sympathy, **will** to act.

Do you believe the sight of your own eyes? How far and how much is seen? Critical faculties operate at every level. Features of a face reveal more than the skull beneath the skin. Instant perception, apprehension, soul open to soul, is revealing. *Light, sight,* insight, *spark* realisation. Revelation, begotten by belief out of commitment, clears pursuit of what is true, illuminated by and in energy of **light**.

Plato presupposes the Good as object and fulfilment of what is true. Advancing consciousness, conscious and confident, moves to further frontiers to *find* food for thought and action. The nature of limits change from physical, practical and literal, to mathematical, metaphorical and metaphysical. Speculation goes beyond analysis of *number, form, size* and *shape* (mathematical) to further realms of knowing where distinctive departments of knowledge reunite. Plato's discussion of the Line is followed by his Cave allegory. Humans, like cave dwellers, live in interior darkness, ignorance, inside each singular and collective cave. **Light** from outside the cave casts shadows within. Seeing shadows draws cave dwellers towards the light to enquire, explore, search for light itself. This light is the light of reason. Outside the cave, day and night distinguish light and darkness. Cave-dwellers become philosophers who learnt to live delivered from darkness and shadows. (*Republic*, VII. 514 A- 521 B, translated Cornford, pages 222-230.)

Metaphysic, to Aristotle, came 'after physic'. Medical study, interaction of body and mind, led him from physic to metaphysic, integration of body and soul. His last work, *De Anima*, considers vitality, life-force referred to as soul, not quite the same as spirit. (The translator of the Penguin Classics edition, 1986 discusses use of 'soul', English, for 'psyche', Greek. *De Anima* is retained since the psyche, for Aristotle, is that in virtue of which something is alive.) (See pages 11-12.) **Change** involves movement. Metaphysical moves from one form to another, maggot into fly, chrysalis into silk worm or butterfly. (See VI i-iii.) Plato's cave-dwellers see shadows but move to light to reason and realise further reality; metamorphosis from cave-dweller to philósopher.

Physical expression, action, engages transmission from impulse, instinct, to refine and be refined, body to soul, metaphysical.

Animus and Anima, opposing principles of animation, coexist in human being. Their tension has led to recognition of divided self, human nature faced with dilemmas, alternatives, inner schisms. A person who becomes conscious of deliberation and capability of decision, acts of *will* are first expressed in physical and material ways retained in memory for future reference. Such decisiveness increases maturity. Thinking, judging, referring to conscience, have been discussed as helping will to decide. Attention to sense and instinct but no longer imprisoned by them sharpens need to accept *will* as capable to *order* and initiate: to *trust* and obey. Senses join into common sense with intelligence and knowledge. Higher, deeper purposes benefit and enhance appreciation of the functions of senses integrated, reconciled, in true and ordered purposes.

Does inward capability to criticise, to appraise, require *confidence* to **control**? Such confidence affects personal *will* to find **power** of self-control. This question requires affirmative or negative response. The response affects behaviour.

Control, believed to be impossible, is not achievable.

Control, believed to be undesirable is not desired — unless feared for other reasons.

Control, believed difficult might suffocate initiative: **WILL** itself

Learning to distinguish levels and differentiating between them promotes cooperation and integration. The concept of innocence in childhood includes all levels of consciousness, unrealised, undamaged, uncomplicated. Responsibility, then, is more joyful than burdensome. Weighty words such as subterfuge, shame, disgrace, misery, failure, inadequacy become relevant when experienced. Temptation, desire resisted, recognises alternatives of good or evil in personal behaviour; genuine possibility to decide and act freely; to *control*.

First unity: one body, *head and heart*, mind and *will*, are ingredients of soul. Your and my body, outwardly still, is inwardly still moving, heart beating, blood circulating, lungs breathing, alive, mind and soul able to contemplate beyond sense distractions.

What is, as it is, in being? You are. I am. As a body, embodied, each person is a unit. Each is capable of unity, duality, trinity, squaring up, circulating, (here we go again) in body, emotion, thought and *will*; revolving, solving, revolving and resolving with resolution. Descended from ancestors and veritable origin of species, diversity devolves from sources unknown; becoming more known, common and uncommon; investigated in wondering what is true. Recognition and realisation of outward things and people occurs inwardly but derives from elsewhere, outwardly and enables astonishing discoveries and developments.

Second: duality, out and in, in and out; dialogue: pro and con, impersonal and personal, object/subject etc in steps and paces, breath, pulse, heartbeat, rhythm to march together, 'by the right', on the ***beat*** going somewhere, to a destination, a target, a war, a destiny, home to peace or different sorts of battle. Parades, pageants of purpose and hope: singular and plural, positive and negative, are occasioned by events. For participant or non-participant, dancing as well as marching, alone or together accompanied by music of destiny, or emptiness, nothing.

Third: triples, the third dimension, up and down as well as along; forward, backward, sideways. Triangle and waltz are patterns of structure and movement; liberating in space, time and place. Triangles: survey by triangulation, trio in sound, trinity in being: knowing, willing, doing. The order changes: learning, thinking, before doing.

Fourth: a square accords within or surrounded by its circle, distinct, autonomous, yet interdependent in shape and concept: plane, solid, spherical, global, symmetrical, balanced, sharing ***one centre***. The rhythm of Common Time, four square, two times two, wreathes and is wreathed with seasons; cycles; moving, rotating, measured, repeating yet at any moment its centre is ***still*** and for ever. Encircling diversity renews unity, universal universe, all moments in this one: ready, imminent, unceasing, unending. The fourth stage becomes the first through discerning threefold nature, whole and complete in true spirit in and of things. Thus our world rotates repeatedly yet with fresh, refreshed ingredients and opportunities, differently each time.

Repetition, cycle, in the sky above from shape and movement of Sun; Moon, full, then waning and waxing in phases; cycles which fascinate young and old; contemporary and ancient. The moon shines with remote geometrical beauty and perfection; other than bright light and heat of the round sun, always round, even in occasional eclipse. Ideas increase and decrease, come and go in mind. A brilliant idea opens radiant possibilities: suggestions, guesses, hypotheses. Questions are raised, evidence collected (practical at the first level, actual, material), to be enjoyed (felt), explored in hope of discovery (thoughtful, third level) of solutions to problems, partial and impartial conclusions, limited and far reaching. Evaluation (fourth level) is occurring: will it work? Is it functional, valuable, useful? *Is it true? Is it good?*

Suggestions do or do not become statements in light of what is believed, recognised, as true. 'So far, so good' or 'good so far'; or dead end, negative, untrue, a bad idea. False statements, enticing, fascinating, do not provide genuine basis for advance, but an end, a *cul de sac*, terminating that route of enquiry. 'Counter-intelligence' side-tracks, diverts, perverts exploration. Genuine mistakes: errors: mislead, deceive, are deceitful. Led astray, to err by innocent or ignorant mistake, an explorer who realises error endeavours to correct it. Deliberate fabrication, concealment, 'cover up' draws into an under-world of falsification, of lost innocence where others are caught, 'framed'. Good faith sustains innocence which strengthens good faith: **trust** that the good and true, to have and to **hold**, although loyalty incurs suffering, possible martyrdom.

Transition from believing to knowing, to objective knowledge, has two practical aspects. First, confidence that the reasoning mind (yours or mine?) can enquire, learn, and discover towards the Good. Guesses lead to something discerned, tested, recognised, understood and accepted as true. Second, belief that enquiry worth making, if true is shared to become common. To pre-suppose something discoverable, knowable, sustains **will** to affirm, continue, persist to conclusion for evil or good, often both. Ends are not always bitter since glory, true glory, emerges from tragedy.

Plato's vision is old and new; fresh, profoundly relevant to asking: is it true? This question concerning a particular **idea** may discover a **principle**, a **pattern** in essence and substance, systematic *form*, as enquiries are pursued.

An ideal has consequences which affect attitude and behaviour. Effort of mind driven by intense curiosity sharpens appetite. Discoveries and conclusions permeate 'formal' education influencing a wonderer to become a believer. The Good as sovereign in every sphere of life: personal, social and political concerns what is true. Plato and Aristotle embraced cardinal virtues, including what is just, in action. Their formative influence endures.

If the life of the mind brings knowledge and understanding, questions as to the nature and sources of joy and happiness continue to challenge heart: peace of mind. Exploration through speculation need not stop at intellectual joy-riding. Why not? Like lightning safely earthed, ideas *spark* between body and mind, mind and mind to return, realised and realisable. Living human life on earth is embodied, manifest, consuming and consumed, capable of being redeemed from appearances, possessiveness, error, evil. The concept of 'intellectual property' did not limit Plato, Aristotle, Augustine whose teaching, (a function of philosophers) engaged and influenced followers who use, used, their names without copyright. The seven liberal arts: trivium of grammar, rhetoric and logic, were followed by *quadrivium* of arithmetic, geometry, astronomy and music — engaged in pursuit of the good and true, to nurture, foster, exemplify. **To philosophise aims to think clearly. To intellectualise is to define. A gap opens between intelligence and virtue.** Belief taught as 'rules' may not bring joy nor empower obedience. Reaction from 'scholastic' into predominantly 'scientific' thought exaggerates 'materialism', tends to lose touch with wisdom, moral responsibility, the sovereignty of good. Independent thought, an independent mind, risks thinking wrongly, falsely, rather than truly. 'Dissociation of sensibility' follows.

Mind and memory experience partial detachment from sense perception. If this increases, intensifies into contemplation, we are 'taken up', static to ecstatic. Body 'ticks over', apparently still, but heart-beat, breath, pulse, are ready to re-engage in practicalities. To *work*: to receive, respond, initiate thinking action, active thinking. A body, quiet for a time, meditative, resting, asleep, perhaps dreaming, is refreshed, available, reminds when nourishment, refuelling, is needed. Concentration enables mind to wonder, ponder, estimate, evaluate, with and without external movement. Looking up, fetching a book, finding a reference, recording by ordinary physical activity (including keying in and out on a processor, assisted by 'search engines') promotes insight, knowledge.

From embryo presupposition, belief opens access towards expanding fields for what is true; to knowing. *Plato's presupposes the Good as object and fulfilment of what is true.* Advancing consciousness, conscious and confident, moves to further frontiers finding food for thought and action. The nature of limits change from physical, literal, to mathematical, metaphorical and metaphysical. Speculation goes beyond analysis of number, form, size and shape known as mathematics to further realms of knowing where separate departments of knowing reunite.

Aristotle pursued medical studies; interaction of body and mind for healing. These led him from physic to metaphysic, integral unity of body and soul. His last work, *De Anima*, already referred to, considers vitality, life-force referred to as soul, not quite the same as spirit. Psyche, for Aristotle, is that in virtue of which something is alive. Change involves movement: from one form to another. Plato's cave-dwellers, in shadows, move into light: *reason*, from cave-dweller to philosopher. 'The Lady of Shallot' saw life reflected in her mirror where 'shadows of the world appear'. Warned never to look directly from the window, she must stay at her loom, weaving, seeing only mirror images. One day, Lancelot rode by, singing. The Lady could not *control* or contain her *desire* to see him. She left her loom and looked out. The mirror cracked. The sight was fatal. Her end was dramatic. Witnesses observed her body floating by.

275

Lancelot mused with sympathetic detachment and a prayer. Tennyson's poem fascinates girls of poetic sensibility and romantic inclination who await a perfect knight, alive, not a mirror image. Is this true?

Belief which makes sense of experience verifies what is true. Such experience verifies belief, so far as it goes; is more evident when seen with our own eyes. To believe what is not true has unhappy consequences as unhappy as trust misplaced or betrayed. Wonder becomes wondering, followed by enquiry and exploration, outward/inward/outward, objective/subjective/subject/object through the levels. Questions of quality prompt discussion of *value*: of quality: equality and inequality, of privilege and privation. Ability and energy are uneven and opportunity is affected by conditions and circumstance, infinite variety, potential integration of head and heart; thought and feeling: integrity.

XIII I viii Interaction and Intersecting

Time, place and continuity are significant. A promise made now could be singular, this once. A continuing commitment is now and always. Elemental and fundamental in any exploration is that prior things exist to be explored before people became capable of exploring. Having emerged in human form, from formed embryo with energy of life, human beings have become capable of recognising and being recognised, named and naming, spoken of and speaking, listening and hearing: performing.

Areas of activity emerge out of immeasurably great creative, sustaining energy, constructive and destructive, expressed in practicalities. Qualities of virtue; of JUSTICE and mercy; enduring virtues of FORTITUDE, TEMPERANCE (moderation), HUMILITY and PRUDENCE concern behaviour.

To value the good for its own sake extends to, from, and for one another; humane in action, appreciation and use of things.

Performatives: to affirm, testify, plead, judge, forgive, swear, confess, repent are not always obvious from physical processes in nature but, when known, are manifestly beneficial; demonstrable in practicalities. Realised in heart and mind from living examples, models, *show*, disclose, inspire imitation. Awe and wonder, fear and love, these are desired and emulated in action, doing. Analysed in mind, remembering, studying and thinking, beget history, philosophy, natural and moral science. Theology, seeking sources of true from untrue, good from evil, becomes academic when separated from practicalities: from living reality of good behaviour. To prefer and promote *will* for good is vision of the *will for good*; envisages theos, God, operating through gift of faith: **grace**. A soul grown in union of flesh and spirit, matter and mind, looks for, longs to know and enjoy elemental and primal sources: food for thought, fruit of the **seed** of the word.

Noun plus verb make a sentence. The briefest sentences are two words. I am. It is. You do. We see. They tell. I hear. I wonder. I might. I will. Will you? Finding words to state intention moves from present and past to intended future. To formulate, express, sympathise, explain; to inform, encourage or warn, are performative: intention with commitment by saying.

To catch and imitate sounds; to order, reproduce and develop; to make a song to sing; performing, plucking harp and heart strings. Melody and harmony, scale, octave, chord and discord are identified. Pattern in sounds discerns theory which enables notation. Compositions noted, written, read, can be repeated, rehearsed, practiced, performed. Personal participation, direct, witnessed, interacting, heard with our ears, seen with our own eyes, arouses response in sense, mind and spirit; nourishing the soul. Music enables participation in the **heat, light, sound:** the **fire** of life; energy moving creative and performing art: composed, danced, dramatised, staged, enacted, depicted, painted, spoken and written about. Experience returns: interacts, intersects, disturbs, soothes, inspires, ignites appreciation and understanding. Sense impression filtered through heart and mind becomes other, revealing, digestible matter.

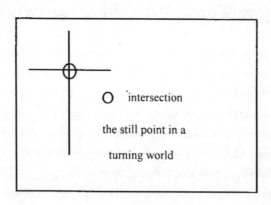

O intersection

the still point in a

turning world

XIII II

True

'Vocabulary is the Everest of a language..
Where does the vastness of the lexicon come from?'
(David Crystal, *Cambridge Encyclopedia of the English Language*,
Cambridge University Press 1995, page 17)

'I am not yet so lost in lexicography, as to forget that words are
the daughters of earth and that things are the sons of heaven.'
(Dr Johnson, *Preface to the Dictionary of the English Language*, 1755)

'But what is freedom? Rightly understood
A universal licence to be good.'
(Hartley Coleridge, *Liberty*, 1796-1849)

XIII II 1 Finding Words, Refreshing Language

English has had comparatively few centuries of language development but in periods of expansion, mobility, comparative stability, growth is exponential. Words and phrases heard are caught before taught. Guiding principles raise questions in the mind of speaker, listener, reader or writer. Grammar becomes recognised. Principles acknowledged lead to 'rules' memorised, not always digested, understood, but helpful to clarify a difficult message. Instinctive communications use grammar, not indoctrinated but examined to warn, delight, agonise.

Correct usages and constructions encourage respect for thinking, speaking, doing truly, but ignorance or disregard tends to inadequate, inappropriate, unsuitable, even false communication. Appreciation of what is true is obscured, hidden, often lost. Superficial error becomes decay unless corrected. Deeper meanings evaporate without commitment and responsibility. Words adopted, adapted, applicable as far as they go, go only so far as the limits of knowledge and understanding, from source to recipient.

'Icon' is used to popularise, personify a trend setter, leader of fashion, new style, **distinctive**, and is widely regarded as a 'process' term.

Principles of grammar and knowledge of vocabulary, necessary for clarity, draw power and energy from who speaks, writes, when true to the Good. Those who think, write, speak, may, **ought** to aspire to learn and communicate truly; but sink, swim, soar **according to absence or presence of integrity which none can recognise in themselves, however much hoped for**.

The skeleton of language structure; the bones and joints that give form and shape to its limbs are clad with muscles and sinews, nerve and skin, parts of speech, words and phrases for fluent movement. Strength and agility of mind, voiced into words, develops quality of speech. Inward personal form and shape need living organs, heart and lungs to receive and give expression, nerved, minded, made manifest. Sensibilities of consciousness, conscience to reflect, remember, formulate, evaluate, judge, describe, and move attempts to find words. Each of us, free and able, may do this for ourselves, more and less effectively. We are fortunate when introduced to words well constructed to nourish appetite of enthusiasm, enjoyment and understanding from early childhood and truly spoken, expressive.

XIII II 2 Outward and Evident

XIII II 2 i Virtue

Justice, Temperance, Fortitude, Prudence, **ancient virtues**; later known as 'cardinal'; now as Fair, Courageous, Moderate, Wise, or Prudent. Each virtue has opposing vice. Absolute Virtue suggests complete freedom from vice: perfection.

Faith, Hope, Love, energy for good, are regarded as **'spiritual virtues'**. Language of opposites, paradoxical, moves when responsibility and conscience become central in cultivating resistance to temptation and sin. Vice, (vice-versa, reversal), imprisons in attitudes which beget bad/wicked/evil actions. Pride, lust, envy, covetousness, gluttony, anger, sloth: **'seven deadly sins'**: contrast with virtue and goodness: humility rather than pride (arrogance, self-satisfaction etc). Sense and virtue link good sense with good behaviour: easier said than done.

Endowed with senses, we learn to interpret, amplify, cultivate. Word promotes inward cognition, consideration, and memory adds to recognition. Received thoughts nourish inward understanding, outward discussion. Words increase consciousness of will, good or ill, to receive or reject, take, give, deny. Virtues known are criteria of behaviour. Virtue in common life is needed for the sake of other people. Hope to be just, prudent, brave and temperate, shows care, concern and control in every sort of activity and relationship. Good behaviour benefits others since objective good inspires and calls for genuinely objective action: good-will, joy, to both receiver and giver.

Generosity is in three stages: first, resources and will to give; second, knowing what to give to whom and when; third, the consequences of giving depend on receiver, not giver. Is genuine generosity known pleasure of giving? Is to deny this true? Is will to give, to share, genuine generosity? Reciprocal quality permeates good-will as thoroughly and oppositely as deceit entangles and spoils, including self-deception. Is it the thought that counts? Thought-motive-action are distinct. Thought and act are capable of conjunction, unity of being and doing. Motive, motion and make, are not **donouns**, but *move* is. Action, *ACT*, exemplifies unity of being and doing professed: *judge, doctor, minister, nurse;* but speak, teach and write do not. Each needs to profess, affirm that their words, spoken, taught, written, are **true**. This means as far as we believe and know in our imperfect world and incomplete knowledge. Who is sufficient for these things?

Mysteries wondered, pondered through faith are unverifiable until evidence is recognised: outward to inward, then outwardly expressed. Science, philosophy, theology need one another. Science took a leap upwards as well as forwards when experimental methods enabled the mind of the Creator to be read in works of nature. Barriers have developed in European thought, evident in the attitude of those who summoned Galileo to Rome, 1632 to answer for his verification of Copernicus (1543) that the Earth revolves and moves round the Sun, not that the Sun moves round the Earth. Galileo was 'vehemently' suspected of heresy, (unorthodoxy), forced to recant under threat of torture and, if he refused, sentenced to imprisonment. He was imprisoned, but after some months, allowed to return to Florence. Francis Bacon (1561-1626) believed that *control* of the natural world would be found by studying and understanding forces at work in nature. A theory must be verified in practice by experiment before a general principle could be acknowledged. Bacon died from a chill caught when stuffing a chicken with snow to see if this would extend its freshness. Bishop Joseph Butler (1692-1754) in *The Analogy of Religion, Natural and Revealed, to the Constitution and Course of Nature* (1736) explored nature and sacrament. He foresaw danger in separating natural philosophy (science) from moral philosophy and theology. Charles Darwin, after extensive travel and meticulous research saw evidence of change as evolution and natural selection; how life in its astounding variety and manifestation evolved, is evolving. Some supposed that revised hypothetical time-scale, denied belief in seven-day wonder of creation as emanating from the *mind*, energy and *order* personified as One, the Creator. Those who wrote the book of Genesis had no archaeology, documents or prehistoric specimens. They were inspired to believe that *form* and *order, light* and dark, *land* and *water*, vegetation and life were, are, the Creator's gift in creating. No human beings were present at the beginning to observe sequences on uninhabited, uninhabitable earth, to measure time or observe what was going on. Reconstructed by study, by reading present conditions and processes to discern past does not deny seven stages, 'days'.

There are moments when time stands still and others when it extends to infinity. Eras and epochs understood by studying rocks derived from types of rock evidently different in origin (igneous, sedimentary, metamorphic: *fire, water* and transformation). Evidence of life emerges in sediments, strata with fossils, sequences of process and order, now reckoned to have taken millennia, billennia, as 'days' of creation. (See **XIII I**.)

XIII II 2 ii Hero, Idol, Icon, Martyr, Saint

Actions of great bravery involve personal danger, *risk* to *save*, rescue, protect or deliver others. Legendary courage of Theseus, hero who slayed the Minotaur (greedy ferocious beast with body of a man and the head of a bull, repeatedly depicted by Picasso) who demanded young girls to placate his appetite. Theseus rescued them and their parents from this evil. The hero who risks his life may lose it. Sacrifice remembered, cultivated, becomes a cult. The ultimate hero is ready to give his life, to die for others.

Heroic action is remembered with gratitude, perpetuated as example sometimes elaborated so much that myth, legend, history are indistinguishable. Charles Kingsley's *Heroes* inspire wonder at their exploits. Did they really live? Their names appear as constellations, Perseus, Andromeda, Cassiopaeia, Orion; accentuating distinction between terrestrial and celestial stardom.

Hero, legendary priestess of Venus, was loved and beloved of Leander. He swam each night across the treacherous water of the Hellespont guided by a light she held for him. One night a storm extinguished the light. Leander drowned. Hero plunged in to rescue him but drowned too. Other lovers: Dido and Aeneas, Caesar and Cleopatra, Romeo and Juliet suffered separation by distance, culture, circumstance, family enmity, tragic in consequence.

A hero's courage does not fail, even in extreme danger, but develops to become heroic. Personal order, self-control in everyday matters maintained under stress tests behaviour with objective *control*: neither intemperate nor temperamental. To know of, know, a wise person whose example and influence is beneficial, whose counsel is sought; who laughs with you, not at you, whose sparklingly serious wit discerns, stimulates and enlivens, is true and good. Physical, emotional, mental and moral courage are heroic qualities. 'Moral' expresses, ***will***, needing ***power***, energy and strength.

Greek heroes of 'godlike' repute were reminded of their humanity by Nemesis, personification of jealousy from Olympus. Legend interweaves myth with history. The courage of Ulysses, Hercules, Theseus to perform exceptional exploits inspired emulation. Greek sculptors endowed rulers, philosophers, heroes with superhuman quality and character still evident in their statues. Temples were dedicated to divinities, Apollo, Athena, god, goddess, rather than to heroes. This avoided danger of a hero idolised becoming an idol. At Athens, the Theseum is below the Parthenon, in the area of the ancient Stoa, market place, scene of trade and debate (stoic). Admiration, emulation and worship are distinctive. Hero-worship is an ancient and modern phenomenon, other than 'celebrity'. Idol-worship, idolatry, persists in some cultures but is excoriated in others. Cult of particular characteristics, personified, finds devotees in traditions vulnerable to natural catastrophes. Vulcan, divine blacksmith, forged Jove's thunderbolts in his workshop. Volcanic eruptions were, are, catastrophic.

'Icon' suggests an 'image': function of imagination. A picture is a visible representation on a flat surface, drawn, painted, photographed. Images model, offer imitation, but pictures depict. Picture and image, representing the same thing, are incapable of being identical, exactly alike. A passport photograph identifies the holder, permits to cross a frontier, a port, to enter another country. A statue and a model may or may not be true to life. Word processor 'icon' identifies a function and gives access to it. Pictorial image, an imagined picture, enters memory, performs a different purpose and function. Greek ideals of immortality, gods, goddesses, sculpted as statues at places of worship, adorned temples. The Parthenon friezes, processions, honour Athena, in masterpieces of sculpture on grand scale. Icons developed from these early inspirations. The Iconostasis in Greek churches illustrates figures from biblical events visible, manifest to strengthen believers. This painted screen is placed between believers and priests, custodians of mysteries of life, birth, death, resurrection. Like Plato's Line, the screen separates wondering and believing. Icons at home assist meditation.

Heroes and heroines whose lives bring good to the world through grace known in Christ: Son of God the Father, of Mary his Mother and the Holy Ghost, dove descending Comforter are painted as *presences*, ICONS. An icon is more than a picture, an image, a representation, although seen at these levels too. Christian believers, Greek and Russian (who learned from Greek usage), find access to **grace** and **power** known in the person pictured: a life empowered. The icon draws the eye of faith, to, from, beyond what is seen, drawn and painted, sometimes decorated, embellished, with dramatic intensity. The icon focuses concentration and invites seeker to find and receive strength through devotion. Lives lived in **will** for good, souls empowered, are painted in ways which draw eyes and memory in reversed perspective to participate in virtue of this strength. Icons assists worship. Lives known to transmit particular **grace**, humility, do not draw attention to themselves but are remembered with benefit, *beatitude*. Grace is infinitely beneficial energy of virtue. Virtue expresses grace, fundamental to iconography, strengthening faith and **will** and strengthened through **trust**, faith, belief.

Hebrew monotheism grew when and where idol worship was common. Personal command, disobeyed by Adam, led to personal call voiced to Noah, Abraham, Moses, who ascended Mount Nebo to receive the law. Needing clarification, he ascended again and left below a Golden Calf and worshipped it. (*Exodus* 32.) Material substitute for genuine but unseen presence was forbidden; ought not to be imagined. No man-made substitute for invisible reality must ever be worshipped. This Law was second only to the principle of unity in divinity. ('One is One and all alone; and ever more shall be so,' became a refrain.)

The law, the Ten Commandments were believed as God's will: His Law in words. No thing could represent the unseen presence of Jehovah. The Tablets of Stone, engraved, were carried on all journeys in a container known as the Ark of the Covenant. The Law ever present, to be learnt, to enter into and be written in hearts and heads, as surely as the Ark of Noah protected and saved from flood and tempest. The golden calf was destroyed. The Temple at Jerusalem, with its 'holy of holies', was built to house the Ark of the Covenant. Neither Jewish nor Islamic belief allows statues or representations of God, Jehovah or Allah. Angels are revered as messengers. Fine scripts, manuscripts, inscribe scriptures, sacred writings; to communicate words.

Mathematics, earliest in Egypt and Mesopotamia, were, are studied. Proportion and shape, decorated, ornamented, expresses Islamic culture. Mount Moriah, (site of Abraham's call, tested to sacrifice his only son Isaac) is crowned by the Dome of the Rock near the site of Solomon's Temple, destroyed and rebuilt. Jesus, presented in Hebrew custom, heard the Law questioned, discussed, understood and later himself taught, renewing consciousness of the will of God: Old Testament promise, prophesy, New Testament beatitude, parable and sacrament, transforming.

Icons communicate the beauty and magnetism of blessedness. Worship of an icon, a thing turned into a 'charm', is not right use. Icons developed in political and social turbulence, uncertainty, instability and fear felt during distress and upheavals culminating in the fall of Rome, AD 411, which concerned Greek Christians who needed strength. Icons present Incarnation: their true purpose is not routine formality or superstitious substitute. Controversy about the use of icons became fierce in the seventh and eight centuries. Iconoclasts claimed authority from the second commandment. Icons separated believers in Athens and in Rome, Greek from Latin; 'orthodox' from 'catholic' traditions. The crucifix is not an icon as such.

Statues, memorials, wall paintings, characteristic in western Christendom, aroused disputes in sixteenth and seventeenth century England. Zealous puritans were 'Iconoclasts'. Among Cromwell's troops some regarded statues in churches and cathedrals as idolatrous, and destroyed them. Affirmation and denial, accusation and counter-accusation, disagreement was deep and bitter, aggressive and violent. The firmer the belief, the stronger the conviction and commitment to it. Councils, synods, seek consensus and consent, but do not obviate zealots and fanatics unable to tolerate convictions other than their own. Concern for what is true includes paradox and balance in apprehending it, watchfulness for real dangers of distortion, exaggeration and abuse. At worst, controversy generates more heat than light. Battle lines form and reflect division. Maximum conflict, war, occurs between intensely serious seekers for what is good and true, who cannot tolerate differences. Benefit and blessing of *trust* and vision in the name of love are lost.

The Roman (Latin) Church maintains procedures for identifying saints and cultivates devotion to them. In England, sixteenth century reformers realised that exaggeration led to corruption, e.g. Chaucer's Pardoner. Hospitals, schools, churches, cathedrals continue to commemorate and celebrate saints: St Paul's in the City, St Peter's at Westminster and many parish churches. Patron Saints: Andrew, Patrick, George are remembered on their days and by flags. Luke, Greek physician and writer, is particularly associated with healing.

Alban, Roman soldier, found faith in Christ through a priest he sheltered from persecution, punishment by death. They exchanged clothes, Alban dressed as a priest, died in his place, (circa AD 209), first British martyr. Offa, King of Mercia, (circa 757-796), builder of the Dyke, began building the Abbey using Roman bricks and stones, enduring centre of Christian life and faith, St Alban's diocese.

. Transformation occurs and changes experience: natural, metamorphic, metaphor and metaphysical, spiritual; words within worlds, and worlds discovered through words, to multiply meaning and significance.

To face and accept being put to death without fighting for life is, in principle, to reject violence. Martyrdom witnessed, is an enduring event in history, experienced as vocation. Ten twentieth-century martyrs are commemorated above the Great West Door of Westminster Abbey, their lives described in *The Terrible Alternative: Christian Martyrdom in the 20th Century* (edited Andrew Chandler, Cassell, 1998.) Some martyrs are remembered as saints: some saints are martyred: Stephen, Peter, Andrew, Paul among them, but suicide is not martyrdom.

XIII II 2 iii Genius and Talent

In ancient Rome, genii were attendant tutelatory spirits, two for each person, not unlike guardian angels. Persian and Indian genii, believed to live in Ginnistan, were hostile to humanity. Occasionally visible, then compelled to serve as slaves, like the slave of the lamp in the story of Aladdin.

Genius suggests innate, generic talent, exceptional insight, a capacity to see clearly into things, ideas and things discerned together with power and talent in original ways, fresh from the heart of creation: 'beauty so old and so new' (Augustine, *Confessions*, X xxvii). Natural aptitude is paired with intuitive comprehension.

Inner consciousness plus constructive capability to express: these unite insight with talent to interpret experience and express it: twin aspects of genius: simple, complex, soaring. Memory and intelligence respond and expand exponentially when inspired and cultivated.

Many words for things/actions are symbols: *step, fold, stage, tie, shape, mould, design, tax, eye* itself, are thought of as concept symbols; mini-parables; **donouns**: words which identify; announce, pronounce, denounce, renounce what is identified. Recognition of good and evil require evaluation.

The moment a word is heard, read, it is ***present***. Like a gift, a *present* is present;

presented to receiver from giver; a presentation. An *offer* accepted (or not), communicates, *a true word given and received*. In some cases, without preparation or opportunity, unprepared, unable, unwilling to listen, to receive, we cannot or will not hear. The word is not received. To hear without attending, intending; to overhear what was not meant for us may be ignored but seeps into memory and needs wise digestion. Sometimes we prefer not to listen or hear, or are tempted to wish we hadn't. Unwanted words heard may be disregarded when feared, hoped untrue, even when suspected that it could be true. This risks pretending, deceiving, self and others, as to what is, or is not, true.

Genius is evident in dramatisation. Words written, spoken, are performed to stage experience. Actions lived which inspire re-enactment, are told, retold, performed and staged for deeper understanding; common experience enlarged, to entertain, edify, be appreciated and enjoyed.

Early story tellers, Homer, Herodotus, recount heroic quality which exemplify the glory and tragedy of life. Sophocles, circa fifth century BC, composed poetic drama from exploits of heroic characters. Convention, unity of time and place, was achieved as familiar epics were staged with high style, rhetoric and eloquence. Festivals included competitions. Work performed, poetic, dramatic, together with sports and games, famous at Olympia.

Theatre, attended by all the local community, gathered even more together for festivals and exercised profound influence. Pent-up feelings, laughter and tears, fear and pity experienced together, moved personal and communal catharsis. The 'sacred way' at Delphi ascends to stadium and theatre, higher than treasury and temple, towards the summit of Parnassus. Greek drama continues to be produced, to influence subsequent production and performance, challenging dramatists, directors, actors and students. Original audiences were more than spectators. Tragic events re-enacted drew them into personal participation. Cultural authority was, is, moral when action portrays, reflects, engages moral capability: felt/thought, thinking feeling in action: performers and audience together.

Theatre, centre of Greek city and festival life, spread round the Mediterranean during the empires of Alexander and of Rome. Hot dry summers, hillsides sites where stone seats were banked for effective seeing and hearing, intensified performance in beautiful settings that enhanced profound participation still seen and felt at Epidaurus, Ephesus, Taormina; Roman Africa, Carthage, in Augustine's youth.

Thomas Babington Macaulay (1800-1859), historian, ballad writer, renewed memory of heroes. *The Lays of Ancient Rome* include verse tattooed in memories of generations of youthful English readers; heroic, historic words as spoken by Horatius when he stepped forward to hold the bridge over the Tiber against invaders:

> 'To every man upon this earth
> Death cometh, soon or late.
> And how can man die better
> Than facing fearful odds
> For the ashes of his fathers
> And the temples of his gods?'
> (Macaulay, *Horatius* xxvii)

Plays written and performed represent classic epic: tragic, comic, are barometers of life and taste of their time. In Medieval England, Mystery play cycles were enacted by players on carts at street corners; York, Chester, Wakefield. In Tudor times, pageants and masques were performed at Court and great houses. Burbage, one of the Earl of Leicester's company of players, opened a wooden theatre at Shoreditch in 1576 and a theatre at Blackfriars, 1597. Local hostility caused a move to Southwark, to the Globe, 1599, shared with Shakespeare: now rebuilt.

Elizabethan and Jacobean drama flourished, wide range of experience and high literary quality, poetic, heroic, tragic; comic, ribald, licentious. Ben Jonson's *Bartholomew Fair* was suppressed by Cromwell The Restoration Court relished diversion, post-puritan indulgence; satire, cynical such as *The Way of the World*. Shakespeare's plays continued performed. John Gay, Goldsmith, Sheridan held eighteenth and early nineteenth century audiences but economic and social change altered and were altered by the climate of belief and thought. Fight for independence by some North American colonists; revolution in France followed by Napoleonic wars, disturbed European neighbours, particularly England. Regency extravaganzas gave way to reform; to revival of faith, to comparative stability in Queen Victoria's reign. Prosperity concealed poverty, cruelty, adversity, reflected by Charles Dickens. Naval and military heroes, Nelson and Wellington had prepared the way for *Pax Britanica*, successor to *Pax Romana*. The long reign and distinctive character of the Queen herself, heroine of the 'Victorian' era, seemed to echo Elizabeth I, Elizabethan England.

Victorian taste and theatre are contrasted with Charles II's court. During the eighteenth century, actresses and actors became stars brighter than the characters they performed. Charles Kemble and his daughter Fanny, David Garrick, Edmund Kean held London audiences; themselves theatrical heroes and heroines of their day as would Henry Irving (1838-1905), performing Shakespeare, actor/manager at the Lyceum, with Ellen Terry.

Heroes, not imagined or invented, but 'larger than life' characters whose actions are embroidered in the telling, in mind and words of writer, speaker, actor who 'dramatises' them. Protagonists and propagandists are tempted to exaggerate what is true. 'Spin doctors' succumb to temptation. Genuine heroism deserves best evidence from persons and records, without embroidery. Nelson's death at Trafalgar, famous victory, is remembered in monumental statues and paintings.

The Greek hero, triumphant in battle, might not, could not, live happily thereafter, as in fairy tales. The story-teller poet, custodian of common memory and tradition, conscious of conflict, describes heroism in the face of danger ending in tragedy, nemesis. Plutarch, priest at Delphi for the last thirty years of his life, includes civilising virtues: just and prudent action, in lives he described.

Heroism in the *Bhagavad Vita*, Icelandic sagas, the Arabian Nights, epics of their place and day, continue to interest and ring true. Exceptional experience, wherever it occurs and survives, continues to inspire, encourage, warn, edify. Shakespeare found in Plutarch reflections of the psychological insights of Greek civilisation plus Roman culture of conquest, administration and law. He made plays of *Pericles, Coriolanus, Julius Caesar, Anthony and Cleopatra*. Great stories of the death of Kings and of Queens, more recent lives encompassed, endowed and enriched reality of royalty in English and Scottish history, *Richard II, Henry V, Macbeth, King Lear*; and in *Hamlet*, Prince of Denmark. As in life, intense tragedy is relieved with wit and laughter comedies: *Twelfth Night, As You Like it, A Midsummer Night's Dream*, reflect his universal, creative genius.

Manners; civil, stylised, 'vulgar' as natural and commonplace, uncouth, 'rude', are essential theatre. 'Character' actors make the most of contrasting events which shock, elate, divert, alternating misery and grief, delight and high humour. Morals, manifested in action rather than in didactic speeches, but soliloquy reflects anguish, conscience: intense feeling and thought, inward high/low experience in head and heart, expressed in words. Dialogue with advice, exhortation, mastered by Jane Austen particularly in *Pride and Prejudice*, 'fiction' enduringly true, challenges film makers in wit, verisimilitude of characters whose manners and morals are exquisitely observed, scrutinised, integrated in context, vivid and humane genius.

Biographers record and enhance lives of general and special interest to readers.

Stranger than fiction, closer to history, theatre continues to challenge with dramatisation. Emlyn Williams emulated Charles Dickens, singular performance, made exceptional 'theatre'. Fiona Shaw spoke *The Waste Land* with memorable range and intensity.

T. S. Eliot dramatises Thomas à Beckett wrestling in conscience with four tempters. They leave. He speaks, preaches what he and his listeners know is his last Christmas Sermon. The Tempters become assassins, the Knights who kill him. Over the dead body of the Archbishop, they turn and speak to the cathedral congregation, who bear witness throughout, to explain and justify themselves. Monks, clergy, more seen than heard: the Women of Canterbury who speak, like a Greek Chorus, with feeling, sympathy, concern, need to understand the power and meaning of what they have witnessed. This great drama was commissioned by the then Dean of Canterbury, George Bell, for performance in the Chapter House there. The National Youth Theatre made a fine production in Southwark Cathedral, near the rebuilt Globe. Beckett is regarded as hero, martyr, saint.

Heroes are vulnerable; Achilles' heel, Helen's beauty, Othello's rage. Greek dramatists saw heroes as persons whose destiny was in the hands of Fates and Furies, inevitable, ineluctable. Destruction by hubris, nemesis, tragedy inherent in mortality was foreseen when oracles were consulted; Oedipus at Delphi, Ulysses at Cumae. Apotheosis, eligibility for Olympus, was not believed to be in their own hands. A hero, son of Zeus, has diverse versions of origins, events and relationships which do not fit together in reconstituted history from records. Heroes reappear with other names and different relations. Legend reflects essences of human soul tested in extremes. Hercules, Jason, Theseus, Achilles, performed exploits of courage and strength immortalised, told and retold. Hebrew heroes were conceived and referred to as sons of God by the daughters of men (*Genesis* 6. 2); their lives recorded as histories of patriarchs, prophets, priests , judges and Kings. Disaster was due to weaknesses of their own: *failure to seek, hear and obey the voice of their originator, creator, Jehovah*, whose providence was believed, known in the created world, listened to, heard, to be obeyed. Tragedy in Greek consciousness was unavoidable, personified by forces more powerful than mortals who had no protection from them.

The words of the sybyll, 'know thyself' indicate inward exploration to face, or avoid facing ourselves as sovereign persons, who wonder and know the ultimate source and energy of life recognised in our own nature and origin. Divinity is acknowledged in diverse cultures, personified as Nature, Reason, Beauty, Dance,

Destruction, with rituals reflecting observation and worship. Singular Divinity: Creator, lawgiver speaks through prophets.

All hope to unlock the mysteries of existence, of vitality, virility, energy, fertility and power; and to transcend misery, error and failure. Who can save, be saved?

XIII II 3 Inward

XIII II 3 i Sincerity

'Since', in reason and mathematics, refers to information authenticated, reported, accepted as true. Since the event in life, (whatever it was) happened, and since you heard about it from someone whose sincerity you are confident of, you believe their report. 'Material fact' is information relevant to enquiry, particular or general, in any case, question, problem, issue: practical, legal, mathematical, philosophical. Hypothesis needs supporting evidence. Suppose, propose, expose, oppose, dispose, accuse and defend; an 'advocate' endeavours to 'establish facts'. Difficulties emerge. From recent actions (motive, intention in doing) to historical sequence, consequences of events as well as events themselves need to be ascertained. Interpretations result from inward terms of reference; information, knowledge, opinion, belief.

Systematic belief opens insight, understanding, knowledge. Belief, last, becomes first (See Figures 1 and 2.) False witness, untrue evidence, may or may not determine conclusion. 'Since' ignorant, insincere, deliberately false is sometimes believed, conclusions follow that destroy authentication of what is true. Evidence apparently relevant in time loses substance. 'Since', then, is not appeal to true evidence but recalls, refers, to something falsified. The witness was not only wrong but false. Was this error, or deliberately insincere?

Sincerity includes feeling and intention, to 'mean well', but may arouse as much doubt as confidence. Custom respected, convention followed with willing participation; is acceptance that springs from courtesy, good manners as civility, inclined to give 'the benefit of the doubt'. A 'thank you', more than polite custom, is appreciated. Cool convention warms with genuine feeling; glad, confident sincerity.

A *promise* (still, yet, again) is a commitment, an undertaking given, intended to be fulfilled. Delay and postponement may be unavoidable but if the promise was genuine it is a responsibility. If not, the one who promised was not sincere; the 'promise' is an unhappy performative. A promise may be lifelong commitment.

Changed circumstances may conclude an obligation; relief sought may be obtained. Some promises are contingent without disclosing contingencies. The sincerity of the person who promises is **integral** to its fulfilment. The context of fulfilment, in *trust* and confidence between giver and receiver, is its essence.

Feelings, opinions, beliefs live beneath surface appearances. Courteous and gentle, rude, aggressive, hostile or friendly attitudes affect expressed sincerity from near indifference, minimal conformity, to genuine respect and commitment. All are vulnerable to dissimulation, sham, hypocrisy. Good manners survive: are expected in stable civilised conditions; some more formal than sincere.

Courts require *order*. Courtesy is personal *form*. **Control** enables discussion of disagreements; diplomacy without acrimony, politeness as politic, political activity with civility. The High Court of Parliament first met when summoned to the Presence of the Crown. Parliament continues summoned by the Sovereign, opened in State, wearing symbolic regalia, proceeding in majestic formal *order*, appreciated when understood and valued. The Wonderland characteristic of Alice was to take things exactly as they seemed, literally, seriously, until she discovered more of what they really were and meant. The effect is highly humorous. When the March Hare tells her she should say what she means, she replies 'I do, at least I mean what I say – that's the same thing you know'. 'Not the same thing a bit!' says the Hatter. 'Why, you might just as well say that 'I see what I eat' is the same thing as 'I eat what I see!' Mad? True, but not always altogether true. The Queen of Hearts and her Court were outraged when Alice exclaimed they were 'nothing but a pack of cards'.

Undigested *change* imperils *form*: sometimes impossible to replace. Stylised manners and custom understood, valued, become sincerely respected by successive generations.

To pretend, delude, deceive are forms of deliberate insincerity. True purpose is concealed, kept secret with every effort to avoid disclosure. To *stage* an *act* performs a part other than one's own. Self-projection, private and public, inward and outward, apparent and real *purpose* are eventually revealed as one or both. An act modified by worthy considerations such as tact, protection of confidences, keeping secrets, includes discretion rather than duplicity, indistinguishable sometimes. **Cheat** and **lie** are **donouns**, not performatives.

Self-deception engages delusion, make-believe vulnerable to destructiveness, untrue. Identity is confirmed in, by, from true sources for genuine confidence, not invented. Fresh presentation may cultivate confidence but a new 'image' devised to 're-invent' does not genuinely transform personality. Appearance, skin deep, is business of 'spinners' for popularity. Transfiguration discloses what is true but unseen, unrealised until 'transfigured'.

Tennyson in *Lancelot and Elaine* described an extreme case of ambiguity in human nature: 'His honour rooted in dishonour stood, and faith unfaithful kept him falsely true'. (Line 870.) Who was this man? Did he have hang-ups? Was he uncertain which way to turn, an honest man grappling with inward contradiction, paradox, un-resolved facing irreconcilable dilemma? Is he to be pitied? Lancelot, the very model gentle knight honoured for courage and high style, was devoted to Guinevere, peerless beauty, wife of King Arthur; susceptible to love of an 'unknown maiden'. (*The Idylls of the King; Lancelot and Elaine.*) Tears, swoons, explanations, renunciations and sacrifices occur in 'romantic manner', chivalry interpreted in the nineteenth century poetic style.

Contexts and attitudes to relationships: emotional suffering is common. 'So groaned Sir Lancelot in remorseful pain, not knowing he should die a holy man.' Inward tension, agonised effort for ***control***; un-consummated passion were part of his emotional ***sacrifice***. Self-respect is as near to personal honour as sincerity is to conscientiousness. Self-knowledge, filtered feelings, can survive intense emotional agony with minimal distress to others. Unconscious, unable or unwilling to cultivate this capability allows feelings to dominate until they run their course in floods of emotional overspill drowning those involved. Disengagement, detachment, non-commitment dilute feeling. Blushes, pallor, laughter, choking sobs are symptoms of spontaneous feeling, sincere, too deep for tears. *Laugh, blush* and *sob* are **donouns**.

'My word is my bond' but some insist on having it 'in writing'. Without good faith, words are not worth the paper written on. To conceal more than is stated may intend to mislead. Temperamental inclination to dramatise, exaggerate, over-reach, overstate inclines speech to run ahead of balanced analysis; careful reference to known thought-out intention. Impetuous words spoken but regretted later cannot be unsaid. Withdrawal, apology, is accepted or not. Credibility lost, trust forfeited, are serious consequences of indiscretion since suspicion of insincerity resembles suspicion of exaggeration which amounts to deceit. Respect for what is true, but modified for convenience, may be discretion rather than insincerity. Temperate words encourage thoughtful consideration. Blind to feeling, deaf in mind, are handicaps. To think or not think this or that; to say or not say; to do or not do requires consistent mind and clear of intention. Trust reciprocates confidence. Even then, things go wrong. Yours truly, yours faithfully, yours sincerely. Yours ever?

Unity of being and doing, essence of **donouns**, tests sincerity. 'I love my love and my love loves me' is happy. If my love turns to another that happiness remains a memory, a *present* no longer *present*: a loss. We *mean* to say, *mean* what we say, say what we *mean*, like Alice. *Mean* may *mean* average, point of balance. If feeling and *mind change* there is temptation to deny. Taking refuge in insincerity adds to deceit, to danger of untrue words. To keep quiet avoids saying what is not true. It is not complimentary to be told that you '*mean* well'. And yet, from each volcanic island of individual volatility, scorched debris sees only *desert*, desertion, being deserted. To find fertile, cultivable areas, words are needed to reflect and define what is true: audible, to who can, who *will* hear. Discretion promotes hope beyond despair, to forward paths of renewal. Human beings are capable of sincerity with one another. Sincerity cultivates and is cultivated in and through trust, fidelity, loyalty: divine humanity and humane Divinity.

> 'Let me not to the marriage of true minds
> Admit impediments. Love is not love
> Which alters when it alteration finds,
> Or bends with the remover to remove:
> O, no! it is an ever fixed mark,
> That looks on tempests and is never shaken;
> It is the star to every wandering bark.
> Whose worth's unknown, although his height be taken.
> Love's not Time's fool, though rosy lips and cheeks
> Within his bending sickle's compass come;
> Love alters not with his brief hours and weeks,
> But bears it out even to the edge of doom.
> If this be error, and upon me prov'd,
> I never writ, nor no man ever lov'd.'
>
> (Shakespeare, *Sonnet*, 116)

XIII II 3 ii Sacrifice and Suffering

> 'The sacrifices of God are a broken spirit: a broken and contrite heart,
> O God, thou wilt not despise.'
>
> *(Psalms,* 51.17)

Sacrifice is an *act* by a person **willing** to offer, to *act*, to *sacrifice*. Motives are singular, plural, sometimes communal. An offering is offered, surrendered, sacrificed. Offer is performative. *Sacrifice* is **donoun** and performative.

'For the sake of...' refers to intention, motive for *sacrifice*. 'Sake' originally implied context of strife, contention, sometimes guilt; words that suggest need of and desire for reconciliation. Sacrifice for the sake of sacrificer may relieve guilt, shame, hoping for forgiveness, peace of mind, giving thanks. Sacrifice offered for the sake of another person; rescue from danger, redeemed from captivity, hostage held by hostile power. For the sake of a loyalty, an allegiance, a principle, sacrifice is inward response to call of duty, devotion, restitution, peace.

Commitment of trust: faithful, true, objective service, obedient love, can promote awe, fear, occasionally alternating with hatred. Motive(s) move individuals; initiate intention to resolve and *act*. An action, a thing, offered, sacrificed for the sake of another, a greater good, defines the action, the thing as a *sacrifice*: more than a gift, a due, debt or duty, but those too. Pain causes suffering; sacrifice is suffering and pain in any of their many forms, in soul: head, heart and body. Generosity is willing giving. The essence of sacrifice is that it is willing, willed, not extorted or compelled. Willing obedience may be indistinguishable from compulsive *fear*, another paradox.

Will to *sacrifice* is stimulated by *need*, emotion, thought, obligation, devotion; one or more in personal consciousness and conscience. *Hope* and *fear* are experienced for good and evil: recognised, personally evaluated. Self-assessment, inward judgment, includes guilt, shame, remorse, penitence: need for forgiveness, reconciliation. True sacrifice, however reluctant, is voluntary. To suffer wounds, pain, misery, agony, violent death is individual but multiplied in war. Peace stirs survivors to remember with gratitude those who suffered, died, or survived with physical, emotional, mental and psychological injuries. Remembrance is intensified by guns and music, sound and silence, reflections in doubt and faith, disbelief and belief, *sacrifice* remembered:

'O God, our help in ages past; our hope for years to come;
Our shelter from the stormy blast.'

Inexplicable disaster causes suspicion and superstition. *Fear* urges *will* to placate unknown power, seek protection, ward off danger of judgment, retribution. Sacrifice was customary until reason, knowledge, understanding, altered custom.

Hope to relieve the evil of pain, suffering, misery, guilt, injustice: these disturb good order and weaken best effort and intention: guilt for fault acknowledged; blame accepted. *Will* endows humanity with potential for liberty and responsibility. Early evidence of sacrifice suggests recognition and *fear* of anger known, power to be placated, reconciliation needed.

Systems of 'do's' and 'don'ts' include 'taboos'. Philosophers wrestle with ethics, hoping to identify and promote virtue, order, civility. Hebrew texts describe the original voice of the one creator-benefactor in the Garden of Eden. Disobedience caused, causes, eviction, paradise lost. Noah, faithful and obedient, survived flood; Abraham was tested, called to sacrifice his only son than whom nothing could be more precious to him.

Wrestling with angels offers profound psychological analogy. Inward struggle, vocation resisted. Temptation overcome brings quires of ministering angels.

Beatitude calls for changed attitudes without triumph: pure in heart; poor in spirit, meek, conscious weakness, hunger and thirst after righteousness: need for help. The windows of heaven pour blessings into hearts open to them. Believers cry 'Lord, have mercy upon us' adding prayer for motive and grace 'incline our hearts to keep this law'. Law identifies dangers: blasphemy, idolatry, murder, infidelity, false witness, covetousness. Divine order, principles disclosed, revealed, known, differ from constructed codes. Moses heard the voice from fire on Sinai as from the burning bush.

An 'ode' addresses source of particular inspiration in lyric verse, in sonnet or, after death, in elegy. 'Ode' is generic lexeme: bode, code, hode, lode, mode, node: 'inclination'. Exceptionally intense consciousness honed with expert workmanship enables a poet to aspire, become inspired, to make lyric, symbolic, metaphysic poetry. One, as ingredient of a word, is even more fruitful than ode in alphabetic flight: bone, cone, done, gone, hone, lone, none; tone, zone. Compounds include condone, intone, undone, begone. Looking for guilt and shame, reasons for sacrifice, leads on and on beyond limits of genes, inherently selfish, to promise of freedom. The song of a bird on the wing suggests sweet soaring freedom emancipated from shame, earthly constraint, responsibility; a blithe spirit hailed, envied, aspired to by Shelley in his *Ode to a Skylark*. Keats' *Ode to a Nightingale* reflects human reality, an aching **heart**: alive in **head**:

> 'Where but to think is to be full of sorrow,
> And leaden-eyed despair.'

Giving unwanted things is not sacrifice as such. Effort, thought, time for the sake of needy, suffering persons supports those who transmit practical help. 'Live simply that others may simply live' encourages systematic life-style; consistent consideration, sacrificial.

Giving requires having something to give. 'To give, and not to count the cost; to fight and not to heed the wounds, to toil and not to seek for rest.....' calls for resources, means, motive, concern and sympathy to supports those desperate for relief.

Receiver and giver *benefit* in the good of a gift. Charity is motivated by *love* and *love* means charity. The words are often interchangeable but *love* is a **donoun**; give, gift, charity, are not. Gift may involve sacrifice; sacrifice expressed in a gift, but 'sacrifice' differs from giving but may overlap. Debt, duty and love connect gift, sacrifice, with receiver to whom it is offered. Sometimes rejected, sometimes received with satisfaction, pleasure, gladness, relief, pure joy. 'Sacrificial giving' refers to gifts not readily spared. Sympathy, skill, knowledge, care, understanding and wisdom, helpful and valuable in themselves, are comforting and strengthening. The spirit of the thing derives from good-will, often of anonymous giver. Appreciation of a gift received invites *will* to discover joy in giving. Generosity expresses good-will, promotes good feeling, trust between receiver and giver. These intangibles qualities of feeling, mind, intention give significance to gifts. Patience, gentleness, tact, kindness, wisdom endow gifts with concern of giver to receiver. Catastrophes destroy livelihoods. Deliberate cruelty; racial hatred, power abused, occur in and disfigure all ages including present times.

Paying a bill settles a debt. Price known, cost estimated, responsibility is accepted beforehand. Creditors expect payment. A defaulter has reason to feel aggrieved if persecuted or prosecuted when innocent. Deliberate fault is another matter. Some feel more foolish than guilty when private deceit has public consequences. Motives and circumstances are complex, difficult to see clearly, understand fully, deal with effectively. Self-justification and anger can conceal uncertainty, inadequacy, resentment with or without just cause. To make amends and seek reconciliation are forms of sacrifice. Vocabularies overlap from level to level, debts measured in money for things, obligations of emotion, error or ignorance in thought, custom, convention and in law. Debt paid differs from debt pardoned. To beg pardon mixes apology with hope for offence to be overlooked, excused, forgiven. Plea for mercy acknowledges **need** that prompts sacrifice: for offence concerning principle of life, high crime such as murder. The sacrificer, fearing retribution, believes possibility of sin mercy: recognised, identified as concepts of penitence, admission, confession, absolution, forgiveness. Since mercy springs from compassionate love; an offender is freed, not by personal sacrifice as debt paid but by realisation and response to, in, of, for, by, from and with *generous* **love**.

Direct witness is first-hand evidence. False witness is perjury. Each witness contributes a piece of the jigsaw. Missing pieces, unknown, may not come to light. Unintended offender can truly say: 'I did not mean to harm'. Responsible purposes, good intentions, best available at the time, are rarely faultless. The sovereignty of good is occluded in ignorance, insensitivity, exclusive self-interest regardless of others. Conscience, crucial, may be inactive, suppressed, suffocated, frightening. Testimony needs courage and **sincerity**.

Systematic belief and trust, integrity cultivated, develop ways of living inspired by and sometimes referred to as religious. Belief which becomes a 'religion' has accompanying strengths and hazards. Augustine, throughout his life, before and after his conversion to Christianity, read every Greek and Latin text he could plus the Hebrew scriptures, Old and New Testaments. He synthesised what he learned in written dialogue, soliloquy, letters, sermons and treatises: *Confessions, Encheridion, De Civitate Dei*; 'the City of God', are evergreen classics. Later life, experience, mature experience, thought and further reading, led him to write *Retractions*. On his understanding and use of the word 'religion' in his work *Of True Religion* Augustine commented:

'Tending to One God, and binding our souls to him alone [religantes] whence religion is supposed to be derived, let us be without superstition.'
(Augustine: *Earlier Writings*, translated J. H. S Burleigh, page 22.)

'The account which is given in these words of the derivation of the word 'religion' pleased me best. To be sure I was not unaware that authors of the Latin tongue have given another derivation, from *religere* which is a

composite verb from *legere*, to choose. *Religio* seems the proper Latin form, following the analogy of *eligio*.'

English derivatives include legible, readable or decipherable. Eligible means to measure up to required quality or standard. Religious from *religere*, to bind fast, not as imprisoned is as personal commitment of *will*. Religious life as life of faith, trust, belief is essentially voluntary as is *sacrifice*. Many tragedies occur through attempts to impose it. Rules and regulations are subsequent and consequent to principle of *order* believed: thought of as helpful and beneficial rather than as oppressive and punitive since obedience, in this context, is willing alignment of personal *will* with belief in the *will* of God. Study and thought, thinking and studying assist the learning process. To read, mark, learn and inwardly digest what is legible, communicated in script, scripture, communicates and inspires faith tested in experience, and found to be true. Guiding principles, trusted and believed, are helpful. The re - in the word religion re-curs repeatedly, re-examined, required, relevant.

Both receiver and giver ***benefit*** in the good of a gift. Charity is motivated by *love* and love is charity. Sympathy, skill, knowledge, ***care***, understanding and wisdom, helpful and valuable, are comforting and strengthening. The spirit of the thing derives from its source and meaning transmitted willingly, often anonymously.

A true gift unites them all. Appreciation of a gift promotes ***desire*** to give; to discover joy in giving. Generosity expresses good-will, good feeling encourages ***trust*** between receiver and giver. These intangibles change transaction of barter, exchange, payment, to generous feeling, head, heart, mind, intention signifying gift. Patience, gentleness, tact, kindness, wisdom are intangibles, virtues, communicating concern of giver to recipient. Catastrophes cause death and destroy livelihoods. Greed, cruelty, anger, hatred; materialist, racist , sexist pride and arrogance when they pervade human being cause suffering: need for penitence, forgiveness, sacrifice.

Word, words heard and read, communicate what is true, unsure, or not true. Discrimination, evaluation, verification are continuing responsibility. Mistake, falsification, deceit require recognition; each listener and reader to believe it or not. To expect, assume in good faith, that words are true is a formidable cultural tradition not to be taken for granted. Responsibility for behaviour is individual. Can we be blamed for what we do not know? This question of innocence and ignorance connects with honesty, *integrity*, ***trust*** and good faith: pre-eminent in PERFORMATIVE UTTERANCES, unhappy when insincere, untrue.

Money, in so far as it measures, estimates and quantifies, provides language of evaluation. Credit and debt, assets and liabilities are accounted for, checked and balanced for profit and loss, spending and saving: *cost, measure, price*. A friend or a relation spoken of as an asset and/or a liability, valued or not, cannot, or surely ought not to be bought or sold: that concept is shocking.

Trade, commerce, manufacturing and transport depend on varieties of material and *work*, but 'deals', 'accommodations', may be agreed. Measuring skills in money, paper and figures attempts to value the invaluable: the indispensable, inestimable benefit of good-will. Gold was, is hoarded: the 'gold standard' thought necessary due to its intrinsic quality as currency, exchange value. Time, effort, sympathy, kindness are needed in any circumstances, and occur in presence of principle, personal goodness and generosity, willing *sacrifice*.

Debt represents what is owed without offence or grievance; wiped out when paid. Concepts of ownership and wealth change when material things are realised to be benefactions, endowments; responsibilities rather than rights demanded, claimed, deserved, self-made possessions. Trustees are entrusted, not for personal advantage but for objective benefit shared wisely and generously according to the purpose of the trust. Farsighted public-spirited bankers know they are trustees. Wise employers do not regard employees as bought, subservient, enslaved, but as responsible persons sharing a livelihood, contributing *will* to *work* with strength and skill, real and potential, of particular gifts. Competence and efficiency emerge as contemporary 'hunger', easily ruined by over-reaching greed, lust, unjust behaviour without regard for 'cardinal' virtues nor resources of 'spiritual'.

Coin, cash, time and *profit* are **donouns**; spend and debt are not. *Mind* and *matter, sign* and *wonder*, known in thought, disclose meaning. *Will* expressed in *act*, **matters**.

Mind requires matter to witness its activity. Effort of mind with purpose and intent expressed in practical, material ways. Evidence does not convince or convict until motive becomes evident and makes sense of action: purpose and intent disclosed, pattern and order emerge towards comprehending what was incomprehensible. Flights of fancy, romanticised imagination, change when realised in genuine purpose, action disclosed in physical, material manifestations confirm that they are true. Such disclosure occurred, occurs, was made manifest, in the reality of the mystery of the Incarnation. This was, is and will continue to be light shining into darkness. Darkness does not, cannot comprehend or overcome *light*. When and where there is no light, it is dark. *Light* is **donoun**; **Dark** is not.

Giving and sacrificing, personal and communal, were not, are not, required by law. Taxes and debts, enforceable, have bailiffs at their disposal. The Welfare State includes cash benefits and social services which reduce former fear of 'bankruptcy'; imprisonment in Marshalsea via Carey Street. Governments whose election policies promise to eliminate poverty and destitution find that 'Welfare' does not iron out human frailty, weakness, failure, debt. Cheating leads to crime; violence wounds. A society whose material expectations rise is no less vulnerable to greed, deceit, cruelty, any form of uncontrolled lust causing suffering at every level. Healing, mending, cure are increasingly difficult to achieve when 'private 'wickedness' is regarded as separate from 'public' veneer. Those who operate 'welfare' services need evidence of need.

Pawn brokers are fewer and farther between. A possession pawned is surrendered to raise cash on security of its estimated value. Possession is forfeited until redeemed, bought back. Failure to repay loan plus interest on it means loss of item pawned; of its redemption.

Samuel Butler imagined exchanging prison with hospital and hospital treatment with prison; guilt treated as sickness and sickness as guilt, culpable. (*Erewhon*, 1872.) Anxiety, uncertainty and guilt make people more vulnerable to illness but not necessarily guilty of bad behaviour. Vigour and vitality, self-indulgence, seem to add zest, popularity. Influences, good or ill, are caught and spread. Epidemics of bad behaviour suggest comparison to a harmful infective virus but, given recognition of personal *will*, responsibility, guilt is deliberate *fault*. This adds essence of authority to the function of judgment since justice is a virtue, a quality of character cultivated. Fair and equitable behaviour cannot be taken for granted although exaggerated *blame* is itself an abuse of power by those who bear responsibility: parent, teacher, employer, magistrate, priest, if their functions are distorted. Systematic counselling, if available, responds to assist healing. Conscience awakened is personal inward counsellor and requires *light* and *love*, knowledge of good and evil.

Love and hate engage *sacrifice*, the *grace* of forgiveness: imprisonment to evil redeemed.

Ethics emerge from custom, habit, practical lived experience towards codes of conduct and criteria for law. Tastes, styles, fashions and manners change. Methods and needs vary, new materials, procedures, pills, become available, but the principles of stability do not. Ethics differ from laws, but freedom depends on following principles of good behaviour. Respect for life, liberty, property and work increase with regard for what is true. Personal needs (practical, emotional, thoughtful, evaluative/moral) lead to opportunity and constraint. Property, rapaciously or virtuously acquired but unevenly distributed, raises concern for disparity between 'haves' and 'have-nots'; social justice and injustice. Redistribution of wealth claims an ethical basis. Entitlement to welfare has followed. Motive for work, for enterprise and effort are stimulated by competition, not necessarily greedy. This concern is explored with reference to various criteria, practical, political and economic, traditional and, in extreme situations, experimental or revolutionary. Philosophical idealism modifies and is modified by the culture which nurtures it, and has developed with its sustenance.

Ethics emerge from practices, customs and values of particular cultures. They are challenged by other schools of thought, not necessarily idealistic or virtuous. Ethics are thought about, explored, for ways to enable people to make the best of each other; people with themselves and with things, practicalities in search of principles. Dictators, tyrants, impose practices for their own satisfaction and convenience. Work requires and demonstrates its own integrity.

Generosity and *sacrifice* are not ethics as such, but responses inspired by realisation of the energy and power of *love* as dynamic of virtue. *Hate* and anger are powerful motives too.

Individuals act with appetites, motives, intentions not always orderly or ethical. Guidelines, codes, are static rather than dynamic, philosophical rather than energetic although generated by mixing practical experience with intellectual effort and moral sensibility. Ethics suggest routes to circumnavigating dangers and difficulties rather than inner purposes although virtue is traditional inspiration. Navigating is no analogy for map-reading because a ship does not travel on a 'right path' but sails on water navigated to its intended destination. Ethics do not in themselves energise or empower deliverance from evil. At best they seek to define virtue. Virtue accepted as the aim and criteria of human behaviour enables paths towards it that are gradually explored. Ethical definition arises in retrospective analysis of behaviour discerned in practicalities. Access to true essentials, integration, the essences of what is true, is thus defined.

Respect for property has led to ethics and law. Both reflect the strength and benefit of the old maxim: 'thou shalt not steal' and relate to covetousness or greed. The primacy of *need*, the function and use of personal belongings appeals to security; to confident recognition of 'ownership'. *Will* to *share* and give becomes known in the liberty of *love*: generosity of heart, *mind* and spirit liberated through *love*. Private ownership and profit, stimulated by competition, are acquisitive. Communal property shares benefit. These opposing principles coexist with tension, paradox. One is emphasised at the expense of the other. Adam Smith propounded theory of wealth: Capitalism; Karl Marx of Communism. Malthus and Jeremy Bentham looked for different balancing factors. Material advantage, competition, primary for prosperity displaces joy when built on greed and envy.

Respect for life itself is primal principle. Believed to devolve from the greatest good requires language of disclosure of what is true, given, recognised. But revelation of what is true is verified by discovery that it works well in practice: for pragmatists the only source of ethics. Idealists look for the ideal. **Saints** realise and aspire to higher vision of perfection, of revelation believed to be the *will* of God. This paradox between ideal and pragmatic stimulates wonder, wondering and believing.

Wondering, learning and knowing through integrated experience finds meaning which discloses and exemplifies principle. 'Calling' experienced as 'vocation', invocation, brings disclosure. Good exposes evil; absence of good is its enemy. This is negative *power*: ignorance, deprivation, corruption, disease. Reclaiming the good is experienced as *grace, light,* energy, potential strength: dependent on and restored through *grace*, elusive to define but realised as clear presence between beloved and loved in the light of experience: integrating. To affirm, believe and live by faith, is to learn to know and experience this *grace* in continuing presence of *love: life* on a sustaining, continuing escalator powered and in company with living Christ: humanity sacrificed to redeem humanity, upwards through knowing 'the means of *grace* and hope of glory'.

Civilisation, civility, courtesy, are fragile, dependent on dynamics beyond ethics and law. Civilising customs arise from and reflect right use, the **sovereignty of good. Belief in possibility of control includes sublimation. Hatred and *fear* cause people to give way to behaviour which makes ethics and law irrelevant.**

Personal obligation is discerned in recognition of good and evil, the fulcrum of moral responsibility, the 'ought' and 'ought not' of considered action. *Will*, healthy and engaged, enables sacrificial action.

Augustine declared that **to believe is to think with assent**. No one can assent or deny on behalf of another person who is of age to decide, to resolve for themselves. Help and support may strengthen resolution but personal assent is unique to the person who makes it: who affirms willingly, with genuine belief. Yes, no, perhaps, tomorrow, but not as a child counting cherry pips for 'this year, next year, sometime, never' and yet with childlike trust. *Hope* looks forward with sure confidence, not certainty: not tuned to the inevitable, 'whatever will be will be'. *Assent* is yes, now, for you, for me. What causes hesitation? What impedes *will*?

Each *face*, unique, individual, reminds that no two persons are identical. *Light* that follows *assent* is true dawn of discovery, light towards what is true; a climax of commitment sometimes described as **second birth**. New vision, fresh horizons, recognition of change, seeks different destinations. Sense of destiny suggests pre-destination, not inevitability, another paradox. Affirmation is not an invented choice but an acknowledgement of what is true, *light* illuminating dark. Decision leads to action such as strengthened with *form*, formality such as in wooing and wedding, agreeing, signing, continuing, enduring, suffering. Performatives, happy, integrate inward and outward action. Ill-will, false words, **deceit**, cause trouble, unhappy.

Soul, essence of personality in living being, may mature in course of life. Soul, or psyche, embodies energy of spirit in human form; from soul to body (See Figure 2.) Anima and animus, opposing principles of animation, coexist in human being. This tension recognises divided self, human nature faced with inner schisms, irreconcilable alternatives; dilemmas. A person capable of deliberate, decisive action: thinking and judging is attentive to but no longer imprisoned by instinct. This liberates personal function of *will* to *order* rather than blindly obey. Senses join into common sense; *will* with intelligence to serve higher and deeper purposes which benefit and enhance the senses integrated in their true functions. But, paradoxically again, pleasures surrendered to ordered purpose involve *sacrifice*.

Light and dark, good and evil are thought of, known to illuminate and illustrate, like love and hate, bringing heart and mind, body and soul together. This vital move develops instinct from sense-intelligence into feeling and thought, desire, purpose and intent. Ability to balance and refine behaviour, to learn to think about what we are doing, then to think beforehand, indicates *purpose*, intention, **control**. Resources of mind and will to act, call upon energy of spirit fertilised in the soul through faith: *trust*, *hope* and *love*. These are divinely human capabilities, forward looking, variably developed and realised.

Will can be experienced as strength and weakness of spirit; good-will, no will, ill-will (good-will perverted), dynamic behaviour for good or evil. Sometimes *will* moves willy-nilly, overpowering, irresistible. Sometimes there is inertia, incapacity to activate or initiate. Much scope, too, for surface appearances and frivolity: 'Daisy and Lily, lazy and silly' and seriously high/low humour, clowns and jesters, fools, witty with pity, pitiable and comical, pathetic and sympathetic, not apathetic.

Spiritual virtue stimulated by the active faith, hope and love brings *light*, illumination, deliverance from the ever-present recurring reality of darkness and of evil. Despair: 'the dark night of the soul', is known inwardly. The plight of a lost soul is to lose *hope*, to find no *light* in the darkness. The awful paradox is that the most intense longing for *hope* is aroused in prisons of its absence. The prisoner has no key.

Material things, with distinctive *form, pattern* and *order* disclose conformity to inward ingredients and with given external principle: e.g. the law of gravity: to stillness and motion. The simple concept of Earth Mother and Sky Father who give birth with infinite fertility embodies creation and procreation. Voltaire recognised original creation, saying, that if God did not exist, it would be necessary to invent him. Hegel saying that 'every truth has become so' appeals to idealists as to evolutionists. True recognitions are not made incompatible by paradox. It is in the nature of belief that assent, the first step beyond reasoned evidence is where sensibility, no longer dissociated, is restored: integrated.

Exploration and fresh thought thrive with freedom of expression and action. All available faculties and resources of mind, memory, imagination, are promoted by *desire*, feeling and *will*; put into words. Speech is intended to communicate; to inform, discuss, amuse, educate and entertain. A writer endeavours to reflect glimpses of what is true, *light* in any, every form.

Hope to find words which reflect recognitions in *light* of what is true liberates mind; expands interest, enquiry, reflection, further opportunity. In 'fiction', imagination envisages life: imitative, representative, not merely fictitious. The appeal of a 'novel' is to introduce the reader to people whose lives tell more of life than the reader has known or imagined. Heroines such as Natasha in *War and Peace*; Dorothea Brooke in *Middlemarch*; Jane and Elizabeth Bennett, particular favourites with Bingley and Darcy in family and society, where serious folly, tragedy and comedy experienced in their time and place, recur since. Villains; people who behave wickedly: Bill Sykes; Leverkuhn (Thomas Mann's *Dr Faustus*) are imagined characters who enlarge consciousness of readers.

The voluntary nature of 'offering' is that the offerer offers, is obliged, not contracted nor compelled. A *sacrifice* is not a payment as such. The offering made and the consequences of making it include *need, desire* for forgiveness; propitiation not negotiation. Self reproach, self-examination, looks for and finds mistakes, faults of one's own, needing forgiveness.

Sacrifice arises from *need* known which seeks satisfaction through sacrifice believed effective. It is a moral and theological concept expressed practically; a peace-offering for deep-seated human need for forgiveness and reconciliation. Once practiced, it provides an example to be imitated, repeated. Ancient burnt offering: the blood of bulls and goats has changed into sacrificial charity, offering and expressing devotion. The vision of the highest magnetises us, calls us to ascend and then look down and see our frailty, frivolities, futilities, failures. Again, 'that than which nothing higher can be thought' is higher than the highest summit. In this light we realise we are soiled; are humbled and ashamed. **Sacrifice** is not legislated, not outlawed by legislators; not recognised in fines imposed by judges nor accepted to redress grievances and make peace in daily life as, when and if we offend one another. Rationalists do not emphasise spontaneous emotional ingredients: they tend to think ethics the best code human reason can construct. Expectation that reasonable people will accept is one thing: but **power** and **grace** to practise them is another.

What is meant by blessings and cursings? Are we dependent on human, subjective, relative judgment as to what is true? Is there any way of approaching aspects of the source itself, of 'that than which nothing higher can be thought'? If so, we have leapt into affirmation of essence: the veritable source of what is true. To affirm that God is **love** is high, magnificent, affirmation. Conscious that the highest and best is knowable, known, personified in Christ. Actions fall short. Responsibility for what is done, or left undone, occurs when we know truly what we have done and are doing. Deliberate evil is **sin**: a notable **donoun**.

Many ordinary words, practical, emotional, intellectual, and theological, are performatives such as *promise, sacrifice, identify, affirm*. To speak the word is enough. Pretence, deceit, conscious, even subconscious, reservation dilute motive and word. Heart and *mind*, feeling and though unite into true performance. Untrue to one another, *integrity* is not found.

Sacrifice is the need and desire for reconciliation between receiver alienated from giver; from user who has abused. It is from creature to creator, offence to offended, shame which illuminates guilt. Usual, day-to-day earth bound, side-by-side view of each other in habitual contexts changes by looking up towards ultimate, invisible, integrating whole in light and in healing perspective of what is true: made manifest, revealed. It happens at and in every level of our experience; the highest restores the meaning of the first. This completes the reversion, the reconciliation of low and high, outward and inward, sense in the flesh and realisation in mind revealed in and through the spirit. Natural appetites, lust to take, become capable of transformation, changed by love to give. Rhythms of time and place, season and cosmos, breath and heartbeat in every creature manifest of creation, created **work. Sacrifice** includes what is due: ***praise*** and thanks for all the blessings of life; penitence for shortcomings and excesses: vision of complete integration healed, mended wholeness: recognised in saintliness.

XIII II 3 iii Excrement and Increment

Bodily waste is offensive and causes disease unless disposed of. At first and last, excretion is uncontrolled. Control is gradually established. When warning signals occur they are heeded.

Natural precipitation, unable to dry or soak away, trickles into a *stream*, river, to *drain* into seas. Wind dries ground, vegetation, scatters ***seed*** assisted by creatures above and below flying, creeping, crawling, burrowing, growing. Natural processes are imitated to purify water and prevent infection, epidemics.

Routine helps to regulate personal habits. Unusual urgency and frequency are symptoms of disturbance. Human waste matter, as of other animals, fertilises. Dunghills were common before sanitation and piped water. Systematic treatment is needed in heavily populated areas. A cholera epidemic prompted the government (after the 1832 Reform Act) to define and establish urban and rural areas to ***control*** water supply, drains, and introduce sanitary inspectors. Since then, recycling and environmental concern is increasingly understood.

Male and female organs of digestion are alike but physique, procreative functions with accompanying emotions, responses, aspirations, differ. Wooing and pairing for conception and birth are normal but varieties of physical, psychological diversities and affinities, idiosyncrasies are known in experience: studied by specialists whose criteria for behaviour: amoral, moral, immoral; constructive, destructive, vary. ***Desire*** and ***control*** do not coincide unless ***control*** is desired, affirmed, believed possible. Human beings are humane and cruel, capable of virtue and of anarchic passions. To surrender is to give way: unable or unwilling to ***control***, to abandon willingly to another.

Pleasure is sought for its own sake, separated from ***purpose***, context and meaning. Pure pleasure, purely for pleasure, is suspect to 'puritans' for 'impure' motives, indulged for ends other than good and true. Depravity and decadence are not virtuous. Pleasure itself can become addictive. Addicts find difficulty in controlling their addiction. Some pleasures: normal, natural, vital appetite, *thirst* intensify beyond ***control***. Care and sympathy need ***balance***: freedom to express devotion in harmony, physical intimacy, responsibility with respect.

An increment increases, augments, something already there. Salaries, originally salt distribution, now measured in money, lucre, are lucrative income. Wages paid in coin and notes, currency for specified labour, recognise **work** done 'by hand and by brain', listed on paper pay-slip, numbers noted, sums transferred, 'credited to your account' as salary. On-line dispenses with paper, but many, including banks, require paper records. An increase is an increment, sometimes regular, expected. Decrement, rarely used, is a decrease. Secrement, not used either but secretion is a familiar spontaneous involuntary physical process: mouth watering saliva, eyes in tears, perspiration, general sweat impossible to control though sometimes possible to avoid, evade, minimise, postpone. Intimate functions, emissions, not secret since widely experienced, are so personal that shyness, reserve, modesty and the sensibilities of others make privacy preferred.

The instincts, desires, appetites that animate human beings to reproduce are potent in other animals. Human characteristics and character can differ from those of animals. This affirmative has crossed Plato's line. Consciousness of cause and effect, felt thought, conscience, decision and **will** are distinctive human characteristics. Cultivation and habit strengthen capability and add fastidiousness to **desire** and responsibility in action. Incapability to restrain, to **control**, removes impediment to do other than gratify appetite. No effort is made to resist if resistance is believed impossible. Tension between natural appetite and self-control is a peculiarly human dilemma, intensified in urgency that accompanies virility. **Will**, good-will informed by mind, learns to acknowledge scruples. Conscience prompts **will** to regard and follow them. Effective interaction between thinking/doing, felt/thought, inclines individuals towards control by **reason**. Without this, cultivation does not develop, but **reason** alone is rarely strong enough for **control**.

The culture of control, of expectation of responsibility, dilutes when the culture changes or is repudiated, thought 'old fashioned'. Propriety gives way to impropriety; licence to licentiousness. The dilemma is not new but is sharpened by climate of 'permissiveness'.

A. E. Housman described poetry as a secretion expressed. Change: inward, secret, private experience wrung out of intense feeling and thought into words with rhythms, rhymes and patterns that become poems, often regularly paced like steps, breath and pulse. Physical exertion, competition, accelerates breathing and emotional excitement towards climactic, sometimes hysteric conclusion. The poet, artist in words, participates in and reflects human experience at its maximum intensity, range and diversity. Instincts, emotions and ideas, thinking action, joy and sorrow, glory and misery are recaptured by striving to integrate every facet of felt/thought known and experienced. Milton's 'mirth which wrinkled care derides and laughter holding both his sides' coexists with 'loathed melancholy' (*L'Allegro and Il Penseroso*.) T. S. Eliot wrote hilarious poems collected as *Old Possum's Book of Practical Cats* when composing *Murder in the Cathedral*, *The Rock* and *Burnt Norton*, first of the *Four Quartets*.

XIII II 3 iv Sacrament

A sac is a containing membrane of a living body. Bees collect nectar into their sacs and work it up into honey, gathered and stored in carefully prepared honeycomb. Testicles are in a sac, a scrotum. A womb is the sac where new life conceived is contained, protected and nourished until, at full term, rhythmic contractions, labour, are spontaneous indication of imminent birth. Once protective waters of the womb break, birth is irreversible. Bleeding continues for a time; and the womb returns to normal size. Cycles recur. A *cul de sac* is not a through route; the way in and out are one and the same but birth has no re-entry. Knowledge and understanding of 'the facts of life' are vital equipment without which people cannot be other than slaves to instincts. Recognition of pleasure and pain, intention, purpose, and *will* include knowledge of and concern for consequence; responsibility with *control*.

Joy and awe at birth leads to welcoming the new arrival with special appreciation known as baby-worship. This profound expression of love is stimulated by anticipation; released at the sight of new life: the baby. *Wonder* has led to knowing and understanding these physical processes. Mind considers cause and effect, even the origin of life. *Wonder* promotes *wonder*, fascination, awe at mystery. Generating and regenerating reaches for and discovers unknowns. Curiosity enquires, explores for what is true. Thought encourages definition. Belief, verified as true, becomes regarded as definite. Fertilisation, conception, pregnancy, labour, giving birth to new baby is truly, a new life, generated, original, ancestral, descent. Awe and wonder, deep happiness are experienced by mother, father, family, midwife, *doctor, nurse*.

Sac- prefixes sacred, sacrosanct, sacristan and sacrifice. Each concerns, respects, refers to what is distinct, separate, holy, extraordinary essential quality of being. Sacrilege is denial or contempt for this quality. Lack of understanding may not tolerate others affirmatives, different needs. Intolerant words and actions, sacrilege lead to desecration. A sacred place, grove, memorial, cenotaph invoke remembrance, solemn devotion. A *chair* specially placed for a particular person is *the* Chair, *the* Throne. As symbol of sovereignty, it enthrones. Allegiance derives from sacred *trust*, loyalty, fealty.

Sacrilege is blasphemy if deep faith is rudely challenged or insulted. Words of sacrilege include blasphemy. Acts include desecration. A sacristan looks after things kept for use in a sacred place, supplies, furnishings kept clean, in order, ready for rite, ritual observed. A sacrifice is offered for the sake of cause, person, personification, deity.

Human life is rarely secure. Danger, *risk*, may be continual, repeated, but death, like birth, comes only once. Sacrifice recognised and remembered develops words, actions, repetitions, when believed and accompanied by concentrated thought: prayer.

Words ending with -ment (comment, torment, ferment, incre- and excre-, de-, frag-, govern-, experi- ment ... etc) involve move-ment: change promoted, retrieved, directed, controlled. 'Ment' prefixes essential words: mention, mental and mentor. Dementor may dement. Thoughts ment-ioned in words include **comment**. Information and ideas, experience considered in mind is mental activity, funded into funda-ment-al development of opinion and knowledge. Growth is organic because thinking is a living activity before being expressed in actions and reproduced in words, doing and making. Technic- and mechanic come later, suggested by organisation, organic. *Change* as transformation is begotten by ideas in mind, first abstracted from matter, material; thinking and doing to *make* making.

Revelation inspires and inspiration reveals, interacting in mind to disclose primary, primal principal. Human generation commonly referred to 'facts of life', means acts that promote fertilisation, conception, birth. These are not human inventions. They were enacted, performed, repeatedly, before being understood. Order, pattern, consequence, cause and effect have become known. Changes of form; metamorphoses in pregnancy, birth, show new life. Ideas in mind may be realised, planned, formulated, developed, manifest in physical *form*. Ideas occur from material needs, problems to solve, questions to ask and try to answer. **This order of mind into matter is an interchange that stimulates, releases creative energy freely for growth.** Ideas occur to be evaluated, discarded or pursued. An idea believed good is tested to see if it works. If pursued, realised, ideas become usable, delightful, enjoyable; reproduced, imitating creation and recreation.

Sacrament communicates power through personal faith. Consecrated elements received, having been once offered, are accepted repeatedly, joyfully, devotedly. Conscious need for forgiveness precedes receiving the promise. Generosity typical of father to son, parent to child, creator to creature are merciful: forgiveness, the gift of *grace*. Love received in trusting head and faithful heart: needing, pleading for strength, new life, refreshment intention and confident inclination towards virtue.

(A 'virtuous and godly' life may seem beyond comprehension to twenty-first century persons.)

Water, bread and wine are sources of physical energy, food for the body transformed into energy of feeling, thought, evaluation and *will*, invigorating purpose. Sacrament, food for the soul, offers grace in heart and mind of believers, receivers through inter-communication with the heart and mind of Christ. Personal *will*, inward, intimate, frail, unsure, conscious of need, humbled in failure, known fault responsibly realised, acknowledged. Water in baptism is outward sign of forgiveness, refreshed with *promise*, intention, resolve to enter and live in closer, continuing communion with the Creator's *love*.

Creation continually in tension with destruction reflects *conflict* of good and evil, love and hate. The power of *love* over hate is experienced in the life of Jesus, human and divine, tempted, resisting, ministering, suffering, dying, restoring; redeeming and healing, restoring. Generalisation that 'all have sinned' affirm all to be capable of goodness, deliberation, responsibility, purpose and control, *need* and *hope* to resist temptations. Outrageous scandals among Christian believers, clergy and people, seem worse because known commitment raises hope and expectation. Temptation intensifies in extreme danger, *fear, need*.

Peter wept bitterly after his denial. Judas betrayed, then hanged himself. Hope for amendment of life requires *time, grace* and courage; energy and power of *love*.

Sacrament was introduced at a time and place. John the Baptist called people to repent. Jesus went to John for baptism. John thought himself unfit to baptise Jesus. When he did so, a dove descended and voice heard were witnessed, authenticated (*Matthew* 3. 16-17.)

Risks, dangers, are common experience. Temptation to be foolish, to fail to identify evil endangers others and ourselves. Physical senses, body knowledge, vital necessities as these are, often confine a person to themselves, to first level practicalities. These essentials become destructive when abused. Temptation to excess, uncontrolled, upsets balance and looses natural benefit, meaning and joy. The spirit of the thing: the principle of the *need* and the true fulfilment of its *function* are undiscovered.

The first temptation concerned material things: are these ends in themselves? Is food, 'bread alone' enough for life? Bread, daily bread, made from good seeds grown and cultivated gives strength and energy. For a starving man to make stones into bread seems impossible. One thing cannot be made into another, unless secret *power* over natural *process*, miracle, alchemy, science, enables such *change*: transformation.

Such power can be abused. Jesus recognised temptation to abuse power over natural, material things, seeing their limits. 'Man shall not live by bread alone, but by every **word** ..... from the mouth of God'.

The second temptation challenged Jesus from the highest pinnacle of the Temple, sacred place of *worship*, to assert his *power*, 'Heaven Born', by casting himself down, certain of divine protection, from destruction on the stones below. Jesus again quoted scripture: 'thou shalt not tempt the Lord thy God'. Hence proverbial 'tempting Providence', refusal to abuse power to demonstrate one's own.

The third temptation offered all *power* for the *worship* of *power* itself, not of God but of the Devil. (See **X**.) 'Get thee hence, Satan...' (*Matthew* 4. 1-11.)

A wise old friend says: 'sow a habit, and reap a character; find a character and reap a destiny'. Love may be love of a good thing abused. When good things are known and experienced, without their meaning, the benefit of their true *purpose* is lost. Instinct, impulse, sensation become 'sensationalism': misguided, shallow, without responsibility, integrity. Most of us know this by learning 'the hard way', from our own fault, 'own goals' if you like.

Bread broken in remembrance, nourishes communion and fellowship, sacramental faith known in Son of, with Father: origin, creator; whose Spirit is *light* and energy of *love*, healing, integrating wholeness, the Comforter. Since this New Passover, the Last Supper, this sacrament has been disputed, particularly concerning 'transubstantiation'. Ordinary bread and wine, symbols of body and blood, are believed to *change* when swallowed and digested as normal, but consecrated bread and wine, reserved, symbolised by a lighted lamp in red glass near an altar, are believed to represent real presence; elements available for dying persons. This 'ever ready' provision reduces priestly function, but is believed to conserve communion communication. The second and third temptation concern authority and power: temptation to demonstrate personal charisma, ascendancy and magnetism; power abused. These temptations, summarised as of **the flesh, the world, the devil** include greed, avarice, arrogance and domination: ever present in personal, social, political and economic, moral and spiritual life, now as then, to weaken and corrupt; vicious, not virtuous. Baptism by water and the Spirit, water and the word, was and is believed to be the watershed between old and new life, the old law made new. Energy of *grace*, love, the new law: Jesus humanly tempted, divinely empowered. Isaiah foresaw that people who walked in darkness would see a great *light*. John, the forerunner, called for penitence. Baptism enacts cleansing forgiveness, washing in water, faith to be born again in the Spirit, awakened, desire to become integrated with the will of God, the Holy Spirit known in *love*: promised in infancy by parents and godparents; by adults themselves.

Sacrament manifests what is true through grace and comfort known in the healing life suffering, presence beyond death through faith.

XIII II 3 v Cohesion, Coherence, Co-inherence

Things fall apart. Centrifugal and centripetal forces are emotional, mental/intellectual and moral as well as physical. Evident in natural movement, they recur in private and in public relationships now as throughout history. Disintegration, decline and fall, is another aspect of falling apart. Repairing, mending, healing requires patient *love, trust, hope*. Tragedies occur, not because one person is right another wrong but that their understandings and wills are opposed.

Analytical thought requires concepts formulated to clarify and be clarified with feeling, interest, zest. Intellectual conception is fertilised from *seed* of practicalities, practical needs, that give birth to **words**. Elements, ingredients, already present, born of *fire*, water, earth, air, first uttered word: then water and blood, became animated, embodied. Since human thought, philosophy, conceives concepts, these require gestation; form, definite and definable.

Thought processes, thesis, hypothesis, antithesis, pro-thesis, synthesis — and increasingly abstruse, exotic terms — emerge from infinitely fertile interaction in mind, between minds, abstracted from practical *form* and *sense* unless and until theoretical discussion becomes realised again in practicalities: **made good**. Concept and thought process is more readily comprehended in action; observed, demonstrated, evident. Experiment and demonstration show processes: **'how'**. Metaphor and parable search into mystery of **'why'**. Sacrament promotes understanding, integration: nourished experience of *grace: power* for good.

Illustration in light and dark, reality and shadow, colour, time and space, weighing and balancing become more and more significant. Light is reproduced in the energy of electricity.

Some minds dislike abstractions, find difficulty and will not engage with them. Others find access through music, mathematics, poetry, drama, indicative signs and symbols. Poets weave wonders in words that cultivate the sacred *flame*. Others find interest, excitement in theoretical analysis, controversy, political and philosophical dialogue and debate, rarely and not necessarily conclusive. No area is exclusive to itself. **Co-inherence**, coined by Charles Williams, (an 'Inkling' with Tolkien, C. S.

Lewis and others) engages **coherent** thoughts with **inherent** emotion. **This enables head and heart to find cohesion and coherence: integration between specialisms.** Integration between specialists who look at other subjects hope but not to lose sight of the whole. Specialist work such as nuclear energy, fission, fusion, clones, genetic modification, transplants, observations from 'space' share psychological stress and need confident understanding with virtue of humility.

Belief in one source of energy and power, 'monotheism', envisages the mind of the creator as readable; to be read in creation, itself dynamic, changing. Abstracted theory is a stage towards recognising created *order* of things before proceeding to possible explanations. Why is, what is, as it is, day and night, light and dark, soon approach questions concerning good and evil.

Early Christian thinkers, 'Fathers', valued and absorbed influences of Plato, Socrates, Aristotle. Later 'literalism', Earth between Hell below and Heaven above, confined later minds so that leading seventeenth century ecclesiastics could not, would not, comprehend Galileo's discoveries. Some leave shelter of familiar concepts and become explorers; risk their lives. Mission, pre-mission (not premonition, but that too) per-mission, commission precede transmission to active adventure and achievement. Astonishing discoveries follow; earth, life, world unimaginably vast in expanse and minutiae of detail. Physical evidence seemingly dissociated from vision: metaphysical, spiritual: integration between them was lost.

Answers to questions of *cause* and *effect*, of *order* and *pattern*, were, are sought. Questions of whose *will, power* and energy worked such *work*: **CREATING** continues to *challenge* supposition, conjecture, *wonder*. Belief does not deny *reason*: exploration depends on both: a *step* at a *time* with moments of deliberation, deliberate intent, decisive. Some persons experience dramatic inspiration and revelation; others proceed with cautious confidence.

Sacrament, infinitely varied in experience, sustains energy of faith. Unrealised, unknown, unacknowledged, unseen energy, believed but not seen, is transmitted.

Theology presupposes disclosure, 'theos', divine wisdom of what is true through logic, *logos, word*. Physical senses plus ingenuity of mind recognised heat, light and energy of the sun as nourishing life discovers compatibility of *order: mind* to *mind*: *tuned, toned and expressed in creation, thought of as the mind of the creator*. Theology, reason and science, integrated, are energised, inspired, **led** to discover and recognise what is true. Knowing, willing, doing: spinning triangle, trinity, whose apex of origin, (first cause,) is not a plane; nor even a spatial concept such as the plane of the ecliptic, important as that is, but **the point: the whole point:** expanding, enlarging, sometimes exploding motion, dynamic within and yet beyond material confines; realised to verify principles of *form*, essence and substance. The *key* to this disclosure, the logos, is the 'word made flesh': spirit incarnate, manifest, known in individual soul through gift of faith; pro-genitive, generating source, **origin personified**. This mystery of the Word, in the beginning, made flesh, embodied, was and is thought of as *the 'still point'*, the centre that holds life and things together. Flesh is mortal and becomes disintegrated remains. Embodied life, animated, endowed with energy, makes sounds. The first *cry* uttered becomes a word; more words in response to what exists, the essence and substance of being. External to internal, inward to outward; cycles repeat, develop, over and over again. Thought and reason, the life of the mind, engage definition, grammar, remembered, recorded, apprehended, communicated, learned. Plato said that to intellectualise is to define. Concern for life, for the planet which supports life, emerges with wondering, knowing, understanding; increasingly urgent.

From 'supposing', increasing, multiplying: from 'wondering', questions arouse further enquiry. Supposition theorises; a theory is doubted, invalidated, or believed, affirmed, *recognised when verified*. Physics approaches metaphysics and believers experience accelerated access through faith. Sciences, philosophy, theology *need* each another. Natural Science took a leap forward when experimental method was applied to reading the mind of the Creator. Serious barriers, insuperable to many, developed in European thought when hearing that Galileo was summoned to Rome, 1632, to answer for having verified Copernicus' recognition (1543) that Earth revolves and moves round the Sun, not that the Sun moves round the Earth.

Galileo's observations showed that earth, in the solar system, travels and revolves round the sun. Human life, earth based but neither cave-bound nor earth bound in mind, releases energy of perception into unimagined spheres. In London, the Royal Society, 1662, nurtured mathematical and scientific genius: Newton, Hooke, Halley, Wren among them. The Solar system itself is being reviewed by contemporary astronomers with new equipment and advancing knowledge.

Exploration, discovery, ingenuity applied energy (wind, water, coal, electricity) to manufacturing. The Royal Society for the Encouragement of Arts, Manufactures and Commerce, founded 1754, fostered cohesion between nature, inventions, industry and technology with the 'polite' arts, decorative and creative, and offered awards. The Royal Academy of Arts, 1764, opened schools of painting and sculpture and held, holds, Exhibitions.

Charles Darwin, a century later, saw evidence of evolution and natural selection; of how life in its astounding variety and manifestations evolved, is evolving. (See **XIII I**.)

Local and universal knowledge extends from subjective personal experience to become objective, verified, temporary or permanent: transient, possibly 'classic', eternal. Francis Bacon reacted to Aristotle's philosophical theorising by returning to practicalities; experimental tests. He and his followers proceeded on scientific method of exploration. Archimedes had used it: 'Eureka!' as did Ptolemy and Augustine of Hippo. Michelangelo dissected bodies; Leonardo, highly original observer, experimenter, inventor; both great artists, persons of genius, *sure of the integrity, ultimate unity, wholeness, in created things.*

A font is made to hold *water*. **FONT** is the **word** for *print*, **words** printed. A fount is a source, a natural *spring* bubbling to the surface. A basin of *water* forms naturally and is also constructed for many purposes. Underground and overground supplies of water are replenished by rain. Wells are dug, sunk, for underground *water*. Mercy, needed for forgiveness, replenishes soul, is compared: since it:

> 'Droppeth as the gentle rain from heaven
> Upon the place beneath: it is twice blessed;
> It blesseth him that gives and him that takes:
> Tis mightiest in the mightiest: it becomes
> The throned monarch better than his crown...
> It is an attribute to God himself.'
> (Shakespeare, *The Merchant of Venice* III. 2,
> lines 165-169 and 175)

Mercy, like rain, falls to form streams, rivers, springs with *water* of life; mercy, like water, is sacramental; baptism; communion, *grace* abounding. It happens, not always predictably nor wholly understood but essential refreshment to all faithful suffering mortals who trust. As water cleanses mouth and staunches thirst; mercy sustains a trusting, faithful heart. Font, mentioned as an old word with an additional meaning recurs now, at the beginning of the end, although there is no end to unending inquiry. From generation to generation, generating and regenerating, birth and rebirth, first birth experiences, second birth by water and word is continuity eventuating beyond time into eternity. (*John* 3.1-22.)

Schemes of coherence and order are needed, sought, in human relationships: children with parents, sisters, brothers; parents with children. Pairing; marriage, is increasingly treated as 'suit-yourself', 'suit-myself', unless, until, it fails to suit either. This conditional rather than permanent commitment intensifies suffering: painful tensions, disputes, contradictions in attitudes and behaviour. Ideas, ideals, hopes, raise expectations. Intentions are high, at least for a time, while sustained by strong attraction, mutual interests. Deepening affection, understanding may mature and grow. Shortcomings disenchant. Infidelity destroys trust. Sometimes a marriage dissolves in the acid of gossip, suspicion, or in extreme cases, even rumour; press publicity. Continuity and stability need protection. The illusion that 'private' is not 'public' is impossible to sustain without pretence. One of a pair can cause breakdown; either or neither may resist dissolution. Both suffer, as do children, relatives, others. All need mercy, grace, reconciliation since interdependence, secrets, secretions, good and ill, are embedded experience.

The operation of faith, believed and celebrated in baptism and communion is strengthening in adversity, for worse as well as for better. 'Holy Matrimony', public, good-will, support and prayer, is commitment, holy as making whole, the pair united in a secret, sacred world where **grace** is needed. Mozart's *Mass in C* commemorated his 'nuptials' and continues sung at many others. Expectation of chastity before marriage and fidelity within it is believed to be firmest foundation for deep, stable joy: in sickness and in health, prosperity and adversity, 'until death us do part'. Milton viewed husband and wife as 'he to God, and she to God in him'. Another view: 'each to each and both to God' suggests balanced, reciprocal responsibility. Water into wine at the wedding feast at Cana (*John* 2. 1-11.) Jesus blessed the occasion.

Sacrament exemplifies an act of acceptance; received with confident **trust**, faith, whose inward meaning is true through that faith. If this were not so, the practice would have disappeared long ago. Water and bread are daily sustenance. Wine gladdens the heart and is itself water transformed, absorbed through strong deep roots sustaining vines through seasonal drought. The fruit of the vine ripens in **heat, light,** energy of the sun. Grapes ferment into celebratory wine. The sacrament of communion engages a penitent self-surrender to the love of God in Christ: enduring presence in the Holy Spirit, healing Comforter. Sacrament brings union, reconciliation, between outward and visible with inward and spiritual. Confession of fault and need for mercy engage self-surrender to ineffable quality of **grace**. Baptism, confirmed and strengthened at confirmation: intended with marriage and vocation, ordained fellowship followed.

The words of the sybyl, 'Know thyself' indicate inward exploration to truly face truly, or avoid facing, ourselves. Hebrew recognition of unique divinity of Creator, is heard to speak through patriarchs, law, prophets in diverse cultures, personified in Nature, Reason, Beauty, Dance, Destruction. Accompanying rituals, images, are observed and worshipped where people endeavour to unlock the mysteries of existence, of vitality, energy, fertility and power to transcend misery, error and failure. Sacrament manifests perennial sources true from Father to Son whose presence continues in Spirit, whole, holy, comforting, energising.

XIII II 4 SOUL

XIII II 4 i Beyond words

'Soul' represents invisible, indefinable essence of human being. Physical senses connect and nourish consciousness in **heads and hearts**: potentially integrated.

Words 'read, marked, learned and inwardly digested' *draw* mind and soul towards indescribable realms and inexplicable resources. Mind proceeds to wonder, awaken, discover, attempt to define experience beyond obvious practicalities. Singularity becomes plurality; multiplies again and again: towards (once more) 'that than which nothing higher can be thought' in new levels of consciousness, disclosure, vision, revelation. (See **XIII I**, Figure 2.)

Like in the invisible sac of energy where pollen collected by bees becomes honey, appetite finds nectar when nourishing words of faith are activated, believed. This promotes *grace*: strength and *power* to accept *order* to *form* in second birth. Each person who ascends Plato's Line awakens to think, recognise the good and seek for what is true. The destination, common objective to each open thinking mind is universal. The language expressing what is to be found, the good and true, varies: differently cultivated with contrasting aims, values affirmed and denied, accepted, rejected from available custom, inherited civilisation, occasionally renewed with transforming vision requiring, finding, **new words and language**.

Sources of 'the good' include personal exploration of experience: earthly passions and powers sometimes personified, enhanced by 'divinities'. How, where, when can we make sense of experience: our own and that known from others? Trust, belief in one sure, certain hope experienced in direct disclosure, voice heard, words remembered, recorded, recurs in this inquiry. Monotheistic faith focuses minds of believers into strong conviction, sometimes exclusive, intolerant, but capable of re-opening, continuing open to further search.

Where and how to seek for and *find* true home in universal heart and soul of creation; personified Creator need not abandon respect for old and new awakening. William Blake spoke of 'emanation'. Music reflects composed intensity, innovative. Poetry follows music into words: words inspired by and exemplifying sounds of music, repeated theme, themes. Voice, inimitable; instrument; rhythm, march, waltz, quadrille/quartet, choir, chorus and orchestra, in and out of step, in harmony and discord, seek conclusion, ultimate unison. Enduring quality, appeal, bears repetition, fresh interpretation, conducted and performed. Motion, emotion, dance and march, stimulate and are stimulated in rhythm: rhythmic, melodic sound; music to follow, enlarge, replenish energy.

Bodily need and action: impulsive instinctive necessities, if they mature and refine, are refined to enhanced soul. **Anima** and **animus**, opposing principles of animation, coexist in human being; their tension felt, recognised in dichotomy, dilemma, paradox, challenging decision. Deep inner schisms are evident in a 'divided self', 'unable to resolve and decide'.

Conscious deliberation, capability to decide, resolves and activates *will* to *act* in physical and material ways retained in memory for future reference. Such decisiveness indicates *change*, possible maturity. Thinking, judging, referring to conscience have been much discussed as helping *will* to decide. Here is an ENCORE. Attentive to sense and instinct but no longer imprisoned by them releases *will* to initiate, to *order* as well as to obey. Senses join into common sense; intelligence and knowledge. Higher, deeper, purposes benefit and enhance the functions of senses into true, ordered purposes. Belief involves commitment to another, an other Person, Purpose, Project, Principle, calling for *transfer* of self-interest: **objective**.

Ethics stem from enlightened self-interest, convenience rather than objective, ultimate good. When no one else is involved or thought to be involved, personal behaviour seems private, personal, no other person's business. Habits form, become known, some harmless, others damaging, scandalous, dangerous. Constraints and restraints emerge from *need* and *fear*, sometimes for the sake of others. **Virtue**, identified and classified in antiquity, continues accepted: justice, prudence, temperance, fortitude. Saul of Tarsus, PAUL, interprets the *mind* of Christ and identifies **spiritual virtues,** *trust***: faith,** *hope* and *love*; forward-looking, needing **GRACE** to empower goodness. (*1 Corinthians* 13.) Generous *love* involves suffering and sacrifice. Writing to persons of faith; believers at Philippi, city of Philip of Macedon, father of Alexander the Great, tutored by Aristotle, Paul says:

'Rejoice in the Lord always, and again I say Rejoice. Let your moderation be known to unto all men: the Lord is at hand. Be careful for nothing, no-thing but in everything by prayer and supplication, with thanksgiving, let your requests be made known unto God. And the peace of God which passeth all understanding shall keep your hearts and minds through Christ Jesus. Finally, brethren, whatsoever things are **true**, whatsoever things are **honest**, whatsoever things are **just** are **pure**, are lovely, are of good report if there be any **VIRTUE** and if there be any **PRAISE, think on these things**'.

Soul needs nourishment for growth, elusive if denied, easily ignored in first world of practicalities, material preoccupations. Soul, health discerned, believed, becomes valued and cultivated; if not, recognition of spiritual virtue fades, dissolves. Each personal kingdom, sovereign identity, grows if confirmed, increasingly illuminated in *light* **of what is true**. A *spark* ignites for good; or evil, **love and hate**. We cannot see *light* but we know that *light* **enables sight**. Created light, given, is reproduced in fire, flame, lamp and candle: electric energy in electric-light bulbs. Parables of darkness include ignorance, error, blindness, misapprehension of what is true. **Eyes**, minds-eye, see, perceive and discern. *Heart* represents emotion, feeling. *Mind* in *head* seeks to learn, know, understand. These three: insight, feeling and thought advise *will* to respond, resolve, intend to do. Interchange of energy, *light, heat, sound,* physical and metaphysical, is true *sacrifice*, seen, felt, known, **understood in soul, beyond words,** Love unknown, known of, knowable through gift of faith, by *grace*.

Augustine thought of memory as stomach of the mind (*Confessions* X xiv) and discussed recollection as rumination. He described 'four perturbations of the mind': **'cupidity, gladness, fear, sadness'**.

Observing, listening with sympathy and intelligent sensibility are functions of friendship, pastoral support. The burden of decision, of responsibility, rests with individuals; some willing to accept by direction, obedience. Decision, difficult to achieve, can seem impossible even to contemplate. The more individual liberty is valued, the greater becomes the burden of decision-making. Normal tension accelerates into acute stress, distress, suffering; but when ignored, denied, suppressed, other problems occur. Formal counselling or analysis is devised to assist understanding and manage difficulties. **Jung** identified 'individuation' as necessary challenge to distressed individuals in acute need of confidence. Physical nourishment supplies energy for body routines but needs to be supplemented, challenged, redirected, by discerning further sources of nourishment; nervous, emotional, thoughtful, evaluative. Soul health is disturbed by disconnection between any *level* of this intricate, invisible system of balanced well-being. Self-examination may disclose *cause*; talking about it may *help* to identify, comprehend and encourage re-connection and integration. **Donouns** spotlight capability to *integrate*, to **confess** and **profess**: in being and doing together. Jung recognised 'archetypes' within universal archetype and counselled many with therapy of increasingly informed, objective integrating friendship: learning from each.

Motive can *form*, reform and transform intention towards co-operative service with another, others purposes and needs. How far we are wholly, partly, self-seeking, self-indulgent, self-gratifying in conscious purpose is much debated: genes or stars blamed for failures, for talent cultivated or dissipated. Attempts to shift responsibility tells something about **need, sin, guilt**. *Need* multiples needs. Carefully constructed processes of considering, consulting, contemplating, promote **order**. Rules become recognised personal and communal. Ignoring, breaking them, weakens cohesion. Reproof, correction, intend and *hope* to assist mending, forgiving, but are ineffective without cooperative *will*. **Hope** is needed in prisons of its absence.

Aristotle considered the movement of a boat rowed and the movement of the oarsmen who row it. The boat is in motion in itself. The motion of the oarsmen is intrinsic to men rowing, different to that of the boat. Is the soul in itself moved to participate in production of motion as the boat participates in the motion of the oarsmen? Aristotle identified four types of movement: **locomotion, alteration, *decay*** and **growth**. These types of movement, when they pertain to the body, have a spatial location. If the soul takes part in this movement it will be moveable by force or forced not to move. **Soul** at *rest* remains so unless, and then until forced to *move*. However, just what these force-produced movements and states of rest of the soul will turn out to be, he does not find it easy to say.

Aristotle's search led him to essence of personality, the **soul**, which he explored inwardly in outward contexts, the external world. He considered movement itself, sure that *soul does move* but what promotes its movement he finds difficult. He notes an absurdity 'in common with most theories about the soul'.

'The soul is connected with the body, and inserted into it, but no further account is given of the reason for this nor of the condition that the body is in. Yet this would seem to be required. For it is by their partnership that the body acts and the soul is affected, that the body comes to be moved and the soul produces motion. And none of these is possible for things whose mutual connection is contingent.' (*De Anima* I. 4.)

Aristotle compares the need of soul for body with the need of skills for tools. He identifies disjunction between action and the sources of action, absence of motivation (*De Anima* III. 9 and 10) now spoken of as dysfunctional and, in severe cases, as breakdown. A discussion of sense perception (*De Anima* III. 1 and 2) is followed by considering imagination as, 'not one of those faculties that are always correct, such as knowledge or intellect; for imagination can also be false. It remains, then, to see if imagination is the same as belief, as there is both a true and a false variety of belief. Belief, however, is followed by conviction, as it is not possible for those that hold belief not to be convinced of the things in which they believe'. (*De Anima* III. 3.)

'To be subject to an appearance will just be to believe non-incidentally in what one perceives. There are, however, false appearances, in connection with whose objects true supposition simultaneously occurs. For instance, the sun appears to be a foot across. Yet we are convinced that it is greater than the inhabited world. If then imagination is belief, there are two possibilities: either the subject has cast aside the true belief that he had, without any change in the facts and without his having forgotten it or been persuaded to the contrary, or, if he retains the true belief, then the same belief must necessarily be both true and false. However, the belief would only really become false in circumstances in which the facts changed without his noticing. Imagination, then, is neither one of these things nor a combination of them.' (*De Anima* III. 3.)

Aristotle's limitless interest, balanced, tuned originality of mind enabled him to open up, explore and analyse spheres of thought and to formulate discoveries. Whatever came to mind caught his wonder, consideration and will to think and write. Senses and sense, (physical, medical, psychological) led him to recognise ten categories or predicaments: 1. Substance or being; 2. Quantity; 3. Quality; 4. Relation; 5. Place; 6. Time; 7. Posture; 8. Having or Possession; 9. Action; 10. Passion.

In Ethics, Politics, Metaphysics, Poetics, the Soul, Aristotle's ordered words continue to communicate his insatiable curiosity, open mind, clear reflection, classic directness. Conscious that motives come from **desire** and thought; a **mind** with intelligence and intellect promotes motion, movement.

'Every movement being a push or a pull, there must be a "still point" as with the circle, and this will be the point of departure for the movement.' (*De Anima* III. 10.) The fact that animals move led him to compare animal and human motivation.

'Can animals that have sensation only by touch have imagination also? Can they have appetite? Well, there is no doubt that they have pain and pleasure, whose presence entails that of appetite. But how could they have imagination? Or perhaps they have these faculties but in an indeterminate way; after all, their movement is indeterminate. The presence even in non-human animals of perceptive imagination has already been noted. It is in those with reason that deliberative imagination occurs, it being a task for reasoning to decide whether to do one thing or another. It must be against a single thing that the options are measured and the better pursued, which implies the power to produce a single thing from many images....Already, then, we count three types of movement. **Supposition, thought,** and **reason** are on the one hand of the general and on the other of the particular. The first prescribes a kind of action for a kind of agent, while the second says "but this action is of the appropriate kind, and I such an agent". We can either say, then, that it is the second and not the first that produces movement, or that it is both, though the first, unlike the second, remains more in a state of rest while doing so.' (*De Anima* III. 11.)

Stillness is seen as necessary for perception but no non-stationary body has a soul without perception. To move deliberately combines activity of mind and body, with *soul as* **hinge** *between them*. Aristotle argued, debated, reasoned and thereafter assumed that perception is essential for motive and thus for movement. **He recognised paradox that the 'still point in a turning world' must be still and still moving.**

High points, promontories, particular features help explorers to navigate, to move to objectives hoped for. The 'still point' may represent pause for reflection, hesitation before decision, decisive action, contemplation, inner sovereignty of soul. Aristotle exercised his mind, sovereign seat of intellect, with all pertaining benefits: reason, imagination, belief. **The gods, then, were not thought of as planners, manipulators, interventionists, but as personifications of natural forces,** *power* **capable of seeming to intervene in lives where destiny, tragedy, fate were believed to be inescapable.**

Hegel's statement that 'every truth has become so' appeals to idealist and to evolutionist philosophers. It is the nature of belief to begin without proof: to propose, suppose, then presuppose a statement which, if verified, is believed true. Areas of experience inaccessible without faith are realised and experienced by faith. (Paul's *Epistle to the Hebrews* 11. 12). Nevertheless, 'Clouds of Unknowing' persist. Questions are raised in hope of answers; problems seek solutions. Subjective, relative judgments limit apprehension of what is true. Are there ways to approach the source of truth itself? If so, we have leapt into affirming source of what is true.

Hypothesis, hypothetical, derives from a theme: a **thesis** proposed. Discussion, consideration for and against proposed **thesis** engages antithesis, pro-thesis, eventual **synthesis**; a compound combining its elements.

Thus humanity approaches divinity. Cultures of *trust*, faith, belief, are formed, systematised, when found and known to *WORK*.

In Hebrew tradition revelation came from the *voice* heard and obeyed. Patriarchs received *promise*, then **law**, later interpreted, or disregarded. Law, the law of God, unified nature with creation: the Creator's will to be followed in and for life beyond disobedience, *sin*. Among priests and judges, kings and prophets, chosen participants heard and heeded **words, orders, commandments, promises**. Not all obeyed. Who was chosen? 'Word' and 'choose' are not **donouns**. Response is to *voice*, persona that utters, to words heard, ignored or obeyed. Failure, defeat, captivity by the waters of Babylon did not destroy *hope*. The *promise* believed was trusted by believers. Expectations of deliverance, liberation, redemption, return to the 'promised land' soon coexisted with messianic expectation: suffering servant: redeeming, healing, restoring presence foreseen by Isaiah. Ezekiel surveyed desolation. 'Can these bones live?' (*Ezekiel* 37.) **Breath of life breathed into them brought them together, bone to bone, clothed with flesh and inspirited with life.**

Augustine believed that the soul of man was alive in the life of the ever-living creator, originator, sustainer. The soul derived life from that life, the living Word, the living God.

'What then do I love when I love my God? Who is he that is higher than the highest element in my soul? Through my soul I will ascend to him. I will rise above the force by which I am bonded to the body and fill its frame with vitality. It is not by that force that I find my God. I will therefore rise above that natural capacity in a step by step ascent to him that made me.' (*Confessions* X vii, viii.)

Augustine experienced conversion, *change* of heart, in clear and memorable circumstances. In the garden at Milan in the summer of AD 386 *light* dawned in his soul as self-surrender, *trust*, commitment, became possible and was accomplished. (*Confessions* VIII xi-xii.)

Great new kingdoms of wonder, glory, happy conjecture followed. Augustine's new consciousness of **soul** led him to consider the mysteries of interaction, interconnection **between *will* and spirit, body and soul. At the core, the heart of human wellbeing, he found conjunction of being and doing: integration: *WILL* to *ACT*.** Believing in **ONE, the source of life and energy of creation,** his thinking developed from and in commitment to that belief. His *Confessions* are to this ONE in direct conversation. ***Wonder***, inquiry, exploration, discussion, analysis, lead from and to outbursts of awe and prayer. His starting point: 'You have made us for yourself, and our heart is restless until it rests in you' (*Confessions* I i.)

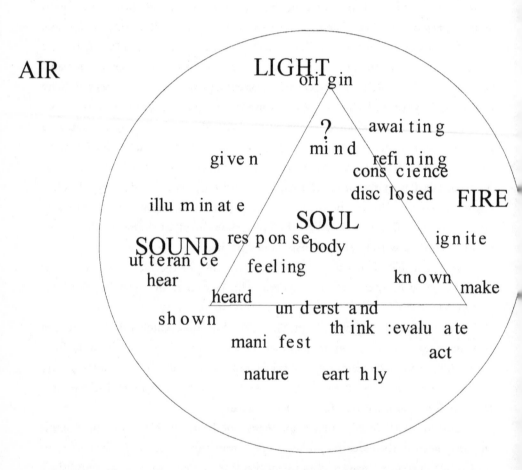

Figure 3: Radiation occurs to and from source; creative origin of *LIGHT*. Sun sheds light transmitted to earth, radiant energy; life manifest in life divine: disclosure to illuminate and nourish human SOUL.

Recognising the four levels simplifies these intricate, interactive complexities woven together in personality and character. Each individual may seek practical, emotional, intellectual integrity, distinct from fully co-ordinated wholeness. Delight in simple things reflects innocent balance: functional human being, some from childhood, others who mature slowly, unevenly, with difficulty. Imprisoned by weakness, failure, their own, others, some lose heart in *despair*; some survive hell; some experience dramatic *change*. conversion, such as Paul, Augustine, Bunyan, John Wesley, and many others, bequeath accounts in **words**. Individuals, families, communities, tribes, cultures, are strengthened; influenced; co-ordinated by what is true and good or in want of them.

Soul to soul, wonder igniting trust, to believe and learn; to communicate, make and act.

Songs without words, beyond words, assist and disclose. The circle represents unlimited sphere open to and offering clues, providing patterns experienced to open hearts and heads.

XIII II 4 ii Breath and Spirit

Hebrew poets, psalmists, regarded soul as seat of emotion; of morale: 'Why art thou cast down, O my soul? and why art thou disquieted within me?' (*Psalms* 42. 5.)

The Oxford Dictionary refers to Beowulf's use of 'sawol' as the principle of life in human and animal being, and to King Alfred's use as the principle of thought and action in man. The Dictionary includes twenty-five distinctive uses of the word 'soul' and refers to King Alfred's understanding of **soul coupled with body in life and thought**; with and without the definite article; soul individual, personal and universal. Boethius (AD 480-524, translated by King Alfred) was already drawing on Augustine (AD 354-430) and on early Christian thinkers, 'Fathers', who connected the soul with deep seated consciousness in earlier traditions of thought: Hebrew prophets and poets, in Homer, Plato (BC 429-347), Aristotle (BC 384-322). Much 'scientific' and contemporary understanding separates soul and body, sad, indeed tragic dissociation of sensibility.

Air is breathed in and out, inhaled and exhaled, is changed from oxygen to carbon dioxide. Air breathed is breath of life. Vegetation restores the balance.

Lungs and heart, body's pumps, *work* for intake and output of air breathed and *pump* blood to circulate. This vital process sustained life long before it was identified, named, understood by people whose lives it sustained. Movement of air, wind, accompanies temperature *change* when hot air expands, rises, circulates. Vents such as doors, windows and chimneys contribute to this movement. Draughts occur. 'Fug' builds up in absence of ventilation.

Ideas are ventilated in discussion; informal and spontaneous; formal, systematic, in words. Many sources, inspirations of thoughts, ideas, reach *beyond words*, unutterable.

Encounters, meetings, parties social and political, occur, in and out of professional organisations: medical, scholarly, educational, legal, clerical. Reasoned discussion breathes heat and light to ventilate points of view: problems needing resolution: decision: majority. Government by committee, safeguarded by procedures, 'democratic', is not always effective, even efficient, but hopes for consensus if possible; ways to limit, prevent, personal domination by dictatorial rulers who avoid listening, refuse to discuss, will not negotiate. Opposition intensifies into open conflict, revolt, revolution, unless accepted, recognised procedures enable constitutional solutions, votes of confidence or of rejection, resignation, fresh elections. 'Winds of change' recognised, discerned by rulers, political sailors, who discern shifts of opinion, cultural changes, and use them to retain *power*.

Air moves, felt but not seen, unless cloud forms. Ideas are ventilated in discussion, tested in different ways and places, informal and formal; at home, in pubs and clubs, offices, common room and committee, among civil servants, in political Parties and in parliaments. Leaders popularise unpopular intentions, plans, especially when 'personality' disguises absence of 'policy'; when support for a *'project'* displaces loyalty to party principles, 'spin doctors' are employed to propagate and popularise unpopular change.

Con and *vent*; to learn and to refresh air, to ventilate, amalgamate into **convent**. Individuals who experience vocation to live according to habitual organised *order*, to cultivate faith, *hope* and *love*, spiritual virtues, in prayer, thought and work, enter a **convent**. Essential practicalities, shared, balance worship with service such as scholarly, medical, educational ministry: strengthening personal and **communal soul; breath and spirit.** Seclusion from distractions is intended to assist concentration, but temptations are inescapable. Some convents are closed from the outside world except for minimal necessities; others open for hospitality and charity. Convents are associated with nuns; monasteries with monks but convent applies to either.

Vent leads to venture; embarking on new activity. Pre-vent, going ahead to prepare or possibly to *stop*. **Advent** is preparation. Invent is act of discovery originating and developing from natural order realised: a **well**; an axe; a sundial; a **shelter** from trees whose **wood** makes houses, boats; structures for better, not worse. Words need breath to communicate, describe, encourage and warn.

Convention suggests *consent* to good practice, well mannered genuine acceptance and respect for custom. A convention is also an assembly looking for consensus, common mind, clear *purpose*. Subvention, prevention, re-invention recognise supporting, forestalling, rediscovering and renewing. **Consensus: *consent*, common mind**, gather recognition of what is 'generally acknowledged': a well founded expectation: what has become regarded as **'orthodox'** manners, behaviour, stronger than convention when faith is confident but weakened when faith dwindles or dilutes: challenged by revision which may or may not refresh, renew, from sources which formed prevailing faith. Loss of consensus, common mind, brings other problems: leaders becalmed are tempted to try to regenerate confidence in purposes promoted by 'charm offensives', not to offend but to create emotional gales, egocentric whirlwinds.

Convention, accepted principle of behaviour, customary to social mores (loosely moral but better not morally loose) of particular groups or communities of people are, for the time being, 'the done thing'. Manners are needed to maintain and sustain relations, relationships, in awkward, difficult, sometimes impossible circumstances. What is 'done' or 'not done' depends on social orthodoxies generally accepted by individuals who respect them enough to follow consistently if inconveniently, to avoid embarrassment, dissenting fights, active rebellion, revolt. An occasional rebellion is tolerated in hope of retaining, restoring, stable connections. Persistent flouting wears away the underlying freedom protected by convention: the courtesies, decencies and civilities which shelter from rude, crude, coarse behaviour: words spoken in hate and anger which incite violence. The soul develops lungs of its own to ventilate personality with intake of fresh air of the *love* of good rather than evil: peace than war: capable of clearing confusion, burning away waste, firing *will* to find reasons, motives to act well. Each soul grows when exercised; strengthened, ventilated, drawing breath for health, 'wholeness', 'holiness'. Characteristic openness clarifies every level for health and wellbeing. Pollution, fog, darkness cause grave difficulties. Refreshing air seems unattainable in conditions which destroy hope and tempt to despair but, like mercy, it descends, blows clarifying draughts of remembered good: knowable, known, received.

Convention has immense unwritten strength when practised as a Constitutional principle of 'the body politic', understood and respected. It emerges in experience of action, example, rather than statement made. A Ruler rules, makes a *rule*, initiated, 'authorised' as an act to constitute an *act* of *state* but precedent respected is stronger than legislation. *ACT, STATE, RULE* are powerful **donouns**. Proclamation, acclamation, appointing, summoning and dissolving, chairing, proceeding, according to order, recorded in minutes, delegated: these are a few words for activities which, since first practised for orderly recorded decisions, become justified in experience, **conventional**. Not laws which depend on statute, but procedures, precedents, found to *work* in *practice*, respected and adhered to; easily lost in ignorance, disregard, indifference. The 'in and out' of breath and spirit are evident in every sphere of life where living activity discovers virtue of wisdom inhaled, civil, civilising, a civilized freedom.

A **convent** is a distinct community where people accept rules, more or less strict discipline; schedules ordered to cultivate and strengthen spiritual virtues of faith, hope and love through prayer, thought and work. Essential practicalities accompany study and worship to nourish individual and communal **soul**. In the lifetime of Jesus and John the Baptist, the community of the Esseenes, near the Dead Sea, studied, preserved and copied Hebrew texts. Fearing destruction by Roman invaders, scrolls were packed into clay jars, hidden in high caves for safety. Two thousand years later , they were found to include copies of texts, Isaiah and others, now displayed in Jerusalem. Masada, earlier fortified hill store near the Esseenes 'convent', became last refuge of Hebrews who killed their families, then themselves rather than surrender to Roman siege, A D 70.

New movements begin with one or two, who *form* groups, secret if threatened. Leaders encourage, teach, remember, write. Jewish families elsewhere, scattered, kept, keep, Passover. This became Eucharist to first Christians with Jesus, and scattered, cultivated communities grew around the Mediterranean where transport was facilitated by roads and sea-routes available to itinerant missions. Paul, leader among them, visited Phillippi, city of Philip and his son, Alexander (tutored by Aristotle). Having established a community of believers there, Paul wrote to inspire, encourage and strengthen in words linking virtue, already known, renewed with fresh air: breath and wind of the Spirit of Christ: 'Whatsoever things are true, honest, just, pure, lovely and of good report'...'if there is any virtue, any praise', to think on these things and there find blessedness and peace. Grace through sacrament was central to sustain this new vision and faith. Persecutions, fierce and cruel, led some to seek seclusion, safety, protection from distraction, hope to assist concentration.

High thinking, idealism, sometimes intensifies temptation to excessively critical oversight, intolerance, rigidity over details. Monastic and convent communities, devoted and dedicated union of heads and hearts to promote and extend culture of every sort; agriculture, horticulture; good food and drink; fasts, feasts, hospitality; sanatoria and hospital for healing; devotion expressed in music, writing, scholarship and good government. Representation and consent, customary in Dominican houses, friars based in places, was known to Archbishop Stephen Langton (died 1228), to Simon de Montfort, and adapted for support and for accountability to the King, and by the King, according to law. Magna Carta, signed 1215, could be invoked when monarchs exceeded their customary powers.Feudal magnates, Barons, other than Abbots and Superiors of Monasteries, were backed up by armed supporters when they confronted King John at Runeymede. Words set down in Magna Carta set a new tone to justice, jury, representation and good law in England.

An invention is devised to **work** effectively and efficiently: such as pot, basket, scarecrow, wheel: leads to energy saved and efficiency promoted, worth advertising. Inspiration comes from an idea, ideal; a model, inwardly cultivated and developed. Technical resources to learn; to do, to make something, enhance confidence in ability to make. The Chinese say that a journey starts with the first step. A word, a gesture, a switch, a button pressed, are actions of **WILL**.

Consciousness of wholeness, of healing integration, challenges and is challenged by believing it is possible. Nicodemus, Jewish lawyer, leader, was baffled by the impossibility of 'second birth'. Jesus speaks to him of 'water and the Spirit'; of Moses, leading deliverance from Egypt, who crossed the waters of the Red Sea; whose rod became a serpent, symbolic tempter, then upheld the brass serpent at Sinai, symbolising law: 'so must the Son of Man be lifted up, raised, to save through faith those drawn to respond in faith, believing.' (*John* 3.) Nicodemus had heard of Jesus and wanted to meet him, secretly, and question him directly. The context of this encounter was **baptism**, new birth. (*John* 1 15-34.)

John the Baptist's call for penitence, need for forgiveness, literal washing in the water of the river Jordan, symbolic in Hebrew history became new sacrament of baptism: **light**, new birth, **change**, 'conversion'. Later, when Jesus faces death and knows his friends, disciples, are troubled, he consoles, warns, gives **promise** of the gift, the presence of the Comforter as he invites them to share depths of sorrow, hatred, agony, suffering **pain**, foreseeing joy and delight fullness of **LOVE**. John (disciple and friend) heard and recorded these 'farewell discourses' (*John* 14-17) as also extraordinary events in Jerusalem for Passover, Last Supper: the, betrayal, arrest, crucifixion; the race with Peter to the empty tomb and the astonishing supernatural appearances on the road to Emmaus, to Galilee: fishing again with Jesus waiting on the shore. John is the disciple who testifies to and wrote these things 'and we know that his testimony is true'. (*John* 21. 24.) John adds that 'there are also many other things which Jesus did the which, if they should be written every one, I suppose that even the world itself could not contain the books that should be written. Amen.'

The intrinsic order of the four levels becomes evident in these extraordinary events. Practicalities apparent in present life, our first world, are always (like the body) the *place*, context and material of life on earth. Body, of the earth, earthy, grows like plants which succeed with ***light, water***, nourishment for root, stalk, leaf, flower, fruitful fulfilment. Persons grow too with senses together: common sense, open to inspired purpose and responsible activity capable of realising principled insight and vision. Breath of spirit, beyond first sense world, separable for purposes of analysis and description is, like wind, invisible. In the table opposite, Figure 4, feeling, thought and judgment, experienced in that order, 2nd, 3rd, 4th, in the first world, stimulate and are stimulated to achieve foresight, vision, with evaluation and judgment, 4th level directed by spirit of good or evil. Integration, integrity, may occur within a person in each level, increasingly mature when further attained.

Imagination runs riot, sensationalist wish fulfilment, unless tempered with reality to reason, evaluate, judge, recognise good and evil to ***plan*** with vision, committed to good or evil ***purposes***. Evaluation is essential for judgment before action, scruples scrupulously censoring impulse and spontaneity without losing the vitality and joy of true good. Judgment requires criteria, evidence of action enlightened by principle to inform and be informed by thought and feeling (felt-thought) for ways and means, practical realisation, fair and good, or unfair, wrong, false, evil. These distinctions may seem beyond easy reach but applied to practicalities, first level problems, they disclose priorities and assist clarification. Knowledge and understanding proceed from subjective to objective, from hypothesis to thesis, antithesis to synthesis, to the heart of the matter, the spirit, personal, veritable essence.

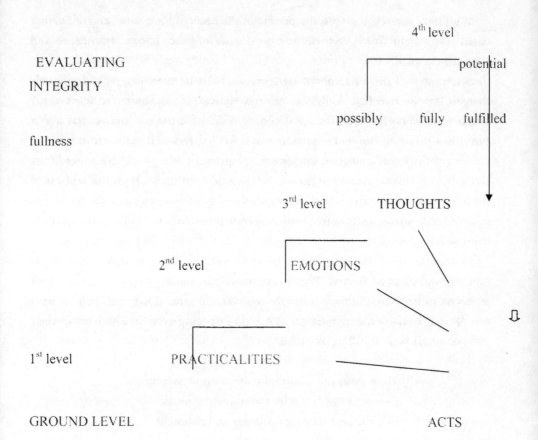

Figure 4

In Henry Vaughan's poem *Peace*, soul is living presence with metaphor, and metaphysic:

> 'My soul, there is a country
> Far beyond the stars,
> Where stands a winged sentry
> All skilful in the wars:
> There, above noise and danger,
> Sweet peace is crown'd with smiles,
> And One born in a manger
> Commands the beauteous files.'

Vaughan's vision is a simple, direct echo of the Book of Revelation, and of Dante's Paradise, wrought from good-will and good news of peace known, learned, in and from the Gospels.

Spirit and soul are sometimes thought of and said to be interchangeable. Soul needs energy and power in action. Souls need spirit: operative spiritual power but 'Spirituality', of one sort or another, many with common ground of virtue and vice, is that which energises a person whose soul is open to it, as it were, to receive it in their soul.

Songs of the slaves, Negroes working the plantations of the southern states of the U.S.A. before Emancipation are known as 'spirituals'. In such a tradition we hear of the death of 'John Brown's body', but that his soul goes marching on. The Spirituals were songs of sorrow, endurance, souls desperate for strength of faith, hope and love, living word.

Philosophy and theology have been thought to be separable, to divide fundamentally and be divided. Poetry expresses high intensity of personal experience in words which reunite them. Lorenzo and Jessica, after elopement, behold with wonder and soul-joy the inspiration of creation opening areas of love beyond their own, wonderful and fulfilling as that is:

> 'How sweet the moonlight sleeps upon this bank!
> Here we will sit, and let the sounds of music
> Creep in our ears: soft stillness and the night
> Become the touches of sweet harmony.
> Sit Jessica. Look how the floor of heaven
> Is thick inlaid with patines of bright gold:
> There's not the smallest orb which thou behold'st
> But in his motion like an angel sings,
> Still quiring to the young eyed cherubins;
> Such harmony is in immortal souls;
> But whilst this muddy vesture of decay
> Doth grossly close it in, We cannot hear it.'
> (Shakespeare, *The Merchant of Venice*, V. 1)

Between decision and baptism, Augustine withdrew into retreat, not solitary, but ordered for quiet study and thought. *Soliloquies* (he coined the word) record discussions between himself and Reason in newly discovered perspective of belief in divine authority. Of sense and reason, sun is to eyes as reason is to mind, given, found in the first place by faith. (*Soliloquies* VI 12.) Augustine is praying for light and to be recalled from error. He ventilates the problem of falsity: that what is false is both like and unlike what is true. Reason says:

'So far as I remember, we concluded that Truth could not perish because if the whole world, nay if Truth itself perished, it would still be true that the world and Truth had perished. But nothing is true without Truth. Hence Truth cannot perish'. (*Soliloquies* XV 28.)

Use of the word TRUTH expresses ultimate unison of all that is true, comprehended into its integrity personified in being of God, apprehended in part 'for the time being'.

Augustine, like Plato, wrote in dialogue form. 'The Teacher' conversed with his sixteen year old son, Adeodatus. *Contra Academicos* (AD 386) concerned the limits of scepticism, of detachment, of suspended judgment, sitting on the fence. *On Music*, begun before baptism, finished two years later, became six books.

'It will appear that the ancients were not inventing anything, but that they were discovering something that already existed in the world of nature, and finding names for it'. He notes that rhythm exists alone, in sound such as water dripping, beat without voice or instrument. Rhythms in sound are separated from rhythms in our hearing, but rhythms which are in our hearing are not separable from those which are in sound. There is 'ascent from rhythm in sense to the immortal rhythm which is in truth'. The faculty of assent or dissent from rhythms shows 'judgment by natural right'. Discussing soul and body with consciousness, harmony, digestion or indigestion, Augustine sees soul as becoming 'keyed up' for perception. The soul is fragile, readily enslaved to habits of body, to emotions initiated at will and difficult to extinguish. Soul, potential ruler of body, will become clarified after resurrection of the body. Meanwhile, the mind has power to recall music without actually hearing it. This theme repeats and is developed thirteen or more years later in *Confessions*. (X xxxiii-xxxiv.)

In Christian theology, the name of the **discloser**, the Paraclete, also referred to as the Holy Ghost, unites the soul of the believer into unison with the Creator, Father, in creation: **manifest** in teacher, Son, one mind and soul at one with one another exemplified in continually available **presence** with the Holy Ghost the Comforter, each being of one substance in whom all things live, move, and have their being. Heart, soul, mind and strength are called together in conscious surrender to the integrating energy beyond each individual and operative daily in increasing power of **love**. If the first **word is of life, in being, *light* is mediating energy of growth and disclosure.** (Paraclete comes from Greek, *para-kaleo*, to call to. A student theologian thought of it as a sort of bird but descent precedes ascent, not 'high flyer'.)

Life is made manifest with breath, rhythm, energy (heat, light, sound); distinct and in interactive unison to promote growth. What is made awaits enjoyment, knowledge and understanding of what is made and this directs attention, interest to its maker, to wonder why as well as how it was made. Human beings learn and become makers, beyond the immediacy of instinctive day-to-day adaptation, selection by thought and judgment as unified reality. The circle represents what awaits exploration. Within it is the interest of exploration in form of the three points of outward source and inward appreciation. The 'still point' of the soul is central in every sense and dimension, when awakened. Father, Son, Holy Spirit (Ghost) personify the three persons, the Trinity. The Paraclete, invisible, cannot be indicated at a point. The circle turns and is also an unlimited sphere, within which life is lived within its culture, whose limits extend and shrink, uncircumscribed. 'Study of mankind is God' extends to every aspect of Creator and Creation, including humanity with all that this implies. Alexander Pope re-centred emphasis when he echoed the inscription at Delphi, 'know thyself'.

> 'Know then thyself, presume not God to scan,
> The proper study of mankind is man.'
> (Alexander Pope, *Essay on Man*)

Pope's dictum for humankind diminishes recognition that the sum, the whole, is greater than its individual parts; that each individual, unique, is open to explore and discover source and origin. Humanity is not a self-invented species. That notion, sometimes applied to personality, is a psychological reduction developed out of need for confidence building in the absence of that which confirms identity and personality in the soul; the Kingdom waiting to be received, within, in childlike trust (*Luke* 17. 21 and 18. 16) with confidence in 'that than which nothing higher can be thought'.

Conversion presents an experience of unity between soul and body, humanity and divinity. It is a metamorphosis of *will* and spirit. It occurs in nature, natural, like seed bearing fruit, like water when it dries, is vaporised and condenses into rain. It is emotional since feelings change, warming and cooling, blowing hot and cold. It occurs in thought; reasoning, understanding, analysing, defining, stating, interpreting, changing mind. It is an act of *will*, a decision, sudden or gradual but decisive. For Paul, conversion proved to be the first step towards unimagined realms in, by, through, with the light, power and energy of faith. 'Spiritual gifts', diversities, uniting one body in wholeness, newness of life and being whose different limbs, organs, faculties and functions co-ordinate into unison, personal and communal. (*1 Corinthians* 12.)

Mind and body, head, heart and *will* unite into soul; personality reborn in the energy of life that makes 'all things new'. Personal response of love manifests 'diversities of operations' but 'it is the same God working all in all'; the heart known and knowing love; peace that passes all understanding. To speak with the tongues of men and angels is nothing without love; its joy and music. To *rise* in love is not the same as to *fall* in love. Rising, resurrection, is second birth. Charity, caritas, is distinct from eros. In the parable of the sower, the **word** is *seed*, sown on good, bad or indifferent ground for ears to hear; choked by thistles, brambles, thorns: by cares, difficulties, vanities to thrive or not, heard or unheard. (*Mark* 4. 1-20.) Paul interprets the parable of the sower as demonstrating and integrating second birth, reborn into new life. His hymn of transcending glory, eloquent vision uniting new life, faith fulfilled, moves from earthly present: 'through a glass darkly; but then face-to-face: now I know in part; but then shall I know even as also I am known. And now abideth faith, hope and charity, these three; but the greatest of these is charity'. (*1 Corinthians* 13.)

XIII II 4 iii Living Word

New life is conceived when seed finds a place to fertilise and grow. Growth, health, fruitfulness follow unless ills and cross accidents: partial or terminal, early or late prevent it. This attempt to simplify and review human growth began from familiarity with eggs, hats, stars and hearts must end, only to find a new beginning, unending. Recognition of word as seed to fertilise and be itself fertilised, reproduced, in human heads and hearts is the end which begins again, unique in who ever welcomes it.

Predicaments weigh on heart and burden mind when problems defy comprehension, exceed understanding and challenge management of *need*. Words to describe, diagnose and look for help emerge from personal difficulties, acknowledged, known in suffering and fear experienced and observed. All faiths look for solutions, prescriptions, which include praying. Habit of heart, mind and *will* to pray is not pious optimism but soul searching urge to face difficulty, danger, possible preparation for disciplined effort. A prayer, at first, in fortunate circumstances, resembles approach to trusted, generous parent who will clarify, understand, encourage. Unavailable in desperate contexts such as war, poverty, prison, community suffering, the seed of life in head and heart looks for words, something heard, remembered. Desperation becomes personal beseeching.

Sources of supply turned to in need may not be physical. Material need includes seeing fault; causes of upsets, wrongs; mercy of forgiveness for ignorance, inadequacies.

Hope to learn, to improve, to find true goodness, wisdom, encourages towards the highest and best from simple need to realise virtue and strength to perform and act well. Learning to ponder, to reflect, meditate with open heart and mind; move to *wonder*. To awaken, find words of *hope*, until *trust* ventilates the soul; fresh breath to refresh: to assist digestion in this inner sanctum of personality unformulated until the breath of *air, light, fire* and *love* enables fertile seed to grow, to reach for and find fusion, integration, *will* to *act*, energy of soul to perform in vitality of living word, word of life.

One word can make all the difference in the world; true or false, yes or no, saved or lost, living or dead. Speaker and hearer find life in a word; a word alive. Life is in the reality. Symbols promote understanding to cultivate its message: the true condition is the Word itself, true to itself, inspiration and model to a helpless bewildered soul.

Words without meaning, arid and empty, recall Job hearing the voice from the whirlwind: 'Who is this that darkens counsel by words without knowledge? Gird up now thy loins like a man; for I *will demand* of thee, and *answer* thou me...' (*Job* 38. 41.) Job answers in total humility. (*Job* 42.) *The Book of Job* recounts integrity tested to extremity. (*Job* 2. 1-3.)

The vocabulary of the vision of immortality, known, fuses in experience. Elemental and theological **donouns** unite levels of meaning towards wellbeing, health, wholeness.

Flesh is perishable, contingent, demanding, and dependent. Physical passion moves, inspires and also frustrates, causes anguish and consumes: destroys unless spent. Persons discover capability of becoming ordered; of finding, in *order* and *control*, clarification of right action; true and best health, body and soul, flesh and spirit, together. Living Spirit is disclosed in created being, all things made, *work* done, learned, shared *function* and destiny, good rather than evil: a fair wind, not an ill-wind. The circle is universal reality in pupil of eye, seen and seeing, opening and closing, participating participles cycles experienced, wheels within wheels, unending, enlightening, wise.

Good and evil are realised, not in things, but in intent, *will, purpose,* done and undone in harmony and discord, just and unjust, timely, in time and timeless, continuing, enduring in memory, indestructible. Mercy, repair from devices and desires, temptations, weakness or illness of *will* which afflict so often, in so many ways. The interaction of flesh and spirit is realised in sensibility, in nerves and psyche, soul growing within body for the time being, often in tension, contradictions, paradox, impossibly difficult situations and dilemmas, excruciating pain. Ears listen when open; hear words, living Word, spoken, read, remembered; in *light* which lightens, occasionally in dreams, clarifying and uniting heartfelt thought, mind, body and soul together.

To write attempts to find and set down words that communicate living, lived life of a hungry unending exploration. John Bunyan's pilgrim embarked on a journey from this world to the world which is to come, burdened until relieved of his burden; frightened until increasingly confident, valiant in faith against all disaster. 'Who would true valour see......' (John Bunyan's *Pilgrim Hymn*).

Aesop, a Phrygian slave, contemporary with Pythagoras, sixth century BC, invented wise and powerful metaphors told as fables of animals anthropomorphised with human beings. His tales were collected and written in verse by Babrius, third century BC, translated into Latin by Erasmus and into English since. Seeing, or rather, reading of Aesop's animals who speak and behave as human, and humans as animal, is sensible, funny and wise.

Ovid, in *Metamorphoses*, pre-supposes cause and effect between human suffering and exaltation, tragedy and glory as result of divine intervention including punishment by gods and goddesses of antiquity. They were jealous of their immortality. Thus:

> 'Minerva, goddess of weavers,
> Had heard too much of Arachne.
> She had heard
> That the weaving of Arachne
> Equalled her own, or surpassed it.'
> (*Tales from Ovid: Twenty four Passages from Metamorphoses*,
> Faber and Faber, 1997, page 174)

Minerva accepts Arachne's challenge. How could Arachne win this uneven contest? Her sentence is her destiny: unceasing weaving from her stomach: the mother of all spider's.

Ted Hughes verse translation re-presents these mythic dramas with breath-taking directness and intensity, starting with *Creation; Four Ages; Flood; Lycaon:*

'Now I am ready to tell how bodies are changed
Into different bodies.
I summon the supernatural beings
Who first contrived
The transmogrifications
In the stuff of life.
You did it for you own amusement.
Descend again, be pleased to reanimate
This revival of those marvels.
Reveal, now, exactly
How they were performed
From the beginning
Up to this moment.'

In length and metre, the *Metamorphoses* resemble an epic but the opening lines describe the very different kind of poem that Ovid set out to write: an account of how from the beginning of the world right down to his own times bodies had been magically changed, by the power of the gods, into other bodies'. (Introduction, page vii.) Judgment for Ovid was seen as ineluctable consequence, without mercy, without scope for penitence, forgiveness, new start although *change*, metamorphosis, is described. Prayer and pity accompany agony in Venus and Adonis (ibid page 124). Pyramus and Thisbe, mortals whose love immortalised gained immortality when they die together (ibid page 246), as Shakespeare recognised in plays, poem, not least 'Venus and Adonis'.

Two thousand years on, in present 'scientific' climate, it seems 'natural', acceptable, to introduce metamorphosis from 'natural science', geology, botany, butterflies, rather than poetry, ancient and modern. Geology discloses fossils: life turned to stone. Organic development of life, organisms, seed to plant, fruit and so on, is, since Darwin, thought of as evolved, evolving life, rather than as 'metamorphosis'. Metaphor uses words as (and including) signs and symbols to express *change*, transformation. Metaphysics embrace union of tangible and intangible, flesh and spirit, growth of the life of the soul. Individual response to and cultivation of consciousness of the spirit of things raises questions of meaning and purpose in life from sources not only of the earth, earthy. *Will* as spirit, spirit as *will* are energised, energetic with energy , electric, *divine*.

S. T. Coleridge (1772-1834), poet and critic of genius: addicted to words and occasionally to opium: wrote letters to a friend, *On the Inspiration of the Scriptures.* Coleridge's *Aids to Reflection and Reflections of an Inquiring Spirit* were edited and published after his death (George Bell, London, 1904, page 288.) On reading *The Confessions of a Fair Saint* in Carlyle's translation of the Wilhelm Meister 'it might, I think', be better rendered literally: 'The Confessions of a Beautiful Soul'. Reflecting on his own religious experience: 'of one who is neither fair nor saintly, but who — groaning under a deep sense of infirmity and manifold imperfection — feels the want, the necessity of religious support...'. (op cit, page 291.) Coleridge's letters, edited by H. N. Coleridge as *Confessions of an Inquiring Spirit*, his criticism and his poems have been much studied for their common sense and for co-ordinating faith and reason, philosophy and divinity.

As a synthesis is a unity that results from the union of two things, so a prothesis is a primary unity that gives itself forth in two things, a prothesis is LIVING WORD.

THESIS, something laid down, the starting point for the THEORY leads to

PROTHESIS, placing publicly, on show (derived from 'shewbread')

MESOTHESIS, (See *O.U.D.*), now rare, is 'something interposed, serving to connect or reconcile antagonistic agencies or principles'. Hurrell Froude (1803-1836) is quoted from *Nemesis of Faith*, page 157: 'the final mesothesis for the reconciling of the two great rivals, Science and Revelation'.

HYPOTHESIS, supposition, basis of argument, supposition (conjunctive, disjunctive, syllogism) proposition laid down: statement: thesis: starting point for true theory. (*O.U.D.*)

SYNTHESIS, ingredients integrated: critical, reasoned acceptance, credible, accepted, believed.

Coleridge recognised and used **THESIS** as itself and as suffix, to identify levels, stages of affirmation. His **Pentad, (pentagon, pentameter, Pentateuch)** injects the word **mesothesis, crucial to his attitude of inquiry.** Like Little Piglet, he really wants to know. His exploration: neither indifferent nor dogmatic, does not inhibit consuming appetite in **search for what is true**. Research begins with question, proceeds towards **thesis**, etc as Coleridge's **Pentad** illustrates:

THE PENTAD OF OPERATIVE CHRISTIANITY

PROTHESIS
CHRIST THE WORD

THESIS   MESOTHESIS   ANTITHESIS
              or the Indifference

THE SCRIPTURES   THE HOLY SPIRIT   THE CHURCH

SYNTHESIS

THE PREACHER

CREDENCE, (*O.U.D.*) is mental attitude of believing: accepting as true. **Trust** is **engaged for confidence in and reliance on, some person or authority. Belief is that which is believed. A letter of credence was, is, a commendation, a recommendation.** A Credence table in a church is where bread and wine, elements, are ready for use in sacramental celebration, not 'reserved'.

Renewal of Christian faith, the Evangelical revival and the Oxford Movement, gathered momentum in the nineteenth century. Coleridge's position, not static, is less known now than his poetry.

Being of one substance: *light,* **life**, and **word** conjoin, ignite, re-unite human soul into unison with creation and creative energy. The Creator who has created, creates and will continue to create, becomes known in three ways, three parts, **origin**, manifest in *time* and *place*, three together in one. Reality realised in music, poetry, and theology ministers metaphysical renewal, re-association of sensibility: healing from disabling dissociation between feeling and thought. A cultural climate that disregards, even discards realisation that *light* draws growth and that growth requires healthy nourished roots could lose it. Growth and roots cultivated together are interdependent on *water, light,* food for growth in light of what is true, only survive when those who depend on them (as all do) continue to understand and retain knowledge of reality of *light* and life at every level, *head light* first, **food for thought, words.** Urban children who do not see bulls and cows, calves fed with milk; or hens who lay eggs, miss essential experience of natural life and food.

The Bible, collected texts which stand the ***test*** of ***time***, has been, continues to be read and re-read: subjected to critical and uncritical appreciation by generations of ordinary readers and increasingly by scholars and critics. Scripture is recognised to communicate ultimate things, highest and deepest, the very origin of Word, divine utterance; sources of words, spoken, written, to find and use language: to find and reveal revelation from, for and of what is true. To hear and read scripture, in any tradition, is to participate in faith, belief; to benefit through increased knowledge: verification of the source disclosed. Readers experience access through faith or miss it in absence supposing faith has been denied, repudiated, betrayed. Reasons to read vary from curiosity, doubt, faith, devotion of those who ***share*** what is revealed.

Without belief, the essence and substance is not reached, nor responded to. Absence of faith, earlier or later denial, arises from or becomes the **indifference**; neither interest nor will to verify. Faith springs from affirmative qualities of ***love*** and ***hate***, not indifferent, but able to nourish or to hurt the soul. Faith, ***trust***, engages confident, effective action, in vitality of living word. Many lives are lived in unending inquiry, exploration, not seen as successful. Coleridge experienced this.

Augustine was moved to sudden and complete assurance at his conversion. He retells how he had been sitting in the garden at Milan with Alypius but moved apart when deep agitation led to floods of tears. ('Solitude seemed to me more appropriate to the business of weeping.')

'I hurried back to the place where Alypius was sitting. There I had put down the book of the apostle: when I got up. I seized it, opened it and in silence read the first passage on which my eyes lit: "Not in riotous and drunken parties, not in eroticism and indecencies, not in strife and rivalry, but put on the Lord Jesus Christ and make no provision for the flesh in its lusts". (*Romans* 13. 3-14.) I neither wished nor needed to read further. At once, with the last words of this sentence, it was as if a light of relief from all anxiety had flooded into my heart. All the shadows of doubt were dispelled.' (*Confessions* VIII 29.)

Alypius asked Augustine to show him the text. Together, they read the next sentence: 'Receive the person who is weak in faith!' Alypius took this to himself. 'Without any agony of hesitation he joined me in making a good resolution and affirmation of intention, entirely congruent with his moral principles in which he had long been greatly superior to me.'

Augustine emerges from his writings as a person who felt, thought and learned with exceptional consciousness, intelligence, range and intensity. Exploration of experience in words led to poetry, drama, rhetoric, philosophy. Delight in the natural world took him to mathematics, astronomy and music, and all forms of science. In his *Confessions* Augustine is addressing the source, the goal of his exploration believed, by then, to be the Lord from whom all thoughts of truth and peace proceed, for 'our heart is restless until it finds rest in you'. (*Confessions* I i.) Augustine in his explorations and discoveries discerns and finds happiness in realising true love through love if what is true; its source and nature. (*Confessions* X.)

Augustine found himself confronted with transcendent presence, the **living word**: 'You are the Lord God of the mind. All these things are liable to change. But you remain immutable above all things, and yet have deigned to dwell in my memory since the time I learnt about you. Where then did I find you to be able to learn of you?

You were not already in my memory before I learnt of you. Where then did I find you so that I could learn of you if not in the fact that you transcend me? There is no place, whether we go backwards or forwards; there can be no question of place. O truth, everywhere you preside over all who ask counsel of you. You respond at one and the same time to all, even though they are consulting you on different subjects. You reply clearly, but not all hear you clearly. All ask your counsel on what they desire, but do not always hear what they would wish. Your best servant is the person who does not attend so much to hearing what he himself wants as to willing what he has heard from you. Late have I loved you: beauty so old and so new'. (*Confessions* X xxiv 35. xxvii 38.)

Human experience bounded by time has been perceived as journey to God. Dante's vision of Paradise is of something attainable through the changes and chances of this mortal life. It leads through *present* hell experienced in life, now as then, then as now, in absence of *reason*. Dante's infernal regions were populated by tormented people, identified by name, imprisoned by habits of deeper and deeper evil.

> 'Abandon hope, all you who enter here.
> Can *hope* abandoned be renewed'

Dante's poetic allegory describes how the guidance of Virgil, personifying *reason*, enabling him to survive infernal regions until they reach a frontier that *reason could not* pass. Here, in his vision, is Beatrice, adored since childhood, ever *present* in his heart. Transformation, restoration, seem possible. Dante then describes cleansing from evil, purgation, rehabilitated, beyond hell. Angels of mercy, each of relevant virtue, hover over him as each deadly sin is faced on this healing path to paradise.

Virgil, *reason*, had accompanied Dante through misery, suffering, torment, tragedy without hope, hell, to meet Beatrice, personification of human love. The company of angels sing and strengthens him in face of each temptation.

Personal purgation is a *process* of recognition: realising what is wrong and, by faith through **grace**, to transcend and become able to love truly; *hope* and faith restored, ready to explore paradise. The Empyrean, ultimate sublime place, is envisaged beyond material worlds yet essential to unity in existence, **essence and substance together.** Heaven is not SPACE because it is fulfilment, glory and peace, not emptiness, nothingness. Dante composed his trilogy in the everyday spoken language of his time, the common tongue, the vernacular, vernal.

Human search, not alone, is in company, carrying possessions, rich confusions and complexities of the human condition; in poverty, imprisoned, enslaved, inescapably travelling through life. Chaucer's procession of pilgrims, a convivial party, are named by place or function: the Wife of Bath, the Knight, Miller, Cook, Friar, Pardoner weave a tapestry of lived experience; some embroidered in imaginative recollection from old legends during travel and as they stop to eat and rest with the Host as a sort of compère, commentator. Drawn together in common purpose, practical, pragmatic, appreciative of the momentous significance of Beckett's martyrdom: they travel to where holiness was tested in martyrdom, aware of their own need and hoping to find benefit, beatitude, blessing. Their penitence is in having suffered from their errors in ordinary life, sins familiar to those to whom they tell their tales and to readers in every generation since. Quintessentially English follies, vanities, illusions, delusions: lust, virility, greed, cupidity, lies, tempered with down-to-earth pragmatism, accompanied by commonsense longing for something better. There are excursions into deep questions such as God's foreknowledge, pre-destination and free choice, in the Nun's Priest's Tale. The Merchant recalls Ovid's Pyramus and Thisbe. The last tale is the Parson's, his verse is followed by sermon in prose, on proper preparation for confession 'on that perfect, glorious pilgrimage that is called the celestial, to the Heavenly Jerusalem'. Chaucer's Parson affirms that God desires none to perish and that 'One noble way is Penitence, the lamenting for sin and the *will* to sin no more'.

The root of the tree of Penitence is **contrition**, the branches and the leaves are **confession**, the fruit **satisfaction**, the *seed grace*, and the *heat* in that seed the *Love of God*.

For John Bunyan (1628-1688), the seventeenth century journey of Christian was a *progress*, intensely personal, written as allegory of his life journeying 'from this world

343

to that which is to come'. Imprisoned in Bedford jail for refusal to conform, Bunyan proceeded as an 'Independent', seeking the celestial city beyond the social, judicial, political, ecclesiastical establishment of that stormy period. An archetype of individualism; undaunted, undismayed, he knows true valour through faith: the *grace* of God to those who seek it. (*Ephesians* 2. 8). The slough of despond, the valley of humiliation, the distracting company of Mr Worldly-Wiseman, Vanity-Fair, Doubting Castle presided over by Giant Despair: these are hazards to be survived; personified prototypes of *present* temptation and danger. He saw ways to hell even from the gates of heaven. At last he came to the river, Jordan rather than Lethe since no ferryman was there to carry him across. Dying to this world as in baptism, Bunyan's passage from mortal life awaited transformation in the next:

'So he passed over, and all the trumpets sounded for him on the other side.'

In the turmoil and destruction of the twentieth century, T. S. Eliot, philosopher, poet and dramatist, documented his personal development in essays of criticism and self-criticism, poetry and drama, throughout his life. His poetry: subtle, allusive, satirical, ferocious and sympathetic, became transparent beyond metaphysical. *Four Quartets* exemplify highest and deepest union, without need for conceit, of a 'spirit unappeased and peregrine' between two worlds, earthly and heavenly; low and high dreams in faith, hope and love towards ultimate peace.

The places are not invented; each is significant in the poet's personal history, native of St Louis, Missouri, retained New England connections at East Gloucester, sailing near rocks known as the Dry Salvages, close to where Andrew Eliot had landed, 1669. After Harvard, T. S. Eliot came to Europe and began to reclaim roots and vicissitudes in France, Germany, then England, English. Fire at *Burnt Norton*; blood and ancestry at *East Coker* where plague and post-civil-war had led Andrew Eliot to embark are echoed as New World awaiting exploration: to be explored; dangerous waters, shipwreck, baptism, off and on *The Dry Salvages*; history destroyed and renewed at *Little Gidding*, place of refuge in seventeenth century civil war, ('I think of a King at nightfall') where Pentecostal fire of the Blitz (Eliot was an Air Raid Warden in London) is the theme. Each of the four places is a poem constructed with movements; a quartet within the Four. Each co-ordinates the four levels of experience within its own movements and into the whole. The four combine, interconnect each theme, woven and interwoven into tapestry of life, as, and into one. Three conditions often look alike: ATTACHMENT, DETACHMENT, and between them, INDIFFERENCE. Attachment to self, to things, to persons, analysed and expressed in philosophical poetry; poetic music of Four Quartets. Reference to Dante and to Coleridge is evident in the third movement of the fourth quartet. (CPP, page 195-196.)

T. S. Eliot's fascination with metaphysical poetry, ignited when a student at Harvard, intensified his sympathy for their ways of expressing need and hope for resolution between head and heart, body and soul. He became obsessed with Laforgue, enamoured with the moon, and with other eighteenth and nineteenth century French 'Parnassan' symbolist poets. Familiar writers made sense in new ways; soul-searching to himself and stimulating extensive reading E. K. Rand introduced Eliot to Dante, to Boethius and to Augustine whose Confessions, in a pocket edition, accompanied him everywhere. George Santyana's Three Philosophical Poets drew him to realise the ideal of 'philosophical poetry', felt /thought, reasoned faith, and to realise belief as the root of culture.

Eliot described his lifelong appreciation and love of Dante in the Egoist, 1919; in the Clark lectures, Trinity College Cambridge, 1926; the Turnbull lectures at John Hopkins University, Baltimore, 1933, (since edited by Ronald Schuchard and published by Faber and Faber, 1993); and in a talk given at the Italian Institute in London, 4th July, 1950, 'What Dante means to me' (To Criticise the Critic, 1965). Laforgue and Dante showed him poetic genius young and old; immature and mature, as he himself strived to experienced and achieved.

Augustine, least discussed by Eliot but quoted crucially, was most powerful influence of all in Eliot's heart, mind and faith, as in Dante's. Augustine's virility, passionate nature; mercurial, brilliant intelligence, classical philosophical erudition and inexhaustible memory enabled him to scale heights and depths of experience unshadowed by puritan heritage into biblical, theological and ecclesiastical insight, scholarly method, omnivorous reading, skilful rhetoric and enhanced delight in mathematics and astronomy, love of music and poetry and, above all, ever increasing devotion and prayer. Eliot found temperamental and intellectual affinity with Augustine, words that ignite in speaking belief, conversion; commitment, that set him on fire to realise, explore, comprehend and discuss the primacy of citizenship, earthly and heavenly, in the City of God. The Idea of a Christian Society was written in the gathering storm of 1939: Notes towards a Definition of Culture in the aftermath of the war, as he had written Ash Wednesday after the first.

Eliot's 'confessions' are within his poetry and plays, distanced through what he called an 'objective correlative', an effort to de-personalise, to universalise self-revelation. The 'conceit' in English metaphysical poetry was designed, intended, to project detachment, observation of self, in order to overcome conscious 'dissociation of sensibility', separation of thought from feeling. Eliot's early crying need to unify is expressed in Prufrock and caricatured in Sweeney, the low dream of the earlier poems. Personal voice emerges in Gerontion, originally part of *The Waste Land. The Hollow Men* is transition to the 'higher dream of *Ash Wednesday. The Fire Sermon (The Waste Land III),* concerns physical lust, unsatisfied and unquenched; common and royal; dense with references within Eliot's reading, criticism and work. His life in London culminates in conversion. He quotes Augustine's *Confessions*: 'To Carthage then I came, where a cauldron of unholy loves sang all about my ears'. (See notes CPP, page 79, including references to Eastern and Western ascetics.) Eliot's feet were at Moorgate, going to work in the overseas section of Lloyds Bank, and to Margate, to recover from illness, breakdown, October-November 1921, where he began to write *The Waste Land.*

Augustine's mind permeated Dante's as both, plus Chaucer, pervade Eliot's work, not always acknowledged. Eliot did not waste words. Drafts for *Murder in the Cathedral* and *The Rock* went into *Burnt Norton.* Both reflect Augustine's fascination with time. Words from *Confessions* (IX) appear in *Burnt Norton I* and *II* where Eliot adopted Augustine's use of Aristotle's 'still point in a turning world' (*Burnt Norton II, IV* and *V*: c.f. *Confessions* XI 16-40). Culminating in eternity, the end and the beginning, ever present, are taken up at once in *East Coker*, birthplace of Andrew Eliot (who emigrated 1669) and London, where Eliot spent his working life, 1915-1965. (*East Coker I* and *III.*)

History: full of cunning passages, contrived corridors and burning issues in *Gerontion*, 1920, (CPP, page 37-39) became implied place of the intersection in time of the timeless, still and still moving, where past and future are conquered and reconciled. (*The Dry Salvages III* and *V.*) A people without a history is not redeemed from time since history is a pattern of timeless moments in time. 'History is now, and England.' (*Little Gidding V.*) The intersection in time and yet beyond time is timeless; Birth and Death, Christmas and Good Friday: birth and death await resurrection: Easter: then Pentecostal fire.

The cross is symbol of incarnation and resurrection. Good Friday is historical event and eternal reality. Between Parts I and II of *Murder in the Cathedral* the Archbishop gives his sermon on Christmas morning, AD 1170. The congregation is present with him, celebrating Christ's birth, life and death and resurrection, the gospel; impending martyrdom, with Augustine's Christmas sermons seven centuries earlier.

Narrative speaks sometimes in words, living words leading to God. Words read anywhere, as in the garden at Milan come alive: **living word**. Sacrament offers union with God, affirmation experienced. Augustine defined sacrament as visible form of invisible grace. Those present at the Last Supper met to remember Passover. Jesus spoke words as bread was blessed, broken and shared as his body: wine was drunk, blood shed; these are remembered, re-enacted in sacrament. The next day, the Friday, Jesus was sentenced to death and crucified. His words of the night before, etched in memory of those who heard them, became new confident knowledge of continuing presence. They were, are, written and spoken, translated, repeated: 'This is my body which is given for you: this do in remembrance of me. Likewise also the cup after supper, saying, this cup is the new testament in my blood which is shed for you.' (*Luke* 22. 19-20.) Matthew's account says the same, heard with distinctive emphasis: 'And as they were eating, Jesus took bread, and blessed it, and brake it and gave it to the disciples and said, "Take eat, this is my body". And he took the cup, and gave thanks, and gave it to them, saying, "Drink ye all of it; for this is my blood of the new testament which is shed for many for the remission of sins. But I say unto you, I will not drink henceforth of this fruit of the vine, until that day when I drink it new with you in my Father's kingdom."' (*Matthew* 26. 26-29.)

In years to come, penitence acknowledges shame for evil motive and *act*; destructive thought, word and deed, mild and mortal wickedness which calls for mercy, for forgiveness; responding to word of *promise* spoken and heard; renewed by grace through faith, believed transmitted through living words of Christ the Word. Baptism enacts faith and hope for new beginning, to be confirmed and sustained in continuing communion, renewed resolve, *grace* at every stage through the changing scenes, troubles and distresses encountered in life towards eventual death of the body in perspective of ultimate ends.

Fifteen hundred years after the Last Supper, debate on the question of *change* became sharp dispute: what happens to the elements received: the bread and wine? The Queen, Elizabeth I, was asked about the meaning of the Eucharist. Her reply:

> 'Twas God the Word that spake it,
> He took the bread, and brake it.
> And what that word doth make it.
> This I believe, and take it.'

In baptism, *water* is blessed to cleanse: to be seen to wash outwardly; the visible sign of invisible second birth, regeneration. The inward, invisible need is for cleansing, healing renewal requested for infants by parents and god-parents who *name*, christen, pray, *promise* continuing support, *gr ace* for the gift of faith, when divisive argument, perennial debate on 'transubstantiation' recur.

In years to come, penitence is for shame of evil motive and act; destructive thought, word and deed, calling for mercy, for forgiveness; response to *promise* spoken and heard.

Renewed by grace through faith, transmitted through living words, words of Christ the Word, baptism enacts new beginning, to be confirmed and sustained in continuing communion, renewed resolve, replenishing grace at every stage through the cycle of life towards ultimate ends.

Birth and death of the body are singular, but reproduced, re-enacted, awake to each new day and to sleep, at night. In family of faith in Christ, Christmas, Good Friday, Easter, Whitsun are remembered as particularly high days, holy days. Knowledge in experience is re-enacted faithfully: rediscovery, knowing again, being and doing, despite pains, calamities, tragedies, in enduring unbroken union.

There is no end to exploration, personal, general, cosmic. It is the challenge and opportunity of human life: faith affirmed, initiative taken: responsibility, faith assumed or ignored in any sphere where and when faith, hope and love bring head and heart together towards integrity of heights and depths, agony and delight: joy.

APPENDIX A

Four Levels

This summary, more suggestive than definitive, clarifies interaction between head and heart, body and soul.

FOUR LEVELS: *practical* (operative), *emotional* (felt), *cognitive* (known?), *decisive* (intended).

Human consciousness awakens capability to wonder, affirm, towards deliberate action (See **XIII I** Figures 1 and 2.)

Action, doing, involves activity at one or more level: single, dual, triple, quadruple:- *physical: emotional: thoughtful: moral*...particular motives, purposes, may be subconscious, denied, unknown until realised, increasingly cultivated towards ordered, conscious, realised awareness.

1. *Instinctive*: **NEED, DESIRE, FEAR** engender intention to move, **WILL** to think, speak, act **in thought-word-deed: well/ill**, good and/or evil intention and purpose, spontaneous, lateral. *Sense*; feeling; analyse; evaluate; consider with **WILL**: energy of **SOUL: SPIRIT**; able to learn, to **REASON; conscience** in **HEAD** to **DECIDE** for **GOOD and/or EVIL. Body, HEART,** *mind/head*, intent, motive, *ACT*; ACTUAL-DOING.

2. *Ascent* from *sense*; outward and inward references, interdependent, distinctive, to formulate intention.
APPETITE...*PURPOSE*...*CONTROL*...DUTY/OBLIGATION...*WILL*.
iv. judging: evaluating, intending, **conscience**/control, deciding, performing, deliberate. **i**
iii. reasoning: analysing: mind, recall, remember, enquire, consider, conclude doing determine. **ii**
ii. feeling: desire: heart, responsive, emotive; impulse, *control*, active/passive. **iii**
i. *sense*, intelligence: body, conscious (un-, sub-); instinctive, intuitive sensible, wise? impulsive/active. **iv**

3. These *stages*, LEVELS, are distinguishable, separable, interdependent: capable of vital **integration**. Evaluation and judgment *require criteria*; precedent to inform, evidence to recognise principle, conscience to advise, *will* to determine, up and down, in and out; outward to inward: out to *ACT*; lit by general, *conscious knowledge of good and/or evil*. The **order** reverses when **control**, desired, is established: *good-will* intended. Some terms interchange, to sharpen meaning: e.g. *limit, cost, waste, form, practice, urge.*

   Prefixes: **affirm, modify, deny**: e.g.: aff, con- in-, re-, (firm suffix); di-, in- ,con-, per, re-, ob-(verse); in-, per-, con-, re-, de- form. Kiss is not reversible. (*TEST* each thought, word, deed at each and EVERY *level*.)

Evaluate	intend	***purpose-*** object/subject	Determine
Think	*mind*	Formulate	define, *plan*
Feel	respond : emotion	*need, desire*	*will*, direct *urge*
Do — *act*	Practicalities	Perform — enact	Achieve? fail/succeed

4. **WILL** as **ACT**: engages what is needed, felt, intended, informed, resolved, determined, done. Ordered intentions *need* **energy**: to **control** and perform, positive and negative: + **and** -.

5. **WILL** in general behaviour may be exceptional, characteristic, habitual self-determined, (co- non-, un-, cooperative, obedient, disobedient), concerned, responsible, indifferent. Other criteria include other *will*(s): individual, communal, *human, super-human*; felt, thought, reasoned, (rational/irrational), imperfect, perfectible: *Vision divined: imperfect, perfectible, perfect*. **Sovereignty of good** realised; personal, social, communal, universal: civic, cooperative, divine (divined/revealed).

6. ***WILL*** as spirit: intended good, not ill, evil. ***Will*** embodied in persons: individual 'spiritual bodies', bodies inspirited: well/ill, capable/incapable; able/unable, disabled. Consciousness opens discerning and knowing. Levels elucidate intentions: ***will*** *to* **control**, *deliberate,* ***act*** *needs* **power** *and strength.* Consciousness of custom, manners, ethics, law, virtue, derive from realising, affirming, knowing good and evil in ***light***, not dark, with **conscience**. Will-power, ***will*** **empowered**, emerges from instinct in **each** *sense* **and level, unified as common-sense**; increasingly refined, available, complex, paradoxical, potentially integrated, resolved, determined.

7. ***WILL***/SOUL: intangible, invisible essence, essential presence, links body/mind/ spirit; animates physical with moral vitality, energy for ***will*** **to do**: well/ill, good/evil. Broken, separated, divided souls need mending: dis-ease healed: rescued, saved, redeemed from denial, rejection, falsity, despair, hatred, hurt, heart, warped mind. Evil: ill-will, ***will*** to EVIL endangers each SOUL. ***GRACE*** known of, accepted, believed, becomes accessible energy of SPIRIT, at ***work*** in soul through ***trust, hope, love***, spiritual virtues, cardinal: c.f. classic virtues.

APPENDIX B

Performatives

Performatives and **donouns** draw this inquiry together. English is now widely spoken and read. Words, more and more specialised, increase exponentially. This slightly literate castaway on Prospero's Island; neither *desert* nor deserted, was told of J. L. Austin's work collected together after his death and edited by J. O. Urmson and G. J. Warnock, published 1961, by Oxford University Press as *Philosophical Papers* in this order:

1st. Austin's critique of H. A. Richard's article (Philosophy, X, 1935) concerning discussion of Pleasure, Virtue and Happiness in **Aristotle's** *Nicomachean Ethics*.

2nd. *Are there A Priori Concepts?*, addressed to the Aristotelian Society, 1939.

3rd. *The Meaning of a Word*, 1940, to the Cambridge Moral Science Club and Oxford Jowett Society. After his extraordinary contribution to the War effort planning D-Day, 1944, Austin returned to Oxford.

4th. *Other Minds,* Paper 1946.

5th *Truth*, 1950.

6th. *How to Talk* – some simple ways.

7th. *Unfair to Facts* to the Oxford Philosophical Society, 1954.

8th. *A Plea for Excuses*, Presidential address to the Aristotelian Society, 1956.

9th. *Ifs and Cans*, reprinted from the proceedings of the British Academy, 1956.

10th. *Performative Utterances*, transcript of an unscripted BBC Third Programme talk, 1956, in which Austin summarised and amplified his William James Harvard lectures: *How to Do things with Words*, 1955.

11th. *Pretending*.

12th. *Three ways of Spilling Ink.*

13th. *The Line and the Cave in Plato's Republic*, carefully reconstructed from sources such as lecture notes.

1. A *performative utterance*: something we **DO**, are doing, by saying it, e.g. agree, argue, bet, warn, date, locate, value, agree, bequeath...a word uniting intention with action: to say is to do.

2. Statements are true or false. Performative utterances ARE; the word spoken is ACT DONE. Must pre-suppose genuine, true intention. If not, if they are *infelicities*, unhappy.

3. 'My word is my bond': 'My tongue swore it, but my heart did not'. Not all, statements, true or false are descriptive but we do not speak of '*a false bet or a false christening'. We do speak of good and bad faith, good and ill will, good and evil intentions.*

4. ***Ethics are not physical but have physical consequences.*** Something believed, verified, known, explained, taught is verbalised/realised, manifested, but a lie is untrue, a false promise.

5. Performative: to say something is to do something; to make explicit. *It is different from stating or describing.* Sincere, genuine, as far as known, trusted believed, hoped. The utterer is the performer, true or lie, felicitous or infelicitous.

6. Austin distinguishes utterances as *performative* (happy or unhappy word/act) from a constative statement, true or false **action in word (e.g. go, begin, end.)** Essential simple test for performative: **act performed by speaker**.

7. True/false and value/fact can be 'fetishes' but are not dispensable. Performatives are:
   i. *Verdictive:* a **finding** e.g. assess, estimate, judge, describe..
   ii *Exercitive:* **exercise of powers**, rights, influence e.g. order, warn, pray, enact, give: also as fact with opinion e.g. appoint, bequeath, vote, advise, warn (knowledge & opinion of....)
   iii. *Commisive:* **promise, commit, plan, covenant;** also declaration of intent, e.g. espousal, siding with.
   iv *Behabitive:* **attitudes**, expressed in social behaviour: e.g. apologise, congratulate, curse, challenge.
   v *Expositive:* fitting utterances into **context** e.g. reply, argue, concede, illustrate, assume: or doubt? know? believe?

Austin adds that iv and v above are troublesome, unclear, cross-classifiable and that all types of performatives are 'present in all my classes'. He sums up:

'the verdictive is an exercise of judgment,

the exercitive is an assertion of influence,

the commissive is an assumption of an obligation or declaring of intention

the behabitive is the adopting of an attitude

the expositive is the clarifying of reasons, arguments, and communications.'

Austin wonders how to define performative more clearly and he considers:

a) *vocabulary* ...and suggests making a list of all verbs with this peculiarity or

b) through *grammar*: first person, active, present tense looks appropriate (e.g. I vote, bequeath, reply, assume...). But another distinction shifts performatives from particular to general in some cases e.g. vote, done once, or intended or to be counted on now or in future; reply as replied, stated. Some performatives require object e.g. bequeath needs bequest, assume needs assumption, warn needs warning. **Implicit performatives are not immediate e.g. I intend.**

Between actual as explicit or implicit is possibility of change from present to future, from intention to action.

APPENDIX C

Donouns

Donouns express being and doing in a word: one word for doing and deed. Each **donoun** is a verb and a noun. Doer may be distinct from deed. **Donoun** unites doer (will to act) with deed e.g. *act* an *act*, *peel* the *peel*, *order* the *order*, *cry* a *cry*.

Participles are verb adjectives (judging, feeling) or noun adjectives (flower, flowering). They express participation: doing in being; being in doing. A participle partakes of the nature of a verb and its adjective is a derivative of a verb with function and construction of an adjective (qualifying a noun) while retaining some of those of a verb (e.g. tense, government of an object): a verbal adjective.

Donouns embody being and doing, *will* the *will*, *act* the *act*, *vote* as *vote*, *work* at *work*, *'I work the work'* (c.f. fly in flight, deny in denial, bequeath the bequest, sing a song).

Many **donouns** are performatives but not all. Many performatives are **donouns** but not all.

A verb that cannot be used as a noun without modification is not a **donoun**: e.g. I speak the speech, say the word or words. I say, speak, hear, write, make a sentence. A *judge* in a *sentence* pronounces *sentence*. The *judge* is *judge*.

To state or make-a statement: speak, write, state, make, are performative but not **donouns**. To *ACT* you (or I or anyone else) *act* the *act*. An action is separable from actual doer who is not necessarily actually doing that action. (Delegation, conformity, obedience may occur.) *Act, order, plan* are not always intended, determined or done as direct action but will be done by another whose *will* is obedient (or disobedient). *Search, purpose,* principle and meaning involve the spirit of the *act, order, plan*, singular or plural; personal, universal in good or ill-will, virtuous or vicious intent.

Performatives are not statements unless they are intended action. Argue is performative but the argument is not. Discuss is performative but not the discussion; decide but not decision.

Perform is performative but not a **donoun**. In action, acted out, perform becomes performance. But performing (a participle) includes acting and acting is performing. *Stage, level, place, time, light, dress* are **donouns**, not all in the same category. (See **XIII I iii**.)

Dress may *change*, be changed, in *time* and *place* according to *need, supply, taste,* choice chosen, the *will* of the dresser, their own or another, the wearer who is dressed.

PERSONIFIED DONOUNS identify and do: e.g. *name* the *name, taste* the *taste, love* my *love, judge* the *judge, love* my *love, will* the *will*. Each, many others, are known and experienced at all levels.

Donoun as embodiment begins as *desire*, possible intention, *purpose*, principle, meaning disclosed; word to identify and comprehend; comprehension comprehensively comprehending *value*, good or ill, in *thought*, word and deed. **NAME** and **WILL** are quintessential **donouns**. Theory and practice in union, living experience, conscious, sub- and un-conscious, become **WORK, PLAY**: realised **donouns. They provide a way to detect integrity:** union in being and doing.

Donoun incorporates levels together: e.g. **call** (heard, responded to, considered, answered, ignored, disregarded), **will** (yes, no, perhaps) and **act** accordingly. If unconnected, or if connection fails, mending is needed.

Mend is a **donoun**. Connect is not. **Point** unites indicating with indication in action; to **will, move, act, object**. Subject may or may not be a **donoun**. **Test** each in a context.

Donouns embody union, **power** in being and doing experienced: a simple, living, everyday way of realising word embodied. The key to unlock this is in three parts: **I AM, I KNOW, I WILL**. Outside, externally, beyond ourselves, known of in creation; with and from other human beings, in beneficiaries and participants who discover union with the original principal revealed in vision, prophecy and incarnation (historic, unified, made perfect, complete, eternal) **word** made flesh. (Flesh is not a **donoun**, deceptively, although 'flesh it out' is idiomatic: c.f. use of 'icon'). Principal and principle, **power** with energy of origin; all things begun, derive, continue, have their being, unending, realised first in *TIME*, timely, sometimes timeless, transitory, ETERNAL?

The source of this three way persona: in being, knowing, willing, unifies one divine/humane origin, beginning, source: Spirit itself being 'that than which nothing higher can be thought'; expressing and expressed in power of three way being, knowing, doing, to *create*, all forms of created things into eventual being, knowable, gradually understandable, disclosed through utterance: to *reveal* mysteries; word as works, word in life, cells, embodied, into living flesh unique/universal, inimitable yet imitable, able to *act* through *power* of this same spirit, in *form* and *order* with *reason*, inspired through faith, *hope*, and *love*.

DONOUNS OF ENERGY: *WILL: heat, light, sound, might, move, state, fight, break, sign, order, act* etc. (*search mind,* memory, dictionary).

DONOUNS OF QUANTITY *count, number, measure, survey, contract;* vital moral and practical value.

DONOUNS OF VALUE AND QUALITY: true, accurate. Trustworthy when dealing with trusty persons, **value, dream, test** etc.

SEARCHING FOR INTEGRATION

LIGHT

SOUL   CONSCIOUS

MYSTERIOUS   *MIND /* **HEAD**

believing /doubting/ affirming/denying

HEARTFELT

IDEALISING   RENEWING   REALISING

INTUITIVE   RECOGNISING

????? WONDERING   APPREHENDING   DISCERNING TRULY ?????

analysing

IMAGINING   HYPOTHETHESIS   DEFINING

THEORETICAL

THESIS   believed

4 **DECIDING** - COMMITTING   **ACTION IN THOUGHT**

GOOD ---------EVIL

REFLECTING   right/wrong   **JUSTIFYING**

EVALUATING : CRITICISING

ANTITHESIS   **SYNTHESIS**

3 **REASONING -THINKING**   **DISCUSSING**

REFERING   ACTION IN WORD

TRUE /UNTRUE/FALSE

RESPONDING

2 **EMOTIONAL RESPONSE**   **EXPLAINING**

YES / NO

1 **DIRECT SENSES**   **PRACTICAL**   **PLANNING**

GROUND LEVEL   **ENACTING**

RECEIVED   + ve   __ ve   ACT IN DEED

LIFE GIVEN   CONSTRUCT /DESTRUCT

FOUNDATIONS

VITALITY   ROOTS   GROWTH

ENERGY   ? UNDERGROUND ?   KNOWN / UNKNOWN

ORIGINAL

BALANCE   STABLE / UNSTABLE   RESEARCHED -INFORMED

357

Faith and belief are not donouns: *TRUST* and *DOUBT* are; Chaos is not. *ORDER* is. **Trust** and *doubt* open criteria to *light of reason* towards recognition, understanding. *Heat* suggests *desire, fire.*

Sound, *echo*, invoke *name* and *voice*. **HOPE** is expectation; **LOVE** manifest in **delight**(s), appreciation, communion to please, enjoy, longing to perfect theory into practice revealed in **love** incarnate. (*John* 14. 6.)

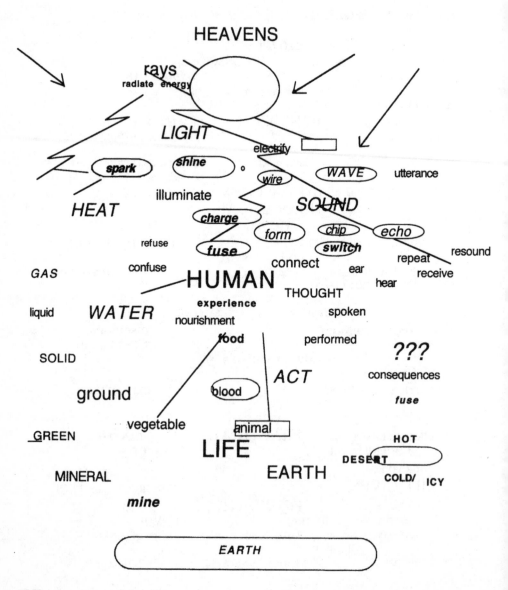

APPENDIX D

The Parson's Tale

summary:
Nevill Coghill's translation of Chaucer
into modern English.

God desires no one to perish; there are many spiritual ways to the celestial city. One noble way is Penitence, lamenting for sin and will to sin no more.

The root of the tree of Penitence is contrition; the branches and leaves are confession; the fruit satisfaction; the seed grace; the heat in that seed is the Love of God.

Contrition is heart's sorrow for sin, venial or deadly. Venial sin is to love Christ less than fully. Deadly sin is to love a creature more than the Creator. Venial sin may lead to deadly sin. Of the seven deadly sins, pride is first.

Pride is in many forms: arrogance, impudence, boasting, hypocrisy, joy in having done harm etc. Outward pride is like a tavern sign showing wine in the cellar. It may show in too many clothes or too few; in the carriage of the body, as when buttocks jut out as the hind parts of a she-ape in full moon; retinue, ostentatious hospitality, one's strength, one's gentility. The remedy for Pride is Humility, or true self-knowledge.

Envy is sorrow at prosperity of others and joy in their hurt. Against all other virtues and goodness, it is the worst of sins, flatly against the Holy Ghost, source of Bounty. Backbiting and grumbling are the Devil's Paternoster. The remedy for envy is to love God, your neighbour and your enemy.

Anger is wicked will to vengeance. Anger against wickedness, wrath without bitterness, is good. Sudden or premeditated anger is wicked. Malice aforethought chases the Holy Ghost out of the soul; the devil's furnace that heats hatred, manslaughter, treachery, lies, flattery, scorn, discord, menaces, curses. The remedy is for anger is patience.

Sloth, rotten hearted sin, does all tasks with vexation, slackly, without joy, and is encumbered by doing good. It restrains one from prayer and leads to despair. The remedy is fortitude.

Avarice is a kind of idolatry; a lecherous desire for earthly things. Every florin in one's coffer is an idol. It leads to extortion, to fraud, to simony, gambling, theft, false-witness, sacrilege. The remedy is mercy, pity.

Gluttony is an immeasurable desire to eat and drink. Drunkenness is horrible sepulchre of man's reason. The remedy is Abstinence, Temperance, Sobriety.

Lechery, cousin to gluttony, has many forms. It is the greatest sin of theft for it steals body and soul. The remedy is chastity and continence: not to eat and drink too much. When a pot boils strongly, it is best to withdraw the fire.

Confession must be freely willed in full faith, of one's own sins only, spoken truthfully, without subtle words, considered, frequent. Satisfaction consists in alms-giving, penance, fasting. Its fruit is endless bliss in Heaven.

Chaucer follows this 'Tale' with his Retractions. Some of his earlier writing he revokes as worldly vanities. His translation of Boethius 'De Consolatione' and other books of Saints' legends etc he is thankful for.

Chaucer went to Canterbury as pilgrim in 1388, aged 48. The Tales were unfinished when he died and unprinted until Caxton, circa 1476-7, at Westminster (hence 'chaple' and 'font'). The vocabulary, albeit modernised, is of its time. Rigorous self examination endures, variously expressed for different times such as Jeremy Taylor's *Holy Living*. Unlike allegories: e.g. Kingsley's *Water Babies*, Chaucer's pilgrims and Bunyan himself in *Pilgrim's Progress* are persons whose lives make and describe their, our, history in their journey, then as now, in England.

References:
Particular and General

Quotations from the Bible (A.V.) and Shakespeare have references in the text.

Epigraphs and quotations in context include author, publisher, date of publication, not necessarily the first edition.

J. L. AUSTIN (1912-1960) was still revising *How to do Things with Words* (William James lectures at Harvard, 1955) for publication when he died. *Philosophical Papers* (OUP, 1961) edited by J. O. Urmson and G. J. Warnock includes *The meaning of a Word*, (read to the Moral Sciences Club, Cambridge and the Jowett Society Oxford, 1940). *Performative Utterances* is the transcript of an unscripted BBC 3rd programme talk, 1956. *Three ways of Spilling Ink* (unfinished, incomplete, but edited for The Philosophical Review, vol. 75, 4, 1966). *The Line* and *The Cave in Plato's Republic* were edited by Urmson.

Sense and Sensibilia (OUP, 1962) is Austin's lecture notes reconstructed by G. J. Warnock.

G. J. Warnock, *J. L. Austin*, (Routledge, 1989, in the series *The Arguments of Philosophers*) was 'conceived as a book about Austin, rather than about Austin and his critics and commentators'. See also *Morality and Language* (OUP, 1983) etc.

Isaiah Berlin's *Personal Impressions*, (Hogarth Press, 1980) includes 'J. L. Austin', pages 108-115 etc. See also *Isaiah Berlin* by Michael Ignatieff, (Metropolitan Books, NY, 1998)

[Translations of classic texts and Biographies (specialist or introductory) include invaluable bibliographies.]

AUGUSTINE: *Confessions and City of God*, English translation (Everyman and Penguin editions). *Confessions*, translated by Henry Chadwick, (OUP, 1991); *De Doctrina Christiana*, translated by R. P. H. Green, (OUP, 1995); *Augustine: Earlier Writings and Augustine: Later Works*, (volumes VI and VII in Library of Christian Classics, SCM Press, circa 1953)

Amor Dei, by John Burnaby, (London, 1938); *Augustine of Hippo*, a biography by Peter Brown, (Faber and Faber, 1967); *Augustine* by Henry Chadwick, (OUP, 1986) Boethius, *The Consolation of Philosophy*, (Penguin, 1969).

Henry Chadwick: *Early Christian Thought and the Classical Tradition*, (OUP, 1966); Boethius: *The Consolations of Music, Logic, Theology and Philosophy*, (Clarendon Press, 1981); *The Early Church*, (Pelican, 1967); *Tradition and Exploration*, (Canterbury Press, 1994); *The Church in Ancient Society: From Galilee to Gregory the Great*, (OUP, 2001); *East and West: The Making of a Rift in the Church*, (OUP, 2003, paperback, 2005); *Studies on Ancient Christianity*, (Ashgate, 2006, Variorium Collected Studies) etc.

Rowan Williams: *Arius, Heresy and Tradition*, (Darton, Longman and Todd, 1987 and Canterbury Press, 2001); *The Making of Orthodoxy*, essays in honour of Henry Chadwick, (CUP, 1989); *On Christian Theology*, (Blackwell, 2000); *The Wound of Knowledge*, (Darton, Longman and Todd, revised 2002) etc.

John Oman: *Grace and Personality*, (Fontana 1960)

Bede: *A History of the English Church and People*, (Penguin Classic and OUP, 1969) Benedicta Ward, SLG: *The Venerable Bede*, (Chapman, 1998); *High King of Heaven*, (Mowbray, 1999) etc.

Douglas Dales, *Dunstan*, (Lutterworth, 1988); *Called to be Angels*, (Canterbury Press, 1998)

Anselm: *Prayers and Meditations*, translated and introduction, Benedicta Ward, foreword by R. W. Southern, (Penguin Classics, 1973)

H. Mayr-Harting: *The Coming of Christianity to Anglo-Saxon England*, (Batsford, 1972) etc.

R. W. Southern: *The Medieval Church*, (volume II, Pelican History) etc.

Dante: *Divine Comedy*, 1, 2, 3 (translated Sayers, Penguin)

The Life and Lyrics of Richard Rolle of Hampole, edited by Frances Comper, (Dent, 1928)

Chaucer: *The Canterbury Tales*, edited by N. Coghill, (Penguin, 1960),

G. G. Coulton: *Chaucer and his England*, (Methuen, 1921)

Julian of Norwich: *Revelations of Divine Love*, (Penguin Classics, 1966)

Everyman and Medieval Mystery Plays, edited by A. C. Cawley, (Dent, 1977)

Piers the Ploughman, Langland, (Penguin, 1959)

William Tyndale: *The Obedience of a Christian Man*, (Penguin Classics, 2000)

William Tyndale: a biography by David Daniell, (Yale University Press, 1994)

Erasmus: *Praise of Folly and Letter to Maarten van Dorp*, 1515, translated by Betty Radice, (Penguin Classics, 1971)

Thomas Cranmer: Diarmaid MacCulloch, (Yale University Press, 1996)

Jeremy Taylor: *The Liberty of Prophesying*, (facsimile reprint, Scolar Press, 1971)

Holy Living, foreword by Henry Chadwick, abridged and edited by Anne Lamb, (Langford Press, 1970 and Harper & Row, NY)

The life of Isaac Newton, Richard S. Westfall, (CUP, 1993)

Charles Darwin: *The Origin of Species*, (John Murray, 1859) edited by Gillian Beer, (OUP, 1996); *The Voyage of the Beagle: The Beagle Diary*, edited by Richard Darwin Keyne, (CUP, 1988); *Charles Darwin*, a biography by John Bowlby, (W. W. Norton, 1991) etc.

From Cranmer to Davidson: A miscellany, edited by Stephen Taylor, (Church of England Record Society, 1999)

George Bell: *Life of Randall Davidson*, (OUP, 1952)

William Temple: *Nature, Man and God*, (Gifford lectures, 1932-3 and 1933-4, Macmillan, 1934); *Citizen and Churchman*, (Eyre & Spottiswood, 1941); *Readings in St John's Gospel*, (Papermac, 1961);. F. A. Iremonger, *William Temple: His Life and Letters*, (OUP, 1948)

Michael Ramsey: *F. D. Maurice and the Conflicts of Modern Theology*, (CUP, 1951) etc.

Owen Chadwick: *John Cassian*, (1968); *The Reformation,* (Pelican History, III); *The Victorian Church*, two volumes, (A & C Black, 1970); *The Secularisation of the European Mind in the 19th Century*, (Gifford Lectures, CUP, 1976); *Hensley Henson*, (OUP, 1983); *Michael Ramsey: A life*, (OUP, 1990); *Early Reformation on the Continent*, (OUP, 2001) etc.

The Education of Henry Adams, Henry Adams, (Modern Library, 1931, from Massachusetts Historical Society, 1918)

T. S. Eliot: *The Sacred Wood*, (Methuen, 1919); *Tradition and the Individual Talent; What is a Classic?*, (1945); *Notes towards the Definition of Culture*, (Faber and Faber, 1948); *The Complete Poems and Plays*, (Faber and Faber, 1969); *The Use of Poetry and the Use of Criticism*, (Charles Eliot Norton Lectures, 1932-3); *On Poetry and Poets; To Criticise the Critic*

The Criterion, (1926-1938) editorials and reviews etc.

C. G. Jung: *Memories, Dreams, Reflections*, (first published 1863, Fontana paperback, 1995)

Hannah Arendt: *The Life of the Mind*, volume I; *Thinking* volume II; *Willing* and appendix: *Judging*, (Harcourt Brace Jovanovich, NY 1977); *The Origins of Totalitarianism*, (Deutsch, 1983) etc.

Miloscz: *The Witness of Poetry*, (Charles Eliot Norton Lectures, 1981-2, Harvard University Press, 1983)

European Literature and Theology in the 20th Century: Ends of Time, edited by David Jasper and Colin Crowder, (Macmillan, 1990)

Solzhenitsyn, *A Day in the Life of Ivan Denisovich; August, 1914*, (Bodley Head, 1972) etc.

Andrew Chandler: *Brethren in Adversity*, (Church of England Record Society, 1992); *The Moral Imperative* (Westview Press, 1998); *The Terrible Alternative, Christian Martyrdom in the C20th*, (Cassell, 1998); *The Church of England in the C20th*, edited by Chandler and Anthony Harvey, (Boydell Press, 2006)

Hermann Hesse: *Narcissus and Goldmund*, (Bantam, 1971)

Andrew Louth: *Discerning the Mystery: An Essay on the Nature of Theology*, (OUP, 1983) etc.

Hans Kung: *Christianity and other World Religions*, (Doubleday, 1986) etc.

Iris Murdoch: Existentialists and Mystics, edited by Peter Conradi, foreword by George Steiner, (Chatto & Windus, 1997) includes *The Sovereignty of Good* and *On Rereading Plato*

William Anderson: *Dante, the Maker*, (Crossroad, NY, 1982); *The Face of Glory*, (Bloomsbury, 1996)

Theodore H. White: *In Search of History*, (Harper & Row, 1978)

Alan Bloom: *The Closing of the American Mind*, (Simon & Schuster, NY, 1987, Penguin, 1988)

Thomas M. Frank: *Race and Nationalism: The Struggle for Power in Rhodesia-Nyasaland*, (Fordham, NY, 1960); *Word Politics: Verbal Strategy among the Superpowers*, (OUP NY, 1972); *Secrecy and Foreign Policy*, (Studies in Peaceful Change, OUP, NY, 1974); *Resignation in Protest*, (Viking, NY, 1975); *Fairness in International Law and Institutions*, (OUP, 1995); *The Empowered Self: Law and Society in the Age of Individualism*, (OUP, NY, 1999)

Balthasar, at the end of Modernity, Gardner, Moss, Quash and Ward, foreword by Fergus Kerr, afterword by Rowan Williams, (T & T Clark, 1999)

An Architecture of Invitation: Colin St J Wilson, Sarah Menin and Stephen Kite, (Ashgate, 2005)

A Memoir, People and Places, Mary Warnock, (Duckworth, 2000) etc

Schools of Reconciliation: issues in Joint RC/Anglican Education, Priscilla Chadwick, (Cassell, 1994)

The Making of the Republican Citizen: Political Ceremonies and Symbols in China, 1911-1929, Henrietta Harrison, (OUP, 2000) etc.

Anthony Harvey: *By What Authority?*, (SCM Press, 2001)

Catriona Bass: *Education in Tibet: Policy and Practice since 1950*, (Zed Books, London and NY, 1998)

Jeremy Begbie: *Theology, Music and Time*, (CUP, 2000)

Hope, Anne and Kenneth Lamb, (Watts, New Thinkers Library, 1971)

Hope Against Hope: a memoir, Nadezhda Mandelstam, (Athenaeum, NY, Harvill, London, 1971)

The Progress of Human Knowledge and Culture, D. C. G. Allan, (Calder Walker Associates, 2005)

Life On Air. David Attenborough, (BBC, 2002)

365

John Polkinghorn: *The God of Hope and the End of the World*, (SPCK, 2002)

Susan Greenfield: *Tomorrow's People*, (Penguin, Allen Lane, 2003)

Michael Ignatieff: *The Lesser Evil: Political Ethics in an Age of Terror*, (Gifford Lectures, Edinburgh, 2004)

Alexandru Popescu: *Petre Tutea: Between Sacrifice and Suicide*, (Ashgate, 2003, paperback, 2004)

Thomas Traherne, edited by Jan Ross, (volume 1, 2005, volumes 2-8 to follow)

GENERAL REFERENCE

The Oxford Dictionary, (OUP, 1971)

The Shorter Oxford English Dictionary, (OUP, 1965)

The Cambridge Encyclopaedia of the English Language, David Crystal, (CUP, 1995, superb facsimiles and illustrations)

Words on Words, David and Hilary Crystal, (Penguin, 2000)

Petit Larouse Illustre

Roget's Thesaurus, (Penguin, 1970)

Dictionary of Phrase and Fable, E. Cobham Brewer, (Cassell new and enlarged, pre 1920, undated)

Oxford Classical Dictionary, (second edition, OUP, 1979)

Oxford History of the Classical World, (OUP, 1986, including maps, illustrations, bibliographies)

Oxford Companion to Philosophy, edited by Ted Honderich, (OUP, 1995)

The Oxford Dictionary of the Christian Church, revised, Cross and Livingstone, (OUP, 1974, new edition 1997, with bibliographies)

Lives of the Poets, Michael Schmidt, (Weidenfeld & Nicolson, 1998)

Index